America and the Armenian Genocide of 1915

Edited by

Jay Winter

Yale University

CAMBRIDGE
UNIVERSITY PRESS

PUBLISHED BY THE PRESS SYNDICATE OF THE UNIVERSITY OF CAMBRIDGE
The Pitt Building, Trumpington Street, Cambridge, United Kingdom

CAMBRIDGE UNIVERSITY PRESS
The Edinburgh Building, Cambridge, CB2 2RU, UK
40 West 20th Street, New York, NY 10011–4211, USA
477 Williamstown Road, Port Melbourne, VIC 3207, Australia
Ruiz de Alarcón 13, 28014 Madrid, Spain
Dock House, The Waterfront, Cape Town 8001, South Africa

http://www.cambridge.org

First published 2003

Printed in the United Kingdom at the University Press, Cambridge

Typeface Plantin 10/12 pt.   *System* LATEX 2$_\varepsilon$ [TB]

A catalogue record for this book is available from the British Library

Library of Congress Cataloguing in Publication data
America and the Armenian Genocide of 1915 / edited by Jay Winter.
   p.   cm. – (Studies in the social and cultural history of modern warfare)
Includes bibliographical references.
ISBN 0 521 82958 5
1. Armenian massacres, 1915–1925 – Foreign public opinion, American.
2. Genocide – Turkey – Foreign public opinion, American.   3. Armenians –
Turkey – History.   4. World War, 1914–1918.   I. Winter, J. M.   II. Series.
DS195.5.A47   2003
956.6′2015 – dc21   2003046119

ISBN 0 521 82958 5 hardback

America and the Armenian Genocide of 1915

Before Rwanda and Bosnia, and before the Holocaust, the first genocide of the twentieth century happened in Turkish Armenia in 1915, when approximately one million people were killed. This volume is the first account of the American response to this atrocity. The first part sets up the framework for understanding the genocide: Sir Martin Gilbert, Vahakn Dadrian, and Jay Winter provide an analytical setting for nine scholarly essays examining how Americans learned of this catastrophe and how they tried to help its victims. Knowledge and compassion, though, were not enough to stop the killings. A terrible precedent was born in 1915, one which has come to haunt the United States and other Western countries throughout the twentieth century and beyond. To read the chapters in this volume is chastening: the dilemmas Americans faced when confronting evil on an unprecedented scale are not very different from the dilemmas we face today.

JAY WINTER is Professor of History at Yale University, a former Reader in Modern History at the University of Cambridge, and Fellow of Pembroke College, Cambridge. He is the author of many books on the First World War, including *Sites of Memory, Sites of Mourning: The Great War in European Cultural History* and, with Jean-Louis Robert, *Capital Cities at War: Paris, London, Berlin 1914–1919*. He was chief historian and co-producer for the Emmy-award winning television series "The Great War and the shaping of the twentieth century," first screened on PBS and the BBC in 1996, and subsequently broadcast in twenty-seven countries. He is also a director of the Historial de la Grande Guerre, an international museum of the First World War at Péronne, Somme, France.

Studies in the Social and Cultural History of Modern Warfare

General Editor
Jay Winter *Yale University*

Advisory Editors
Omer Bartov *Brown University*
Carol Gluck *Columbia University*
David M. Kennedy *Stanford University*
Paul Kennedy *Yale University*
Antoine Prost *Université de Paris-Sorbonne*
Emmanuel Sivan *Hebrew University of Jerusalem*
Robert Wohl *University of California, Los Angeles*

In recent years the field of modern history has been enriched by the exploration of two parallel histories. These are the social and cultural history of armed conflict, and the impact of military events on social and cultural history.

Studies in the Social and Cultural History of Modern Warfare presents the fruits of this growing area of research, reflecting both the colonization of military history by cultural historians and the reciprocal interest of military historians in social and cultural history, to the benefit of both. The series offers the latest scholarship in European and non-European events from the 1850s to the present day.

For a list of titles in the series, please see end of book.

Contents

Contributors

ROUBEN PAUL ADALIAN is Director of the Armenian National Institute, Washington, D.C.

LLOYD E. AMBROSIUS is Professor of History, University of Nebraska-Lincoln

PETER BALAKIAN is Donald M. and Constance H. Rebar Professor of the Humanities in the Department of English at Colgate University

JOHN MILTON COOPER, JR., is E. Gordon Fox Professor of American Institutions, University of Wisconsin-Madison

VAHAKN N. DADRIAN is Director of Genocide Research, Zoryan Institute, Cambridge, Mass., and Toronto, Canada

SIR MARTIN GILBERT is a Fellow of Merton College, Oxford

SUSAN BILLINGTON HARPER is an independent writer

RICHARD G. HOVANNISIAN holds the Armenian Educational Foundation Chair in Modern Armenian History at the University of California, Los Angeles

THOMAS C. LEONARD is University Librarian and Professor in the Graduate School of Journalism at the University of California, Berkeley

SUZANNE E. MORANIAN is a historian and an independent writer

DONALD RITCHIE is Associate Historian in the US Senate Historical Office

JAY WINTER is Professor of History, Yale University

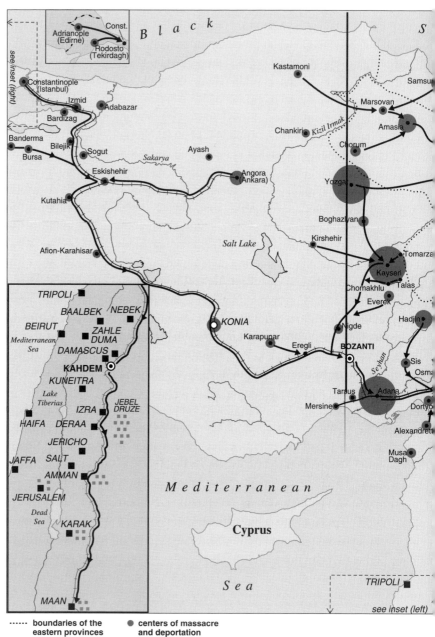

Black Sea

Adrianople (Edirne)   Const.
Rodosto (Tekirdagh)

Kastamoni   Samsu
Constantinople (Istanbul)   Marsovan
Izmid   Adabazar   Amasia
Bardizag   Chankiri   Kizil Irmak
Banderma   Chorum
Bilejik Sogut   Ayash
Bursa   Sakarya
Eskishehir   Angora (Ankara)   Yozga
Kutahia
Boghazlyan
Kirshehir   Tomarza
Afion-Karahisar   Salt Lake
Kayseri
Chomakhlu   Talas
Everek
KONIA   Nigde   Hadjin
Karapunar
Ergli   BOZANTI   Sis
Osma
TRIPOLI
BAALBEK NEBEK   Tarsus Adana Doryo
BEIRUT   ZAHLE   Mersine
Mediterranean DUMA
Sea   DAMASCUS   Alexandret
KAHDEM
KUNEITRA   Musa Dagh
Lake
Tiberias   IZRA   JEBEL
DRUZE
HAIFA   DERAA
JERICHO
JAFFA   SALT
AMMAN
JERUSALEM
Dead
Sea   KARAK

Mediterranean

Cyprus

MAAN

Sea   TRIPOLI
see inset (left)

...... boundaries of the   ● centers of massacre
eastern provinces   and deportation

⊙ concentration   O principal points
camps   of transit

→ principal routes of   ▪ subsidiary points
deportation   of deportation

+++++ rail lines   ■ principal destination
points of deportation

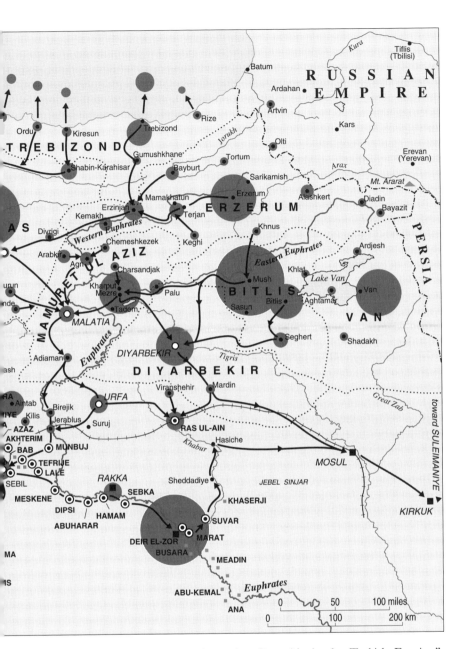

Figure 1. "The 1915 Armenian Genocide in the Turkish Empire."
Originally produced by, and reproduced with the kind permission of,
the Armenian National Institute (ANI) (Washington D.C.), and the
Nubrarian Library (Paris). © ANI, English Edition, copyright 1998.

Acknowledgments

The chapters in this volume arose out of the conference, "The American Response to the Armenian Genocide," held in Washington, D.C., on 27–28 September 2000. All have been revised to enable scholars to extend their work and its documentation.

The conference was co-sponsored by the Library of Congress and the Armenian National Institute, in cooperation with the US Holocaust Memorial Museum. The participation of these three institutions opened a new phase in the public and scholarly discussion of the Armenian genocide and its implications.

It is a particular pleasure to acknowledge and thank the following individuals for their assistance in organizing and realizing this event: James H. Billington, The Librarian of the Library of Congress; Prosser Gifford, Library of Congress Director of Scholarly Programs; Levon Avdoyan, Library of Congress Armenian and Georgian Area Specialist; Irving Greenberg, Chairman, Sara Bloomfield, Director, and William Parsons, Chief of Staff, of the US Holocaust Memorial Museum; Robert A. Kaloosdian, Chairman of the Board of Governors, Armenian National Institute; and Carolyn Mugar, of the Armenian National Institute Board of Governors. Particular thanks are due to Sir Martin Gilbert, whose keynote lecture forms the first chapter in this book.

We are grateful to many others whose help was essential; among them are Richard G. Hovannisian, Chairman, Armenian National Institute Academic Council; Sylvia Parsons, Armenian National Institute Conference Coordinator; Rouben P. Adalian, Director of the Armenian National Institute; and Jackie Abramian, editorial assistant.

JAY WINTER
Yale University, January 2003

Introduction
Witness to genocide

Jay Winter

> Between the idea
> And the reality
> Between the motion
> And the act
> Falls the Shadow.
>   T. S. Eliot "The Hollow Men" (1925)

The Armenian National Institute convened a meeting in Washington in September 2000 out of which this volume emerged. The meeting had two venues: first in the United States Holocaust Memorial Museum, and then in the Library of Congress. The location of this meeting in the heart of the nation's capital, and in two such monumental settings, had a particular importance. For this meeting of scholars from both sides of the Atlantic was testimony to the increasing prominence of the subject of the Armenian genocide in public discourse as well as in contemporary scholarship. It has taken many decades to grow, but by the end of the twentieth century, a consensus has emerged that the Armenian genocide of 1915 is of universal significance. It disclosed much about the century which followed, and, in particular, its history illuminates uncomfortably the obstacles which block international action in situations where genocidal acts appear possible or likely.

This book does not address the question of the justification in general of American or international intervention in "trouble spots" around the world. The disastrous record of US foreign policy in Vietnam, in Chile, and in many other parts of the world where ruling or insurgent movements appeared to threaten American interests or bolster Soviet power precludes any easy argument for the deployment of American power. This book is restricted to a set of events where the murder of a people is in question. How Americans have related to the phenomenon of genocide is the subject of this book. Its particular reference is to American responses to the first genocide of the twentieth century, the Turkish genocidal campaign against its Armenian population, which resulted in approximately one million deaths in 1915–16.

This volume is not a story of heroic intervention. On the contrary, the book catalogues the enormous distance between full recognition of an unfolding catastrophe and effective action to mitigate it or stop the perpetrators before they realize their objectives and complete their plans. Mass murder happened, and the world let it happen. In T. S. Eliot's imagery, between the idea of saving the victims and the reality of their fate fell an international shadow. This book is about the shadow. For the Armenian genocide was not a crime done in the dark; there were hundreds, indeed thousands, of eye witnesses whose reports made it from Anatolia to Constantinople to Berlin, London, and Washington. Genocide happened in the presence of journalists, physicians, soldiers, diplomats, missionaries, writers, and teachers. They knew what was happening, and told millions of others about it while it was going on.

Knowledge bred out of relatively rapid means of communication led nowhere. The recognition that innocent civilians were dying was not enough. Between reliable reports and action fell a host of shadows of many different kinds. Who could have acted to stop the killing? The first failure was German. Inaction was a policy which arose out of the alliance between Germany and Turkey, fighting a war on an unprecedented scale against Britain, France, Italy, and Tsarist Russia. German diplomats felt that their hands were tied, because their ally in the Middle East faced both invasion at Gallipoli south of Constantinople and sporadic fighting in the Caucasus in the north-east of the country. Other European powers were closer to Turkey than were the Americans. Inaction in Western Europe was hardly surprising, given the state of war between Britain, France, Russia, and Turkey, and besides, Western European attitudes were marked by massive ignorance about the Orient, an ignorance deep enough to lump together Armenian Christians and Turkish Muslims in one undifferentiated mass of people who – supposedly wise heads nodded – share eternal and uncompromising hatreds. That Turks and Kurds were killing Armenians appeared another chapter in an atavistic tale without a beginning and without an end. This kind of argument blocked European action against genocide at several stages of the twentieth century; 1915 is simply the first.

There were many reasons why America did not act to save the Armenians. As this book shows, outrage was evident, but the problem of turning it into action was multiple in character. First, American isolationists resisted being drawn into any corner of the world conflict; this was another mess brewed up by the Old World not the New. In addition, there were substantial populations of German-Americans, about as numerous as those of British extraction in the country, and some ethnic groups – Irish-Americans or Jewish-Americans – were not predisposed to rally to the cause of an alliance including both Britain and Tsarist Russia. It was to get away from these imperial powers that many immigrants had moved to the United States in the first place. Why should they stand for an alliance which embraced their enemies?

When the bulk of the killings took place in eastern Turkey in 1915, there was a clear majority in American public opinion for staying out of war. Intervention in Turkey or anywhere else was simply not on. Woodrow Wilson was in his first term in the White House, and he won re-election in 1916 as the man who had kept the country out of war. Then Germany forced his hand, but the resulting war effort did not change the underlying strength of isolationism. This is evident in Wilson's failure to secure Senate ratification of the Treaty of Versailles in 1919 and 1920.

Isolationism in Europe was matched by imperialism in the Western Hemisphere. In 1915, the United States was a country whose universalist principles had no purchase – and, I suspect, were not intended to have purchase – in international affairs outside of the Western Hemisphere. What such principles meant in Mexico or Cuba is another question, which need not detain us here. Suffice it to say that Anatolia was in another world.

Some see in this selective application of principle, substantial evidence of American hypocrisy, and, to be sure, the United States has had no immunity from that condition. Even when we allow for hypocrisy, however, we need to reflect on the ways the Armenian genocide of 1915 exposed the limits of American liberalism. On the one hand, liberals have decried "gun-boat diplomacy" and international policing as thuggery or as the defense of special interests. On the other hand, American liberals were prominent among those who called for action in the face of evidence that genocidal acts were in preparation or under way. This was true with respect to the Armenian genocide, and it was true during the Second World War and later, in Cambodia, in Rwanda, in Bosnia. The same question returned time and again: can anyone advocate selective intervention after the risk of genocide is established without opening the floodgates to unilateral military action of a more undifferentiated kind? No one has a clear answer to this question today, and no one had one in 1915.

One point emerging from this book is that different cases of victimhood elicit different responses in the United States. The government traditionally has shrunk from any action until and unless substantial numbers of American citizens were directly attacked or maltreated. How many are "substantial numbers?" There were American citizens among the victims of the Armenian genocide, but their fate seemed to matter less than the nearly 200 Americans who went down on the *Lusitania*, sunk at the same time as the expulsions and murders of Armenians were occurring 5,000 miles away. Some victims are more American than others.

As Samantha Power has recently shown,[1] political action in the face of evidence that genocide is in the making, is both possible and difficult. The primacy of domestic concerns placed the Armenian genocide outside the reach of practical politics in 1915. And now nearly a century later, with a host of other genocidal crimes indelibly etched in history, that set of limitations still creates a yawning gap between knowledge and action in times when atrocities loom as likely outcomes of communal conflict. To read the chapters in this volume is chastening; the dilemmas Americans faced when confronting evil on a scale not seen before are not very different from the same dilemmas confronted today. To study this history is no pathway to smugness or certainty, or even to a kind of cynicism all too easily mistaken for wisdom.

The structure of this book reflects the multiple facets of the Armenian genocide, and the complex dilemmas it revealed. In the first part, Sir Martin Gilbert locates the story of genocide in the history of the twentieth century; Jay Winter places specific emphasis on the context of total war as a critical element in the unfolding of the crime. Vahakn Dadrian then provides an interpretation of the genocide as a cluster of crimes of different kinds and of different origins, many of which foreshadow the Nazi Holocaust of the Second World War.

The second part of the book moves away from the European and Asian theatres of the war and the genocide, and elucidates the way American politicians, intellectuals, and social activists responded to the stories of atrocities which reached the United States. John Milton Cooper and Lloyd Ambrosius both discuss President Wilson and the evolution of his policy, coming to different interpretations of the reasons why he was unable or unwilling to act effectively at this time. As Rouben Adalian shows, the information available to Wilson and other political figures was voluminous, detailed, and damning. The National Archives have materials which simply place out of the court of human opinion any effort at holocaust denial. The intellectual, cultural, and social response to the holocaust is the subject of the following three chapters. Peter Balakian shows how widely discussed these crimes were among American

---

[1] Samantha Power, *"A Problem from Hell": America and the Age of Genocide* (New York: Basic Books, 2002).

writers and literary figures, and both Susan Billington Harper and Suzanne Moranian point out how many Americans were deeply engaged in direct assistance to those who were in danger or who managed to survive it. Many Americans bore witness, and some shared the sufferings of the victims. Their voices emerge powerfully and movingly from these chapters.

Post-war commissions and congressional inquiries, as Richard Hovannisian and Donald Ritchie show, reinforce our sense of an open and vivid discussion of these issues in the United States both during and after the war. Together with Thomas Leonard's chapter on the press, they underscore the view that the Armenian genocide was a subject scrutinized, analyzed, publicized virtually everywhere at the time. Yet the outcome of all this attention was relatively meager. Those who have argued recently that the human rights project is aided and abetted by modern communications should take pause when confronting the story these scholars have told. The paralysis of policy was not a function of ignorance, but of a willful turning away from a fully documented catastrophe. Consciences were made "uneasy," as Peter Balakian's chapter shows, but it is evident that that sense of discomfort has rarely informed effective action to prevent genocide.

Scholarship of this kind should lead away from what E. P. Thompson called "the enormous condescension of posterity." There is little reason at all to think that the present generation is any more likely to move quickly and efficiently when non-American lives are being taken by the tens of thousands. There have been too many invasions and interventions, direct and covert, in too many parts of the world for anyone to make an ironclad case for unilateral American action as a valid principle of international order.

Yet, the case of genocide is so extreme, so beyond the powers of normal reasoning, that we rightly ask whether, in such cases, exceptions not only can but must be made. That question was posed in 1915; it was not answered clearly then, but even so, the question – and the terrifying images of genocide underlying it – has not gone away.

In the absence of international action, we are left with the record of individual witnessing. Here too the story of the Armenian genocide was a harbinger. When states fail to act to stop neighbors or adversaries from killing their own people, individual people have found ways to try to ensure that the voice of the victims is heard. That is what witnessing is all about: witnesses stop the killers from lying with impunity about their crimes. The historical record of American witnesses to genocide helps ensure that genocide denial is treated with the contempt it deserves.

To be sure, this story shows that there are dangers in unilateral action just as there are dangers in unilateral inaction. This volume illustrates them all. It shows the men and women who stood by the victims, who witnessed the evil, as well as those who heard what they had to say and, at the end of the day, remained inert. Now, nearly a century later, we are not far from their dilemma, which arises time and again whenever the menace of genocide appears.

Part I

The framework

1   Twentieth-century genocides

Sir Martin Gilbert

The twentieth century witnessed some of humanity's greatest achievements – in medicine, science, agricultural production, communications – and some of its worst excesses. By any scale of values, looking back one – or even two – millennia, it was a century of improvement, at times vast improvement, in the quality of life for millions of people; yet the twentieth century was also one of decline in many parts of the world.

In much of my recent scholarship, I have touched on many of the attempts made in the century that is now behind us, to destroy a whole people. No episode, however horrific, resembles another. Each has its own appalling characteristics. In recent years, the researches of pioneer scholars – among them George Andreopoulos, Martin van Bruinessen, Frank Chalk, Israel Charny, Helen Fein, Leo Kuper, and Richard Hovannisian – have shown just how widespread the barbarism of governments can be, once they set as their aim the destruction or curtailment of a particular people.

Winston Churchill was once asked why the twentieth century was called the century of the common man. He replied to his questioner: "It is called the century of the common man because in it the common man has suffered most."[1] The often tragic fate of that "common man" – and woman and child, – the young and the old, runs like a dark thread through twentieth-century history.

When the twentieth century opened the European empires, Britain, France, Turkey, Russia, and Germany – as well as the United States (which in 1898 had acquired the Philippines in the Pacific and other Spanish territory) – possessed among them enormous power: primarily military and naval, but also industrial. It was therefore not difficult for them, in a conflict with smaller nations or weaker peoples, to act, if they so wished, with ruthless, even murderous efficiency. Ottoman Turkey had already, in 1894 and 1895, massacred 100,000 Armenians, looted and

---

[1] Martin Gilbert, *A History of the Twentieth Century, 1900–1933* (New York: William Morrow and Company, 1997 vol. I, p. 2.

set on fire several thousand Armenian homes, and forced many Armenians to convert to Islam. The Turkish Sultan, Abdul-Hamid, was almost universally known as "Abdul the Damned."

In 1900, in the very first year of the century, in the distant eastern regions of the Ottoman Empire, Kurdish villagers attacked and murdered at least 60 Armenians – some accounts say as many as 400 – in the mountainous countryside along the upper reach of the Tigris River. One village, Spaghank, was surrounded not only by Kurds, but by a force under the direct control of the local Turkish military commander. When a group of Armenians took refuge in the village church, the troops surrounded the building and set it on fire, suffocating to death those inside, including the local priest. In the eastern Turkish town of Van, the British Vice-Consul, who had attempted to protect the local Armenians, was himself attacked by Kurds. When the British and other governments protested to Constantinople, the Sultan removed the regional military commander, but the violence against the Armenians continued.[2]

Thus the century began, and the fate of the Armenians was at its core. In the hundred years ahead, not only war, but racist, genocidal impulses that sometimes hide in the fog of war, were to be the grim counters to progress in the medical, technological, and environmental sciences, and the civilizing influences of the arts. It was only a narrow line between hatreds which generate war and the killing of soldiers and civilians, and genocides which set out to destroy a whole race. Also in 1900, in an attempt to weaken the Boer guerrilla movement in South Africa, the British Government seized thousands of women and children and forced them into what were called, at that time, "concentration camps." The idea was not to exterminate the Boer people, but to cut the fighting soldiers off from their homes and isolate them to the point of despair. Seventeen concentration camps were established. They had little food and almost no medical facilities. A further thirty-five camps were set up for Black Africans who worked on the farms of the absent fighters, so that they too would be unable to plough, or harvest crops, or look after livestock.

The death toll in the camps was high. A British woman, Emily Hobhouse, who visited the camps, wrote:

I began to compare a parish I had known at home of two thousand people, where a funeral was an event – and usually of an old person. Here some twenty to twenty-five were carried away *daily* . . . The full realisation of the position dawned on me – it was a death rate such as had never been known except in the times of the Great Plagues . . . The whole talk was of death – who died yesterday, who lay dying today, who would be dead tomorrow.[3]

2 Gilbert, *Twentieth Century*, vol. I, pp. 31–2.
3 Gilbert, *Twentieth Century*, vol. I, p. 38.

Returning to Britain, Emily Hobhouse led a campaign against the camps, which were forcefully denounced by the Liberal Party leader, Henry Campbell-Bannerman. "When is a war not a war?" he asked, and gave the answer: "When it is carried on by methods of barbarism in South Africa."[4] The British Government quickly instituted improvements, and the death rate fell. The final toll, however, was far higher than that of the battlefield: 28,000 Boer women and children died in the camps, and more than 50,000 Africans.[5]

The cruelty of the concentration camps in South Africa was certainly barbarism, but it was not genocide. The Boers and British signed a peace treaty in 1902 and the Boers flourished – so much so that within fifty years they were imposing their own tyrannical apartheid ideology on the Black African majority.

Elsewhere in southern Africa a more sustained attempt to destroy a whole people took place in that same first decade of the twentieth century in German-ruled South-West Africa (now Namibia), where the local people – the Hereros – found their land and livelihood taken away by a group of German colonists, less than 5,000 in all, who had been acquiring land with what the German colonial department itself described as "fraud and extortion."[6] The Hereros rose in revolt. In the punitive expedition launched against them, thousands were killed. When news of the severity of the punitive measures reached Europe, there was widespread indignation, including in the German Parliament, that such savage destruction had been inflicted by a colonial power. The Herero people survived; so too does their folk memory of the cruelties inflicted on them.

The fierceness of colonial reaction to local "native" rebellion was often fuelled by racial, dehumanizing animosities – hatred, scorn, contempt – that could certainly be described as genocidal. In the Dutch East Indies nearly 1,000 local women and children were killed when the Dutch suppressed a rebellion there in 1904. There was indignation in Holland at what had happened, not only amongst the socialist Opposition, but also within the government. One member of the governing party declared the Dutch soldiers had behaved like "Huns and Tatars" massacring the women and children for the commercial ends of mining and oil exploration.[7]

Since May 1903 news of a reign of terror in the Belgian Congo was reaching Europe as a result of the efforts of Edmund Morel, a shipping clerk in Liverpool. Morel published graphic accounts of atrocities which arose out of the system of forced labor which was imposed by the Belgian

---

[4] Gilbert, *Twentieth Century*, vol. I, pp. 38–9.
[5] Gilbert, *Twentieth Century*, vol. I, p. 39.   [6] Gilbert, *Twentieth Century*, vol. I, p. 99.
[7] Gilbert, *Twentieth Century*, vol. I, p. 100.

authorities – under the direct rule of King Leopold – on the local inhabitants.[8] What he described had all the hallmarks of genocide: Belgian punitive expeditions which, on their return to base, brought baskets of human hands as proof of their ruthlessness.

Nine months after Morel's first published exposure of the crimes, Roger Casement, the British Consul in the Belgian Congo, sent an eye-witness report of Congolese women and children chained in sheds as hostages, and men beaten up for failure to produce sufficient rubber at collection points. He wrote of mass executions, and terrible mutilations inflicted on the natives by white officials. Casement estimated that as many as 3 million native Congolese had died of disease, torture, or shooting during the previous fifteen years. A Congolese soldier who was sent to get rubber, and had to open fire to do so, had to bring back a right hand for every bullet he expended. At one rubber collection site, Casement reported, the soldiers had used 6,000 cartridges, "which means," he noted, "that 6,000 people are killed or mutilated; it means more than 6,000 – for the people have told me repeatedly that the soldiers kill children with the butt of their guns."[9]

As news of the Congolese atrocities spread, President Theodore Roosevelt, Mark Twain, and Joseph Conrad were among those who protested.[10] It was only after two years of international protests, however, that the Belgian Parliament debated the situation in the Congo, and another two years until Leopold agreed to hand over his personal control of the Congo to the Belgian Parliament. The atrocities ceased. International protest had prevailed, though long after the initial cruelties were made known.

Within the Russian Empire, the fires of political and national dissent that had been lit at the beginning of 1905 continued to smolder and burst into flame. In the Armenian provinces of Russia, where resentment against Russian anti-minority policies had been smoldering for most of the year, the conflict was made all the more bloody when, in September, Azeris (a Muslim people then indentified as Tatars) attacked Armenian homes in Baku, Tiflis, and Erevan. Fearing Armenian national ambitions, and noting that the Armenians had been joined in their protest in Baku by Russian revolutionaries, the Tsarist authorities took the side of the Tatars. For their part, the Tatars raised the green banner of Islam and proclaimed a Holy War against the Armenians. Hundreds of Armenians were killed, and dozens of Armenian villages destroyed.[11]

[8] Gilbert, *Twentieth Century*, vol. I, p. 94.
[9] Gilbert, *Twentieth Century*, vol. I, pp. 94–5.
[10] Gilbert, *Twentieth Century*, vol. I, p. 95.
[11] Gilbert, *Twentieth Century*, I, pp. 112–13.

In 1906 it was the turn of the British Government, then a Liberal government – led by those who had condemned the "methods of barbarism" in South Africa six years earlier – to suppress a Zulu revolt in southern Africa with great severity. More than 3,000 Zulus were killed.[12] A racist attitude of mind underlay the brutality of the action, which amounted to an exercise in extermination. That same genocidal potential was in evidence a mere three years later, in 1909, when 20,000 Armenians living in Adana and Tarsus, in southern Anatolia, were massacred by the Turks.

There were episodes during which Armenian men, women, and children were forced into churches, which were then set on fire: those who tried to run out were shot dead by armed Turkish soldiers.[13] Thirty years later, in September 1939, in German-occupied Poland, Jews were driven into synagogues which were then similarly set alight – the SS then shooting dead those who broke out.[14]

I now come to the First World War and the fate of the Armenians at the hands of Turks. With Russia at war with Turkey since October 1914, the large Armenian Christian population in Anatolia, which had long been denied any national rights by the Turks, hoped against hope that a Russian victory over Turkey might lead to the recognition of Armenian national aspirations. The Russians tried to woo the Armenians. On 30 December 1914 the Tsar, on a visit to the Caucasus front, declared: "a most brilliant future awaits the Armenians."[15] As Russian troops pushed deeper and deeper into eastern Turkey, the Turks accused the Armenians of being secretly and even actively loyal to Russia. Starting on 8 April 1915, Armenians throughout Anatolia were attacked and massacred. Armenian soldiers serving in the Ottoman army, who had already been segregated into unarmed labor battalions, were taken out of their battalions in small groups, and killed.[16]

Henry Morgenthau, the American Ambassador in Constantinople, himself a Jew, reported to Washington on the atrocities which took place between 15 April and 20 April. His report reveals an intensity of terror with which students of the fate of the Jews a quarter of a century later will be familiar:

[12] Gilbert, *Twentieth Century*, vol. I, p. 131.
[13] Donald E. Miller and Lorna Touryan Miller, *Survivors: An Oral History of the Armenian Genocide* (Berkeley, Los Angeles, London: University of California Press, 1993), pp. 63–4.
[14] Martin Gilbert, *The Second World War: A Complete History* (New York: Henry Holt and Company, 1989) p. 7.
[15] Martin Gilbert, *The First World War: A Complete History* (New York: Henry Holt and Company, 1994), p. 108.
[16] Gilbert, *Twentieth Century*, vol. I, p. 356.

The Turks' army turned aside and invaded their own territory of Van. Instead of fighting the trained Russian army of men, they turned their rifles, machine guns, and other weapons upon the Armenian women, children, and old men in the villages of Van. Following their usual custom, they distributed the most beautiful Armenian women among the Moslems, sacked and burned the Armenian villages, and massacred uninterruptedly for days.

On April 15, about 500 young Armenian men of Akantz were mustered to hear an order of the Sultan; at sunset they were marched outside the town and every man shot in cold blood. This procedure was repeated in about eighty Armenian villages in the district north of Lake Van, and in three days 24,000 Armenians were murdered in this atrocious fashion.[17]

Djevdet Bey, Governor of Van, then demanded 4,000 Armenian men from the city of Van to serve in the Turkish army. Believing this was an attempt to deny the Armenians of Van their only means of self-defense, the Armenians refused. Morgenthau's report continued:

On April 20, a band of Turkish soldiers seized several Armenian women who were entering the city; a couple of Armenians ran to their assistance and were shot dead. The Turks now opened fire on the Armenian quarters with rifles and artillery; soon a large part of the town was in flames and a regular siege had started. The whole Armenian fighting force consisted of only 1,500 men; they had only 300 rifles and a most inadequate supply of ammunition, while Djevdet had an army of 5,000 men, completely equipped and supplied.[18]

As the massacres intensified, the Armenians appealed for protection to Germany, the European – and Christian – power whose officers and men were nearest to them, and which, as Turkey's ally, might be able to exert a restraining influence. The Armenian appeal was rejected by the German Government on the grounds that it would offend the Turkish Government. By 19 April 1915 it was known in Berlin that more than 50,000 Armenians had been murdered in the province of Van, and that the predominantly Armenian town of Van was besieged, with 1,300 armed Armenians defending the 30,000 Armenian civilians in the town, many of them refugees from the surrounding countryside.

Details of the Armenian massacres circulated far outside Turkey.[19] The German Government, troubled by the international outcry that Germany was doing nothing to restrain its Turkish ally, instructed the German Vice-Consul at Erzerum, Max Erwin von Scheubner-Richter, to intervene.[20] He was warned, however, not to do so in any way that might give the

[17] Henry Morgenthau, *Ambassador Morgenthau's Story* (Garden City. N.Y.: Doubleday, Page, 1918), p. 297, as quoted in Miller and Miller, *Survivors*, p. 76.
[18] Morgenthau, *Ambassador Morgenthau's Story*, p. 297, as quoted in Miller and Miller, *Survivors*, p. 77.
[19] Gilbert, *Twentieth Century*, vol. I, p. 357.
[20] Gilbert, *Twentieth Century*, vol. I, p. 357.

impression that Germany wanted "to exercise a right of protection over the Armenians, or interfere with the activities of the authorities."[21] The muted protest was duly made; the massacres continued. Seven and a half years later von Scheubner-Richter was shot dead while advancing through the streets of Munich, at the side of Adolf Hitler, during the attempt in November 1923 to overthrow the Bavarian Government.

There was one brief moment of respite for the Armenians, when Russian forces reached the besieged town of Van, and rescued those Armenians who had been trapped there under Turkish bombardment for thirty days. In a huge area of Turkish Anatolia, however, from the western town of Bursa to the southern town of Aleppo, and eastward to the Russo-Turkish front-line, the killings went on. In Bitlis, 15,000 Armenian civilians were killed in eight days. In the Black Sea port of Trebizond, in the course of a two-week orgy of destruction, an estimated 15,000 Turkish troops murdered all but 100 of the 17,000 Armenian inhabitants of the town. The Italian Consul-General was an eye-witness to the terrors of Trebizond, writing to his government a month later, having returned to Italy:

The passing of gangs of Armenian exiles beneath the windows and before the door of the Consulate; their prayers for help, when neither I nor any other could do anything to answer them; the city in a state of siege, guarded at every point by 15,000 troops in complete war equipment, by thousands of police agents, by bands of volunteers and by the members of the "Committee of Union and Progress"; the lamentations, the tears, the abandonments, the imprecations, the many suicides, the instantaneous deaths from sheer terror, the sudden unhinging of men's reason, the conflagrations, the shooting of victims in the city, the ruthless searches through the houses in the countryside; the hundreds of corpses found every day along the exile road; the young women converted by force to Islam or exiled like the rest; the children torn away from their families or from the Christian schools, and handed over by force to Moslem families, or else placed by hundreds on board ship in nothing but their shirts, and then capsized and drowned in the Black Sea and the River Deyirmen Dere – these are my last ineffaceable memories of Trebizond, memories which still, at a month's distance, torment my soul and almost drive me frantic.[22]

In Constantinople, on the night of 23–24 April, the Turks arrested 235 Armenian political, religious, educational, and intellectual leaders, took them away from the city, and put them to death. The Armenian nation was in despair, its only protection being in the east, within the regions conquered by Russia. "There are no words in the dictionaries," the

[21] Gilbert, *Twentieth Century*, vol. I, p. 357.
[22] Richard G. Hovannisian, "Etiology and Sequelae of the Armenian Genocide," in George J. Andreopoulos, ed., *Genocide: Conceptual and Historical Dimensions* (Philadelphia: University of Pennsylvania Press, 1994), p. 125.

Armenian poet Avetik Isahakian wrote a few months later, "to describe the hideousness of the terrors."[23] Today those "terrors," which extended for the following year, are known as the Armenian Genocide. The British, French, and Russian Governments, each of them at war with Turkey, issued a joint public denunciation, on 24 May 1915, of the Turkish "mass murders" of the Armenians, describing the killings as "a crime against humanity and civilization."[24] From that day the term "crimes against humanity" entered the universal lexicon.

The eminent Armenian historian Vahakn N. Dadrian, a member of the international editorial board of the *Journal of Genocide Research*, pointed out in the first issue of the journal, in March 1999, a parallel between the Armenian Genocide and the Holocaust: that in both cases, the killing followed a premeditated plan.[25] On 1 November 1916, the American Secretary of State, Robert Lansing, informed the American Ambassador in Berlin of "the studied intention on the part of the Ottoman Government to annihilate a Christian race. The true facts, if publicly known, would shock the whole civilized world."[26] Dadrian also cites German documents that show the same word used by German observers for what they saw happening to the Armenians in 1915 as was later to be used by the SS in describing what was happening to the Jews. Thus Scheubner-Richter refers to 'die ganzliche Ausrottung' of the Armenians, and later to the 'Ausrottungspolitik': the "policy of extermination."[27] This same word, *ausrottung* – extermination – was used by the SS to describe the mass killings of Jews after June 1941 in German-occupied Russia.

The death toll of Armenians in a mere eight months was horrific. Between April and November 1915 more than 600,000 Armenian men, women, and children were murdered in the area of Lake Van, the towns of Bitlis, Erzurum, and Diyarbekir, and along the upper reaches of the Tigris and Euphrates rivers (the location, ironically, of the biblical Garden of Eden). As an example of the scale of the killing, of the 82 members of the Terpandjian family in Diyarbekir only 2 survived, seven-year-old Missak and his five-year-old brother Dikran. Their grandfather Megerditch, the head of the Terpandjian clan, was among the leading Armenian citizens of Diyarbekir whom the Turks put on a barge on the Tigris, sent towards Mosul, and killed on the way. The boys' father Garabet was among 600 Armenians taken to a Turkish army barracks in Diyarbekir and killed. Their eldest brother Paul was seized by the Turks and never

---

[23] Gilbert, *Twentieth Century*, vol. I, p. 357.

[24] Gilbert, *Twentieth Century*, vol. I, p. 357.

[25] Vahakn N. Dadrian, "The Determinants of the Armenian Genocide," *Journal of Genocide Research* 1:1 (March 1999), pp. 68–71, 76–9.

[26] Dadrian, "Determinants," p. 70.   [27] Dadrian, "Determinants," p. 72.

heard of again: it is believed that he was tortured and killed. Their mother, Touma, and their brothers Shukri, aged fourteen, and Philip, aged three – the youngest – were among several thousand Armenians deported from Diyarbekir and murdered in the vicinity of Mardin. The two boys who survived were also on that deportation, but were taken off by Kurds to work in the fields.

More than half a million Armenians were deported by the Turks southward to Mesopotamia (modern Iraq). Of these deportees only 90,000 survived repeated attacks by the Turks, beatings, and executions, as they were driven southward. A French naval attempt to take off as many Armenians as possible from the coast of Syria led to the rescue of 4,000.[28] Of those who could not be taken off, 200,000 were forcibly converted to Islam.[29] The rest continued to be forced southward into Syria and Mesopotamia. "The greatest torment," writes Richard Hovannisian, "was reserved for the women and children, who were driven for months over mountains and deserts, often dehumanized by being stripped naked and repeatedly preyed upon and abused. Intentionally deprived of food and water, they fell by the thousands and the hundreds of thousands along the routes to the desert." "In this manner," Hovannisian concludes, "an entire nation was swept away, and the Armenian people were effectively eliminated from their homeland of several millennia."[30] To this day, that homeland is under Turkish rule.

One eye-witness to the terrible suffering of the Armenian deportees was a 25-year-old Jewish woman, Sarah Aaronsohn – a member of a Jewish espionage group working for the British against the Turks – who had set out from Constantinople to her home in Palestine, and traveled that December through the Taurus mountains to Aleppo. Her biographer, Anita Engle, has written:

She saw vultures hovering over children who had fallen dead by the roadside. She saw beings crawling along, maimed, starving and begging for bread. From time to time she passed soldiers driving before them with whips and rifle-butts whole families, men, women and children, shrieking, pleading, wailing. These were the Armenian people setting out for exile in the desert from which there was no return.[31]

Captured by the Turks two years later, Sarah Aaronsohn was taken to Damascus, tortured, and took her own life to avoid betraying her companions.[32]

---

[28] Gilbert, *Twentieth Century*, vol. I, p. 357.
[29] Gilbert, *Twentieth Century*, vol. I, p. 357.   [30] Hovannisian, "Etiology," p. 124.
[31] Anita Engle, *The Nili Spies* (London: The Hogarth Press, 1959), p. 62.
[32] Gilbert, *The First World War*, pp. 365–6.

In the early months of 1918, Russia, under its new Bolshevik rulers, signed a peace treaty with Germany, Austria-Hungary, and Turkey, and withdrew from the fighting. Turkish troops, seizing the opportunity of Russia's military weakness and political isolation, drove eastward through the Caucasus to the shores of the Caspian Sea. Several former Russian imperial cities fell to the advancing Turkish army, among them towns with large Armenian populations: Ardahan, Ardanuj, Kars, Erevan, and Baku. During this Turkish military advance, 400,000 Armenians were killed.[33]

The First World War ended in November 1918. Turkey was defeated and the Sultan fled on a British warship. In central Turkey, Armenians living in the cities of Marash, Sivas, and Kayseri became the victims of a renewed upsurge of violence. In 1920 more than 30,000 Armenians were killed in Cilicia.[34] Tens of thousands more were living in refugee camps in Mesopotamia, among them Torkom Manoogian, born in 1919 in a refugee camp near Baghdad; at the beginning of our new century he was the 96th Armenian Patriarch of Jerusalem.

There remained one further tragic act in the destruction of Armenian life and livelihood. In September 1922, with the loss of tens of thousands of lives, the Armenians living in the western regions of Anatolia, particularly in Izmir and Aidin, were driven from their homes and forced into exile in distant lands. By the early 1930s, the Turkish Government had formally confiscated all their property.[35] Among those who were forced to leave their homes in this final expulsion was Charles Mahjoubian, then aged fifteen: seventy-eight years later he remains a powerful voice for remembrance and justice.[36]

---

[33] Gilbert, *Twentieth Century*, vol. I, p. 496.

[34] Stanley K. Kerr, *The Lions of Marash* (Albany: State University of New York Press, 1973), and Paul Du Véou, *La Passion de La Cilicie 1919–1922* (Paris: Librairie Orientaliste Paul Geuthner, 2nd. edn., 1954).

[35] Marjorie Housepian Dobkin, *Smyrna 1922: The Destruction of a City* (New York: Newmark Press, 1998); Christopher J. Walker, *Armenia: The Survival of a Nation* (New York: St. Martin's Press, revised 2nd. edn., 1990), p. 347; Kévork K. Baghdjian, *La Confiscation, par le gouvernement turc, des biens arméniens . . . dits abandonnés* (Montreal, Quebec: published by author, 1987); Dickran Kouymjian, "Confiscation and Destruction: A Manifestation of the Genocidal Process," *Armenian Forum* 1:3 (Autumn 1998), p. 7.

[36] Gilbert, *The First World War*, p. xxiii; Charles N. Mahjoubian, *America's Conscience: Gorbachev's Dilemma* (Wayne, Penn.: [Mahjoubian's books cited here were published by the author, revised edn.; [1995]) Mahjoubian, *Scoundrels and Bashi-Bozooks in the Armenian Genocide* (Southeastern, Penn.: Mahjoubian, [1995]); Mahjoubian, *Supremest Tragedy of All History: Armenian Civilization under Geopolitical and Religious Conflict* ([Southeastern, Penn.]: Mahjoubian, 1995); Mahjoubian, *Garbis to America: Fifteen Years in Konya (Holy City of Turkish Islam) and One Year in Greece During the Years of the Armenian Genocide* (Southeastern, Penn.: Mahjoubian, 1995).

Between April 1915 and September 1922, 1,450,000 Armenians had been murdered. In the anguished words of Richard Hovannisian, "Our generation didn't have grandparents. Why didn't we have grandparents?" As with the Jewish Holocaust, so with the Armenian Genocide, the statistics are overwhelming, but it is possible to focus on many thousands of separate episodes, incidents, and individual stories. The story, for example, of the massacres in Sivas – of the fate of so many of those potential grandparents – has recently been told by Agop J. Hacikyan, a scholar and expert on the fate of the Armenians, in his novel *A Summer Without Dawn: An Armenian Epic* (written with Jean-Yves Soucy).[37] In 1916, in the immediate aftermath of the massacres, a starkly factual report endorsed by a leading British jurist, Viscount Bryce, *The Treatment of Armenians in the Ottoman Empire, 1915–1916*, detailed the killings with unequivocal documentation: the author of the report, Arnold Toynbee, stressed that the Turkish claim of Armenian treason and rebellion against the Turks could not "bear examination" and was "easily rebutted."[38] Another powerful portrayal of the Armenian fate, in the form of a novel, was Franz Werfel's book *The Forty Days of Musa Dagh*, first published in 1933.[39] Werfel, an Austrian Jew, had spent three years in the Austrian army on the Russian front in the First World War. Like so many of the Armenians about whom he had written, he too became a refugee, fleeing Austria for France in 1938, and when the German army invaded France in 1940, making his way to the United States.

Out of the hundred places about which I could give an account in miniature, I have chosen the town of Kharput, the home town of Richard Hovannisian's family. As Turkish soldiers rampaged through the town in the summer of 1915, an Armenian mother hid her baby boy in a mulberry bush and prayed to God that the Turkish soldiers would not find him. Mother and baby survived.[40] Most of the Armenians of Kharput were massacred. That baby, Michael Hagopian, now eighty-six years old and living in California, completed a documentary film in 2001 entitled *Voices from the Lake*. In it he tells the story his mother told him of how, whenever soldiers came knocking on Armenian doors with deportation orders, his mother would rush to the field where tall poplars shielded the mulberries,

---

[37] Agop J. Hacikyan and Jean-Yves Soucy, *A Summer Without Dawn: An Armenian Epic*, trans. from the French by Christina Le Vernoy and Joyce Bailey (Ontario: M&S, 2000).

[38] Viscount Bryce, ed., Arnold Toynbee, compiler, *The Treatment of Armenians in the Ottoman Empire, 1915–1916: Documents Presented to Viscount Grey of Falloden by Viscount Bryce* (London: His Majesty's Stationery Office, Miscellaneous no. 31, 1916), p. 627.

[39] *Die vierzig Tage des Musa Dagh, Roman* (Berlin: P. Zsolnay, 1933); *The Forty Days of Musa Dagh*, English trans. Geoffrey Dunlop (New York: The Viking Press, 1934).

[40] J. Michael Hagopian, *The Witnesser*, vol. I: *Voices from the Lake: A Film about the Secret Genocide* (Thousand Oaks, Calif.: Armenian Film Foundation, 2001).

and would make him a safe cradle in the foliage. In Hagopian's words: "The mulberry bush is symbolic. It has a purpose in the film in that by the time the leaves had fallen in that one year, the genocide had been completed."

Hagopian found a detailed account of the killings in the diaries of Leslie Davis, United States Consul in Kharput. Hearing reports that bodies had been seen floating in nearby Lake Geoljik, Davis took his camera and went to investigate, recording what he saw. In his diary he described finding what he estimated to be 10,000 bodies of Armenians in (and around) the lake.[41] Hagopian's family was spared because his father was a surgeon whose skills were needed by influential members of the Turkish community. Visiting Kharput in 1967, Hagopian found no trace of Armenians there. All buildings in the Armenian quarter had been leveled to the ground.[42]

While the Armenian massacres were at their height, a 21-year-old Polish Jew, Raphael Lemkin, who was then studying law at Lvov University, found himself in discussion with his professors about one of the dramatic events of the day.[43] On 15 March 1921, Soghomon Tehlirian, a survivor of the Armenian massacres, assassinated one of the leading Turkish politicians involved in them, the Minister of the Interior, Talaat Pasha. Lemkin's professors defended the Turkish action against the Armenians invoking the argument about sovereignty of States: "But 'Sovereignty of States,' I answered, 'implies conducting an independent foreign and international policy, building of schools, construction of roads, in brief, all types of activity directed towards the welfare of people.' Sovereignty, I argued, cannot be conceived of as the right to kill millions of innocent people."[44]

In addition to the million and a half Armenians murdered between 1915 and 1922 there had been an enormous death toll in the four years fighting between 1914 and 1918 which constituted the First World War. Although there had been no genocidal intent in the conflict of the European Powers (into which the United States was drawn in 1917), the propaganda of hatred had been deliberately stimulated by governments in

---

[41] Leslie Davis, *The Slaughterhouse Province: An American Diplomat's Report on the Armenian Genocide, 1915–1917*, ed. Susan K. Blair (New Rochelle: Aristide D. Caratzas, 1989), p. 87.

[42] Hagopian, *Voices from the Lake*.

[43] Frank Chalk, "Redefining Genocide," in George J. Andreopoulos, ed., *Genocide: Conceptual and Historical Dimensions* (Philadelphia: University of Pennsylvania Press, 1994), p. 47.

[44] From the manuscript autobiography of Raphael Lemkin (ch. 1, p. 26, deposited at the New York Public Library, Main Branch), quoted in Chalk, "Redefining Genocide," p. 47.

order to demonize each enemy and impress upon the soldiers that the human beings in each facing set of trenches were in some way inhuman. For the British, French, Italians, Romanians, and Russians it was the German, Austro-Hungarian, Turkish, and Bulgarian soldiers who were to be destroyed – mown down in vast swathes by machine-gun fire, pulverized by artillery shells, bayoneted to death, or blown to pieces by aerial bombardment. Genocidal images had to be created in order to maintain motivation, to foster first the ability and then the zeal for killing in soldiers who, in civilian life, had been innocent and ignorant of the realities of war.

When the First World War ended, the Allied Powers had suffered 5,200,000 dead; the Central Powers, 3,500,000. In the Allied naval blockade of Germany an estimated 500,000 German civilians died of starvation as food supplies were ruthlessly blockaded – the same number of Germans that were killed in the bombing raids of the Second World War.

Reflecting on the first twenty-two years of the twentieth century, Winston Churchill told his constituents in Dundee in 1922: "What a disappointment the Twentieth Century has been." A long series of "disastrous events" had darkened its first twenty years. He went on to ask:

Can you doubt, my faithful friends, as you survey this sombre panorama, that mankind is passing through a period marked not only by an enormous destruction and abridgement of human species, not only by a vast impoverishment and reduction in means of existence, but also that destructive tendencies have not yet run their course? And only intense, concerted and prolonged efforts among all nations can avert further and perhaps even greater calamities.[45]

In the early 1990s, as Communism fell and the Soviet Union disintegrated, I was present in the Ukrainian capital, Kiev, for the first international conference held in a post-Soviet setting, even as the hammer and sickle was being replaced by the blue and yellow flag, and Lenin's statues being toppled to the ground. The conference opened with a distinguished Ukrainian professor telling those present (it was a Ukrainian Jewish colloquium) that he wished to announce formally that Ukraine now recognized that millions of Jews had been murdered in the Holocaust, but hoped that for their part the Jews would recognize the equally terrible suffering of the Ukrainians during the Stalin period.

Undoubtedly the fate of the Ukrainians in the late 1920s was tragic. Several million Ukrainians were then farmers struggling to make a living from agriculture at a time when Communist institutions and economics were being ruthlessly imposed. The peasant farmer was known as a "kulak." From Moscow Stalin characterized the kulaks as "an evil

---

[45] Gilbert, *Twentieth Century*, vol. I, p. 648.

to be uprooted." In his book *Life and Fate*, written after the Second World War, the Soviet-Jewish writer, Vasily Grossman, noted: "Just as the Germans proclaimed that the Jews are not human, thus did Lenin and Stalin proclaim, Kulaks are not human beings." Grossman has left a powerful account of the Soviet demonization of the Ukrainian and other Russian peasants (not unlike Hitler's demonization of the Jews). "They had sold themselves on the idea that the so-called 'Kulaks' were pariahs, untouchable, vermin," Grossman writes:

They would not sit down at a "parasite" table; the "Kulak" child was loathsome, the young "Kulak" girl was lower than a louse. They looked on the so-called "Kulaks" as cattle, swine, loathsome, repulsive: they had no souls; they stank; they had all the venereal diseases; they were enemies of the people and exploited the labour of others. And there was no pity for them. They were not human beings, one had a hard time making out what they were – vermin evidently.[46]

An official Soviet estimate of peasant deaths, in the Ukraine alone – published in Moscow in 1990, just before the disintegration of the Soviet Union – is about 4 million.[47] Robert Conquest put the number at about 5 million.[48] The final, terrible extent of the deaths will probably never be known exactly, and could well be more.

In 1933, when Hitler came to power in Germany, a British observer linked the imminent fate of the Jews with that of the past fate of the Armenians. After a visit to Europe, Eric Mills, a senior member of the British Mandate Administration in Palestine, wrote in his official report to Jerusalem:

While before I went to Germany I knew that the Jewish situation was bad, I had not realized as I now do, that the fate of German Jews is a tragedy, for which cold, intelligent planning by those in authority takes rank with that of those who are out of sympathy with the Bolshevik regime in Russia, or with the elimination of Armenians from the Turkish empire.[49]

Shortly after Hitler came to power in Germany, the fifth International Conference for the Unification of Criminal Law took place in Madrid, under the auspices of the League of Nations. It was at this conference that Raphael Lemkin (who coined the term "genocide") submitted a proposal "to declare the destruction of racial, religious or social collectivities a crime under the law of nations." Lemkin regarded a central element in genocide as "the criminal intent to destroy or to cripple permanently a human group. The acts are directed against groups, as such,

---

[46] Gilbert, *Twentieth Century*, vol. I, p. 761.
[47] Gilbert, *Twentieth Century*, vol. I, p. 761.
[48] Gilbert, *Twentieth Century*, vol. I, p. 761.
[49] Gilbert, *Twentieth Century*, vol. I, p. 80.

and individuals are selected for destruction only because they belong to these groups." This definition, although rejected – with the whole concept – by the League of Nations, was to form the basis of the United Nations Convention for the Prevention and Punishment of the Crime of Genocide after the Second World War.[50]

With the Japanese attack on China in 1937, a genocidal menace entered China together with the invading army. On 13 December 1937 Japanese troops entered Nanking, the Chinese capital. With an intensity that shocked even those familiar with the savagery of war, the Japanese soldiers who entered Nanking attacked the Chinese civilian population in an orgy of destruction. The "Rape of Nanking" was to take its place among the massacres not only of the century, but of modern times. When the Japanese entered Nanking the total Chinese population was estimated at between 600,000 and 700,000, of whom 150,000 were soldiers. In the ensuing slaughter more than 200,000 civilians and 90,000 soldiers were killed. The first to be killed were the soldiers who had surrendered. The orders for their execution were specific: "All prisoners of war are to be executed. Method of execution: divide the prisoners into groups of a dozen. Shoot to kill separately."[51]

Japanese officers used their swords to chop off the heads of their Chinese prisoners. Soldiers bayoneted prisoners to death, often tying them up in batches first. Old people, women, children, and wounded soldiers were shot down in the streets. Shopkeepers, having been ordered to open their shops, were then killed, and the shops looted.

A Japanese soldier, Takokoro Kozo, later recalled: "Women suffered most. No matter how young or old, they all could not escape the fate of being raped. We sent out coal trucks to the city streets and villages to seize a lot of women. And then each of them was allocated to fifteen to twenty soldiers for sexual intercourse and abuse." Takokoro added: "After raping we would also kill them. Those women would start to flee once we let them go. Then we would 'bang!' shoot them in the back to finish them up."[52] Such was the fate of human beings whose only "crime" – judged to make them worthy of death – was that they had been born Chinese, just as the only "crime" of the Armenians between 1915 and 1922 was to have been born Armenian, the only "crime" of the Jews between 1939 and 1945 to have been born Jewish.

---

[50] George J. Andreopoulos, "Introduction: The Calculus of Genocide," in Andreopoulos, ed., *Genocide*, pp. 1–2. In 1946 Lemkin was an adviser to United States Supreme Court Justice Robert H. Jackson at the International Military Tribunal in Nuremberg, which tried the leading Nazi war criminals.
[51] Gilbert, *Twentieth Century*, vol. II, p. 162.
[52] Gilbert, *Twentieth Century*, vol. II, p. 163.

In the fighting against the Japanese in 1938, a million Chinese soldiers were killed or wounded. Tens of thousands of Chinese civilians were killed in Japanese air raids. If not genocide, then certainly a cruel fate – simply for being Chinese.

In the spring of 1938 the Turkish Government carried out a punitive raid against the Kurds of the Dersim region (now known as Tunceli).[53] On 27 September 1938 the British Consul in Trebizond, after referring to the Armenian massacres in the same region in 1915, reported to the Foreign Office in London: "Thousands of Kurds, including women and children, were slain; others, mostly children, were thrown into the Euphrates; while thousands of others in less hostile areas, who had first been deprived of their cattle and other belongings, were deported to vilayets in Central Anatolia. It is now stated that the Kurdish question no longer exists in Turkey."[54]

More than 5,000 Kurds were killed in that punitive act of destruction, 10 percent of the local Kurdish population: they had been, literally, decimated – the Ancient Roman policy of killing 1 in 10 of their captives. Martin van Bruinessen writes, of the Dersim killings, "what we are dealing with was not merely the brutal suppression of an internal rebellion but part of a wider policy directed against Kurds as such."[55] It was this murderous targeting of an entire community which constituted the element of genocide.

On 1 September 1939 Germany invaded Poland. Five and a half years later, on 8 May 1945, the fighting that had become the Second World War ended – in Europe. As during the First World War, the "enemy" had to be demonized. Decent, moderate Britons had to feel that the destruction of 42,000 German civilians in the city of Hamburg in the course of a few hours in 1943 – of half a million German civilians before the war was over – was a necessary element in war-making against "the vile Hun." The average German citizen had already been taught that the destruction of civilians by aerial bombardment in Warsaw, Rotterdam, Coventry, London, and Belgrade was an essential aspect of war-making, even of national survival. The vast majority of Americans regarded the death of 2 million Japanese civilians in the massive bombing raids over Tokyo and other Japanese cities, as a rightful act – even before the dropping of the atomic bombs on Hiroshima and Nagasaki.

[53] Martin van Bruinessen, "Genocide in Kurdistan?: The Suppression of the Dersim Rebellion in Turkey (1937–38) and the Chemical War against the Iraqi Kurds (1988)," in Andreopoulos, ed., *Genocide*, p. 147.
[54] Van Bruinessen, "Genocide in Kurdistan?" p. 144.
[55] Van Bruinessen, "Genocide in Kurdistan?" pp. 144–5.

That the Japanese were bayoneting to death unarmed Chinese (and also, after 1941, unarmed Allied prisoners of war) roused no moral indignation inside Japan. What rankled for the Japanese was that the two atomic bombs were dropped on them, the demonized "Orientals," and not on "white Europeans." Second World War songs and jingles, in every country, sought to demonize the whole populations of the enemy. These were not genocides; but they constituted a serious diminution of the respect and tolerance which, if it does not prevail among nations and peoples, can produce an atmosphere of hatred whereby some form or other of genocidal policy becomes acceptable.

The Second World War was among the most destructive conflicts in recorded history. Between the German attack on Poland in September 1939 and the surrender of Japan in 1945 as many as 50 million soldiers and civilians perished. In the mass killing of civilians civilized behavior was set aside, and civilization itself was put in danger. Captive Poles, Serbs, Russians, Czechs were murdered by their captors as if they were vermin, and were characterized as such – called "sub-human" – as were the 6 million Jews whose destruction was part of a deliberate genocidal plan (which failed, but only just failed) to destroy all the Jews of Europe.

Both the Jews and the Armenians have survived as a people, but it has taken both of them decades for their numerical strength to return to what it had been before the destructions. In the year 2000 the Jews have just reached the numbers – some 15 million – which they had reached in 1939, just as the Armenians – 7 million in 1915 – have only just reached, after eighty-five years, their earlier figure. The loss, for Jews and Armenians, of what might have been the achievement and contribution of vibrant, creative, life-enhancing, life-perpetuating generations, is incalculable.

There is one little-mentioned element of the Holocaust which I should like to mention. From the moment of the German invasion of the Soviet Union in June 1941, the SS killing squads inside Russia itemized daily and sent back to Berlin lists of the thousands of Jews they had killed.[56] They noted down with pedantic precision, in separate listings, the exact numbers of Jewish men, women, and children whom they had murdered each day. They also listed, from time to time, individual Armenians whom they had killed. Like the Jews, these Armenians were not killed because they were soldiers or partisans, or constituted a threat to German rule, but because they had been characterized as beneath the dignity of human beings. Whenever I am in Lvov, one of the centres of the SS killing areas,

[56] Gilbert, *Twentieth Century*, vol. II, p. 422.

I visit the Armenian quarter there, conscious of this link: that even the Holocaust had an Armenian aspect.

There is another Armenian aspect: three Armenians have been awarded the Medal of the Righteous by Yad Vashem, the Holocaust museum and memorial in Jerusalem, for helping to save Jewish lives during the Holocaust at the risk of their own lives. One of them, an Armenian doctor, Ara Jeretzian, saved at least 200 Jews by sheltering them in the hospital where he worked and in an emergency clinic which he set up in a private home, providing food and, when needed, false documents.[57] Another, Felicia Taschdjian, together with her husband, had hidden a Jew, Valentine Skidelsky, in the attic of their Viennese home for two and a half years.[58]

In 1951 the United Nations Convention for the Prevention and Punishment of the Crime of Genocide (known as the Genocide Convention) came into force. It had originally been adopted by the United Nations almost three years earlier, on 9 December 1948. Its definition of genocide, which the Jewish human rights activist Raphael Lemkin had inspired, reads:

In the present Convention, genocide means any of the following acts committed with intent to destroy, in whole or in part, a national, ethical, racial or religious group, as such:
a. Killing members of the group;
b. Causing serious bodily or mental harm to members of the group;
c. Deliberately inflicting on the group conditions of life calculated to bring about its physical destruction in whole or in part;
d. Imposing measures intended to prevent births within the group;
e. Forcibly transferring children of the group to another group.[59]

Armenians, Ukrainians, Chinese, Poles, Serbs, Jews, were each among the victims of mass murder in the first half of the twentieth century leading up to the convention who came within this definition.

The coming into being of the Genocide Convention did not signal an end to genocide. The second half of the twentieth century was besmirched in that regard, year by year. The fate of Tibetans under Chinese Communist rule after 1951 was tragic. So was the fate of native Indian tribes in the forests of Brazil. So too was the fate of the people of East Timor, a former Portuguese colony which had just declared its independence, following the invasion of East Timor by Indonesian troops in 1975. As new

[57] Yad Vashem Archives, File no. 2002, Buday Tiborne, Dr. Gyori Palne and Dr. Mosonyi Laszlo, letter, 27 September 1977.
[58] Yad Vashem Archives, File no. 4962, Dara Skidelsky, letter, 24 July 1990.
[59] "Appendix I: Text of the 1948 Genocide Convention," in Andreopoulos, ed., *Genocide*, p. 229.

areas of genocidal acts emerged on the globe, it was clear that Churchill's "terrible twentieth century" had yet to run its destructive course. James Dunn, an Australian diplomat who was in East Timor at the time of the Indonesian invasion (he subsequently wrote *Timor: A People Betrayed*) has written:

The genocidal dimensions of the loss of life in East Timor emerged starkly in 1979, almost four years after the invasion, when Indonesian authorities finally allowed a small number of international aid workers to conduct a survey of the humanitarian needs of the province. The human misery they encountered shocked these officials, whose estimates suggested that in the preceding four years Timor had lost between a tenth and a third of its population and that 200,000 of the remainder were in appalling conditions in "resettlement camps," which one official, who had previously been in Cambodia, described as among the worst he had seen.[60]

Also starting in 1975, in order to help secure his border against infiltration by groups hostile to his dictatorial regime, the Cambodian Prime Minister, Pol Pot, ordered the depopulation of a strip of territory along its border. This was done with a barbarity seldom seen even in the severity of South-East Asian conflicts. Pol Pot was also perpetrating terrifying crimes inside his country. The total death toll during five years of Khmer Rouge domination was a million and a half, out of a total population of 8 million. A chill indication of the scale of the killings is found in the words of the historian Ben Kiernan. "I first visited Cambodia in early 1975," he writes; "None of the Cambodians I knew then survived the next four years."[61] In the words of George J. Andreopoulos, one of those who has most enhanced our knowledge of genocide, Pol Pot's regime was – he writes:

an open and shut case of genocidal activities on at least four fronts: the extermination of a religious group, the Buddhist monks (out of a total of 2,680 Buddhist monks from eight of Cambodia's monasteries, only 70 monks were found to have survived in 1979); and the persecution of three ethnic groups, including the Vietnamese community (in more than a year's research in Cambodia after 1979 it was not possible to find a Vietnamese resident who had survived the Pol Pot years there), the Chinese community (reduced by half by 1979); and the Muslim Chams (reduced by 36 percent, from 250,000 to 160,000, by 1979).[62]

On 19 August 1984 the *New York Times* carried a news item about a recent episode in Sri Lanka. The government had rounded up some 5,000

---

[60] James Dunn, "East Timor: A Case of Cultural Genocide?" in Andreopoulos, ed., *Genocide*, p. 182.
[61] Gilbert, *Twentieth Century*, vol. III, p. 514.   [62] Andreopoulos, "Introduction" p. 3.

Tamils over the previous weekend and executed them.[63] Israel Charny, author of *Genocide: The Human Cancer*, has described the persistent killing of Tamils by Sri Lankans as "genocidal massacre."[64] The Tamil militants were not without genocidal tendencies of their own. On 30 May 1990, Amnesty International appealed to the Tamil Tigers to end their "executions" of political opponents.[65] The appeal was ignored. On 13 June the Tamil Tigers captured ninety Sinhalese policemen in eastern Sri Lanka and, having disarmed them, executed them.[66] Tamil Tigers also attacked moderate Tamil groups who were calling for restraint and compromise.

The Tamil Tigers also turned on the Muslim minority in Sri Lanka. On 3 August 1990 more than 100 Muslims were massacred at a mosque in Kattankudy. Two days later, 58 Muslims were murdered in their villages.[67] when Tamil Tigers captured the fort at Jaffna at the end of August, the Sri Lankan air force bombed the fort with considerable intensity; among the buildings destroyed in the bombing was the hospital, which had been placed under the control of the International Committee of the Red Cross. On 23 October the European Community protested at Sri Lanka's "descent into unrestrained killings."[68] What was being witnessed in Sri Lanka was a civil war with a genocidal aspect: hatreds inflamed between race and race, religion and religion: not unlike – though on a far smaller scale – the Catholic–Protestant killings in Northern Ireland, which cost more than 1,000 lives; or, on a larger scale, the Hindu–Muslim killings in the Indo-Pakistan borderlands in and around Kashmir, where according to recent reports[69] more than 30,000 people were killed in the 1990s.

In February 1988 the plight of the Armenians returned to the forefront of international consciousness. As the Soviet Union began to disintegrate, the Armenians of the Karabagh region – which Stalin had awarded to the overall control of the Muslim Azeris of Azerbaijan – took Gorbachev's promise of *glasnost* and *perestroika* seriously, as they did his declarations that the time had come to rectify past errors of the Stalin era. For the Armenians a cardinal crime of Stalin was the award of Karabagh to Azerbaijan.

---

[63] "More Killing in Sri Lanka," *New York Times*, 19 August, 1984, cited in Israel W. Charny, "Toward a Generic Definition of Genocide," in Andreopoulos, ed., *Genocide*, pp. 77, 94 (n. 30).
[64] Charny, "Toward a Generic Definition of Genocide," p. 77.
[65] Gilbert, *Twentieth Century*, vol. III, p. 703.
[66] Gilbert, *Twentieth Century*, vol. III, p. 703.
[67] Gilbert, *Twentieth Century*, vol. III, p. 703.
[68] Gilbert, *Twentieth Century*, vol. III, p. 703.
[69] "Kashmiri Killing Mounts as EU Arrives," Reuters, in *Washington Post*, 27 September 2000, p. A24.

The Armenian population and local government organs of the Mountainous Karabagh Autonomous Region petitioned for the right of self-determination and incorporation into Soviet Armenia. Hundreds of thousands of people in Erevan and elsewhere in Armenia took to the streets in support of the Karabagh movement. The massive demonstrations were unprecedented in the Soviet Union. A wave of optimism engulfed the Armenians both inside the Soviet Union and throughout the Armenian diaspora. Dormant Armenian communities in Russia began to stir, and the Armenians abroad rallied to the cause. Spirits were high and the mood was festive, as it seemed that for once in the twentieth century the continuous process of diminution of the living space of the Armenians might be reversed, since the proposed shift of boundaries could be effected as an internal Soviet affair.

Armenian optimism was dampened at the end of February 1988, by the outbreak of anti-Armenian violence in the Azerbaijani industrial city of Sumgait. The indiscriminate, brutal torture and killing, the mutilation and rape, the looting and burning sent shock waves into Armenian communities throughout the world. Richard Hovannisian writes:

The terms "massacre," "pogrom," and even "genocide" became current. Spontaneous associations with 1915 were made everywhere. The Azerbaijanis, related by race, language, and culture to the Turks, became in Armenian minds the same vicious, heartless people who had perpetrated the genocide in 1915, and the victims of Sumgait were simply the most recent martyrs exacted from the nation since antiquity and especially since the Turanic domination of Armenia.

Seventy years of Soviet mythology about the resolution and elimination of nationality problems and the friendship and brotherhood of all Soviet peoples dissolved in a single instance, and the traumatized Armenians came face to face with the ghost of the past.[70]

That same year, 1988, exactly fifty years after the killings at Dersim when Turks had massacred Kurds, the Iraqi Government of Saddam Hussein carried out a series of chemical weapons attacks against the Kurds in northern Iraq. In March 1991 an Iraqi punitive expedition against Kurdish towns led to renewed killings.

From the outset of its independence on 1 March 1992, Bosnia was beset with internal and external strife. From the first days, Bosnian-Serb soldiers were trying – behind the lines – to bring to an end the Muslim population by the most terrible of all methods, not with expulsion but by mass murder. It became known as "ethnic cleansing." Among the Muslims rounded up that April were several hundred in the village of Vlasenica. It was to be four years before their fate became known, when

---

[70] Hovannisian, "Etiology," pp. 115–16.

Western journalists entered the area for the first time, and discovered the mass graves.[71]

In a ruling on 8 April 1993 the International Court of Justice at The Hague asked the government of the Federal Republic of Yugoslavia to ensure that any military, paramilitary or irregular armed units which may be directed or supported by it . . . do not commit any acts of genocide, of conspiracy to commit genocide, of direct and public incitement to commit genocide, or of complicity to genocide, whether directed against the Muslim population of Bosnia and Herzegovina or against any other national, ethical, racial or religious group.[72]

The evident failure to stop genocide has resulted in the prosecution of the former head of the Yugoslav state, Slobodon Milosevic.

Early in 1994, a 2,500-strong United Nations force was sent to maintain peace in Rwanda, where two groups were in conflict: the majority Hutu, and the minority Tutsi, the latter the traditional rulers of Rwanda. As fighting intensified, Hutu attacks on Tutsi reached a fearsome pitch. Hutu human rights activists who protested against the massacres were killed by their fellow-Hutu. The United Nations Security Council, fearful for the lives of its own men, voted on 21 April to withdraw all but 270 of the United Nations force from Rwanda. Two days later the International Committee of the Red Cross announced that 100,000 people had been killed in Rwanda in the previous eighteen days. Five days later the toll had doubled to 200,000. Some of the worst massacres took place inside churches to which the Tutsi had fled for sanctuary. As the slaughter continued, a quarter of a million Tutsi refugees fled across the border into Tanzania. In all, between 500,000 and 800,000 Tutsi had been killed, as had many moderate Hutu who opposed the killing.[73]

On 8 November 1994 the United Nations Security Council set up an International Criminal Tribunal for Rwanda, charged with prosecuting those responsible for genocide.[74] Four years later the Rwandan courts passed death sentences on those who had carried out the massacres. It was the first time since the end of the Second World War fifty-three years earlier that men had been found guilty of genocide. Those to be executed included Froduald Karamira, who had appealed daily over radio stations controlled by extremist Hutus for the Hutu majority to "cleanse" their communities of Tutsi "cockroaches." A British journalist, David Orr,

[71] Gilbert, *Twentieth Century*, vol. III, pp. 733, 823–4.
[72] International Court of Justice, *Order on Request for the Indication of Provisional Measures in Case Concerning Application of the Convention on the Prevention and Punishment of the Crime of Genocide* (Bosnia and Herzegovina v. Yugoslavia [Serbia and Montenegro]), 8 April 1993, 32.ILM888 (1993).
[73] Gilbert, *Twentieth Century*, vol. III, p. 781.
[74] Gilbert, *Twentieth Century*, vol. III, p. 781.

witnessed the executions, and reported to *The Times*: "A well-dressed man said: 'This is justice being done.' A young man in jeans said: 'This will serve as an example to people who might try to organize genocide in future.' "[75]

On 16 November 1998, in The Hague, three United Nations judges imposed the first international convictions for atrocities committed against Bosnian Serbs. A Bosnian Croat and two Muslims were convicted of murdering, torturing, and raping Serb prisoners in 1992. The trial had lasted twenty months. It was the first in which the tribunal concentrated on atrocities against Serbs – who were blamed for most of the war crimes committed in Bosnia. The prosecutor, Brenda Hollis, had been seconded from the United States Army legal branch. The camp warden at a concentration camp at Celebici was a Bosnian Croat, Zdravko Mucic. He was found guilty of eleven war crimes, having been in charge of guards who murdered nine Serbs and tortured six.[76] His conviction was the first by an international court on the basis of "command responsibility" since the International Military Tribunals at Nuremberg and Tokyo convicted Second World War German and Japanese commanders and superiors for the crimes committed by their subordinates. The accused was sentenced to seven years in prison.[77]

International pressure and effort can end genocidal situations. In 1996 the Dayton peace treaty brought an end to the ethnic fighting in former Yugoslavia, and created a unified yet partitioned Bosnia. Muslims and Bosnian Croats in one geographic area, Bosnian Serbs in another, had to rebuild broken homes and shattered lives, and learn to live in some degree of harmony with the minorities in their midst from each community. There was, however, much unfinished business with regard to the civil war that had just ended. The United Nations was committed to bringing to trial those Bosnian Serbs who had been identified as war criminals, responsible for the "ethnic cleansing" of thousands of men, women, and children.

There were fifty-two names on the initial list submitted to the International War Crimes Tribunal at The Hague.[78] The trials continue to this day. There is much judicial work to be done. In March 1996, a United Nations envoy, Elisabeth Rehn, confirmed that at least 3,000 Muslims had been murdered by the Bosnian Serb army after the fall of the town of Srebrenica in July 1995. As yet "unaccounted for more Muslims"

[75] Gilbert, *Twentieth Century*, vol. III, pp. 864–5.
[76] Gilbert, *Twentieth Century*, vol. III, p. 865.
[77] Gilbert, *Twentieth Century*, vol. III, p. 865.
[78] Gilbert, *Twentieth Century*, vol. III, p. 823.

were 8,000.[79] The United States Ambassador to the United Nations, Madeleine Albright, who was taken in March to see a mass grave near Srebrenica, commented: "It is the most disgusting and horrifying sight for another human being to see."[80]

Mass graves were also being found in Cambodia in 1996, from Pol Pot's reign of terror twenty-five years earlier. The search for graves was being undertaken, as in Bosnia, under the aegis of the United Nations. Funding came from the United States, through a Cambodian Genocide Program. The manager of the program, Craig Etcheson, gave details of the new discoveries at a press conference in Phnom Penh in February. "We had anticipated that there could be about one hundred to two hundred of them in the whole country," he said; "That is so far off, it is ridiculous. We are finding thousands in individual provinces."[81]

The fiftieth anniversary of the independence of Burma from Britain was marked on 4 January 1998. Commenting on this anniversary a British member of the House of Lords, David Alton, remarked bitterly: "A flag hoisting ceremony was suitably subdued as Myanmar, or Burma as most of the world still knows it, commemorated half a century of human rights abuses and oppressive authoritarian government."[82] Lord Alton has been at the forefront of a public campaign on behalf of the Karen people of Burma, of whom 116,000 are in refugee camps inside Thailand, and an estimated 20,000 have died in recent years. "Inside Burma" he writes, "villages continue to be destroyed, women raped, and men conscripted as forced labour or used as human mine sweepers."

Does the desperate plight of the Karen people constitute an aspect of genocide? On 17 January 2000 Lord Alton asked a British Government minister Baroness Scotland (herself a Black peer):

Is she aware that many of the hotels and the tourist infrastructure in Burma have been built by slave labour, often involving in particular the Karen people and others from different ethnic minorities, who have been forcibly exploited and many of whom have even died during the creation of that tourist infrastructure? Is she further aware that in the past five years in the Karen State alone, some 30,000 Karen people have died, 300,000 have been displaced, and that clearly that amounts to genocide?[83]

Baroness Scotland made no comment on the charge of genocide, though she did state that the British government "deplore the forced

---

[79] Gilbert, *Twentieth Century*, vol. III, p. 824.
[80] Gilbert, *Twentieth Century*, vol. III, p. 824.
[81] Gilbert, *Twentieth Century*, vol. III, p. 824.
[82] David Alton, "Burma: The Great British Betrayal – and Another Tragedy is Waiting to Happen," Jubilee Campaign Press Release, 24 February, 1998.
[83] Great Britain, House of Lords *Hansard* Text, Lord David Alton of Liverpool, "Burma: Tourist Advice," 17 January 2000, column 873.

labour used in Burma" which she described as "one of a large number of human rights violations in that country."[84] Two years earlier Lord Alton had stated emphatically, in a statement entitled "The Karen: A Case Study in International Indifference" (2 March 1998):

> What is happening in Burma today is every bit as evil as the atrocities committed by the Bosnian war lords. The Karen people have a rich culture. It is being destroyed. Cultural and physical genocide has been compounded by betrayal and manipulation. Atrocities in Bosnia shocked European sensibilities because courageous reporters ensured that the story was told. Politicians reacted with international and judicial sanctions. Trials for war crimes have been established at the Hague. Compare that with our reaction to Burma or to Cambodia. What is intolerable in Europe should not be any more tolerable because it is in South East Asia. Is a life in South East Asia worth less than a life in South East Europe?[85]

One reason why individuals in Britain took up the Karen issue was that many of them remember the contribution the Karen people made in the struggle against the Japanese occupiers of Burma in the Second World War: 50,000 Karen soldiers fought with the British as allies against the Japanese. Today some 5,000–10,000 Karen troops are in those same jungles fighting against an estimated 350,000 Burmese soldiers.

Lord Chalfont, one of the British officers who had commanded Karen soldiers in the Second World War, spoke during a debate in the House of Lords on 25 March 1998: "There is a cultural factor also which is worth bearing in mind . . . many Burmese have traditionally regarded the Karen as inferior beings. In fact the word Karen, in the Burmese language, means 'a wild man.' "[86] He went on further to refer to the suffering, oppression, and atrocities inflicted on the Karen by the Burmese.

"In the case of the persecution of the Karen it may be a means of averting genocide that such publicity and protest takes place. But the power of United Nations High Commissioner for Refugees, the only international organization with any status at all in the region, is (as we have seen) limited. Who, if the situation worsens," Chalfont asked, "will have the will or power to take action on behalf of a persecuted people?"

News reports at the end of July 1999 told of at least twenty-two Karen villagers, including a baby and two children, aged two and eight, who were massacred by Burmese soldiers. The United Nations Special Rapporteur on Burma, Rajsoomer Lallah, said in his report in 1998 that human rights violations "are not simply isolated acts of individual misbehaviour . . . but

---

[84] Great Britain, House of Lords *Hansard* Text, Baroness Scotland of Asthal, "Burma: Tourist Advice," 17 January 2000, column 873.

[85] Alton, "Burma: The Great British Betrayal," 24 February 1998.

[86] Great Britain, House of Lords *Hansard* Text, Lord Chalfont, "Burma and Karen Refugees," 25 March 1998, column 1298.

are rather the result of policy at the highest level, entailing political and legal responsibility."[87]

About 40 percent of the Karen people are Christians, mainly Baptist. Muslims are also victims in Burma of what is essentially a Buddhist-initiated racism. According to Dr. Abdul Razzak, the Chairman of the All Burma Moslem Union, Muslims have regularly been arrested and pressed into forced labor in Burma. Forty-two mosques have been destroyed and Burmese soldiers subject individual Muslims to humiliations which offend their religious belief – such as being forced to eat pork – and have taken their animals and possessions and destroyed whole villages.[88]

The use of the word "genocide" has become increasingly frequent as a term of outrage against what appears to be the deliberate killing of a particular group of people for no other reason than that they have been targeted as members of that group to suffer some extreme form of suffering. On 2 August 2000 Denis J. Halliday, a former United Nations Assistant Secretary General who had served as United Nations Humanitarian Co-ordinator in Iraq in 1997–8, published an article in the *Guardian* newspaper in London in which he wrote:

Here we are in the middle of the millennium year and we are responsible for genocide in Iraq . . .

We do not care when Unicef reports that 5,000 children under five years old die each month unnecessarily from embargo-related deprivation . . .

Do we not care that the UN allies, in breach of Geneva conventions, destroyed the lives of civilians through direct bombing and destruction of electric power capabilities, clean water systems, sanitation and health care?

Do we not care that Iraqi society, culture and learning, rooted in the cities of Mesopotamia, is dying alongside its people? Are we really that racist? Are we really that anti-Islamic? Could Britain stand by and watch the same holocaust within a white Christian State?[89]

Can sanctions be genocidal? Were the 500,000 German civilians who died as a result of the British naval blockade in the First World War the victims of the demonization, not merely of the Kaiser, but of Germans as a group? Are Iraqi civilians dying because they are likewise demonized – not just Saddam Hussein but the people of Iraq?

---

[87] Rajsoomer Lallah, "Interim Report on the Situation of Human Rights in Myanmar prepared by the Special Rapporteur of the Commission on Human Rights in accordance with Economic and Social Council Decision 1998/261 of 30 July 1998," UN General Assembly Report A/53/364, 10 September 1998.

[88] Great Britain, House of Lords *Hansard* Text, Lord David Alton of Liverpool, "Burma and Karen Refugees," 25 March 1998, column 1295.

[89] Denis J. Halliday, "Time to See the Truth about Ourselves and Iraq," *Guardian*, 2 August 2000.

Another question being asked increasingly at the opening of the twenty-first century is: can genocidal activity be forestalled, or at least halted, in its earliest stages? On 4 September 2000, during a symposium on the future role of the United Nations, a senior Canadian army officer, now retired, Lieutenant-General Romeo Dallaire, warned that unless the United Nations "is allowed to respond to humanitarian emergencies in places like Rwanda with the same resources as it did in the former Yugoslavia, more catastrophes will occur."

Dallaire had been the commander of the United Nations forces in Rwanda when Hutu extremists killed 800,000 Tutsi and Hutu moderates. At that time he had pleaded with the United Nations for more manpower, and a clearer mandate to prevent genocide. Asked at the symposium whether the United Nations could keep the peace around the world, he said that massive changes were needed in the way peacekeeping is approached. In his view the most powerful Western countries, notably the United States, must be willing to shelve self-interest in deciding where their peacekeepers serve, for how long, and at what cost. In some cases the commitment may span decades, as has been the case in Cyprus, divided between Greek and Turkish Cypriot communities.

The United Nations does have military forces, drawn from its member States, most of them on "peacekeeping missions" around the world. Can they be effective in stopping the killing by one group of another, should it break out, or re-occur? As of 9 September 2000 these United Nations forces were, in descending numerical order: in Sierra Leone (12,474); in East Timor, forming a "transitional administration," (9,352); in Lebanon (6,138); in Kosovo (5,748); in Bosnia (1,648); on the Golan Heights, as an "observer force" in the demilitarized zone between Israel and Syria (1,274); in Cyprus, along the Turkish–Greek divide (1,251); on the Iraq–Kuwait border (1,111); in Western Sahara (721); in Georgia (former Soviet Union) (328); in India and Pakistan, without powers to separate the warring factions in the disputed region of Kashmir (124); in Croatia (53). An unarmed United Nations force of 160 soldiers from Norway, Denmark, and Italy was sent to Hebron in 1994 to keep the peace between Jews and Arabs in that Holy City (where the Patriarch Abraham, the father of both Jews and Arabs, is buried).[90] When trouble came six years later, the force had little effect. In addition, in the even holier city of Jerusalem, 355 United Nations troops, based in a former British headquarters on the Hill of Evil Counsel (!), have taken no part since 1967 in trying to separate Jews and Arabs, not even during the "Al-Aksa Intifada" which broke out towards the end of 2000 – they have no mandate for intervention. Was

[90] Gilbert, *Twentieth Century*, vol. III, p. 772.

it a question of mandate or of numbers? Following the Al-Aksa Intifada, both Britain – through the United Nations – and Yasser Arafat from his Chairman's residence in Gaza, pressed for a larger force of some 2,000 United Nations troops to be sent to the flash-point areas. Britain wanted "observers"; Arafat wanted armed men with a mandate to intervene.

We are now in the twenty-first century. Will we have the power, and equally important the will, not only to prevent violent confrontations between groups with deep mutual hostility, but to halt future genocides – future genocidal impulses? That remains the question we need to ponder; that is the challenge of the history presented in this volume. The answer is by no means clear.

2   Under cover of war: the Armenian
Genocide in the context of total war

Jay Winter

It is one of the signal challenges of the historical profession to provide a guide to understanding the century which has just passed while recognizing that the language historians use is in significant ways inadequate to the task. In that historical narrative, to talk of genocide is unavoidable, but the grammar of historical analysis withers when used to encapsulate the history of genocide.

Some have called this problem a crisis of representation, formulated famously by Adorno in the rhetorical statement that, after Auschwitz there can be no poetry.[1] His injunction was to try to write poetry nonetheless. It may be useful to recast Adorno and to say that, after Auschwitz, there can be no linear history, and yet we must try to write it nonetheless. This insight was true long before Auschwitz, however, and the need to recognize it and reflect on it was evident well before the Second World War.

Here is the predicament we face. Dietrich Bonhoeffer wrote that only those who cried for the Jews had the right to sing Gregorian chants.[2] I want to suggest that only by confronting the horror of the Armenian genocide of 1915 can we begin to locate the Holocaust of the Second World War within the history of the twentieth century. For these crimes occurred under the cover of world wars; and both disclosed the devastating logic and power of a new kind of war: "total war".

This contextual issue matters crucially, in part because it provides us with a way out of the absurdity of measuring genocidal acts against each other. All are unique; all require comparison to enable us even to begin to talk about them. The framework for such comparison must remain tentative and incomplete, but at least part of it must be located in the phenomenon of total war.

---

[1] Saul Friedlander, ed., *Probing the Limits of Representation: Nazism and the "Final Solution"* (Cambridge, Mass.: Harvard University Press, 1992).

[2] Eberhard Bethge, "Bonhoeffer and the Jews," in John B. Godsey and Geffrey B. Kelly, eds., *Ethical Responsibility: Bonhoeffer's Legacy to the Churches* Toronto Studies in Theology, 6. (New York: Edwin Mellen Press, 1981), p. 71.

Total war and genocide in the twentieth century

The Armenian genocide unfolded during the Great War of 1914–18, a conflict which began as a conventional conflict and then turned into total war, the first of its kind. When industrialized nations, supported by imperial dominions, took the decision to go to war, and stayed at war over an extended period, they opened a Pandora's box. What they let free was a kind of war unlike any the world had ever seen before. Our search to understand the historical setting of the Armenian genocide of 1915 brings us abruptly to this new framework of violence and international conflict which I call total war.

The notion of "total war" is a term notoriously difficult to define. Let me try. In its constituent parts, total war resembled other conflicts. The elements out of which it was forged were not at all new. There were anticipations and precursors; the American Civil War, as we shall see, is one of them. Taken together, however, the concatenation of the elements of the mass mobilization of industrialized societies produced a new kind of war, total war. Its constitutive parts had existed separately before 1914, but had never before been fused together. Another way of making the same point is to say that the sum of the vectors of international violence was greater in 1914–18 than in any previous war. Here a difference in degree – an exponential increase in the lethality and reach of warfare – turned into a difference in kind.

In elaborating some of the unique features of this phenomenon, I want to reiterate that it is in their multiplicative character, their tendency to amplify each other, that the true nature of total war must be sought. In this case, the whole is much more terrible than the sum of its parts.

The best way of using the term "total war" is less as a description than as a metaphor, suggesting rather than defining a decided turn for the worse in international conflict. Indeed "total war" is never literally total. It is "totalizing," in the sense that the longer it lasts, the more human and material resources are drawn inexorably into its vortex. The spiral towards "total war," begun in 1914, was a process resembling the approach of an asymptote to a mathematical limit; as in Zeno's Paradox, it never gets there. A Weberian view is that the notion of "total war" is an ideal type, a heuristic rather than a descriptive tool.[3] I believe the term has more bite than that, though it needs to be handled with care. When the war of 1914 failed to produce a rapid outcome, when it turned into a form of siege warfare among industrial powers whose dominions stretched across the

---

[3] Roger Chickering, "Total War: The Use and Abuse of a Concept," in Manfred F. Boemeke, Roger Chickering and Stig Förster, eds., *Anticipating Total War: The German and American Experiences, 1871–1914* (Cambridge: Cambridge University Press, 1999), p. 23.

world, it mutated into another kind of war, bigger, more lethal, and more corrosive than any previous conflict. It is to that new kind of war that the word "total" appropriately applies.

Some have viewed the Peloponnesian wars as total; others cite the Thirty Years' War of the seventeenth century, and eighteenth-century warfare among empires truly spanned the globe. From a number of viewpoints, there is force in these arguments. On balance, however, I cannot accept them as extending the category of "total war" prior to the twentieth century. The birth of industrial warfare on the world scale after 1914 was, in my view, a revolutionary event. The intersection of that event with genocidal acts is the critical point I want to explore.

That transformation occurred precisely in the period when the Armenian genocide took place. The fact that Turkey was not among the leading industrial nations is neither here nor there; the transformation in the nature of warfare itself at this very time is the key issue. The war Turkey joined on the side of the Central Powers soon became a new kind of war, whose radicalized character Turkey helped shape through carrying out the Armenian genocide. In effect, total war did not produce genocide; it created the military, political, and cultural space in which it could occur, and occur again.

Another way of putting the central point is to reverse it. The notion of "total war" helps us to see how genocide happened in the twentieth century. To study the Armenian genocide of 1915 and the Nazi genocide of 1941–5, however, enables us see what total war was. My claim is that genocide is part of the landscape of total war. Indeed, genocide helped create what we now understand as "total war," a kind of armed conflict on a scale and with a character placing it beyond what had been framed for centuries as the laws of war.

No one can deny that the Armenian genocide took place under the eyes of the German army and that the killers operated with impunity until after the war was over. Moreover, even then, such justice as was administered under Turkish military law barely touched the surface of the crimes – crimes the very existence of which are still denied by the authorities of the present-day Turkish state. The killers got away with the crime. This is what Hitler meant when, in a controversial and still-disputed set of remarks, he asked "Who remembers the Armenian genocide?" Whatever his precise words, the meaning was clear. Racial war, biological warfare, ethnic cleansing were on the map in 1915 in a way that went beyond the experience of earlier conflicts. When war visited Europe again in 1939, and when it turned into a world war in 1941, Hitler returned to this phenomenon – the phenomenon of genocide in the context of total war. That is when and why he set the Holocaust in motion.[4] In effect, without the Great War and its precedents, Auschwitz was unthinkable.

That is my argument. Other pathways to genocide existed before 1914 and after 1918. My interpretation is about a sub-set of the category, genocide set in the framework of total war. One reason why the category "total war" is the right one to use in this context is that it is embedded in contemporary usage. This is hardly surprising. That something radical had happened in the nature of warfare became apparent within months of the outbreak of hostilities in August 1914. The world-wide reach of the war was evident in the April 1915 landing at Gallipoli by a combined force of British, French, Australian and New Zealand troops. This landing, clearly aimed to knock Turkey out of the war, precipitated elements of the genocide, evidently planned before the assault on the peninsula. The globalization of the conflict, however, describes only one facet of this new kind of war. At virtually the same time, other features of "total war" emerged. In April 1915, the German army first discharged canisters of poison gas on the battlefields of Ypres in Belgium. Soon the Allies responded in kind. In Brussels a British nurse Edith Cavell was arrested for helping wounded British servicemen to evade capture. She freely admitted her actions, and was shot in Brussels in October. In May 1915 the civilian passenger liner the *Lusitania* went down, sunk by a German torpedo off the Irish coast; 1,200 civilians perished, including 190 Americans. Whether or not the ship was carrying munitions, it was certainly entering a combat zone. Zeppelin attacks reached London, causing civilian casualties. Among them were children in a Hackney elementary school. Paris too was bombed by long-range artillery. Investigations of German atrocities against civilians in Belgium were published; we now know that such crimes were not the product of propaganda. They occurred, and were known about and tolerated by the German general staff.[5] Such is the *Schrecklichkeit*, the frightfulness of this new kind of war. On the Eastern front, massacres of civilians occurred in Serbia and in what is now Poland. For Eastern European Jews, 1915 was a catastrophic year; Russian soldiers in retreat brought pogroms to many towns and villages, whose residents were suspected of helping the German or Austrian armies. Perhaps 250,000 Jews were either expelled or fled from Galicia.[6]

---

[4] See the forthcoming study of Tobais Jersak, *Hitler's Decision: August 1941* (Cambridge: Cambridge University Press, 2004).

[5] See John Horne and Alan Kramer, *German Atrocities, 1914: A History of Denial* (New Haven: Yale University Press, 2001).

[6] Mark Levene, "Jews in Poland and Russia," in P. Panayi, ed., *Minorities in Wartime* (Leamington Spa: Berg Publishers, 1995), pp. 22–33.

Once again, there was much here that Europe and the world had seen before. Civilians had always been trampled on by invading armies. What was more disturbing now was not only the scale of the disaster but the implication, visible for all to see, that such acts were not unfortunate by-products of war but were built into the nature of the conflict itself. The boundaries between civilian and military targets were fading fast.

Industrial power exponentially increased the lethality of battle. This is why the bloodbath of the first year of the war was so unprecedented. By the end of 1915, when approximately 1 million Armenians had been killed or perished at the hands of Turks and their subordinates in Western Asia, over 2 million soldiers had already been killed on the war's disparate battlefields. Perhaps twice that dizzying number had been wounded. Yet this was just the beginning: by 1918, 9 million men had died in uniform.[7]

The first year of the conflict, when the war of movement produced stalemate and when the Armenian genocide was perpetrated, was its most costly phase. The brutalizing character of total war starts here, in 1914–15, with massive casualties, and crimes against civilians on both the Western and the Eastern fronts, both of which left a legacy of bitterness and hatred in their wake.

The scale of the carnage was such as to persuade many contemporaries that the first year of the war was the time when the rules of engagement of warfare clearly had changed, and changed forever. Those who waged war in 1914 saw it as a limited conflict, consistent with a nineteenth-century model of belligerency. Some, like the younger Moltke, Chief of Staff of the Imperial German army, wondered whether it would be a long war, but most believed that there would be a clash of arms, followed by a decisive outcome.[8] They were wrong. A year later, that model was shattered, and not only by the level of violence employed. The conflict was then termed "the Great War" – a phrase first used repeatedly in April 1915 – not only because of its scale, but because of its unlimited, revolutionary, character.

To reiterate my position. Elements of total war existed before 1914; and genocide happened under other circumstances. The interpretation I offer applies to genocide under the cover of industrial warfare between 1914 and 1945. Other paths to genocide have appeared – in Rwanda, Cambodia, as earlier in the North American plains. The term "genocide" is of relatively recent coinage, and cannot be taken as a unity but as a general class of crimes of different origins and different character. The

[7] Jay Winter, *The Great War and the British People* (London: Macmillan, 1985), ch. 3.
[8] Stig Förster, "Dreams and Nightmares: German Military Leadership and the Images of Future Warfare, 1871–1914." in Boeneke, Chickering and Förster, eds., *Anticipating Total War*, pp. 343–76.

systematic killing of the subjects of a nation by agents of their own state is certainly genocide; but so is the extermination of others deemed outside "civilization."

My argument applies only to genocide in the two world wars. Locating them in their time and place may help us avoid universalizing the quest for some underlying cause of all genocides, and also avoids the untenable argument that any particular genocidal campaign is outside history. These crimes may – indeed do – challenge our historical imagination, but they must never be allowed to defeat it.

Five facets of total war

Ever since the Armistice of 1918, historians have been arguing about what precisely made the Great War revolutionary. What made it a fault line, a caesura in history? That is effectively what the term "total war" really means. Focusing on five points may help describe the new landscape of warfare, and its linkage to genocide. The five are:
1. the fatal crossing of a military participation threshold;
2. the creation of direct and ongoing linkages between front and home front;
3. the redefinition of the military as the cutting edge of the nation at war;
4. the mobilization of the imagination;
5. the cultural preparation of hatred, atrocity, and genocide.

Genocide is at the end of this path, but it traverses many other features of war which are physically remote from the Armenian tragedy. I raise these issues because they describe conditions of possibility, a context within which to understand this facet of twentieth-century history.

Military participation threshold

First, the military participation threshold. The Great War was a revolutionary conflict in part because, between 1914 and 1918, the proportion of the male population aged 18–49 in uniform passed an arbitrary threshold: about 50 percent of the cohort. Once passed, that participation ratio stayed there or above for an extended period.

Among combatants in the 1914–18 war, France and Germany mobilized the highest proportion of the relevant male cohorts: about 80 percent of men aged 15–49 on the eve of the war were conscripted. Austria-Hungary mobilized 75 percent of its adult male population in the relevant age groups; Britain, Serbia, and Turkey called up between 50 and 60 percent. The Russian case is on the lower edge of what I call "total" mobilization, which is of course never literally total: approximately

16 million men or 40 percent of the male population aged 15–49 served during the war.[9]

Even in this case, however, it is easy to see that total war meant a transformation of the age-composition and sex ratio of large parts of the home population. Not so in the United States, where, in the brief space of eighteen months, about 4 million men or only 16 percent of the relevant cohort served in uniform in the Great War. The United States, or at least its civilian population, neither fought through nor incurred the costs of total war, and its reaction to the conflict reflects this marginal participation.

Secondly, total casualties and losses as a proportion of those who served passed a threshold beyond previous experience: wherever the threshold is, the total of roughly 9 million dead soldiers (according to varying estimates) is beyond it – this constitutes roughly one in eight of the men who served. Adding statistics on other casualties, it is apparent that roughly 50 percent of the men who served were either prisoners-of-war, wounded, or killed.

Here again national variations must be noted: the most murderous theatre of operations was the Eastern Front, where disease and enemy action described the course of a nineteenth-century war waged with twentieth-century weapons. Of all Serbs who served in the war, 37 percent were killed; roughly one in four Rumanians, Turks, and Bulgarians also perished. On the Western Front, where the war was won and lost, combat was about half as lethal: German and French losses were about one in six of those who served; British losses were one in eight.

Another feature of total war may be more surprising. Initially casualties among social elites were higher than among the rest of the population. The longer the war lasted, the greater was the democratization of loss. The reason is that officer casualties were higher than those in the ranks, and the social selection of the officer corps mirrored inequalities in prewar life. Consequently, in its initial phases, the higher up in the social scale was a man, the greater were his chances of becoming a casualty of war. By 1917, elites were sufficiently decimated to require the armies to draw junior officers from wider social groups which in their turn suffered disproportionately higher casualties in the last two years of the war.

Among the poor and the under-privileged, the story is different. Pre-war deprivation saved the lives of millions of working-class men and poor peasants, whose stunted stature and diseases made it impossible for them to pass even the rudimentary standards of medical fitness for military service during the war. In the British case, roughly 35 percent of the

---

[9] For statistics, see Winter, *The Great War and the British People*, chs. 2–3.

men examined for military service were either unfit for combat or unfit to wear a uniform at all. They were the lucky ones.[10]

Linkage

Casualties on this scale tied front and home front together in new and complex ways. It is clear that total war went into high gear when all the combatants were either industrialized or part of a system of world trade based on industrialization.

There is another level, however, on which linkage was more than a metaphor; it was a palpable reality. In 1914–18, despite what many soldiers and journalists wrote, civilians knew how bad war was, even if they did not see the landscape in which the fighting took place. From 1914 they saw millions of refugees streaming away from the fighting in Belgium, France, Serbia, Macedonia, eastern Germany, Russia; soon enough they saw the mutilated; they mourned the dead; they knew the pain of loss which by 1918 in one way or another hit virtually every household in the major combatants.[11]

The cutting edge

War efforts on this scale and duration required the recognition that armies were the cutting edge of the nation at war: well-being at home vitally affected the capacity of armies to go on, and thereby well-being at home directly affected the outcome of the war. This was true not only because armies of workers had to supply armies of soldiers, but also because war of this kind entailed hardship and sacrifice for the families of soldiers, an issue fundamental to *their* will to fight.

This is hardly a revolutionary finding, though it has led to massive misunderstanding about why the Allies won and the Central Powers lost the war. The war came to an end when the morale of *both* the German army and the German home front crumbled in 1918; both front and home front came to see that the war could not be won.[12] The fact that they crumbled together is hardly surprising, though the linkage has been obscured by Hitler's claim that the reason the front-line soldiers had to

---

[10] For a fuller discussion, see Winter, *ibid.*, chs. 3–4.
[11] See Stéphane Audoin-Rouzeau, *Cinq Deuils de guerre: 1914–1918* (Paris: Noesis, 2001); Stéphane Audoin-Rouzeau and Annette Becker, *14–18, retrouver la guerre* (Paris: Gallimard, 2000); Jay Winter, *Sites of Memory, Sites of Mourning. The Great War in European Cultural History* (Cambridge: Cambridge University Press, 1995).
[12] See W. Deist, *Militär Staat und Gesellschaft* (Munich: Oldenbourg, 1991).

surrender was because they were betrayed by cowards at home – the stab-in-the-back legend.[13]

What Hitler said was almost exactly the reverse of the truth: there was a stab in the back – the knife was wielded by the military leadership of Germany that led their country into a war they could not win and then brilliantly shifted responsibility for the disaster onto all shoulders other than those who really bore the blame. Hitler's statement about linkage between front and home front, however, did disclose a feature of total war of great importance, not only to the 1914–18 struggle but to later conflicts. Among the lessons the Nazis took from the Great War was that to undermine the material well-being of the civilian population was to endanger the war effort as a whole. That is one reason why the Nazis kept living standards relatively high for "Aryans" during the 1939–45 war and why they displaced the deprivation suffered by their elders in 1914–18 at home onto the backs of *Untermenschen*: slaves, political prisoners, gypsies, and Jews.[14]

For the Nazis, Aryans were entitled to a minimum standard of living, better than that provided in the 1914–18 war, when the official ration could not keep anyone alive. In the Great War, to avoid starvation, all Germans had to break the law: that meant recourse to the black market, and all the social tensions it entailed.[15]

Democracies were better at waging total war because they took seriously the consent of the governed. This is one significant element which has a bearing both on the way war was waged and on its outcome. While the Allies had a major advantage in aggregate supplies of essential goods and services, distribution mattered at least as much as supply. Distribution is a political issue, one that always entails the question "to whom".

In important ways the nature of citizenship helped determine the military efficiency of the war effort of the Allies and severely limited the war effort of Germany. This contrast was visible on the home front, and operated through the prior existence of what the economist Amartya Sen has called a system of "entitlements," a legal and moral framework upon which distributive networks rest.[16] In Paris and London the entitlements of citizenship – located in the right to a minimum level of subsistence – helped preserve communities at war by *enforcing* a balance of distribution

[13] A. Hitler, *Mein Kampf* (New York: Reynal and Hitchcock, 1939).

[14] L. Borchardt, "The Impact of the War Economy on the Civilian-Population," in W. Deist, ed., *The German Military in the Age of Total War* (Oxford: Berg, 1984).

[15] See A. Offer, *The First World War. An Agrarian Interpretation* (Oxford: Oxford University Press, 1990).

[16] Amartya Sen, *Poverty and Famines* (Oxford: Blackwell, 1976).

of necessary goods and services between civilian and military claimants. In Berlin, a different order of priorities existed. The military came first, and the economy created to service it completely distorted the delicate economic system at home. Allied adaptation and well-being reflected a more equitable and efficient distributive system than existed on the other side of the lines. In both Britain and France civilians got more both because they had more and because their share of the national income was preserved, despite spiraling claims for men and resources from the generals. The Germans disregarded the need for such a balance and created the first military-industrial complex in history, and its record in waging war was an unmitigated disaster.[17]

In 1915, when the Armenian genocide began, this political logic of military effectiveness was not yet evident. German authoritarian rule appeared to have the upper hand over democratic disorder. It was only a matter of time, however, before the fault lines appeared in the German war effort, and the Allies finally got their act together. Then the material advantages of the Allies were multiplied by their political strength. Democracies were simply better at waging wars than dictatorships.

The mobilization of the imagination

So far I have emphasized structural features of total war. Total war is incomprehensible, however, without attending to its cultural history, its capacity to tap the loyalties and prejudices of the home population.[18] It is to this subject that I now turn.

Slaughter on the grand scale needed justification. To keep intact the domestic commitment to the war effort, an elaborate cultural campaign was organized in each combatant country. Of even greater importance than the proliferation of government agencies was the tendency for civil society itself to foster a cultural campaign with two objectives: steeling the will of civilians to go on; and stifling dissent and thereby making it impossible to think of any alternative other than total victory and total defeat. By and large this campaign worked. Anti-war sentiment grew as the conflict dragged on, but with the notable exception of Russia, anti-war activists were unable to shorten the war by one day or one hour.

State-directed propaganda had only a minor role to play in this successful effort at cultural mobilization. It succeeded only when it locked into messages coming from below about the need to go on with the war.

---

[17] Jay Winter and Jean-Louis Robert, *Capital Cities at war: Paris, London, Berlin 1914–1919* (Cambridge: Cambridge University Press, 1997), ch. 1.

[18] See J. J. Becker *et al.*, eds., *Guerres et cultures* (Paris: Armand Colin, 1994).

Big Brother did not create consent during the 1914–18 war. The truth is more frightening: the Great War provided much evidence of the propensity for populations to generate internally a commitment to carry on a war of unprecedented carnage.[19]

Political and social elites tried to manipulate opinion, to be sure. Censorship and imprisonment operated, but neither had much force in formulating public opinion in wartime. The effort to mobilize the imagination in wartime came from below.[20]

The cultivation of hatred

In the effort of cultural mobilization, total war entailed the demonization of the enemy, right from the day war was declared. Some of this story is old – witness the wars of religion or the propaganda of the Reformation and Counter-reformation – but aligned with the other elements in this matrix, the cultural history of warfare entered a new and strikingly original landscape. It is a space in which what Peter Gay has called the cultivation of hatred[21] took place, an effort which provided the context in which war crimes of a revolutionary scale and character took place. I refer here to my central argument, that total war provided the space in which genocidal crimes could and did take place.

It is important to note the contingent nature of this argument. By no means did all nations engaged in total war commit genocide, but total war created the conditions which made it possible for such crimes to be committed with impunity. Total war entailed the brutalization of millions and thereby raised radically the tolerance of state-sponsored cruelty and violence in societies caught up in armed conflict.

Consider this metaphor. Total war is like an infection; it has the capacity to infect many populations, but most – through their legal systems, education, religious beliefs, military traditions, or other convictions and practices – are inoculated against the worst effects of the infection. Those not so fortunate, those (so to speak) without the antibodies,[22] succumb

---

[19] Jay Winter, "Popular culture in wartime Britain," in Richard Stites and Ariel Roshwald, eds., *European Culture in the Great War: The Arts, Entertainment, and Propaganda, 1914–1918* (Cambridge: Cambridge University Press, 1999), pp. 138–59; and Winter, "Propaganda and the Mobilization of Consent," in Hew Strachan, ed., *The Oxford Illustrated History of the First World War* (Oxford: Oxford University Press, 1998), pp. 25–40.

[20] On this theme, see Stéphane Audoin-Rouzeau, *La Guerre des enfants, 1914–1918* (Paris: Armand Colin, 1993).

[21] P. Gay, *The Cultivation of Hatred* (New York: Norton, 1993).

[22] I owe this image to the late George Mosse. For a comparison which emphasizes choice and contingency, see Jonathan Steinberg, *All or Nothing. The Axis and the Holocaust* (London: Routledge, 1990).

to virulent forms of the infection, and then the innocent suffer. Under these conditions, and in the context of total war, war crimes of staggering magnitudes can occur. Genocide can occur. It did during both world wars.

Conclusion

The literature on the Armenian genocide is substantial, and yet, given the refusal of successive Turkish governments throughout the twentieth century to acknowledge either the dimensions or the nature of the crime, the bare outlines of the story remain contested. Some elements are clear enough, and, for a more complete account, readers are urged to turn to the next chapter in this book.

A brief summary may be useful at this point. In the hours before dawn on 25 April 1915, British, Australian, New Zealand, and French forces landed at Gallipoli, the gateway to Constantinople. The aim was evidently to take the Turkish capital, and knock Turkey out of the war. The very same day as the invasion, Turkish authorities launched a new phase of repression of what they saw as internal enemies – the Armenian communities, numbering perhaps 2 million people, concentrated in Anatolia in the north-east, straddling the border with Russia, but also scattered throughout the Ottoman Empire. Under cover of darkness, on 25 April, several hundred Armenian men – intellectuals, journalists, professionals, businessmen, clergymen – were taken from their homes and shot.

That was only the beginning. Over the next two years most of the Armenian population of the eastern provinces of Ottoman Turkey was forcibly uprooted and expelled to the desert regions of Mesopotamia. Some Armenians in western Turkey survived, but overall between 500,000 and 1 million Armenians were killed or died of exposure or disease in camps or in the Syrian desert. The perpetrators were a mixed group. Turkish soldiers and policemen as well as Kurdish irregulars organized the deportations and then robbed, raped, and killed at will. Hunger, starvation, disease did the rest. Statistics on atrocities are never precise or easily verified, but even a conservative estimate of the scale and dimensions of the deportation places loss of life at about 50 percent of the pre-1914 population. In the midst of war, a substantial part of a long-established and prosperous civilian community with identifiable religious and cultural characteristics had been wiped out; they were sentenced to death *because of* who they were and where they were; in effect, because of their ethnicity. Their fate was indisputably a war crime, which constituted a clear precedent for the Nazi extermination of the Jews.

How did this happen, and what did international opinion make of it? Here contextual issues, I believe, are decisive. In general terms, the framework of "total war" helps us to account for the conditions that made the genocide possible and enabled its perpetrators to act with impunity. The context of total war, and its multiple brutalizations prepared the ground both for genocide and for its denial. In the same way as the Cold War created a space where crimes against humanity committed by client states could be shielded, if not openly defended, by their patrons, so, in the Great War, the space in which genocidal crimes emerged was redefined both by the nature of war and by its geographical reach.

Total war created a political environment in which the boundaries between limited violence and unlimited violence were blurred. Limited violence, in the Clausewitzian sense of the term is the application of force to compel an enemy to surrender. Unlimited violence is the application of force, either directly or indirectly, to all enemy nationals, whether or not in uniform, of whatever age or sex, and whether or not they have surrendered. Under certain circumstances, that lifting of constraints on the targeting and intensity of wartime violence opened the way to genocide. My argument, therefore, is a straightforward one. Total war was a necessary, though not sufficient, condition for the emergence of genocide in the twentieth century. Once it had happened, it could and would happen again.

Recently, there has been some discussion of the Armenian genocide as a function of the end of empires. While there are many cases of mass killings following the breakup of imperial hegemony – stretching from India to Bosnia to East Timor, I am unpersuaded by this argument. Turkey did indeed fight a war for its survival in 1915–18 and lost it. So, however, did Russia, Germany, and Austria-Hungary, none of which had democratic traditions to temper their anger at so-called internal enemies. In Armenia in 1915, what turned a massive war crime into a genocidal act was not the end of empire, but rather the context of total war, a context which, with great speed, helped translate deportation inexorably into the mass slaughter, abuse, and starvation of an ethnic group targeted by an authoritarian regime at war, backed up by an even stronger central ally.

The fear of subversion, in and of itself, was not the key to genocide. Every power tried it out. The imperial character of all the major combatants ensured that this would be so. The Germans stirred up trouble in Ireland and Russia, as well as in Mexico; the British and French dabbled time and again in the Austrian Empire; the Russians were active among Armenians on their common border with Turkey. Only in Turkey, though, did the threat of subversion lead to the extermination of so-called "subversives" – men, women, and children in hundreds of thousands.

Genocide then was much more than a reaction to an adversary's probing of the weak links in an unraveling imperial chain. Such an argument was (and remains) useful for exculpatory propaganda, but it does not take us very far, because it misses the key issue of context – the context of a revolutionary form of warfare. Genocide, in 1915 as in 1941, came out of total war. Total war entailed the obliteration of the distinction between military and civilian targets and the ruthless use of terror in the suppression of domestic groups suspected of or having even the remote potential for offering the enemy tacit or active support.

Unlike the historian Ernst Nolte, I see no resemblance in either case to what he terms "Asiatic barbarism."[23] The notion of "total war" came not out of Turkey but out of the West. Napoleonic warfare in Spain and Russia entailed war against civilians and irregular forces. Fifty years later, American civil warfare added another dimension to the cruelty of armed conflict. It was not a Turk but the American General Philip Sheridan who on 8 September 1870 told the future German Chancellor Otto von Bismarck that the "proper strategy" in wartime "consists in the first place in inflicting as telling blows as possible upon the enemy's army, and then causing the inhabitants so much suffering that they must long for peace, and force their Government to demand it. The people must be left nothing but their eyes to weep with over the war."[24] The "people" in question were secessionists, it is true, but they shared the same language, many the same religion, and often came from the same families. What would wartime brutality look like when not tempered by such cultural bonds? What terms would we use to describe it?

Here we confront the challenge stated at the beginning of this chapter. When we begin to explore the history of genocide, we approach some of the limits of the language we use in historical study. Nonetheless, we must confront the nature of genocide, and call it by its name, in order to locate it within the terrifying history of total war in the twentieth century.

In 1919 the Russian poet Akhmatova reflected on the nature of the upheaval through which she was living. Her poem is entitled "Why is this century worse?"

> Why is this century worse than those that have gone before?
> In a stupor of sorrow and grief
> it located the blackest wound
> but somehow couldn't heal it.

[23] Ernst Nolte, *Der europäische Bürgerkrieg 1917–1945: Nationalsozialismus und Bolschewismus* (Berlin: Propyläen Verlag, 1987).
[24] Moritz Busch, *Bismarck. Some Secret Page of his History*, 2 vols (New York: Macmillan, 1898), I, 128.

The earth's sun is still shining in the West
and the roofs of towns sparkle in its rays,
while here death marks houses with crosses
and calls in the crows and the crows fly over.[25]

What they flew over was a landscape disfigured by a new kind of warfare. The "blackest wound that could not be healed" is one way to describe total war. Its scars are with us still.

[25] Anna Akhmatova, *Selected Poems*, trans. Richard McKane (London: Bloodaxe Books, 1989), p. 96.

3   The Armenian Genocide: an interpretation

Vahakn N. Dadrian

Introduction

The Armenian Genocide, perpetrated during the First World War, is significant for several reasons. First and foremost, that Genocide was the devastating culmination of a series of antecedent massacres. These massacres were consummated in the decades preceding 1914, especially those of 1894–6, the era of Sultan Abdul-Hamid, and that of Adana in 1909. The latter massacre more or less coincided with the advent of the (Ittihadist) Young Turk regime. Operating under the designation "Committee of Union and Progress" (CUP), the leaders of that regime came to power by overthrowing Sultan Abdul-Hamid in 1908 in a more or less bloodless revolution. Adopting the clarion calls of the French Revolution, i.e., freedom, equality, and brotherhood, these leaders had proposed to supplant the preceding despotic regime by a constitutional one. Yet, by a twist in the turn of events, they ended up becoming the lethal nexus between the massacres of that preceding regime and those of the subsequent ones, thus ushering in the era of the most comprehensive of all massacres, namely, the World War I Genocide.

Within this perspective, this genocide emerges as a developmental event, punctuated by a history of accumulative tensions, animosities, and attendant sanguinary persecutions. It marks a phenomenon that is anchored on a constantly evolving and critically escalating perpetrator–victim conflict. Such a framework of analysis precludes the consideration of the argument that the Armenian Genocide was more or less a by-product of the exigencies and consuming crises of the first global war. It, therefore, precludes also the companion consideration that the genocide in question was but "an aberration"[1]– as far as the characterization of the

---

[1] UN (United Nations) ESCOR (Economic and Social Council Official Records) Committee on Human Rights Sub-Commission on Prevention of Discrimination and Protection of Minorities 38th session, Item 57, UN Document E/CN. 4/Sub.2/1985/ SR36/(1985). The summary record of the 36th meeting 29 August 1985. This is the report of the British expert, Benjamin Whitaker, who was tasked by the Sub-Commission to research the problem and come up with his evaluation. After eight years of research, Whitaker

behavior of the perpetrator camp is concerned. It is instead maintained that the elements of conflict propelling the earlier massacres persisted to operate up to the outbreak of the First World War. That was the type of war that afforded an inordinate opportunity to deal with these elements of conflict in a draconian way, thereby lethally terminating the conflict itself.

It is further argued that focusing attention on the concept of "impunity" may go a long way in understanding this process of conflict-escalation and conflict-consummation. Indeed, the Abdul-Hamid era massacres, claiming some 150,000–200,000 direct and indirect victims during and in the aftermath of the atrocities, remarkably escaped criminal-legal prosecution, domestically as well as internationally. The mutually suspicious and rival Great Powers, through a number of Accords and Treaties, in particular the 1856 Paris and 1878 Berlin Peace Treaties, had undertaken to "watch" and "supervise" the promised amelioration of the conditions of the Empire's Christian minorities, especially the Armenians.[2] Their continuous inaction in the face of recurrent episodes of massacres was, however, a factor that decisively influenced the First World War Ottoman resolve to resort to draconian measures against the targeted Armenians. Indeed, the sustained absence of deterrence prior to, and of retribution in the aftermath of, episodes of mass murder all but served to embolden the Young Turk leaders to consider seriously the option of a radical solution vis-à-vis the problems they felt the Armenians were causing.[3] Accordingly, the unpunished massacres of before the First World War emerge here as a factor not only conditioning but, more precisely, preconditioning the incidence of the genocide. Hence, the legacy of impunity is to be viewed and treated as a central question in the analysis of the Armenian Genocide. That centrality is further keynoted by the fact that there is

concluded that the First World War Armenian experience was a case of genocide within the terms of the meaning of the UN Convention on the Prevention and Punishment of the Crime of Genocide. Whitaker saw fit, however, to describe it as a war-conditioned "aberration."
[2] Vahakn N. Dadrian, "The Armenian Question and the Wartime Fate of the Armenians as Documented by Officials of the Ottoman Empire's World War I Allies: Germany and Austria-Hungry," *International Journal of Middle East Studies* 34 (February 2002), p. 64. In this study these elements of international concern are identified as being the lingering Armenian Question and the ancillary Armenian Reforms issue that continued to beset the Ottoman Empire in its declining years – internally, as well as in her external relations, in particular, with the Great Powers of Europe.
[3] Vahakn N. Dadrian, "Genocide as a Problem of National and International Law: The World War I Armenian Case and its Contemporary Legal Ramifications," *Yale Journal of International Law* 14: 2 (Summer 1989), pp. 244–51, 317–34; Dadrian, "The Historical and Legal Interconnections Between the Armenian Genocide and the Jewish Holocaust: From Impunity to Retributive Justice," *Yale Journal of International Law* 23: 2 (Summer 1998), pp. 504–7, 554–9.

often an intimate relationship between impunity and denial of the crime. One may even argue that the genesis of new attitudes favoring the commission of similar new crimes is afforded through such a relationship.

The Armenian Genocide acquires, therefore, additional significance in the face of a whole gamut of persistent denials, and the parallel campaign to impose silence on it as a topic of public debate and political discourse, but, most importantly, as a legitimate subject for unfettered academic research and publications. Presently, a major weapon used for denial is the constant reference to the holdings of the Ottoman archives whose documents relating to the Armenian Question are portrayed as state evidence absolutely disputing the claim of genocide – in total disregard of the questionable aspects, and, therefore, the unreliability of these holdings.[4] In order to institutionalize this campaign of denial and try to invest it with an aura of legitimacy, there was established in Ankara a "think-tank" in April 2001. Operating under the name "Institute for Armenian Research" as a subsidiary of The Center For Eurasian Studies, with a staff of nine, this new outfit is now proactively engaged in contesting all claims of genocide by organizing a series of conferences, lectures, and interviews, and, above all, through the medium of publications, including a quarterly. During a recent interview, its President, retired Ambassador Ömer Lutem, offered the following main rationale for the sustained denials:

The conflict [between Armenians and Turks] arises from an interpretation of a historical event. Armenian activists claim that the relocation of the Armenians in 1915–1916 constitutes the crime of genocide, or had genocidal effects on the Armenian population. Turkish historians and writers on their part consider that the relocation did not intend to destroy the Armenians. On the contrary, it intended to protect them and remove them from the war zones, for their own security and also for the security of the Ottoman forces. I am convinced that there is enough evidence to show that the Ottoman Government did not intend to destroy the Armenian civilians.[5]

---

[4] Vahakn N. Dadrian, "Ottoman Archives and Denial of the Armenian Genocide," in R. Hovannisian, ed., *The Armenian Genocide: History, Politics, Ethics* (New Brunswick, N.J.: Transaction Books, 1986), pp. 280–310. For a review of statements by Turkish, British, and American authors, questioning the reliability of Ottoman archives in the matter of the genocide, see Vahakn N. Dadrian, "Documentation of the Armenian Genocide in Turkish Sources," in Israel W. Charny, ed., *Genocide: A Critical Bibliographic Review*, 3 vols., vol. II (London: Mansel, 1991), pp. 137–8; Rouben Adalian, "Ottoman Archives," *Society for Armenian Studies Newsletter* 14:1 (1 June 1989), pp. 14–17.

[5] The interview which actually was a dialogue-exchange with another retired Ambassador, Yüksel Söylemez, was published in Ankara's *Turkish Daily News*, 22 October 2001. Almost around the same time the current President of the Turkish Historical Society, in a similar vein and in considerable detail, extolled the virtues and the benefits for the Armenians of the "relocation" plan. He even ventured to declare that "[t]he Ottoman government had carried out the resettlement in an efficient and orderly way . . . the transfer of Armenians to their new settlements, the first planned population movement of the century, was

Should one discount for a moment the contents of the relevant documents held in "the Ottoman Archives," the independently furnished aggregate testimony of a host of Turkish authors – not to mention non-Turkish, especially German, official testimony – one can readily observe the *non plus ultra* frivolity of this argument of "relocation" with the intent to "protect" the masses being relocated. Particularly trenchant in this respect is the testimony of Turkish General Ali Fuad Erden, the wartime Chief of Staff of Cemal Paşa, the Commander-in-Chief of the Ottoman IVth Army headquartered in Damascus. Referring to the nearby Mesopotamian deserts, the desolate *loci* selected by the Ittihadist leaders for the purported relocation of the multitudes of dislocated Armenians, he wrote, with a sense of derision, "there was neither preparation, nor organization to shelter the hundreds of thousands of the deportees."[6] The pattern of denial had in fact originated from the period of the First World War when the genocide was inexorably running its course. Even during that period, i.e., immediately after the end of the war, a succession of post-war Ottoman governments, anxious to set the record straight, had legally challenged these denials. The series of courts-martial these

conducted in great discipline." Constantly referring to "the Ottoman Archives," which he claims he thoroughly studied, this Turkish historian ventures to come up with the following remarkable data, based on "Foreign and Interior Ministry documents." Altogether "20,000 Armenians were killed by the bandits . . . some others starved to death on the road, while about 30,000 died because of diseases like dysentery or typhoid" Thus, "about 56,610 Armenians unfortunately died" in the First World War: Yusuf Halaçoglu, "Realities Behind the Relocation," in Türkkaya Ataöv, ed., *The Armenians in the Late Ottoman Period* (Ankara: Turkish Historical Society, 2001), pp. 118, 128, 130. For the full monograph of the author see *Ermeni Tehciri ve Gerçekler, 1914–1918* (Ankara: Turkish Historical Society, 2001).

[6] Orgeneral (Full General) Ali Fuad Erden, *Birinci Dünya Harbinde Suriye Hatıraları* (Syrian Memoirs of World War I), Vol. I (Istanbul: Halk Matbaası, 1954), p. 122. See also Refik Altınay, *Iki Komite Iki Kıtal* (Two Committees, Two Massacres), ed. H. Koyukan (Ankara: Kebikeç, 1994; originally published in Ottoman script in Istanbul, 1919). The author was a naval officer, serving in the Intelligence Department of Ottoman General Headquarters. On p. 34 he bemoans the fate of the deportees who "were driven to blazing deserts, to hunger, misery and death." In praising the scholarly contributions of this author who served as Professor of History at the University of Istanbul in the Kemalist Republic, Bernard Lewis, the noted Islamist and Ottomanist, called him "Perhaps the most distinguished among the contributors" to the journal published by the Ottoman Historical Society: "History-writing and National Revival in Turkey," *Middle Eastern Affairs* 4 (June–July 1953), p. 223. The maverick Turkish author Taner Akçam maintains that nowhere during the deportations, nor at their destination in the deserts "were there any arrangements required" for resettling or relocating these deportees, which fact "is sufficient proof of the existence of this plan of annihilation": *Türk Ulusal Kimliği ve Ermeni Sorunu* (Turkish National Identity and the Armenian Question) (Istanbul: Iletişim, 1992), p. 106. For a general review of the problem of the farcicalness of the claim of relocation, see Vahakn N. Dadrian, *The History of the Armenian Genocide. Ethnic Conflict from the Balkans to Anatolia to the Caucasus* (Providence, R.I. [presently New York]: Berghahn Books, 3rd. edn, 1997), pp. 239–43, 246–7.

governments had instituted in the 1919–21 period, having the task of investigating and prosecuting the wartime crimes perpetrated wholesale against the Armenian population of the Ottoman Empire, attained a measure of success. Through the issuance of a string of verdicts, the claims of the innocence of Ottoman Turkish authorities were falsified. Even though the Military Tribunal was unable to administer retributive justice to any significant degree – most of the principal perpetrators had fled the country and had become fugitives of justice – through probative evidence it had established a cardinal fact: the massive deportation of the victim population was but a device to effect the liquidation of that population under cover of the war.[7] What is most relevant to the issue of denial, however, is the fact that the voluminous archives of this Tribunal have simply vanished since the advent of the Kemalist regime. No one seems to be able, or willing, to indicate the fate of these archives.

It is against the background of all these elements of denial that the present study seeks to bring into relief the Armenian Genocide, utilizing a particular type of focus. By way of introduction it first reviews briefly the origin and evolution of the Armenian Question thereby underscoring the importance of the use of a historical perspective. By the same token, it draws attention to the pivotal role of a monolithic political party by depicting the prominence of the Ittihadist Young Turk party leaders in decision making. In this connection, it also reviews the critical importance of wartime exigencies by virtue of which legislative power is displaced and is supplanted by executive power. The expedient amplification of that power inheres the type of dynamics, which under certain conditions, can enable potential perpetrators to subvert a regularly functioning government and thereby carry out an exterminatory scheme.

The core of the study is the exploration of two specific but interrelated features of the Armenian Genocide. One of them probes into the conditions that allowed the perpetrator group to entrap and eliminate the able-bodied Armenian men who were conscripted through the issuance of

---

[7] For full details of these courts-martial see Dadrian "Genocide as a Problem of National and International Law," pp. 503–59; Vahakn N. Dadrian, "The Armenian Genocide and the Legal and Political Issues in the Failure to Prevent or to Punish the Crime," *University of West Los Angeles Law Review* 29 (1998), pp. 43–78; Dadrian, "The Documentation of the World War I Armenian Massacres in the Proceedings of the Turkish Military tribunal," *International Journal of Middle East Studies* 23 (1991), pp. 549–76; Dadrian, "The Naim-Andonian Documents on the World War I Destruction of Ottoman Armenians: The Anatomy of a Genocide," *International Journal of Middle East Studies* 18 (1986), pp. 311–60; Dadrian, "A Textual Analysis of the Key Indictment of the Turkish Military Tribunal Investigating the Armenian Genocide," *Armenian Review* 44:1/173 (Spring 1991), pp. 1–36. Moreover, many of the proceedings of the courts-martial, in particular several indictments and nearly all the verdicts, were published in the special supplements, *Ilâve*, in *Takvim-i Vekâyi*, the official gazette of the Ottoman Parliament.

a decree on general mobilization – months before Turkey had entered the war. The other examines in detail the genocide executed in the province of Trabzon, on the Black Sea littoral, and in Erzincan. Such an examination affords a rare overview of the ingredients of genocide in its manifold forms.

Some key historical and political pre-conditions of the genocide

Some preliminary remarks are necessary about the pre-war preparation of the genocide. At the very core of the historically protracted Turko-Armenian conflict was and remained the Armenian struggle to remedy the problem of inequities stemming from the theocratic underpinnings of the multi-ethnic Ottoman state system. The fixed and intractable prescriptions and proscriptions of Islamic canon law, as expressed mostly through the Koran and codified in the Sheriat, and as interpreted and applied for centuries by Ottoman elites, had given rise to a dichotomous socio-political system. In that system the non-Muslims, relegated to a permanently fixed inferior status, were treated as the subordinates (*milleti makhûme*) of the dominant and super-ordinate Muslims (*milleti hâkime*).

The institutionalization of the practices of enduring prejudice and discrimination against the former were the inevitable by-products of that system. The cumulative consequences of this arrangement were such as to render the Armenians increasingly disaffected, like many other subject nationalities despairing of relief. The Tanzimat reforms of 1839 and 1856, introduced by reformist Ottoman-Turkish leaders, provided the first, tangible signal of relief. The Armenians began to think of entitlement relative to the principle of equality. The contagious impact of the ideals of the French Revolution, on the one hand, and the successes of the Balkan nationalities, which one by one had eventually emancipated themselves from Ottoman dominion, on the other, were developments which energized the Armenians even more to pursue reforms actively.

As the depredations in the provinces continued with unabated violence and the reform movement ultimately proved abortive, Armenian revolutionaries entered the arena of confrontation thereby accentuating the already simmering Turko-Armenian conflict. The Ottoman response was repression through massacres. This pattern obtained throughout the last decades of the nineteenth century and the first decade of the twentieth. These were the general conditions when in 1912 the first Balkan War broke out.

The reviving of the Armenian Reform issue, in the aftermath of the crushing military defeat the Ottoman army suffered in the course of that first Balkan War in late 1912, sent shock-waves through the ranks of the CUP. The outbreak and outcome of that war had ingredients that closely resembled those surrounding the Armenian Question. Indeed that war was intimately connected with Article 23 of the 1878 Berlin Peace Treaty that stipulated reforms for conflict-ridden Macedonia, and was immediately preceded by two massacres the Ottomans, unwilling to implement the stipulated reforms, had perpetrated against the local population. Moreover, the victors in that war were former subject nationalities, Serbs, Greeks, and Bulgarians, who, through the direct and indirect assistance of the Great Powers, especially the Russians, put an end to Ottoman dominion in the Balkans by forcibly evicting them altogether from the region. One may get a glimpse of the striking similarity involved when considering the comparable elements animating the simmering Armenian Question. Involved here were, for example, Article 61 of the same Berlin Peace Treaty similarly stipulating Armenian reforms in eastern Turkey; the serial massacres associated with the stipulation of that Article; the involvement on behalf of the Armenians of the Great Powers, especially of Russia, the historical nemesis of the Empire; and the impotence of the Ottoman government to resist successfully the various pressures. Given the reform-oriented direct and indirect exertions of the six Great Powers, this was, from their point of view, a new milestone in the forging of a new political culture – i.e., humanitarian intervention. When the Young Turk leaders, after protracted, tedious, and, for them, fretful negotiations with these Powers, were finally impelled by them to sign a new Armenian Reform Accord in February 1914, in the framing of which Tsarist Russia played a prominent role, the specter of a repeat Balkan disaster in eastern Turkey galvanized these leaders. They were driven to consider drastic new measures to avert by all means a recurrence.

Coincidental with this development, there erupted in January 1913 a second (Ittihadist) Young Turk revolution (that had the trappings of a *coup d'état*), the first having been accomplished in July 1908. The military and civilian torchbearers of that revolution raided the seat of the Ottoman government, the (Sublime) Porte, overthrowing the regime of the opponent Freedom and Accord (Hürriyet ve Itilâf) Party, and established a new government. The consequences of this second revolution and the attendant violent change of government would prove portentous for the fate of the Armenians – but also for that of the Empire.

The drastic rearrangement of the structure of the Ottoman regime was the most potent consequence of this overthrow. The pivotal organs of the Empire's government were fused with the upper echelons of a political party organization bent on monopoly of power. Not only did the CUP Party hierarchy end up dominating the government, but the organization of the party itself was reinvigorated and extended, especially in the provinces, but also in the ranks of the armed forces. The two arch leaders of the party, Ismail Enver and Mehmed Talât, became Minister of Defense and Interior Minister, respectively. As a result, the overt and covert agendas of the party gradually gained the upper hand in the designing of the internal and external policies of the Ottoman state.

The sudden eruption of a major crisis gave impetus to this development. The new Grand Vizier, Mahmud Şevket Paşa, who was installed in that position by CUP Party bosses, was assassinated in June 1913 by conspirators identified with the opposition Hürriyet ve Itilâf Party that had been thrown out of power five months earlier. The ensuing large-scale purge of the leaders of all opposition parties and factions, attended by the swift court-martialing, sentencing, and execution through hanging of a dozen conspirators, paved the way for the CUP emerging as a monolithic and near-dictatorial party in the months preceding the First World War. The atmosphere of intimidation and terror was reinforced by the continuation of the courts-martial against suspected co-conspirators up to February 1914. For appearances' sake, though, the CUP for the time refrained from banning its main opposition party.

It was under these circumstances that the CUP, which had relocated its main headquarters to Istanbul after relinquishing the one in Saloniki as a result of the Balkan Wars, launched its annual convention in September 1913. At this time the government, i.e., the executive branch, was nearly completely in the hands of the CUP, with all the key ministries being held by Ittihadist potentates who were driven by consuming CUP ambitions. More important, in the aftermath of that convention the party took on a new direction. After an increase in the number of its Central Committee members from seven to twelve in 1911, within a year – i.e., after the first Balkan War in late 1912 – the party's effective leadership on matters of nationality policy was assumed, and thereafter almost monopolized, by two physician–politicians, MDs Behaeddin Şakir and Mehmed Nâzım. They were joined by Ziya Gökalp, the CUP's ideological guru, to form the nucleus of a new alignment in the higher councils of the party that secretly but willfully controlled the essential organs of party and government.[8] Operating behind the scenes but with sufficient resolve to influence the decision of the other party leaders, such as the above-mentioned Enver and Talât, this omnipotent triumvirate eventually

---

[8] Ahmed Emin Yalman, *Yakın Tarihte Gördüklerim ve Geçirdiklerim* (The Things I Observed and Experienced in the Recent Past), 4 vols. (Istanbul: Yenilik, 1970), I (*1888–1918*), pp. 265–66; Tarik Z. Tunaya, *Türkiyede Siyasi Partiler (1859–1912)* (Political Parties in Turkey [1859–1912]) (Istanbul: Doğan, 1952), p. 219; Galip Vardar, *Ittihad ve Terakki İçinde Dönenler* (The Inside Story of CUP), ed. S. Nafiz Tansu (Istanbul: Inkilâp, 1960), p. 83; Vahakn N. Dadrian, "The Convergent Roles of the State and a Governmental Party in the Armenian Genocide," in L. Chorbajian and G. Shirinian, eds., *Studies in Comparative Genocide* (London, New York: Macmillan / St. Martin Press, 1999), p. 103.

became the principal taskmaster in the organization of the Armenian Genocide.[9] Their *modus operandi* was largely dictated by nationalist goals implicit in the switch from inclusive Ottomanism to exclusive Turkism. The devising of a scheme of a correlative Turkification of the Empire, or what was left of it, included the cardinal goal of the liquidation of that Empire's residual non-Turkish elements.[10] Given their numbers, their concentration in geo-strategic locations, and the troublesome legacy of the Armenian Question, the Armenians were targeted as the prime object for such liquidation. To achieve this goal, the undertaking of certain preliminary initiatives were needed to cover the legal, organizational, and operational aspects of the task.

The destruction of large clusters of populations dispersed over large swaths of lands involving a wide range of cities, towns, and villages is not an easy task. Even mass murder requires the application of the rule

---

[9] Reportedly Talât, while in refuge in Berlin in 1918–21, lamented to Nesim Mazliyah, an Ittihadist deputy of Jewish background, about the many mistakes he (and his CUP Party) admitted having made, adding, "Our greatest mistake was our embracing the two or three comrades who had come from Europe in the wake of the establishment of the new regime and who sowed discord in the country"; the reference here is to Drs. Nâzım and Şakir. They are perceived as vindictive and tyrannical men who denounced and persecuted anyone who disagreed with them: Ahmed Bedevi Kuran, *Osmanlı Imparatorluğunda Inkılâp Hareketleri ve Millî Mücadele* (Revolutionary Movements and National Struggle in the Ottoman Empire) (Istanbul: Çeltüt, 1959), pp. 484, 539, 540. The omnipotence of the Central Committee of the CUP – dominated by these men – to which even the two arch leaders of the CUP, namely, War Minister Enver, and Interior Minister – later Grand Vizier – Talât were often accountable, is attested to by German Ambassador Paul Wolff-Metternich. He described the latter two as "powerless" ("machtlos") vis-à-vis the former trio's "fanatical decisions": German Foreign Ministry Archives (Auswärtiges Amt), ["AA" henceforth]), R13536, 1 July 1916 report. Talât is described by his biographer as somewhat skeptical about the merits of the ideology of Turkism as opposed to multi-ethnic Ottomanism; in this respect he considered Gökalp, the high priest of emerging Turkish nationalism, as a dreamer. For the sake of team-playing, however, he went along with him, says this author: Tevfik Çavdar, *Talât Paşa. Bir Orgüt Ustasının Yasam Oyküsü* (Talât Paşa. The Life Story of a Master Organizer) (Ankara: Dost, 1984), pp. 73, 194. For more details about Nâzım and Şakir, see Dadrian "The Naim-Andonian Documents," pp. 328–31 (n. 7).

[10] This point is explicitly emphasized by Halil Menteşe, one of the CUP's top leaders, who had a legal background. In one of the subheadings in his book he used the expression, "To cleanse the country" (*memleketi temizlemek*) to describe Talât's "top priority": *Osmanlı Mebusan Meclisi Reisi Halil Menteşe nin Anıları* (The Memoirs of Ottoman Chamber of Deputies President Halil Menteşe) (Istanbul: Hürriyet Vakfı, 1986), p. 165. For the relevance of this plan to Ottoman Armenians, see Dadrian, "The Armenian Question," pp. 65–6 (n. 2). Commenting on this issue of "top priority," William Yale, noted expert on the Near East, faulted the Armenians for their failure to be cognizant of this Young Turk anteposition in 1908 when with great jubilation they hailed the advent of the new constitutional regime ushered in by the same Young Turks – "They failed to see that the ideas seething in the minds of the Young Turks would result only seven years later in a wholesale attempt to eliminate the Armenians": *The Near East. A Modern History* (Ann Arbor: The University of Michigan Press, new edn., revised and enlarged, 1968), p. 167.

of "economy in lethal violence." The method of spatially concentrating the targeted victim population through a series of deportation procedures that were enacted by the Ottoman government during the war served this purpose of economy. Such a method proved functional as it enabled the perpetrator group to assemble together large clusters of populations, and then to mask the underlying ultimate purpose of the destruction of the deportees. At the 1913 annual party convention the Ittihadists, through the terms of Article 12 of their CUP Party program, embraced in a slightly amended form the Ottoman Constitution's Article 36 which itself had been recast in 1909. Through the scheme of this Article these Young Turk leaders established a legal framework which would empower them later to decree the forcible deportations of large clusters of populations of the Empire through administrative fiat. This constitutional provision namely authorized the Cabinet to issue temporary laws without concurrent legislative debate and approval. For this to happen, the Chamber of Deputies had to be dissolved, suspended, or adjourned. In its 1909 version the law stipulated that the enactment of such temporary laws could only be allowed when there was an acute need for "defending the State against danger or guarding the public security."[11] The Young Turk leaders twisted this provision in Article 12 of their party program to read "in case there is a pressing need and an urgency for speedy action" (*ihtiyacatı âcile ve zarureti mübreme*),[12] thus leaving out the very specific reference to the need for protecting state and public security. They hereby created broad latitude for themselves to enact temporary laws. The entire course of the First World War in the 1915–16 period demonstrated, however, that, as anticipated, this authorization for unlimited deportations found application primarily with the Armenians.

The outbreak of the First World War provided the needed opportunity to develop further the specifics of the scheme. Within hours of declaring war on Russia, the Young Turk leaders signed a secret military and political pact with Germany. At the same time they dissolved the Parliament indefinitely.[13] These acts allowed the CUP leaders to concentrate the decision-making powers, especially war-making powers, in the hands of the executive,[14] but, more particularly, in the hands of the small number of members of the Central Committee of the party. In the end, these men,

[11] Friedrich von Kraelitz-Greifenhorst, "Die Verfassungsgesetze des Osmanischen Reiches," *Osten und Orient* 1 (1919, Vienna), pp. 36, 58.
[12] Tunaya, *Türkiyede* p. 215 (n. 8). See also Tunaya, *Türkiyede Siyasal Partiler* (Political Parties in Turkey), 3 vols., vol. III *Ittihat ve Terakki* (Ittihad and Terakki, i.e. Union and Progress) (Istanbul: Hürriyet Vakfi, 1989), p. 385 (n. 43).
[13] Yusuf Hikmet Bayur, *Türk Inkilâbı Tarihi* (History of Turkish Revolution), vol. III, part I (Ankara: Türk Tarih Kurumu, 1953), p. 64; ibid., vol. II, part IV (1952), p. 658.
[14] Ibid., vol. III, part I, p. 425.

all of whom were at the same time Ministers – e.g., Enver (War), Talât (Interior), Cemal (Navy), Halil (President of the Chamber of Deputies and later Foreign Minister) – one way or another pushed the Empire into war.[15] By way of a preemptive attack against Russian warships in, and coastal installations on, the Black Sea, the Ottoman Turks, led by the Germans, entered the First World War, after maintaining for some three months a state of armed neutrality. Even though a host of considerations were involved in launching this act of aggression, by the CUP leaders' own admission, however, the solving of the Armenian Question, especially removing once and for all the need for Armenian reforms – as conceded by War Minister Enver – weighed heavily in the decision to enter the war. Cemal Paşa, one of these leaders, explicitly made a reference to the inevitability of large-scale massacres, should the Reform movement succeed. He said that, exactly to prevent this, the CUP decided to intervene in the war.[16] The stage was set for action.

The first crippling initiative of the genocide: the conscription and liquidation of the able-bodied Armenian men

Part of the strategy of "economy in lethal violence" is to render the targeted victim population as defenseless as possible. Within hours of the signing of the secret political and military pact with Imperial Germany on 2 August 1914, the Ittihadist regime declared general mobilization. As a result nearly all able-bodied Armenian men were conscripted into the Ottoman army, starting with the 20–45 age group and subsequently extending the call to groups aged 18–20 and 45–60. This was in line with the 12 May 1914 supplementary Temporary Law on Recruitment (*Mükellefiyeti Askeriye Kanuni Muvakkatı*); the original law was enacted on 7 August 1909.[17]

When, during the genocide, Ottoman authorities kept trying to argue that the massive deportations were justified for military security reasons,

---

[15] Ibid., pp. 229–35.

[16] For these statements by Enver, Cemal, Talât, and others, see Dadrian, *History of the Armenian Genocide*, pp. 208–9, pp. 211–12 (nn. 23–8). For the temporary law, see Kraelitz-Greifenhorst, "Die Verfassungsgesetze," p. 25 (nn. 1, 11).

[17] French Foreign Ministry Archives. "Guerre 1914–18. Arménie," Série 887, p. 183. The bulk of the conscripted men were in the 20–45 age group; the 18–20 and 45–60 age groups were mainly conscripted for military transport duties which often meant being used as "pack animals": Austrian Foreign Ministry Archives ("AFMA" henceforth) 16 July 1915 "Confidential" report to Vienna, P.A. I/ 944, No. 274/ KD; AA Türkei 183/36, A388, or R14085 in the new catalogue system (n. 341), German Ambassador Hans Wangenheim's report to Berlin, 29 December 1914. See also S. Zurlinden, *Der Weltkrieg*, vol. II (Zurich: Art Institut Orell Rissli, 1918), pp. 638–9.

German and Austrian officials with duties in Turkey as political and military allies uniformly questioned the honesty of this argument. Aleppo's veteran German Consul, Walter Rössler, in a report of 27 July 1915 to Berlin declared, "In the absence of menfolk, nearly all of whom have been conscripted, how can women and children pose a threat?"[18] For his part German Colonel Stange, in charge of a detachment of Special Organization Forces in eastern Turkey, questioned the veracity of the argument of Ottoman military authorities. These authorities were maintaining that the deportations were a military necessity because they feared an uprising. In his report to his German military superiors, Stange retorted, "Save for a small fraction of them, all able-bodied Armenian men were recruited. There could, therefore, be no particular reason to fear a *real* uprising" (emphasis in the original).[19] Another high-ranking allied officer, Austrian Vice Marshal Pomiankowski, Military Plenipotentiary at Ottoman General Headquarters, provided his answer to these questions. The Turks "began to massacre the able-bodied Armenian men . . . in order to render the rest of the population defenseless."[20] After graphically describing the scenes of these serial massacres of conscripted Armenian men which were "in summary fashion," and "in almost all cases the procedure was the same," American Ambassador to the Ottoman Empire Henry Morgenthau noted with emphasis the same rationale: "Before Armenia could be slaughtered, Armenia must be made defenseless." In this connection, the Ambassador notified Washington on 10 July 1915 that "All the men from 20 to 45 are in the Turkish army."[21]

Examples of this procedure abound but two specific cases involving eyewitness accounts – one of them having been identified as the account of a German officer, an ally of Turkey – are illustrative in this regard. The Kavass of the local branch of the Ottoman Bank in Trabzon, a Montenegrin, under American protection, observed that "Five hundred Armenian soldiers were disarmed, and then deported and massacred on the road." Subsequently the operations of deportation and mass murder began: "The river Yel Degirmeni brought down every day to the sea a number of corpses, mutilated and absolutely naked, the women with their

---

[18] AA Türkei 183/38, A23991, or R14087, K. no. 81/B.1645.
[19] AA Botschaft Konstantinopel ("BoKon" henceforth) 170, J. no. 3841, "secret" report of 23 August 1915.
[20] Joseph Pomiankowski, *Der Zusammenbruch des Ottomanischen Reiches* (Graz, Austria: Akademischer Druck – u. Verlag, 1969), p. 160. Swiss author Zurlinden (*Der Weltkrieg*, vol. II, p. 637) likewise argues that this measure was intended to facilitate the massacres to follow ["um desto leichter massakrieren zu können").
[21] Henry Morgenthau, *Ambassador Morgenthau's Story* (Garden City, N.Y.: Doubleday, 1918), pp. 302–4. The 10 July report is in US National Archives, RG59, 867.4016/74.

breasts cut off."[22] The other testimony comes from a German Cavalry Captain (Rittmeister) who in the course of a ride from Diyarbekir to Urfa had seen innumerable unburied corpses on both sides of the road. The victims were disarmed Armenian labor battalion soldiers "whose throats had been cut" ("mit durchschnittenen Hälsen").[23]

This practice of wholesale slaughter of Armenian conscripts was confirmed by Germany's Vice-Consul at Erzurum, Scheubner Richter, a Reserve Captain. In a 4 December 1916 report to Berlin, he declared that General Halil (Kut), the uncle of War Minister Enver, ordered "the massacre of his Armenian . . . battalions."[24] Halil's policy of extermination of the Armenian soldiers under his command is attested to by a Turkish officer who was part of his First Expeditionary Force (formerly the Fifth Expeditionary Force). As he stated, "All of the Armenian officers and soldiers of our Force were massacred by the order of Halil Paşa." The same officer continues to say that subsequently "Halil had the entire Armenian population (men, women and children) in the areas of Bitlis, Muş, and Beyazit also massacred without pity. My company received a similar order. Many of the victims were buried alive in especially prepared ditches."[25] A Russian-Armenian lawyer disclosed, in the Red Paper he compiled to expose, he said, the falsehoods of the White Paper the Ottoman authorities had published during the war, that "upon orders of General Halil, 800 Armenian and another time 1,000 soldiers, officers, and MDs in his Expeditionary Force were disarmed and killed by the Turkish soldiers of that Force."[26] Halil had been successively

---

[22] Viscount Bryce ed., Arnold Toynbee, compiler, *The Treatment of Armenians in the Ottoman Empire 1915–1916: Documents Presented to Viscount Grey of Falloden by Viscount Bryce* (London: His Majesty's Stationery Office, Miscellaneous no. 31, 1916), Doc. no. 74, p. 293.

[23] AA Türkei 183/44, A24663, enclosure no. 3, p. 4. The English version is in *Germany, Turkey and Armenia* (London: J. J. Keliher, 1917) (no author listed), p. 84. This testimony is corroborated by another eyewitness account in which the number of the murdered Armenian soldiers of this battalion is estimated to be 500: AA Türkei 183/41, A2888, Aleppo's German Consul Walter Rösler's 3 January 1916 report, enclosure no. 1, pp. 1, 4, with the new index numbering system, it is file no. R14090.

[24] AA Türkei 183/45, A33457, or, at new R14094. For similar reports on the mass murder of disarmed Armenian labor battalion soldiers, see below, notes 69, 73, and 79, and corresponding texts, discussing reports made by the Austrian Trabzon Consul, a German Colonel in charge of a regiment comprising felons released from the prisons of the Ottoman Empire, and Trabzon's US Consul Heizer.

[25] Report in Bureau de Correspondance Juif, The Hague, reproduced under the title, "Les massacres d'Arménie d'après un témoin oculaire" in *La Voix de l' Arménie* (Paris, fortnightly) LVA 1:24 (15 December 1918), p. 901.

[26] Gregory Tchalkhouchian, *Le Livre rouge* (Paris: Imprimerie Veradzenount, 1919), pp. 43–4. For a similar Armenian account see Garo Pasdermadjian, "Armenia. A Leading Factor in the Winning of World War I," *Armenian Review* 17:1–65 (Spring, February 1964), pp. 29–30.

commanding several Ottoman Turkish army units, including the Fifth Expeditionary Force, the fifty-second Division, the Eighteenth Army Corps, the Sixth Army, and finally the Army Groups East. In his post-war memoirs he boasted of having killed altogether "300,000 Armenians" adding "it can be more or less. I didn't count."[27] Given the relatively large numbers involved, and given the vicissitudes of war, this process of liquidation inevitably took several months to complete.

The Turkish authorities claimed that the "neutralization" of Armenian conscripts was due to acts of sabotage and betrayal by running over to the enemy side. Undoubtedly these acts occurred in some cases. However, preparatory work of detaching the Armenians from the other recruits and isolating them started long before the onset of major battles. In fact, even the plan to divest them of their weapons and assign them to labor battalion duties started weeks before Turkey entered the war. An official Turkish document containing a cipher telegram issued by General Hasan Izzet, Commander-in-Chief of the Third Army with headquarters in Erzurum, is noteworthy. It demonstrates that already on 24 September 1914, namely seven weeks after signing the secret Turko German political and military alliance, and the concurrent declaration of general mobilization when the able-bodied Armenian men in the 20–45 age category, were conscripted, the disarming of the latter was already decided – in other words, five weeks before Turkey entered the war. General Izzet's order, a copy of which was transmitted to Ottoman General Headquarters, commands the disarming "henceforth, and to the extent possible, of the Armenians" "şimdiden Ermenileri mümkün mertebe". A similar order was issued by War Minister Enver just before he launched the ill-fated Sarıkamış offensive.[28] Furthermore, the same order provides for the eventual formation of "militia" ("milis") units among those Muslims who are not subject to recruitment. As both the late dean of Turkish political scientists, Tarik Zafer Tunaya, on the one hand, and Special Organization Operative, Arif Cemal, on the other, emphasized, however, "militias" were coterminous with "brigands" ("çetes") and "convicts," yet they were "the constitutive" ("yapısal") elements of the Special Organization, the main

---

[27] Halil Paşa, *Bitmeyen Savaş*, ed. M. T. Sorgun (Istanbul: Yedigün, 1972), p. 274. On p. 241, Halil is more emphatic: "I have endeavored to wipe out the Armenian nation to the last individual" ("Son ferdine kadar yok etmeğe çalıştığım Ermeni milleti"). For more details, see Dadrian, "Documentation of the Armenian Genocide in Turkish Sources," pp. 116–17.

[28] *Askeri Tarih Belgeleri Dergisi* (Documents on Military History) 32: 83 (March 1983), Documents on the Armenians Series, special issue no. 2, Doc. No. 1894, p. 7. This is Izzet's order. For War Minister Enver's order of 25 December 1914, however, see *Askeri Tarih Belgeleri* 34: 85 (October 1985), Special Issue on the Armenia Series, no. 3, Doc. No. 1999, p. 23.

CUP instrument in the implementation of its anti-Armenian scheme.[29] Confirming this *prima facie* evidence emanating from the Ottoman Third Army, a German document states that these operations to disarm in some areas of the Empire began as early as October 1914, i.e., within two months of the Armenians' conscription and weeks before Turkey's entry into the world conflagration.[30] Due to the irregularities then endemic in the operational system of the Ottoman army, the implementation was neither uniform nor complete; in some unusual cases the ultimate liquidation was delayed on account of pressing needs for all kinds of labor which some of these disarmed Armenian soldiers could carry out. This was the case of the estimated 2,000–2,500 Armenians engaged in such labor in Sivas. In the summer of 1916 in small batches they were tied together with special ropes and butchered in the valley of Kızıldere near Gemerek, north-east of Kayseri. A chivalrous Turkish army Commander, General Vehib, executed the two arch perpetrators on the scaffold following a court-martial.[31]

[29] Tunaya, *Türkiyede Siyasal Partiler*, vol. III, p. 282; Arif Cemal, *1ci Dünya Savaşında Teşkilât-ı Mahsusa* (The Special Organization during the First World War) (Istanbul: Arba, 1997), pp. 44, 58. Such a militia detachment was secretly constituted shortly thereafter. A Turkish author, with irony, notes that the disarming of the conscripted Armenian soldiers was a measure taken prior to Turkey's intervention in the war, November 1914: Suat Parlar, *Osmanlıdan Günümüze Gizli Devlet* (The Continuation of the Secret State from the Ottoman Era to the Present) (Istanbul: Spartakus, 1996), pp. 92–3. Moreover, as one surviving Armenian officer recounted in his post-war testimony, already in December 1914 – i.e., before the launching of the Turkish Sarikamış offensive – "there was hardly any Armenian conscript left in possession of his arms in the ranks of the III Army." Reduced to "labor battalions, in which capacity they were engaged in the construction of the Erzurum-Tercan-Erzincan highway, these recruits suffered the fate awaiting them. It is an incontestable fact that the extermination in general of the Armenian soldiers was conjointly administered by the government and the army": "Tourk Zinvoraganoutian yev Mudavoraganoutian Teru Hayachinch Sarsapneru Untazkeen" (The Role of the Turkish Military and Intellectuals in the Horrors of Armenocide), *Djagadamart*, 1 February 1919.
[30] AA Türkei 142/41, A27535. Lieutenant Commander (*Korvettenkapitän*) and German Naval Attaché, Hans Humann, in his report no. 241, on 16 October 1914, informed German Ambassador Hans Wangenheim about this measure.
[31] For details on Vehib and his court-martial proceedings see Dadrian, "The Naim-Andonian Documents," pp. 330, 350 (n. 47); Dadrian, "The Armenian Question," p. 77, and n. 111 on pp. 84–5; for the most detailed account of this event in the Armenian language, see G. Kapigian, *Yeghernnabadoum Sepasdio* (The Story of the Mass Murder in Sivas) (Boston: Hairenik, 1924), pp. 570–2. Additional accounts with graphic descriptions of massacres of various Armenian labor battalion companies are provided by a Swiss pharmacist who throughout the war remained in Turkey serving the sick and wounded, non-Muslims and Muslims alike, in a hospital in Urfa: Jacob Künzler, *Im Lande des Blutes und der Tränen* (In the Land of Blood and Tears) (Potsdam, Berlin: Tempel, 1921), pp. 16–23. Another eyewitness of these systematic massacres was a Venezuelan officer who had volunteered his services to the Ottoman army in the First World War. His access to the organizers of these massacres and his presence in the areas of the atrocities impart poignancy to his testimony. His account relates to "the massacre of 1300–1500 unarmed Armenian soldiers in the area of Suverek in Diarbekir province" which he declared as

With the progression of the war, the range of opportunities to initiate new levels of anti-Armenian measures had expanded as well. Two major instances merit special attention in connection with the war against Russia in eastern Turkey. In both instances, in which to various degrees Armenians as combatants were involved, the Ottoman-Turkish military campaign, and the political-strategic designs associated with that campaign, suffered serious setbacks. One of them refers to the crushing defeat at Sarıkamış in January 1915 in which Armenian volunteers, spearheading the offensive as well as the defensive units of the Russian Caucasus Army, were believed to have played some contributory role.[32] The other concerns the 20 April – 17 May 1915 Armenian Van uprising which was mounted as a last-ditch desperate attempt to avert the calamity of imminent destruction, to which a large number of the province's Armenian villages, with their population, had fallen victim through a series of relentless massacres – as attested to and documented by German and Austro-Hungarian official testimonies.[33] These testimonies are remarkably corroborated by two high-ranking Ottoman-Turkish civilian administrators, namely provincial governors, whose official involvement in the events surrounding the insurrection imparts uncommon authenticity to their accounts. In his post-war memoirs Van province's Governor-General revealed that "the CUP was underhandedly instigating the [Muslim] people, prodding them to hurl themselves upon the Armenians" ("el altından halkı tahrik ederek Ermenilere saldırtmış").[34] For his part, Erzurum's Governor-General, who was transferred from the same position he held at Van a few months before the outbreak of the uprising, even then bitterly complained to Interior Minister Talât, stating, "I swear that the uprising in Van would not and could not have occurred. We are responsible for it because we tried to the utmost [to provoke

---

"so hideous a crime against humanity": Rafael de Nogales, *Four Years Beneath the Crescent*, trans. Muna Lee (New York, London: Scribner's, 1926), pp. 141, 150. His military engagement in the Ottoman-Turkish army during the war is confirmed by an official Turkish document: *Askeri Tarih Belgeleri* (Documents on Military History) 34 (October 1985), Doc. No. 2003, cipher no. 3, p. 41. Another account by a Russian-Armenian lawyer describes the mass murder of some 8,000 Armenian soldiers following the completion of a highway, for the construction of which they were employed by the military authorities: Tchalkhouchian, *Le Livre rouge*, p. 44.

[32] Morgenthau, *Ambassador* pp. 327, 333, but especially 337 where Interior Minister Talât is quoted as saying, "They [the Armenians] have assisted the Russians in the Caucasus and our failure there is largely explained by their actions." See also Dadrian, "The Armenian Question," pp. 66–9.

[33] For details of this episode of uprising, see Dadrian, "The Armenian Question," pp. 68, 69, and 82 (nn. 59–66).

[34] Ibrahim Arvas, *Tarihi Hakikatler. Ibrahim Arvas in Hatıratı* (Historical Truths. The Memoirs of Ibrahim Arvas) (Ankara: Resimli Posta, 1964), p. 6. The memoirs can also be found in installment form in the 21 April 1965 (no. 193) issue of *Yeni İstiklâl*.

the Armenians] thereby creating an upheaval that we cannot deal with" ("Kasem ederim ki Vanda ihtilâl olmazdı. Kendimiz zorlaya zorlaya şu içinden çıkamadığımız kargaşalığı meydana getirdik").[35]

There is no doubt that a number of Armenian soldiers enrolled in the Ottoman army did not recoil from deserting that army when in proximity to enemy lines. This is what happened during some of the battles against the Russian Caucasus Army in the east. This was in part due to the unabating abuses many of the Armenian conscripts were being subjected to by their Muslim fellow-combatants. To a greater extent, however, it was due to an inveterate urge to seek deliverance from the cumulative burdens of an oppressive regime. By the same token, there were indeed isolated cases of espionage and sabotage, the commission of which, however, was not limited to the Armenians and was particularly recurrent among Muslim Kurds, and even some Turks. The existence of a plan, however embryonic or tentative in its design, to eliminate the Armenians, made it quite expedient and convenient to embellish the significance of these incidents and consequently intensify the campaign against the conscripts. However, these incidents proved the catalyst in extending that campaign against the bulk of the Empire's Armenian population. The cases of Erzincan and Trabzon are remarkably emblematic in this respect. Therefore, they deserve a detailed exploration.

The cases of Erzincan and Trabzon. A microcosm of the Armenian Genocide

The Trabzon province, at that time, embraced a stretch of land consisting of a long, narrow littoral on the Black Sea coast, west of the port city of Batum, and north of the provinces of Sivas and Erzurum from which it is

---

[35] The Governor-General in question was Hasan Tahsin (Uzer). He was *vali* of Van 27 March 1913 – 30 September 1914. Subsequently, he served as *vali* of Erzerum until 10 August 1916. His cipher was a response to the message of Talât sent the day before with which the latter was ordering the wholesale deportation of the Armenians of that province. In questioning the wisdom of that order, Tahsin was trying to assure Talât that Erzurum's Armenians were not suspected of "revolution and espionage [*bu gayri variddir*] . . . they are in a wretched [*biçare*] condition and many of them do exactly appreciate the dire consequences of such foolish acts [*nereye varacağını takdir edenler çoktur*]." The full text of both ciphers is to be found in the depositories of Jerusalem Patriarchate Archive, Series 17, file H, Doc. Nos. 571 and 572. Confirming Tahsin's apparent carefulness in this whole matter, the Aide-de-Camp of Scheubner, Erzurum's German Vice-Consul, describes the series of meetings the latter held with the *vali*. In the course of one of these meetings Tahsin reportedly decried the whole matter of mass deportations as an "outrage" ("Schmach"): Paul Leverkuehn, *Posten auf Ewiger Wache* (Essen: Essener Verlag, 1938), p. 44.

separated by a string of mountains. The name derives from "Trabizoid," a geometric designation, which meant to the indigenous Greeks a narrow and elongated territory, and its main town was accordingly called "Trapezus." Throughout history that town served as a commercial center, and as a major port city. With the advent of Ottoman rule in the fifteenth century, it became the point of departure for caravans to Persia. Trabzon was not only the capital of the province but also that of the district, likewise called Trabzon (Trebizond). The other three districts were Samsun (Canik), Gümüşhane, and Lazistan or Rize. The less-known port cities of the province were Tirebolu, Giresun, and Ordu (counties in Trabzon district), Samsun, and Ünye (in Samsun district), and of course Rize (in Lazistan).

The demography involved populations which, apart from the Turks, consisted mainly of Lazic (a Caucasian ethnic group) and Greek elements. Kurdish migration centered on the mountain ranges overlooking the coast. Armenian colonies, on the other hand, were concentrated in the towns, ports, and rural areas. The province was under the administration of a Governor-General (*vali*), and his subordinates: i.e., Governors (*mutasarrif*) and Sub-governors (*kaymakam*), who administered districts (*sancak*) and counties (*kaza*) respectively. There were over 1 million Muslims, about 250,000 Greeks, and about 55,000–60,000 Armenians living in the province. While only 8,000–10,000 of the latter lived in the city of Trabzon itself, about an equal number of them resided in the surrounding villages of the city. The majority of the Armenians lived, however, in the rural areas of the province, dispersed as they were in a couple of hundred villages, such as in those of Ordu (about 9,000), of Çarsamba of Samsun district (about 13,000), of Ünye (about 8,000). The province and its capital in particular were under the military jurisdiction of the Third Army whose Commander, Mahmud Kâmil Paşa (February 1915 – February 1916), ruled it with an iron hand. This was done by a complete coordination of the requisite initiatives with his subordinate, Governor-General Cemal Azmi, who politically and militarily, as well as juridically (he was the President of the regional Court Martial), had thereby become omnipotent in the entire province. The supervisory power in the application of all such initiatives was vested in people carefully selected by the CUP's Central Committee. Called "Responsible Secretary," these people were the highest provincial representatives of the party, overseeing the running of the government in such a way as to bring it in line with the directives, and overt and covert goals of the party. Trabzon's Responsible Secretary was Yenibahçeli Nail. He, together with Azmi, reigned supreme in the province.

Discussed below is the first case in Erzincan where a special type of lethal experiment set the stage for medical killings to become a constitutive element of the Armenian Genocide.

Medical killings in Erzincan

As all genocidal campaigns have their peculiar rationales, in the case of the Armenians there was an element of perverted epidemiology leading to a kind of preventive medicine. The leaders of the Special Organization, who mainly carried out that campaign, alternately vilified their Armenian victims as "microbes"[36] and "tumors,"[37] that, according to them, were devouring the Empire. Such a frame of mind allowed the perpetrators to institute lethal medical experiments for which young Armenian males would serve as disposable guinea pigs.

The opportunity presented itself with the wartime outbreak and persistence of a host of epidemics involving a number of diseases, many of them contagious. The existing scanty health and sanitation conditions were particularly exacerbated in wartime Turkey. In no small way they contributed to the decimation of the ranks of the military on all fronts. Referring to these casualties in the Third Army, for example, a noted Turkish military historian underscores this problem of poor sanitation conditions, pointing out the dearth of vaccines to protect the soldiers from the ravages of epidemics. Based on statistics, he states that the Third Army alone suffered 128,698 fatalities as a result of these deficiencies.[38] A Turkish medical authority also touches on this problem declaring that even before the onset of major battles, such as Sarıkamiş, "the typhus epidemics had wreaked havoc in the army, causing the death of tens of thousands of soldiers."[39]

---

[36] Cemal Kutay, *Birinci Dünya Harbinde Teşkilât-i Mahsusa ve Hayber' de Türk Genci* (The Special Organization in World War I) (Istanbul: Ercan, 1962), p. 44.

[37] Celal Bayar, *Ben de Yazdim* (I Too Have Narrated) vol. V (Istanbul: Baha, 1967), p. 1578. The author was one of the operatives of that Organization who later became Prime Minister (1937–9), and subsequently President of the Republic of Turkey (1950–60). Both Bayar and Kutay are quoting Eşref Kuscubaşı, the Chief of the Special Organization, who confided to Kutay that he was personally involved in the implementation of the anti-Armenian measures: Kutay, *Birinci*, p. 78. When justifying his exterminatory campaign against the Armenians, Dr. Mehmed Reşid, Governor-General of Diyarbekir province, likewise debased his Armenian victims as "dangerous microbes." See Vahakn N. Dadrian, "The Role of Turkish Physicians in the World War I Genocide of Ottoman Armenians," *Holocaust and Genocide Studies* 1:2 (1986), p. 175.

[38] General Fahri Belen, *Birinci Cihan Harbinde Türk Harbi* (Turkey's War in World War I), vol. IV (Ankara: General Staff Publication, 1966), p. 194.

[39] Rifat Gözberk, MD, *Hürriyet* (Turkish daily), 28 June 1969. Quoted in Şevket Süreyya Aydemir, *Makedonya' dan Ortaasya' ya Enver Paşa* (Enver Paşa From Macedonia to Central Asia), 3 vols., vol. III, *1914–1922* (Istanbul: Remzi, 1972), p. 441.

Consequently, the Chief of the Third Army's Sanitation and Health Service, army physician Tevfik Salim (he later adopted the surname Sağlam), ordered the launching of typhus experiments in an effort to develop an effective vaccine.[40] The experiments were conducted in the Central Hospital of Erzincan, a city located some 180 km south of Trabzon. Two categories of young Armenian males were selected for these experiments. The main category involved those Armenians who were disarmed and were being used for various types of labor. The other embraced those Armenians who were enrolled in Erzincan's two military schools. One of them was for training reserve officers in a six-month program that was set up at the start of the war (*Yedeksubay Talimgâhı*); 150 Armenians were enrolled there. The other involved a military secondary school for young cadets and some 40 Armenians were enrolled there as well. Some of the Armenian trainees of the Reserve Officers' School were taken out in batches of ten, hands tied, and killed in the valley near Vasgerd village. These operations were conducted under the supervision of Captain Şahin from Erzurum and Imam Hoca Ismail Hakkı. The young cadets of the other school were, likewise, with hands tied, executed, and their corpses were thrown into a shaft near Zenbereg Köprü. However, a large part of the trainees of the Reserve School, along with the labor battalion soldiers, were experimented upon for a typhus vaccine and died as a result. Though no details are available about the specifics of his involvement in this entire episode, one of his close associates, in his post-war memoirs, indicates that Behaeddin Şakir, one of the principal architects of the Armenian Genocide, an MD, was also engaged in the fight against typhus while in Erzurum. He was able to secure the transfer of Dr. Hamdi

[40] Professor Dr. Tevfik Sağlam (Retired General), *Büyük Harpte Sıhhi Hizmet* (Health Service During the Great War) (Istanbul: Military Publishing House, 1941). On p. 76 he disclosed that 88.3 percent of the deaths in the Third Army were due to illness. On pp. 89, 134, and 145, he identified the Turkish physicians engaged in typhus experiments. The author held the same position of Chief of the Sanitation and Health Service with the Second Army before being transferred to the Third to combat typhus. Later in the year, he was promoted to Inspector of Army Group East. After becoming Professor of Medicine at the Medical School of Istanbul University, he was first promoted to Dean of that school, and later to Rector (President) of the University. Marshal Liman von Sanders, the head of the German Military Mission to Turkey and Commander in Chief of the First Ottoman Army and then of the Fifth Army in the Dardanelles, in his post-war tome, reflected on the dire conditions related to the typhus epidemics. Quoting from a report sent by the German Consul at Trabzon, he wrote, "Spotted typhus is raging in all the hospitals of the city. The extent of the epidemics is approaching a catastrophe . . . the daily death rate [among the soldiers] is between thirty and fifty." Two German physicians on duty in Erzincan's Red Crescent Hospital, MDs Theodor Colley and Zlocisti, likewise reported that "Lack of sanitary arrangements and of sufficient medical help is decimating the ranks of the Turkish soldiers in a manner unthinkable under German conditions": Liman von Sanders, *Five Years in Turkey* (Annapolis: United States Naval Institute, 1927), p. 49.

Suat from his work at Istanbul University Medical School to Erzurum, and eventually Erzincan, where at the city's Central Hospital the latter conducted the deadly experiments.[41]

Hamdi Suat (Aknar) was a Munich-trained Professor of Pathology at Istanbul's Medical School. In an effort to generate through antibodies a level of immunity against typhus, he injected typhus-contaminated blood into hundreds of his Armenian subjects. For this, he used the method of defibrillation – the process of separating, through centrifugation, the lighter portions of a solution from the heavier portions and then using these portions as a serum for vaccination. Through the tests the professor was trying to determine the differential impact of the serum obtained this way on such organs of the healthy human body as the heart, the brain, and the liver. As openly admitted by Dr. Suat's Turkish colleagues, the experiments were fatal for the subjects because Dr. Suat deliberately failed to render "inactive" the blood to be tested. When during the Armistice these facts became public and the Turkish Military Tribunal's Inquiry Commission was invited to investigate the matter, Professor Suat was being cared for by psychiatrists in the clinic of the Medical School for "acute psychosis." He was being forcibly restrained during that treatment.[42] Notwithstanding, he is venerated in Turkey today as "the father" of bacteriology in Turkey ("Turk mikrobiyologisinin Babası"). A memorial-museum, erected in his name on the grounds of the University of Istanbul in Beyazit, is expressive of that veneration.

In a comprehensive study on this subject, a German specialist on medical history and pharmacology not only confirms these experiments by Hamdi Suat but discloses that Süleyman Numan, Chief Medical Officer of Ottoman Armed Forces, and Talât's Interior Ministry, together approved of them. Utilizing official documents from the Bayerisches Hauptstaatsarchiv, Abteilung IV, Kriegsarchiv (Bavarian Main State Archive, Münich, Section IV, War Archive), he details the efforts of Professor George Mayer, Süleyman Numan's German deputy, and Marshal Liman von Sanders, the Chief of the German Military Mission to Turkey, to stop these experiments. There were repeated attempts by them to induce Enver, War Minister and de facto Commander-in-Chief of Ottoman Armed Forces, to intervene and forbid "these injections which can infect

---

[41] Arif Cemil, *I. Dünya Savaşında Teşkilât-ı Mahsusa* (The Special Organization During the First World War) (Istanbul: Arba, 1997), pp. 228–9. The same can be found in installment no. 93, the 5 February 1934 issue of *Vakit* (Turkish daily) in which the author, under the pseudonym A. Mil, published his material in serial installments, November 1933 – March 1934.

[42] A. Khandjian, MD, "Keedagan Martasbanountiun" (Scientific Murder), *Nor Giank* (Armenian daily, Istanbul), 3 January 1919.

even the monkeys, and which are not only devoid of scientific merit but are unconscionable as well." Dr. Helmut Becker, the specialist of the book mentioned above, also indicates that Professor Mayer first learned about these lethal experiments from Erzurum's German Consul, and that additionally Dr. Heinrich Bergfeld, the German Consul at Trabzon, informed him that sixty-five people there died as a result of such injections. Without identifying them as Armenians, Professor Mayer voices his indignation at sacrificing the young cadets at Erzincan's Military School and is at a loss as to why the experiments are continuing. He also discloses that the Governor-General of Erzurum province thanked Interior Minister Talât for sponsoring the typhus experiments while allowing that this Governor was either fooled or was instructed to do so "to cover-up [*vertuschen*] the unhappy outcomes." Becker expresses the same skepticism regarding similar sentiments expressed by Sağlam, the Third Ottoman Army's Chief Sanitation Officer, on the quality of the research involved. These doubts were shared, according to Becker, by Professor E. Rodenwaldt, Captain of Sanitation attached to the Ottoman Army; Professor Zlocisti, German Red Cross Chief Physician in an Ottoman military hospital; Professor Viktor Schilling who was in charge of a bacteriological laboratory in Aleppo.[43]

---

[43] Helmut Becker, *Äskulap Zwischen Reichsadler und Halbmond* (Symbol of Medical Art Interposed Between the Imperial Eagle and the Crescent) (Herzogenrath: Murken-Altrogge, 1990), pp. 152–4. On 2 March 1916 Professor Mayer sent to his superior, Major General (med.) Professor Karl Ritter von Seydel, in Munich, Bavaria, a "secret" memorandum in which he described how in the Ottoman War Ministry Turkish officers "with cynical grin were recounting fabricated tales of Armenians dying by natural causes or by [bogus] accidents as attested by official medical reports": Bayerisches Hauptstaatsarchiv, Abteilung IV, p. 13. For a study by Tevfik Salim (Sağlam) on the avowed success of the typhus experiments described in the text, see Becker, *Äskulap*, p. 152 (n. 3). For the involvement in similar efforts, especially in Aleppo, of other German physicians, such as Professors Heinz Zeiss and Viktor Schilling, see Paul Weindling, "German-Soviet Medical Co-operation and the Institute for Racial Research 1927 – c. 1935," *German History* 10: 2, pp. 177–206. For the complicity of Süleyman Numan, whose brief biography is provided by Becker (*Äskulap*, p. 26), in lethal medical experiments and associated initiatives, see British Foreign Office Archives FO371/6503/E6311, folios 37–8. In these pages he is accused of poisoning Armenians and having had Armenian physicians murdered in the area of Erzurum and Erzincan. During the Armistice, surviving Armenian MDs, pharmacists, and other medical professionals filed against him a lawsuit containing twenty specific charges: *Renaissance*, 29 April 1919. An Armenian chronicler of the genocide states that Numan had the sick of a deportee convoy burned to death to prevent epidemics: S. Agouni, *Million Mu Hayerou Tchartee Badmoutounee* (The Story of the Massacre of One Million Armenians) (Istanbul: Assadourian, 1920), p. 156. The post-war Turkish government through its Inquiry Commission had him arrested for trial before the Military Tribunal on charges of having "ordered his staff to murder by poisoning the sick among the populations of Erzurum, Sivas, and Erzincan, under the pretext of safeguarding the healthy part of the remaining population against epidemics and starvation": FO 371/6500, folios 170–4; FO371/6509, folio 51, Appendix C, p. 9;

In order to appreciate the significance of this disturbing precedent in the medical history of genocide, the sequence of events surrounding this case needs to be highlighted. As the post-war Turkish authorities in December 1918 were grappling with the problem of prosecuting and punishing the authors of the wartime Armenian deportations and massacres and their accomplices, a surviving Armenian physician, in an article entitled "The Turkish Physicians Too Are Complicit," disclosed some details about the active involvement of a host of Turkish military physicians in the anti-Armenian extermination campaign, including that part of the campaign especially targeting Armenian medical personnel: physicians, pharmacists, and nurses who were employed in various military hospitals. He offered to identify the culprits in a properly instituted juridical venue and to testify against them.[44] The Health Services Board of the War Ministry promptly denied the charge, challenging the Armenian physician to be specific and name names.[45] The brazenness of this denial sufficiently angered two Turkish physicians with intimate knowledge of the matter to go public and provide details, including the identification of the physician who conducted the experiments. One of those who protested, surgeon Cemal Haydar, complained in a Turkish newspaper that such denials were "customary for Turkish authorities." This fact prompted him to tell the truth as he knew it, he added.

In his open letter addressed to the Interior Minister, Dr. Haydar made the following points:

The blood of typhoid fever patients was inoculated into innocent Armenians without rendering that blood 'inactive.' The subjects were duped [*iğfal*] into believing that they were being inoculated against typhus. The experiments were of the kind whose application medical science allows only for animals slated for vivisection. When publishing the results of these criminal experiments, of which I personally was a close witness, the esteemed Professor simply stated that the subjects were men condemned to death, without identifying them as Armenians whose sole guilt in fact was that they belonged to the Armenian people.

After mentioning the names of the two Turkish Chief Physicians of Erzincan's Central Hospital and Red Crescent Hospital as authorities with intimate knowledge of these tests, surgeon Haydar declared, "I am ready to furnish fully the requisite explanations on the matter"

FO371/4173/83002, folio 470. See also Dadrian, "The Role of Turkish Physicians," p. 174.

[44] Mihran Norair, MD, "Turk Pushignern Al Mechsageetz" (The Turkish Physicians Too Are Complicit), *Ariamard* (Azadamard), 15 December 1918. The French translation of the article appeared the next day in *Renaissance* (a French-language Istanbul daily), (December 1918); the Turkish version appeared in *Yeni Gazeta*, 17 December 1918.

[45] *Ariamard*, 21 December 1918 issue, published the text of the denial.

("bu hususta icab eden tafsilâtı vermeye"). He sought the help of the Interior Ministry's Commission of Inquiry of Misdeeds (Tedkîk-i-Seyyiât Komisyonu). That Commission was created to gather evidentiary material through pre-trial interrogations, administered, orally and in writing, for possible court-martialing of those who were responsible for "Armenian deportations and massacres" ("tehcir ve taktil"). In seeking help Dr. Haydar appealed to the sense of honor and the conscience of the authorities. He further declared that the Tribunal should be able to locate the hospital's records where physicians are expected to register the names of the patients they handle, and verify the fact that these innocent Armenian subjects had no trial and conviction records whatsoever. Surgeon Haydar further argued that it was unconscionable to allow this event to be consigned to oblivion. He declared, "the barbarities committed against the Armenians were not only an administrative but a scientific crime as well [yalniz idâri degil, fenni bir sui-kasd] and as such they constitute a stain for the medical profession."[46]

Dr. Haydar was followed by Dr. Salaheddin, the Chief Physician of the Red Crescent Hospital of the same city, i.e., Erzincan. His statement was published one day later in the same Turkish newspaper. He was, he said, unfortunately completely familiar with the events of Erzincan's Central Hospital, and, if he could assist in apprehending the authorities really responsible for these acts, his conscience would be cleared and the dishonored medical profession and Turkism would have relieved themselves of a large burden. He went on to say that the experiments, to which the Armenians, ever anxious about the atrocities surrounding them, were subjected, were fit only for laboratory animals, guinea pigs, and rabbits. They issued, he said, from a theory not yet validated by science and were essentially chance procedures. Then he went on to say:

a large number of Armenians succumbed to these inhuman experiments, they hardly contributed to the health of others . . . No positive results whatsoever were obtained. The unfortunate Armenians, whose existence was relegated to levels lower than that of animals, were victimized in the name of certain obscure points of science. As far as I remember, the blood taken from these typhus-infected Armenian subjects was used to inoculate Erzurum's Governor Tahsin – after having been rendered "inactive," as required by the ad hoc rules of medicine.[47]

---

[46] *Türkce Istanbul*, Istanbul Turkish newspaper, 23 December 1918. The English translation of surgeon Cemal Haydar's open letter is in Dadrian, "The Role of Turkish Physicians," pp. 177–9. The Interior Minister to whom the open letter was addressed was Mustafa Arif (Deymer).

[47] *Türkce Istanbul*, 24 December 1918; also Dadrian, "The Role of Turkish Physicians," pp. 178–9.

When the Ministry of Defense denied these allegations,[48] surgeons Haydar and Salaheddin each published a second letter. Haydar reiterated his assertion that "hundreds" of young Armenians were murdered by the typhus serum experiments and that these had indelibly stained the reputation of Turkish medicine. He was at a loss as to why so many other medical faculties and physicians were remaining silent in defense of the honor of their profession. Suffice it to point out that the Defense Ministry merely denied the existence of an order or authorization to conduct such experiments without denying the experiments themselves.[49] For his part, Dr. Salaheddin disclosed that "to his surprise" he was being pressured to remain silent on the entire affair while many "ignorant doctors" were denying the facts instead of insisting on the establishment of "the truth."[50]

Due to the political turmoil attending the efforts of a succession of post-war Turkish governments to bring to justice a whole range of culprits relative to the atrocities committed against the Armenians, including a large group of Turkish physicians, along with their administrative superiors, Professor Hamdi Suat and his co-perpetrators escaped prosecution and punishment. He even managed to publish about the results of his experiments, first in the *Journal of Military Medicine* (*Ceride-i Tibbiyi-e Askeriyye*),[51] then in the German *Zeitschrift für Hygiene und Infektionskrankheiten.*[52] As mentioned above, Professor Suat was less than truthful in this article about both the nature of his subjects, whom he described as "condemned" men ("Verurteilte"), and the information he provided to the latter about the purpose of the experiments. Moreover, according to the testimony of his two Turkish colleagues, who had gone public with their exposure of the criminal nature of these tests, Professor Suat's claims about his results were also open to dispute. As indicated by his ultimate superior, Professor Tevfik Salim (Sağlam), who had authorized these tests in the first place, Suat subsequently established a course on pathological anatomy in Erzurum during the war.[53]

The significance of this episode of medical killings could have been limited if it had proven to be an isolated case involving the aberrant, albeit atrocious, behavior of a single professor of pathology and bacteriology.

---

[48] *Ikdam* (Istanbul Turkish newspaper), 27 December 1918.
[49] *Istiklâl* (Istanbul Turkish newspaper), 3 January 1919.
[50] *Alemdar* (Istanbul Turkish newspaper), 8 January 1919.
[51] *Ikdam*, 27 December 1918, indicated that the article was forthcoming.
[52] It was published in vol. 22 (1916) of the journal under the title "Über die Ergebnisse der Immunisierungsversuche gegen Typhus exanthematicus (Aus den Etappenkrankhäusern in Ersindjan)," pp. 235–42.
[53] Sağlam, *Büyük Harpte*, p. 145. On p. 89, Sağlam confirms Suat's experiments in Erzincan. The reference to his Armenian subjects as condemned men is on p. 239.

This man, however, worked within a system, had superiors, had assistants, and, above all, had a host of colleagues who studiously remained silent and some of whom did not even hesitate to exert all kinds of pressure upon the above-discussed two Chief Physicians in order to conceal the facts. Further research on this matter clearly demonstrates that Professor Hamdi Suat, the performer of the murderous experiments, was but a cog in a set-up targeting the Armenians as a nefarious pathogen in the body of the Ottoman Empire. By widening the compass beyond the scale of Professor Suat's medical experiments, voluminous other material bearing on the subject comes to the fore. A US State Department document covering the same period of disclosures described above indicates, for example, that in the Aziziye Hospital of the same city of Erzincan, the anti-Armenian campaign was extended to Armenian physicians of that hospital, as witnessed and testified to by a Greek physician, MD Vassilaki.[54] Some of the victims included Armenian pharmacists and dentists as well. As reported by a pair of nurses, an American and German working in the Military Hospital of distant Bitlis, "All the Armenian nurses, druggists, and orderlies," were likewise liquidated; "It mattered not that they were the most intelligent and faithful helpers and that there was no one left to prepare medicines for the Turkish patients – all had to go."[55]

Medical killings of babies and infants in Trabzon

To return to the Turkish physicians depicted in the American document cited above, one of them is described as having openly boasted that he killed his Armenian patients by having them drink "corrosive sublimate"

[54] Enclosure in Acting Secretary of State Frank L. Polks, 25 January 1918 communication to The Mission of the United States to the Conference to Negotiate Peace, Paris. The enclosure is a duplicate copy of dispatch no. 306 from the American Consulate at Saloniki, Greece, dated 16 December 1918. The report lists the names and positions of ten Armenian MDs as "some of the Armenian doctors serving as officers in the Turkish army who have been murdered": US National Archives R.G. 256, 867 4016/4. For their part, the officials of the British Foreign Office submitted to the same Paris Peace Conference a list containing the names of five Turkish physicians accused of having personally organized the murder, through various devices including poisoning with mercury, of Armenian physicians serving in military hospitals: FO 371/247/8109, I series list, folio 96, 4 January 1919 report.

[55] Grace H. Knapp, *The Tragedy of Bitlis* (London and Edinburgh: Fleming H. Revell Co. 1919), p. 54. The two sister-nurses who were working in that hospital and who reported this liquidation were American citizen Ms. Grisell McLaren, who knew Ottoman Turkish, and German citizen Ms. Martha Kleiss. The book describes a litany of murders of Armenian physicians, surgeons, and other medical personnel in Turkish military hospitals in Van and Bitlis, as observed by many other European and American physicians and nurses working in these hospitals.

potions.[56] In the same document a covert reference is also made to MD
Ali Saib, Director of Trabzon Public Health and Sanitation Services.
During the court-martial proceedings it was revealed that Dr. Saib regularly poisoned Armenian infants, adults, and pregnant women in Trabzon's Red Crescent Hospital as well as at several schools in that city
temporarily sheltering Armenian infants, and that he ordered the drowning at the Black Sea of those who refused to take his "medicine."[57] What
is so significant and particularly instructive about Dr. Saib's case is the
preponderance of testimony supplied by Ottoman-Turkish physicians,
military officers, and governmental officials. One can observe here the
extent to which a trained physician can lapse into the abyss of a multi-
level and sustained criminal behavior vis-à-vis a totally defenseless and,
therefore, highly vulnerable victim population under cover of wartime
exigencies and by resort to disingenuous excuses. A brief review may,
therefore, be warranted.

Dr. Ali Saib was Director of Health Services in Trabzon province.
In that capacity he inspected and supervised the medical activities
at Trabzon's Red Crescent Hospital. During the deportation of the
Armenians in the summer of 1915, he used a variety of devices to exterminate most Armenians who for one reason or another ended up at that
hospital. During the post-war court-martial, the judicial authorities, as a
result of testimony they had secured through pre-trial interrogations and
written interrogatories, sent a Dr. Ziya Fuad, then Inspector of Health
Services, to Trabzon to gather evidence from local Turkish physicians
about Dr. Saib's misdeeds. At the third sitting of the Trabzon trial series,
Dr. Fuad's report was read into the record (1 April 1919). A key finding
of that report was that Dr. Saib disposed of most of his Armenian victims
through poison. At times he would pour the potion into the victim's cup.
As testified to at that sitting by a survivor, once the hospital aides refused
to carry out his order. Thereupon he had someone else force the cup to
the mouth of the victim. Other times Dr. Saib would resort to a device
that reportedly was widely used against many survivors who had become
sick and enfeebled in the deserts of Mesopotamia, especially in the transit camps, namely, injection of morphine or other lethal substances. One
such survivor stated that sick Armenians in her transit camp were taken to
the hospital in Hamam, a town some 200 km east of Aleppo, "and given
a needle and killed."[58] Moreover, several hundred Armenian children
from among the 3,000 orphans left behind were being cared for by the

[56] See note 54.   [57] Dadrian, "The Role of Turkish Physicians," p. 176.
[58] For Dr. Fuad's report, see *Renaissance* 2 and 3 April 1919; *Istiklâl*, 2 April 1919. The
statement about the use of morphine in Hamam is excerpted from an interview provided
by survivor Lousaper Shamlian on 19 February 1980 to interviewer Helen Sahagian as

Greek metropolitan of Trabzon, Archbishop Khrisantos. However, they were soon snatched away by the CUP potentate Nail; some were distributed among Turkish families, others were taken to the Red Crescent Hospital and the others to several school buildings. At the seventh sitting of the Trabzon trial series, Father Laurent, the French Capucin Father Superior in Trabzon, through an interpreter, testified that he personally saw the corpses of the dead, poisoned, children being squeezed into large and deep baskets in the hospital grounds, like animals from a slaughter house, and then dumped in the sea nearby.[59] A similar procedure was followed at some school buildings. Another Turkish physician, Dr. Adnan, Director of Trabzon Public Health Services, who had launched his own investigation, likewise had prepared a report. It too was read into the record at the third sitting (1 April 1919). In it, Dr. Adnan confirmed acts of poisoning of the children in some school buildings and "their disposal through baskets." Apart from using poison potions, a new method that was introduced in a school building involved steam baths, the so-called *etüv*, the sterilizing chamber of super-hot air pressure.[60] Apparently Dr. Saib had had installed there an army mobile *etüv* contraption consisting of boxes that released super-hot steam and, through suffocation, instantly killed the infants, some of whom were mere babies.

Among other Muslim and Turkish witnesses testifying at the court-martial were: (1) merchant Mehmet Ali who confirmed the acts of poisoning as well as drowning of children (at the tenth sitting, on 12 April 1919); (2) ex-Van Governor-General Nâzım testified on the drowning operations (fifteenth sitting, 1 May 1919); (3) Ordu merchant Hüseyin recounted scenes of drowning of women and children (sixteenth sitting, 5 May 1919); (4) judicial Inspector Kenan testified also on drowning operations (seventeenth sitting, 10 May 1919); (5) Cavalry First Lieutenant Fadil Harun, the Aide de Camp and interpreter of German Colonel

part of the Armenian Assembly Oral History Project: File no. GEN 04, Transcripts for Aleppo, Armenian Research Center, University of Michigan, Dearborn, Michigan.

[59] *Istiklâl and Ikdam*, 8 April 1919; *Renaissance*, 9 April 1919.

[60] *Renaissance*, 27 April 1919; The sitting, the fourth in the Trabzon trial series, took place on 26 April 1919. Nearly all Armenian dailies, i.e., *Nor Giank, Zhamanag, Zhoghovourtee Tzain and Djagadamard*, carried this testimony in their 27 April 1919 issue. In my coverage of this incident in 1986, when available data was scant, I was led to believe that Dr. Saib was luring the infants to this "disinfection" chamber in order to smother them with some toxic material such as asphyxiating gases released from cylindrical metal cases that were of German origin. After reviewing new material about the wartime uses of disinfection devices in the sanitation system of the Turkish army, I am now inclined to believe, however, that it was the sudden exposure to extremely high temperatures generated in these *etüves* that, through suffocation, instantly killed the multitudes of fragile Armenian infants. For my original interpretation, see Dadrian, "The Role of Turkish Physicians," p. 176.

Stange who was in charge of the 8th Regiment of the Ottoman Third Army's Tenth Army Corps, testified to the incidence both of operations of drowning at the Black Sea, and of poisoning not only at the Red Crescent Hospital but at school buildings as well, to which procedure, he said, about 300 Armenian orphan children fell victim (eighteenth sitting, 13 May 1919).[61] In that trial Inspector of Health Services Dr. Ziya Fuad repeated his findings about Dr. Saib's procedure of disposing of his victims through administering poison to them. As witnesses he cited three Turkish physicians, Vahab, Raif, and Sadri, who had provided him with the requisite information.[62]

Extermination of women and children by drowning

Even though the bulk of Trabzon's Armenian population was destroyed through the "deportation" procedures that involved the dispatching inland of several convoys,[63] drowning was a means of mass murder, nearly all of the victims of which were women, including pregnant women,

---

[61] *Renaissance, and L'Entente* (also a French-language Istanbul daily), 14 May 1919. For the sources of the other testimonies, see Vahakn N. Dadrian, "The Documentation of the World War I Armenian Massacres in the Proceedings of the Turkish Military Tribunal," *International Journal of Middle East Studies* 23 (1991), pp. 560, 574 (nn. 55 and 56); Dadrian, "The Case of Trabzon Province: The Drowning Operations in the Black Sea," in Dadrian, *The Armenian Genocide in Official Turkish Records* [Collected Works], pp. 44–49 (*Journal of Political and Military Sociology* [Special Edition] 22: 1 [Summer 1994] x–xi and 1-202). Of particular interest is the wartime testimony of a Muslim military officer serving in the Ottoman army. Lieutenant Said Ahmed Muhtar describes the method of drowning in one particular case involving children as victims: "They were taken out to sea in little boats. At some distance out they were stabbed to death, put in sacks and thrown into the sea. A few days later some of their little bodies were washed up on the shore of Trabzon": FO 371/2781/364888, 27 December 1916, Appendix B, report no. 2, p. 7. For a similar Muslim testimony, see FO.WO106/1418, folio 34, p. 506.
[62] *Ileri* (Istanbul Turkish daily), 7 July 1919; 9 July 1919.
[63] In a monographic study which, as far as it is known, is the only detailed exploration in English of that part of the Armenian Genocide that was executed in Trabzon province, the author mentions five such successive convoys in the 1–18 July 1915 period: Kevork Y. Suakjian (Syakjian), *Genocide in Trebizond: A Case Study of Armeno-Turkish Relations During the First World War* (Ann Arbor, Mich. University Microfilms, 1981), pp. 132–7. One can also find in this doctoral dissertation, among others, the series of reports which the US Consul at Trabzon, Oscar S. Heizer, sent to the State Department, in which he narrates many of the details of the on-going mass murder in Trabzon. Eight of these are reproduced in this work, some being incomplete, others bearing wrong dates or no date at all, and several of them being wrongly indexed and carrying wrong document numbers. Another monograph reproduces some fifteen of these reports. See *United States Official Documents on the Armenian Genocide*, compiled and introduced by Ara Sarafian, vol. II, *The Peripheries* (Watertown, Mass.: Armenian Review, 1994), Doc. nos. 1, 5, 7, 9, 13, 14, 15, 17, 18, 19, 20, 24, 27, 28, 29. Both monographs additionally have an important report by W. Peter, US Consular Agent at Samsun, i.e., Doc. no. 35, the original text of which was in French.

though old men, children, and the sick were also targeted. During the post-war debates in the Ottoman Parliament, Çürüksulu Mahmud Paşa, one-time departmental head at Ottoman General Headquarters, twice Minister of Navy, and occupant of several other Cabinet posts, in his 2 December 1918 speech in the Ottoman Senate declared that Cemal Azmi, the province's Governor-General, was responsible for this crime, and that the latter was acting on orders from the CUP's Central Committee.[64] On 11 December 1918, Trabzon province's Deputy, Hafiz Mehmed, who by profession was a lawyer and as such was nicknamed "hukukcu," declared in the Chamber of Deputies of the same Parliament:

God will punish us for what we did [*Allah bize belasını verecektir*] . . . the matter is too obvious to be denied. I personally witnessed this Armenian occurrence in the port city of Ordu [about 155 km west of Trabzon]. Under the pretext of sending off to Samsun, another port city on the Black Sea [about 255 km west of Trabzon], the district's governor loaded the Armenians into barges and had them thrown overboard. I have heard that the governor-general applied this procedure [throughout the province]. Even though I reported this at the Interior Ministry immediately upon my return to Istanbul   I was unable to initiate any action against the latter; I tried for some three years to get such action instituted but in vain.[65]

It is noteworthy that governor Faik, himself of that port city Ordu, located halfway between Trabzon and Samsun, personally executed these drowning operations. At the fifteenth sitting of the Trabzon trial series (5 May 1919), Ordu merchant Hüseyin testified: "I saw Kaymakam Faik one afternoon load two barges with women and children supposedly to take them to Samsun. But the boats which needed two days for the journey, returned in two hours instead, as the corpses of the victims began to be sighted near the shoreline."[66] Deputy Hafiz's testimony is incorporated in the Military Tribunal's key indictment charging the Cabinet ministers and top CUP leaders with capital crimes.[67] When the Tribunal in its two separate verdicts found the Governor-General and his principal co-perpetrator, CUP Central Committee delegate Nail, guilty and sentenced them to death (in absentia), it specified the crime of drowning. That verdict in part reads, "Relying upon repeat criminals

[64] *Meclisi Âyan Zabit Ceridesi* (Transcripts of the Senate Proceedings) 3rd election period, 5th session, 13th sitting, vol. I, p. 148, 2 December 1918 issue.

[65] *Meclisi Mebusan Zabit Ceridesi* (Transcripts of the Proceedings of the Chamber of Deputies) 3rd election period, 5th session, 24th sitting, p. 299, 1 December 1918 issue.

[66] *Hadisat* (Istanbul Turkish daily), 7 May 1919; *Renaissance*, 6 May 1919.

[67] *Takvim-i Vekâyi* (Ottoman Parliament's "Calendar of Events" whose supplements [*Ilâve*] served as a judicial journal covering many portions of the court-martial proceedings, especially the series of verdicts issued by that Military Tribunal in 1919–1921), no. 3540, p. 7. It was read on 28 April 1919 and published on 5 May 1919.

[*cerayimi mükerrere*] . . . and under the pretext of transporting them by the sea route to another place, the male and female infants [*zükur ve inas çocukları*] were taken in split groups on board of barges and caiques to the high seas and, hidden from sight [*gözden nihan olduktan sonra*] were thrown overboard to be drowned and destroyed [*bahra ilka etmekle bogdurup mahv edildikleri*]".[68] Because of its location and direction of flow, a fraction of these victims were likewise drowned in nearby Degirmendere River.

Even though most Trabzon Armenians were destroyed in a variety of ways directly connected with the processes of "deportation", the scope of the drowning operations neither reflected randomness nor was it minimal. The absence of precise or reliable statistics in this respect is somewhat mitigated by the fact that European and American consular representatives considered the drownings numerous enough to provide many details about them in their reports. The three countries involved – Germany, Austria-Hungary, and the USA – had sufficient latitude to gather reliable data and transmit them to their governments. The USA was neutral until April 1917. Imperial Germany as well as imperial Austria-Hungary were, on the other hand, the Ottoman Empire's staunch political and military allies during the war; as such their reports to Vienna and Berlin acquire extraordinary significance because of these critical alliance bonds.

From among many of his reports to Vienna, Austria-Hungary's Trabzon Consul, Ernst von Kwiatkoski, in two separate reports "based on concordant pieces of information," as he put it, describes the drowning operations at the Black Sea of "women and children who are being loaded into barges, taken to the high seas, and drowned there." In the second of these reports the Consul, quoting a Turkish military officer, describes also the mass murder of 132 Armenian labor battalion soldiers near Hamziköy, 53 km from Trabzon.[69] When the war was nearing its end, the same Consul spoke of "the near complete extermination of the Armenians" ("die fast gänzliche Ausrottung der Armenier").[70] Heinrich Bergfeld, the German Consul at Trabzon, a very Turkophile diplomat, felt constrained to report to Berlin that "All my colleagues and I are of the opinion that the treatment of women and children is a form of mass murder" ("Massenmord").[71] In another report he stated his opinion that "The Young Turk Committee is hereby trying to solve

---

[68] *Takvim-i Vekâyi*, no. 3616, p. 1, right column, 6 August 1919. The verdict was pronounced on 22 May 1919.

[69] AFMA, 31 July 1915 report, 38 Konsulate/368, no. 46/P.; 4 September 1915 report, 38 Konsulate /368, no. Zl.54/P.

[70] AFMA, 12 Türkei/380, Zl.17/pol., 13 March 1918 report.

[71] AA BoKon 169, no. 7, folio 135 (4002), 29 June 1915 report.

the Armenian Question."[72] Finally reference may be made to the above-mentioned Colonel Stange who was in charge of an Ottoman regiment comprising a large number of convicts released from the various prisons of the Ottoman Empire. In a lengthy "secret" report to his superior, Marshal Liman von Sanders, he relayed his personal observations about the methods used to exterminate the Armenians. Speaking of Trabzon, he related how able-bodied Armenian men "were marched off to a mountain and slaughtered" ("abgeschlachtet"). In the same city, he said, "The Armenians were taken on board of vessels and dumped overboard in the sea" ("Auf's Meer hinausgefahren und dann über Bord geworfen"). His conclusion was that these acts of "beastly brutality . . . which amplified the torments of the Armenians" and which were mostly perpetrated by Trabzon's riffraff, "the scum" ("Gesindel"), i.e., the brigands, the çetes – were part of an overall scheme of wholesale extermination "conceived a long time ago" ("einen lang gehegten Plan").[73]

Plunder and rape

As is the case in many instances of wholesale and indiscriminate destruction, an integral part of the anti-Armenian campaign in Trabzon involved the rampant practice of rape as testified to by a host of Turkish, American, Austrian, and German witnesses and officials. Trabzon's German Consul, Bergfeld, also a jurist by profession, in one of his reports decried "the numerous rapes of women and girls," which crime he regarded as being part of a plan for "the virtually complete extermination of the Armenians." In the same report he vented his ire, declaring that such mass murder "cannot be condemned with enough severity . . . it is very difficult to explain or to excuse it."[74]

Nor is there a paucity of Muslim and Turkish testimony in this respect. In his testimony as a defendant in the Trabzon trial series, Nuri, the city's chief police officer, was constrained to admit that he took young Armenian girls to Istanbul as the Governor-General's gift to the members of the CUP's Central Committee (ninth sitting, 10 April 1919). Trabzon merchant Mehmed Ali stated that not only were children from the Red Crescent Hospital being poisoned and drowned, but young girls were being raped there and that the Governor-General had been keeping there some fifteen such girls for his sexual pleasures (tenth sitting, 12 April 1919). When his turn came to testify, Customs Inspector Nesim,

---

[72] AA Türkei 183/38, A28189 R14087, 9 July 1915 report; also AA BoKon 170, F. 102, no. 20 (4996).
[73] Ibid., BoKon 170, registry no. 3841, 23 August 1915 "secret" report.
[74] Ibid., Türkei 183/54, A38986, 1 September 1915 report.

with derision, declared that the Red Crescent Hospital had been reduced to a pleasuredome where the Governor-General was often indulging in sex orgies (sixteenth sitting, 5 May 1919). A Muslim military officer, Lieutenant Hasan Maruf, on duty in Trabzon during the war, even then told British authorities that "Government officials at Trebizond picked out some of the prettiest Armenian women of the best families. After committing the worst outrages on them, they had them killed."[75]

Other integral components of the extermination campaign were robbery and plunder. Throughout the records of the Trabzon trials, comprising some twenty sittings, some of which had separate morning and afternoon sessions, rampant cupidity repeatedly emerged as a central theme in the presentation of evidentiary material as well as of witness testimony. The Governor-General, Cemal Azmi; his cohorts, Dr. Saib; Police Chief Nuri; Special Organization Chieftain Acente Mustafa; and CUP potentate, Yenibahçeli Nail – all of them, sometimes in tandem and sometimes individually, robbed and plundered their doomed victims at will. In the process, all of them ended up amassing enormous fortunes through the swift appropriation of the accumulated goods, properties, savings and bank accounts of these victims. In two separate reports German Consul Bergfeld denounced "the ongoing pillage and thievery"[76] and "the shameless enrichment of police officers and civil servants . . . with very few exceptions, all these men are partaking in the plunder of Armenian houses as are the CUP (Ittihad) people."[77]

As to Turkish testimony itself, at the tenth sitting (12 April 1919) of the same trial series, Turkish merchant Mehmed Ali testified that defendant Acente Mustafa, together with Trabzon province's Governor-General, Cemal Azmi, plundered jewelry and other valuable objects from their Armenian victims, worth between 300,000 and 400,000 Turkish gold pounds (at that time about $1,500,000). He further testified: "I personally witnessed Mustafa selling these valuables in Switzerland a year later." The Armenian Genocide was punctuated by prodigious pillage. As US veteran Consul at Aleppo, Jesse B. Jackson, informed Washington, the wartime anti-Armenian measures were "a gigantic plundering scheme as well as a final blow to extinguish the [Armenian] race."[78]

All these pieces of documentation are fully corroborated by Oscar S. Heizer, the US Consul at Trabzon, who filed numerous reports with the State Department while serving in that port city during the war, i.e.,

---

[75] FO37/2781/264888, 27 December 1916, Appendix B, report no. 2, p. 6–7. His testimony is reproduced in *Germany, Turkey and Armenia*, p. 127.
[76] AA Türkei 183/54, A28189 R 14087; BoKon 170, J.
[77] Ibid., A38986 R14087, 1 September 1915.
[78] US National Archives RG59.867.4016/148.

until April 1917, when the United States entered the conflict on the side of the Triple Entente. The one dated 28 July 1915, one of the longest and most detailed, covers nearly every component of the mass murder committed against the Armenians of Trabzon province and one way or another depicted in the discussion above. Heizer directs attention to the fact that, when deporting the Armenians, the authorities were not in the least concerned about the guilt or innocence of the victims: "If a person was an Armenian that was sufficient reason for being treated as a criminal and deported." He describes "a number of lighters which were loaded with people at different times," who were drowned in the Black Sea; "A number of bodies of women and children have lately been thrown up by the sea." He was able to see such occurrences "from the window of the consulate." Part of the victim population in that province consisted of disarmed Armenian labor battalion soldiers who were executed "after being stripped of their clothing"; they had belonged to "a battalion engaged in road construction work near Gümüşhane" ("inşaat taburu"). Some male children were distributed among Turkish farmers. Among the female children "the best looking . . . are kept in houses for the pleasure" of CUP potentates and other members of "the gang," one of whom "has ten of the handsomest girls in a house in the central part of the city."

When a deportee convoy is sufficiently out of sight from a town, or a village, such as in Tots, "the women were first outraged by the officers of the gendarmerie and then turned over to the gendarmes to dispose of . . . the men were all killed and not a single person survived from this group." All the houses emptied of Armenians were systematically ransacked, plundered by police: "A crowd of Turkish women and children follow the police about like a lot of vultures and seize anything they can lay their hands on and when the more valuable things are carried out of a house by the police they rush in and take the balance. I see this performance every day with my own eyes." The Consul ends his report with the remark that he could include many more details about anti-Armenian atrocities, "but it is difficult to verify all the stories circulated and I have confined myself to these I believe to be correct."[79] And, speaking of the CUP's omnipotent commissar in Trabzon, Yenibahçeli Nail, Heizer informed Washington that when Nail returned to his home in Eskişehir he was "laden with gold and jewelry which was his share of the plunder."[80]

---

[79] Ibid./411/128. 28 July 1915 report. See also Bryce and Toynbee, ed. and comp., *Treatment*, pp. 286–9. In a post-war report, Consul Jackson identified that "one person" appropriating for lascivious purposes "ten of the handsomest girls" as being CUP's delegate Nail: RG 59.867.4016/411, no. 169, 11 April 1919.

[80] RG 59.867.4016/411, no. 169.

The entire picture was summed up by W. Peter, US consular official from Samsun, a port city on the same Black Sea coast. This diplomat observed that the goal of the Ottoman authorities was "to finish with the Armenians altogether," and offered this judgment to Washington: "Turkey may not in general be in the front rank as regards to organization and talent, but this time when it was a question of massacres, robberies, etc., it has shown well-planned and very quick action. Only the Turk is capable of dispatching to another world hundreds of thousands of people in a short time."[81]

The unfolding of genocide

This study is an attempt at probing, within certain parameters, into the circumstances of the First World War genocidal fate of the Armenians of the Ottoman Empire. Such an effort was deemed particularly exigent in face of the persistence with which Turkish authorities, past and present, are categorically denying the genocidal character of that fate. The denial is rendered especially intractable on account of the imprimatur that is accorded to it by the Turkish Historical Society. What is so remarkable about this Society, which encompasses nearly all the prominent and not-so-prominent Turkish historians, is that, unlike in any other democratic society, it is an arm of the Turkish state (*devlet*). Under unrelenting pressure to embrace and propound the official historical theses of the State (*resmi tarih*), these historians, with rare exceptions, feel constrained to remain in the vanguard of the school of denial, a denial that presently has assumed the dimensions of a state-sponsored industry in steady growth and expansion.

It is apparent that the genocide was neither a wartime aberration, nor an accidental, temporary lapse into a misdeed that happened to involve a mass murder. Rather it was a distinctive feature of the modern annals of Ottoman political subculture, a subculture that almost as a matter of routine has been allowing recourse to massacre as a state instrument of oppression and repression against discordant nationalities and minorities. This pattern of victimization obtained because the latter were seen as challenging the imperial prerogative of theocratic authority and dominance. Accordingly, this study has seen fit to review briefly, within a historical perspective, the portentous legal and political developments that transpired in the decades preceding the First World War. At issue here was the pre-war radical reorganization of the Ottoman government,

---

[81] Ibid.,/259, 4 December 1915 report. The original French text of this report is in Sarafian, comp., *The Peripheries*, pp. 59–60. Some of the excerpts from Heizer's reports used in this study were taken from Suakjian, *Genocide in Trebizond*.

reflecting the equally important parallel reorganization of the structure
of power relations in the upper echelons of the Young Turk Ittihad party.
The new Central Committee of that party, i.e., the CUP, is thus seen
emerging as an omnipotent body bent on recasting at an opportune moment a new Empire predicated primarily, if not exclusively, on a doctrine
of Turkism rather than Ottomanism. The result is a radical and ominous
new policy on nationalities, presaging, one way or another, the wholesale
elimination of the Armenians from their ancestral territories, and, with
it, a legacy of 3,000 years of culture and civilization.

Given its limited scope, this chapter selected a particular setting of
the Armenian Genocide as a focus of inquiry and exploration. To the
extent that such a case study is more or less typical in terms of the main
elements of the overall genocide, it represents a microcosm of the larger
picture. Accordingly, it may be possible to understand aspects of the first
major genocide of the twentieth century by a measure of extrapolation.
By the same token, it is clear that that regional genocide was part of
a systematic, comprehensive initiative indispensable for implementation
of the general genocide. In documenting the various methods through
which the able-bodied Armenian men were liquidated – as a prelude
to the genocide in general – we can see the operation of the principle
of functional efficiency. All other things being equal, the organization of
mass murder was substantially facilitated when the victim population had
been reduced to a condition of utter defenselessness.

The significance of such case studies hinges on the strength of the
documentation supporting them. There are three major sources to draw
on. Foremost among them is the corpus of inculpatory evidence mar-
shaled by the Turkish Military Tribunal in connection with the Trabzon
court-martial series that started on 26 March and ended on 17 May
1919, involving altogether twenty sittings. As explored in the main body
of this study, the proceedings of this series yielded critical evidentiary
facts developed mostly through official Ottoman documents, pre-trial
interrogatories administered to the principal defendants, and a host of
Muslim witnesses testifying in court in person. Especially critical in this
respect is the verdict of the Tribunal. It should be noted in this respect
that, before being introduced as court exhibits, each and every official
wartime document was examined and authenticated by a competent official of the Ottoman Interior Ministry. To record this fact, the notation
"It conforms to the original" ("Aslına Muafıkdır") was appended on the
upper right corner of the document.[82] This fact alone should go a long

[82] Vahakn N. Dadrian, "The Turkish Military Tribunal's Prosecution of the Authors of the
Armenian Genocide. Four Major Court-Martial Series," *Holocaust and Genocide Studies*
11:1 (Spring 1997), p. 35.

way to vouch for the legitimacy of the Tribunal and its findings. This was precisely the case with the Nuremberg Tribunal which followed a similar track in relying mainly on authenticated wartime official documents rather than witness testimony. In both cases fundamental evidence was harnessed through probative evidence yielding the ultimate conviction of truth, a truth in which fact and reason converged thereby providing the bases for the respective verdicts. Yet, unlike the Nuremberg Tribunal, the Tribunal in Istanbul was a strictly domestic rather than an international tribunal. As such it carried with it elements of domestic – national authority and authenticity that served to transform its findings of culpability and complicity into a measure of national self-indictment and self-condemnation.

The second group of sources is equally, if not more, significant for several reasons. First of all these sources emanate from camps that are identified as partners with the Ottoman Empire. The reference is to imperial Germany and imperial Austria-Hungary, two staunch political and military wartime allies of the Ottoman-Turks. Moreover, their "confidential," "secret," and "top-secret" reports to Berlin and Vienna were intended for internal, in-house use, rather than for public consumption, or for propaganda. The reports filed by the German and Austro-Hungarian Consuls stationed at Trabzon indeed acquire particular significance not only on account of the exigent bonds of an alliance: they are additionally invaluable because they are prepared on the spot at the very time the events were unfolding and as such they antedate the findings of the Turkish courts-martial.

Finally, reference is to be made to two sources that qualify as "neutral." Up until April 1917 the United States were neutral in the First World War. Accordingly, the State Department received a steady flow of material evidence about the wartime genocide treatment of the Armenians from its diplomatic representative in Trabzon, Consul Oscar Heizer. Such neutrality enabled the latter to obtain and relay to Washington invaluable details about that treatment. The US Consular Agent at Samsun on 4 December 1915 characterized that treatment as one intended "to finish off with the Armenians altogether."[83]

Likewise, up until the third week of August 1915 Italy too was neutral. By then the wholesale liquidation of the Armenian population of Trabzon province, estimated to be about 60,000, was all but completed. Upon his return to Italy Signor Gorrini, the Italian Consul-General at Trabzon, lamented and decried the fiendish methods with which this liquidation was executed. Here are some portions of his testimony:

[83] See note 81.

From the 24th of June [1915], the date of the publication of the infamous decree [of deportation] until the 23rd of July, the date of my own departure . . . I no longer slept or ate; I was given over to nerves and nausea, so terrible was the torment of having to look on at the wholesale execution of these defenceless, innocent creatures . . . the lamentations, the tears, the abandonments, the imprecations, the many suicides, the instantaneous death from sheer terror, the sudden unhingeing of men's reason, the conflagrations . . . the hundreds of corpses found every day along the exile road . . . the children torn away from their families . . . placed by hundreds on board ship in nothing but their shirts, and then capsized and drowned in the Black Sea and the river Degirmendere – these are my ineffaceable memoirs of Trabzon, memoirs which still, at a month's distance torment my soul and almost drive me frantic . . . all the cannibals and all the wild beasts in the world [are conjured up].[84]

The Armenian Genocide: a synopsis

Based on this array of documentary evidence, one gains an overview of the major components of the Armenian Genocide; at the same time, however, such an overview may permit us to attempt to reconstruct in outline form what genocide itself was in terms of its major components. According to the verdict, issued at the end of the Trabzon trial series, i.e., 22 May 1919, the aim of the wartime Armenian deportations was "the massacre and annihilation" ("taktil ve ifna") of the deportee population. This crime was "premeditated" ("ta 'ammüden"). The two arch perpetrators were the province's Governor-General, Cemal Azmi, and the CUP's provincial Commissar, Yenibahçeli Nail. Both of them received and relayed the requisite "special secret orders" ("evâmir-i mübellige-i hafiye"). To accomplish their goal, they used convicts as tools, involving in the main "repeat criminals" ("ceraim-i mükerrere") who were released from the province's prisons to form "gangs of brigands, bandits" ("haydut çeteler"). The Armenians, their victims, had been rendered defenseless ("müdafaadan mahrum"). In addition to robbery, thievery, and plunder, the atrocities included drowning operations and serial rapes: "Many of the helpless women were violated" ("ırzlarina tecavüz"). "Young girls were deflowered" ("izaleyi bikr") in the hospital that supposedly had "a humanitarian

---

[84] These statements were part of an interview Comm. G. Gorrini gave to the then-noted Italian newspaper *Il Messagero*, published in Rome 25 (August 1915 issue). The full text in English can be found in Bryce and Toynbee, *The Treatment*, Doc. No. 73, pp. 290–2. In that same interview Gorrini declared, "If they knew all the things that I know, all that I have had to see with my eyes . . . [humanity and government] would be impelled to rise up against Turkey and cry anathema against her inhuman government and her ferocious Committee of Union and Progress, and they would extend the responsibility to Turkey's Allies [imperial Germany and imperial Austria-Hungary], who tolerate or even shield with their strong arm these execrable crimes, which have not their equal in history, either modern or ancient. Shame, horror and disgrace" (p. 292).

mission" ("maksadı insaniyetkârane"). All these crimes were committed with a pretense of patriotism ("güya bir vazifeyi vataniye"). "Groups of women, and male and female children, were in batches taken to lighters and caiques and were told that they were being taken to another port city. In fact, however, they were drowned and destroyed as far out of sight as possible" ("bogdurup mahvettikleri"). In reaching these judgments the Tribunal averred that it carefully weighed all the evidence "from head to toe" ("serapa") and "in its entirety" ("bilcümle"), and became "fully convinced of the fact that the crime was carried out in an organized way and it was ascertained as such" ("müretteb bir sûretde icrâ-i edilmiş . . . numayan olmuş"). The two arch perpetrators, cited above, were convicted and sentenced to death in absentia.[85]

Once we put this evidence, uncovered in the course of these criminal prosecutions, in the context of other evidence unavailable to the courts at the time, we can see some outlines of the genocidal process as a whole. Indeed, vital supplementary material is provided in the official wartime reports of German, Austro-Hungarian, and American diplomats on duty in the interior of the Ottoman Empire during the war. These officials not only confirm and corroborate already during the war the major findings of the post-war Turkish Military Tribunal but, equally important, they help fill many missing links relative to such issues as the hierarchical set-up in genocidal decision making, the administrative network handling the organizational and supervisory aspects of the genocidal scheme, the details of the conspiracy attending that scheme, the role of the military, the procedures of engaging felons and convicts, the prevalence of thievery and pillage, the incidence of widespread rape, especially of underage girls, and the variety of devices of mass murder, including shooting, poisoning, and drowning operations. Moreover, similar types of supplementation are provided through evidence secured in the other trial series that were held by the Turkish Military Tribunal. Finally, the reconstruction effort, predicated as it is largely upon the Trabzon case study, is bound to be further enhanced by drawing on the equally invaluable evidence secured by the Ottoman Parliament in the months preceding the onset of court-martial proceedings.

The most difficult parts of the construction of an accurate and fully documented narrative of a crime of the magnitude of genocide are the tasks of separating the covert, secretive aspects of that crime from its overt aspects, and then of integrating the two. In other words, one has to probe into the secrecy of the conspiracy involved. Inevitably then, one ends up with the problem of locating and identifying a group of conspirators

---

[85] *Takrim-i Vekâyi*, no. 3616, pp. 1–3.

and determining the organizational nature of the interrelationships embedded in that conspiracy. Within this broad conceptual framework, the
Armenian Genocide may be reconstructed in the following manner.

The Tribunal's verdict was that the annihilation of Trabzon province's
Armenian population was "premeditated." The question immediately
arises as to the identity of those who planned and committed the crime.
All evidence shows that the ultimate decision makers were part of a highly
secretive faction within the Central Committee of the Ittihad Party, the
CUP. Three members of that Committee are cited again and again in
many of the official documents and related testimonies as the principal
architects of the Armenian Genocide. Of these, Mehmed Talât had su-
perordinate authority in as much as not only was he Interior Minister,
and as such formally in charge of the deportations, but – equally, if not
more, important – he was an omnipotent party chieftain, and a dominant
figure in the CUP's Central Committee. The other two, MDs Behaeddin
Şakir and Mehmed Nâzım, were the shadowy potentates of the Central
Committee, operating mostly behind the scenes (with Nâzım serving as
Education Minister for a brief three-month stint only). Nearly totally free
from the bureaucratic and regulatory fetters of office, these two, often in
tandem with equally unfettered party boss Talât, are seen in charge of
all the major arrangements relating to the Armenian Genocide. At the
same time, however, to deflect attention from their conspiracy, to cover
up the associated criminal details, Talât's Interior Ministry was used to
issue a string of official orders meant to regulate and control the flow
of the massive deportations that were decreed through a temporary law.
To enhance further the appearance of legitimacy, several of these orders
were sugarcoated with exhortations to the provincial authorities such as:
"protect the deportee convoys," "provide for them bread and olive," "the
purpose of these deportations is only relocation" ("tebdil-i mekân"), etc.

These overt and seemingly solicitous official injunctions were cancelled
and supplanted, however, by the secret use of a second track of communication. The orders relayed through this track did not issue from any
ministerial or other official authority but, rather, from the three Central
Committee members cited above. These orders were most of the time
transmitted orally. Whenever this was difficult or impossible, the method
of written top-secret orders carrying unofficial messages and instructions
was used, with the ancillary order either to keep them secret, to destroy
them, or to return them after reading. In other words, two levels of authority were at work in the organization of the Armenian Genocide. The
one in charge was not formal authority *per se* as embodied in the various Cabinet ministries and other associated governmental organs, but
what may be termed "informal authority" as embodied in the clandestine,

conspiratorial, and highly secretive recesses of the CUP's Central Committee that throughout operated like a Supreme Directorate, a kind of Politbüro. In its key indictment and in nearly every one of its series of verdicts the Military Tribunal focused on this point repeatedly and with emphasis. The most trenchant confirmation of this fact was provided by two high-ranking Ottoman officials, one military and one civilian. In his testimony prepared at the request of the Tribunal, Third Army Commander General Mehmed Vehib (Kaçı) underscored this point, directly linking "the deportation and annihilation of the Armenians to the decision of the CUP."[86] Veteran Ottoman statesman Reşid Akif Paşa, who throughout his career occupied nearly every high post in the Ottoman state system, including Governor-General, Cabinet Minister, President of State Council, and Vizier, on 21 November 1918, in the Ottoman Senate, confirmed the use of the two-track system. Referring to documents that he had secured as President of the State Council in the aftermath of the war, he declared that for public consumption the Interior Ministry issued orders for deportations; this was formal authority. Parallel to the resort to this "deportation" subterfuge, however, "the Central Committee of CUP undertook to send an ominous circular" to all provincial party branches directing them to proceed: "The massacres and the slaughter, which represented the accursed mission of the brigands (*çete*), were the results." Denouncing the CUP Central Committee members as "a deceitful clique, a vile and tyrannical body," Akif Paşa pointed out that these people who "had been trampling on the Islamic world and mankind's humanity," had become more powerful than the regular organs of the government.[87]

The significance of the supremacy of these agents of informal authority in a state system in which an entire nationality is being subjected to mass murder cannot be overemphasized. State authority is seen here as being not only overwhelmed but in the process also subverted and eventually criminalized. The fact of this development is evident in the operational level of the Ittihadist conspiracy to liquidate the Armenians. In order to be swift and merciless in this task, the organizers decided to employ thousands of convicts. Accordingly the latter were serially released from the various prisons of the Empire for massacre duty. The Military Tribunal's key indictment a dozen times makes reference to them as the main instrument of mass murder against the Armenians. Like Akif Paşa, General Vehib, mentioned above, also singles them out as the actual murderers, decrying them as "butchers of human beings" ("insan kasapları"),

[86] Dadrian, *The Armenian Genocide in Official Turkish Records* (Collected Works), p. 63.
[87] Ibid., pp. 85–6.

as actual "gallow-birds" ("ipten ve kazıktan kurtulmuş yaranını").[88] Another Turkish officer who during the war was on duty in Department II of Ottoman General Headquarters as a Reserve Navy Captain intelligence officer, was more specific in this respect. In his post-war memoirs Ahmed Refik (Altınay) identified the Special Organization as the secret body created by the Central Committee of the CUP. Thousands of ex-convicts were enrolled in it and integrated under the control of agents of the Committee. In denouncing their "enormous crime" ("muazzam cinayet"), which he defined as a "crime against humanity," Ahmed Refik wrote, "These felons who were released from the prisons committed the greatest crimes during the Armenian horrors."[89]

The Trabzon trials yielded relevant evidence to verify the sway of this informal authority, the subordination of agents of formal authority, such as Governors-General, district Governors, county executives, Mayors, etc., to that informal authority, and the organization of convicts for massacre duty. Specific testimony inside and outside the court confirmed the power of the CUP's informal authority. During the fourth sitting of the trial series, for example (4 April 1919), it was stated that a few weeks before the order for deportation was issued, Dr. Behaeddin Şakir, the Central Committee member in charge of the Special Organization East, visited Trabzon. That city's Greek Metropolitan, Archbishop Khrisantos, in his memoirs likewise noted that one month before the start of the deportations Şakir, coming to Trabzon from Erzurum where he was headquartered, convened a secret conclave. All the civilian administrators, *valis*, *mutassarıfs*, and *kaymakams*, of the province were summoned. They received "secret instructions" relative to the imminent implementation of the Ittihadist anti-Armenian scheme.[90] Ali Riza, a notable of Trabzon, likewise confirms Şakir's visit and his secret consultations with the principal organizers of the anti-Armenian extermination campaign in Trabzon, i.e., *vali* Cemal Azmi, CUP plenipotentiary Nail, and Azmi's

---

[88] Dadrian, "The Armenian Question," pp. 84–5 (n. 111).

[89] Ahmed Refik, *Iki Komite Iki Kital*, pp. 27, 44, 45. In several sittings of the courts-martial the leaders of this Special Organization revealed that it had two major branches. One of them dealt with external espionage, sabotage, and revolutionary agitation; but the other, which was run by the CUP, was involved in the matter of "deportations" (*tehcir*). See Yusuf Riza's testimony in the fourth sitting (*Takvim-i Vekâyi*, henceforth "TV," no. 3549, p. 59, 8 May 1919); that testimony was repeated in the fifth sitting (TV no. 3553, p. 88, 12 May 1919); Atif's (Kamçil's) and Küçük Talât's testimonies were in the fifth sitting (TV no. 3553, p. 89, 12 May 1919).

[90] Hovagim Hovagimian, *Badmoutiun Haigagan Bandosee* (History of Armenian Pontus) (Beirut: Mushag, 1967), p. 224, excerpted from Athens's newspaper *Esthia* which, in installments published the memoirs of the Greek Metropolitan in the 9 and 10 June 1964 issues.

chief assistant, Mehmed Ali.[91] All this confirms the written testimony of General Vehib that, with a special automobile, Şakir went from province to province to pave the ground for the execution of the CUP scheme, and that the provincial authorities meekly submitted to his orders (*inkiyad*). Vehib too invoked Islam and humanity to condemn the perpetrators.

The procedures relating to the release of convicts in Trabzon province attest to a very distinct feature of the organization of the Armenian Genocide. It appears that all three members of the CUP's Central Committee faction had a hand in enlisting and deploying multitudes of felons, who are described as "bloodthirsty" murderers ("kanlı katil"), as the main instrument of the extermination campaign. Not only Turkish Colonel Vasfi, Chief of Staff at Trabzon, testified that the brigands, the so-called *çetes*, were the same as the killer gangs enrolled in Dr. Behaeddin Şakir's Special Organization (fourth sitting, p.m. segment, 3 April 1919). Merchant Hüseyin from Ordu also testified that Süleyman, Ordu's prison warden, personally formed a *çete* killer band from among the convicts, for massacre duty (sixteenth sitting, 5 May 1919). Lütfi, the province's Director of Revenues, testified that the whole tragedy began to unfold in the wake of Dr. Şakir's visit to Trabzon: "he instigated and launched the whole thing" (seventh sitting, 8 April 1919).

Perhaps the most telling account in this respect comes from one of the leaders of the Special Organization who admitted to having closely collaborated with Dr. Şakir. In his post-war narrative he even reproduces excerpts from letters and ciphers Dr. Şakir reportedly sent to his wife and to Talât while engaged as a Special Organization chieftain. As repeatedly asserted in the Military Tribunal's several indictments and verdicts, the Special Organization was solely the creation of the CUP's Central Committee.[92] After admitting that the central mission of the organization was not what it purported to be, such as intelligence, spying, etc., Cemal Arif, the author of the narrative, makes some important disclosures. The two CUP men, Nail and Artillery Captain Yusuf Riza, who were the

[91] Ibid., pp. 240–1.
[92] For confirmation of this fact by Galip Vardar, Hüsamettin Ertürk, Mustafa Ragıp Esatlı, and Esref Kuşcubaşı, all of them deeply involved in the clandestine operations of that organization and having one way or another recorded their knowledge of "the inside story" of it, see Vahakn Dadrian, "The Role of the Special Organization in the Armenian Genocide during the First World War," in P. Panayi, ed. *Minorities in Wartime* (Oxford and Providence: Berg, 1993). Pages 11–12 describe the intimate links between the Central Committee and the Special Organization; pp. 5 and 12 describe the Special Organization's internal mission aimed at wiping out decisively "the internal, domestic foes," with special reference to the Armenians; pp. 8–11 deal with the role of the convicts in the implementation of the CUP's scheme of genocide through the agency of the Special Organization (*Teşkilât-ı Mahsusa*); and pp. 15–18 highlight the crucial role Dr. Şakir played in conceiving, designing, organizing, and executing the CUP scheme of genocide. Dr. Nâzım was no less effective.

top Special Organization leaders in Trabzon, were joined by two other Trabzon officials. In special swearing-in ceremonies, Cemal Azmi, the omnipotent Governor-General of the province, and MD Yunus Vasfi, the province's Chief Physician, were inducted into the ranks of the Special Organization. In stating this fact the author underscores the latter's "many previous services" to the organization. The liberation of the convicts from the prisons was a task in whose performance the conjoint efforts of the principals of the Armenian Genocide are striking. As the Military Tribunal, in its supplement, to the key indictment, clearly stated, the MDs Şakir and Nâzım were the dominant figures in the Special Organization which they created and ran. In fact, said the indictment, the organization and its leaders were all CUP men (*Takvim-i Vekâyi*, no. 3571, 4 May 1919, pp. 128, 129, 130). To continue Arif Cemal's disclosures, he states that the release and mobilization of the convicts in Trabzon were primarily arranged by Governor-General Cemal Azmi and CUP plenipotentiary Nail. It is most significant that Talât, then Interior Minister, but also party boss, gave the ultimate authorization to both men to proceed in this respect. As indicated above, the Special Organization had a military mission as well. Its abysmal external failure on the Caucasus Front, however, was such as to prompt Dr. Şakir to relinquish completely any and all external ambitions and decide to tackle "the internal foe, the Armenians." He was able to persuade the CUP's Central Committee and, according to Arif Cemil, the result was the promulgation of the Temporary Law of Deportation targeting the Armenians.[93]

The internal enemy included the several thousand Armenian volunteers, some of them Ottoman Armenians, fighting alongside the Russians arrayed against Turkey in the east. The three major battles that the Turks lost, Sarıkamış, Dilman, and the Van insurrection, further inflamed the brewing anti-Armenian hostility on account of a perceived role in these defeats attributed to the Armenian volunteers. Nor can one deny the incidence of isolated acts of espionage and sabotage by individual Armenians. As a host of German and Austro-Hungarian diplomats and military officers uniformly informed their superiors, however, to the extent that these charges were true, they were clearly insignificant in scope and effect. The litany of reports they filed overwhelmingly focus on one major assertion. Namely, from its very inception, the Ottoman Turks were bent on solving by way of an exterminatory campaign the lingering and troublesome Armenian Question, under cover of the war. The events described above provided the pretext.[94] Moreover, the same diplomats and military

---

[93] Cemil, *I.Dünya Savaşında Teskilât-ı Mahsusa*, pp. 20–1, 73–4, 101–2, 240–6.
[94] For a full exploration of this issue, see Dadrian, "The Armenian Question," pp. 60, 71–3.

officers in several reports spotlight the decisive role of the CUP and its lethal appendage, the Special Organization, in the creation and implementation of that campaign.[95] However, the creation and employment of this body provoked dismay and anger among some high-ranking officers, ministerial officials, and lawmakers. One objection was that Ottoman law forbade the enrollment of convicts in the army. Another, raised by a former Ittihadist leader, Ahmet Riza, in the Ottoman Senate, was that these felons were bound to corrupt and demoralize the rest of the army. When countering this argument, the Deputy Director of the Department of the Army in the Ministry of War declared that the felons were meant for special missions, outside the army's province – in blatant contradiction of the text of the proposed legislative draft bill which spoke of "the acute need of patriotic service in the army." The bizarre character of this effort to fool and mislead the Senate, bordering at times on farcicality, became clear when, during the ensuing debate, it was revealed that the CUP leaders were applying a non-existent law through administrative fiat. Therefore, the senators were told that, since the Special Organization had completed its mission, "the law's validity has expired. It is no longer being applied." Indeed, by then, i.e., December 1916, the Armenian Genocide had all but run its course. Notwithstanding, by the strong urging of the CUP power-wielders, the Ottoman Parliament retroactively promulgated this – by now unnecessary – law as an "urgent matter" ("Müstaceliyet").[96]

The impotence of this Parliament and the parliamentarians came into relief a number of times during 1915 when the genocide was in full swing, especially with respect to Trabzon.[97] Hafiz Mehmed, a Deputy for that province, on 11 December 1918 complained in the Chamber of Deputies that for three years he had struggled with Talât's Interior Ministry in order to discipline the province's *vali*, Cemal Azmi, the man who had organized the drowning operations throughout the port cities of that province's littoral (see note 65 for documentation). On 2 December 1918, Çürüksulu Mahmud Paşa, in the Senate, likewise expressed a sense of futility as regards attempts at having the *vali* removed (see n. 64). During the twelfth sitting of the Trabzon trial series the presiding judge, Divisional

---

[95] See a specific discussion on this in Dadrian, "The Role of the Special Organization," pp. 8–10.

[96] For a full coverage of these legislative debates, see Dadrian, *The Armenian Genocide in Official Turkish Records* (Collected Works), pp. 57–61.

[97] The only works in Turkish covering the various Parliamentary Hearings and the proceedings of the post-war Turkish Military Tribunal and the ancillary Parliamentary Hearings are those of Osman Selim Kocahanoğlu, *Ittihat-Terakkinin, Sorgulanması ve Yargılanması* (The Hearings About and Trials of Ittihat-Terakki) (Istanbul: Temel Publication Series no. 98, 1998); Taner Akçam, *Insan Hakları ve Ermeni Sorunu* (Human Rights and the Armenian Question) (Ankara: Imge Publication, 1999), part III, pp. 329–587.

Staff General *(Müşir)*, *Mustafa Nâzım Paşa*, took Naci, Trabzon's other Deputy, to task (16 April 1919) for not stopping the crimes being perpetrated against the Armenians – despite the high authority vested in him as a Parliament member. The judge was particularly incensed about the horrific nature of the drowning operations. On 31 July 1915, Austria-Hungary's Consul-General at Trabzon, Ernst von Kwiatkowski, reported to Vienna as follows: "according to concurrent [*übereinstimmend*] Turkish sources, several hundred Armenian women, children and old men in the months of July and August were herded into barges, taken to the high seas and drowned." In another report he stated, "One has to dig deep into history in order to find a parallel level of atrocity aimed at exterminating a people."[98]

Taking all this information into account, the judge in his cross-examination of Trabzon Deputy Naci got him to agree implicitly that the anti-Armenian campaign of wholesale annihilation was due to "neither security, nor retaliatory reasons but for some other consideration." In the Tribunal's key indictment a similar assertion was made, namely: that campaign was launched "neither as a military necessity, nor for reasons of discipline or punishment" ("ne tedabiri askeri, ne de tedbiri inzibatı cümlesinden olmayıp") (*Takvim-i Vekâyi*, no. 3540, p. 6).

No sketch of a crime of this magnitude perpetrated during a war can be adequate without embodying an assessment of the military factor.[99] The bulk of the Ottoman Armenian population resided in six provinces, namely Van, Erzurum, Bitlis, Sivas, Harput, and Diyarbekir; of these the first three were often geographically denoted by many historians as "Historic Armenia" and, as such, had the highest degree of density of Armenian population. It is noteworthy that this very population was the foremost target in the CUP's design of liquidation; the scale of its destruction was exceeded only by its tempo and relentlessness. Given the exigencies of the war and the state of siege enforced through martial law, the Ittihadist wing of the Ottoman army became ascendant in the councils of the CUP decision makers. The imposition of military authority over

[98] The 31 July report is in AFMA, 38 Konsulate/368, no. 46/P.; the second one, dated 20 July 1915, is in ibid., no. 42/P. At the end of the First World Wars, *vali* Cemal Azmi fled to Germany as a fugitive of justice. During a social gathering in 1921 in Berlin, attended by other Turkish accomplices and their wives, he declared, "Because of these drownings there will be now a rich harvest of fresh anchovy" ("Bu sene hamsi çoğalsın", thereby eliciting loud laughter (Trabzon is famous for its breed of anchovy which at that time constituted the staple food of the area's poor inhabitants): Dadrian, "The Documentation of the World War I Armenian Massacres," p. 574 (n. 55).

[99] Vahakn N. Dadrian, "The Role of the Turkish Military in the Destruction of Ottoman Armenians: A Study in Historical Continuity," *Journal of Political and Military Sociology* 10: 2 (Winter 1992), pp. 276–7.

the combined landscape of these six provinces, plus Trabzon province, through the High Command of the Third Army, was a factor that proved decisive for the swift organization of the ensuing campaign of annihilation. All of the Governors-General of the provinces were repeatedly summoned by General Mahmud Kâmil, the Commander-in-Chief, to Erzurum, the headquarters of that army, for streamlining the requisite lethal operations. The General's political background and the circumstances of his appointment to that post are such as to increase his propensity for the mission assigned to him. He was an ardent Ittihadist, a close friend of Ziya Gökalp, the high priest of Ittihadist political ideology, and adept at embracing the radical, political ends of the CUP. The manner of his appointment confirms and at the same time epitomizes the value of these attributes.

When War Minister Enver appointed General Vehib to the post of Third Army Commander in February 1915, MDs Behaeddin Şakir and Nâzım of the CUP's Central Committee immediately intervened energetically objecting to Enver's choice. As a result Enver felt impelled, if not compelled, to give Vehib an alternative command post and in his stead appoint General Mahmud Kâmil – in compliance with the wishes of the two overweening party potentates. All available evidence demonstrates that with this pivotal appointment the architects of the Armenian Genocide had set their scheme in motion. Shortly after his appointment, General Mahmud Kâmil, in an urgent communication to the Ottoman headquarters, "proposed and demanded" ("teklif ve talep") authorization to "deport" the Armenians in his area of command, which, as expected, was granted through hasty legal and illegal maneuvers. This disposition proved the *alpha* and *omega* of the ensuing Armenian Genocide. Several German diplomatic and military officials, in their reports to their superiors, explicitly identify Kâmil as the arch organizer of the campaign of extermination of the Armenians of this string of provinces.[100] As specified by Y. H. Bayur, the late dean of Turkish historians, already during the turmoils surrounding the revival of the Armenian Question in the years preceding the First World War, the CUP leaders had decided to solve the Armenian Question eventually "with the help of the Army" ("İşi ordu ile görmek").[101]

In the Trabzon case, General Kâmil is portrayed by two Muslim Turk witnesses as the supreme authority controlling the overall anti-Armenian operations. Colonel Vasfi, Chief of Staff at Trabzon, testified that, upon

---

[100] All the details about General Mahmud Kâmil can be found in Dadrian, "The Armenian Question," pp. 74–5.
[101] Bayur, *Türk İnkılâbı Tarihi*, vol. II, part IV (1952), p. 13.

the orders of his commanding officer, General Ali Paşa, he set out to go to Erzurum to investigate reports of massacres against the Armenians. General Kâmil forbade him to proceed, telling him in so many words that it was none of his business (fourth sitting, p.m. segment, 3 April 1919). Ethem, a retired Major, Chief of the Commission in Charge of Military Supplies in Trabzon, testified that General Kâmil gave license to the *vali* Cemal Azmi to be the ultimate authority in the province, including over military matters, and the organization of convict-brigands (fifteenth sitting, 30 April 1919). Even the Commander of Trabzon's military units, Avni Paşa, confirmed this state of affairs in a written statement personally submitted to the Tribunal in its sixteenth sitting on 5 May 1919. In a separate press release, Avni described the *vali*, actually General Kâmil's proxy in Trabzon,

as a man of unlimited power, but also as the most dastardly man you can imagine. A tyrant by nature, he derived a fierce pleasure from massacring the Christians . . . The murder of Armenian physicians, pharmacists and veterinarians, among others, was ordered by him. It is wrong to accuse these people of sabotage. They never attacked Ottoman troops. Talât's responses to my remonstrances were always evasive.[102]

To sum up, it is evident that the Armenian Genocide as an embryonic idea antedated the outbreak of the First World War. Its most distinguishing feature is that its conception, organization, and execution is intimately linked with a monolithic political party rather than with the regular organs of a normally functioning state system. Any understanding of the genocide, therefore, requires us to focus clearly on that aspect of a political party that covertly creates and maintains a conspiratorial network of committed party operatives. The genocidal agenda is covered up as long as possible through a variety of techniques of deception, deflection, the use of a vocabulary of euphemisms and code words, and through ceremonial oaths of secrecy administered to layers of perpetrator groups. To

---

[102] *Journal d'Orient* (French-language Istanbul daily), 24 April 1919. Of a prestigious Kurdish family background, Cemal Azmi developed his sanguinary career in the Balkans where from 1902 to 1905 he led a campaign of suppression against the Bulgarians and the Greeks in his capacity as *kaymakam*, County Executive, then as Governor-General in Saloniki. He too was a close friend of the two CUP potentates, MDs Şakir and Nâzım. He was tracked down by Armenian avengers and assassinated in Berlin on 17 April 1922, along with MD Behaeddin Şakir. In commenting on his penchant for drowning many of his Armenian victims, a British Member of Parliament, Sir J. Spear, on 18 November 1918, made the following declaration in the House of Commons: "Tragedies have occurred throughout the War and tortures have been committed, but nothing moved my people more than the action of Turkey in taking thousands of Armenians out to sea and throwing them into the water to drown": *Parliamentary Debates, Armenia* (House of Lords, 13 November 1918; House of Commons, 23, 24, 30, 31 October, 6 7, 12, 14, 18, November 1918) (London: The Pelican Press, 1918), p. 25.

facilitate a swift execution of the scheme at hand, the victim population is rendered as defenseless as possible by way of disarming, dislocating, and concentrating them, and misleading them about the purpose of the deportation and actual destination of the deportee population. It appears that the more brutal, fiendish, and merciless the genocidal operations are, the greater the chances of a swift success are likely to be. The injection of terror into the minds of the targeted population is in this respect an integral part of these operations. Another component appears to be the application of the techniques of surprise and entrapment – to preempt or mitigate resistance or even counteraction by the members of the targeted group. It appears also that, in order to enlist a degree of popular partic- ipation in the cataclysm, the appetite for common cupidity and avarice has to be stimulated. In this sense the perpetrators of the genocide have to be differentiated and subjected to gradations in terms of the specific nature of their involvement. The downright intention of mass murder by the decision makers was not always in tune with the more mundane motives of lower-echelon perpetrators for whom such murder was but subsidiary to thievery, pillage, and robbery.

Perhaps the most striking element in this synopsis is the reference to the concept of informal authority. Through such authority the CUP po- tentates, adeptly exploiting the channels of formal authority which some of them also controlled, secured unfettered and broad scope for plan- ning and action. Having eliminated all effective opposition, they became almost completely free from the moderating influences of any challenge to their *modus operandi*. The standard constraints and restraints that as a rule are prescribed for and are even imposed upon a regularly functioning system of government were reduced to irrelevance. In the absence of the modalities of accountability and responsibility endemic in such a system, these architects of the Armenian Genocide easily became the execution- ers of that genocide by way of cultivating a web of conspiracy that was as lethal as it was effective. In brief, the principles of accountability and responsibility gave way to the principle of license for the murder of an entire people.

Part II

During the catastrophe

4   A friend in power? Woodrow Wilson and Armenia

John Milton Cooper, Jr.

Two facts overshadow everything else about Woodrow Wilson's relationship with the Armenian Genocide. First, he was President of the United States when those atrocities occurred. Second, he did not intervene to try to stop those atrocities. Wilson's situation *vis à vis* the Armenian Genocide eerily foreshadowed Franklin Roosevelt's towards the Holocaust a generation later. The same question arises about both leaders – why? Why did they act or fail to act as they did? Likewise, with both leaders that question has a necessary antecedent. This is Senator Howard Baker's famous, repeated query to the witnesses at the Watergate committee hearings in 1973: "What did the president know, and when did he know it?" That is the first question that needs to be put to President Wilson about Armenia.

As is rarely the case with historical evidence, it is possible to give a precise, even quantitative estimate of what Wilson knew about Armenia and when he knew it. Thanks to Arthur Link's monumental edition of *The Papers of Woodrow Wilson* (hereafter *Wilson Papers*), it is possible to measure, at least roughly, the attention that Wilson gave to Armenia. The measurements come from the three cumulative index volumes of the *Wilson Papers* that cover the years between his becoming President in 1913 and his death in 1924.[1]

The first of these indexes is for the twelve volumes that cover 1913 through 1916. Under "Armenia" there are three entries; more important, under "Armenians, plight of" there are six entries. The three general references are to documents from 1916. One is a report by the French ambassador to his foreign ministry of a conversation with Wilson's diplomatic agent and confidant, Colonel Edward M. House, which refers to Russia taking over Turkish Armenia. Another is a letter to Wilson from Secretary of State Robert Lansing reporting his conversations with the Germans and the Turks over "the further deportation of the Armenian

---

[1] Arthur S. Link, ed., *The Papers of Woodrow Wilson* (Princeton, N. J.: Princeton University Press, 1966–94), vol. XXXIX, p. 117; vol. LII, p. 133; vol. LXIX, pp. 156, 333.

population." The final reference is to a speech that Wilson gave in Cincinnati at the close of his re-election campaign, in which he declared:

You know the feeling of this nation towards those unorganized people who have no political standing in Europe, like the Armenians, like the people of Poland – all those peoples who seem caught between the forces of this terrible struggle and seem likely to be crushed almost out of existence . . . our heart goes out to these helpless people who are being crushed and whom we would like to save.[2]

The references to the plight of the Armenians in all these volumes come from the latter part of 1915, not long after the massacres began. As early as 1 October, Colonel House told Wilson, "I am wondering whether this Government should not make some sort of protest over the Armenian massacres." Later in the month, a prominent Armenian-American appealed to the President to aid his suffering people. In December, a college acquaintance who had been a missionary in Turkey gave Wilson an eyewitness account of what was happening in Turkish Armenia. That month also, Colonel House forwarded to the President a letter to him from the former British Ambassador to the United States, James Bryce, who would become the foremost international champion of the Armenians, likewise describing their plight. To his missionary acquaintance Wilson replied, "The situation with regard to the Armenians is indeed nothing less than appalling. You may be sure that we have been doing everything that is diplomatically possible to check the terrible business."[3]

Those references answer the question about what and when the President knew about the situation. Wilson did know something about the Armenian massacres, and he knew it early, soon after they began. Also, his letter and speech show that he sympathized with the plight of the Armenians.

The second index is for the eleven volumes of the *Wilson Papers* that cover all but three days of the period when the United States was a belligerent in the First World War. The United States declared a state of war against Germany in April 1917 and against Austria-Hungary in December 1917. The United States never did declare war against the other two members of the Central Powers, Bulgaria and Turkey. In this index there

---

[2] J. Cambon, "Deuxième Entrevue du Colonel House," 7 Feb. 1916, in ibid., vol. XXXVI (Princeton, N. J.: Princeton University Press, 1981), p. 148 (n. l); Lansing to Wilson, 15 Nov. 1916, in *Wilson Papers*, vol. XXXVIII, p. 652; Wilson speech at Cincinnati, 26 Oct. 1916, in *Wilson Papers*, vol. XXXVIII, p. 539.

[3] House to Wilson, 1 Oct. 1915, in *Wilson Papers*, vol. XXXV, p. 3; Haigazoun Hohannes Topakyan to Wilson, 22 Oct. 1915, in *Wilson Papers*, vol. XXXV, p. 104; William Nesbitt Chambers to Wilson, 10 Dec. 1915, in *Wilson Papers*, vol. XXXV, p. 337; Bryce to House, 26 Nov. 1915, in *Wilson Papers*, vol. XXXV, p. 348; Wilson to Chambers, 13 Dec. 1915, in *Wilson Papers*, vol. XXXV, p. 349. See also Wilson to Topakyan, 28 Oct. 1915, in *Wilson Papers*, vol. XXXV, p. 119.

are forty entries under "Armenia and Armenians" – thirty-six general references and four references to "massacre of." As might be expected, most of these references are to reports by diplomats and military observers about what was happening in Turkey and the Caucasus with reference to the Armenians. What becomes clear in these references is how intricately the fate of Armenia had become wrapped up in the competing designs of the Allied Powers on the Ottoman Empire and with the problems and dangers that were emerging out of the Bolshevik Revolution in Russia. For example, less than a month after the United States entered the war Wilson and House discussed how in Anatolia "the secret treaties between the Allies come in most prominently. They have agreed to give Russia a sphere of influence in Armenia."[4]

Few of these references contain statements by Wilson himself. Those few statements show that he had conflicted attitudes about Armenia. His most important utterance came in January 1918, when he delivered the Fourteen Points address. An advisory memorandum by members of the Inquiry, Colonel House's brain trust of bright young men, had stated: "It is necessary to free the subject races of the Turkish Empire from oppression and misrule. This implies at the very least autonomy for Armenia." Wilson had some inclination to follow their suggestion. Colonel House noted in his diary, "After the Turkish paragraph had been written, the President thought it might be made more specific, and that Armenia, Mesopotamia, Syria and other parts be mentioned by name. I disagreed with this believing that what was said was sufficient to indicate this, and it finally stood as originally framed." That paragraph, Point XII, read, in part, "The Turkish portions of the present Ottoman Empire should be assured a secure sovereignty, but the other nationalities which are now under Turkish rule should be assured an undoubted security of life and an absolutely unmolested opportunity of autonomous development."[5]

Dropping an overt reference to Armenia evidently reflected the need to keep American war aims limited, flexible, and realistic, something to which Wilson and House were both acutely sensitive. During the spring of 1918, the British in particular urged the United States to declare war against Turkey. Wilson resisted that move, both because he believed that restraint might tempt Turkey to quit the war and because he distrusted the Allies' designs on the Ottoman Empire. By the middle of the year, he also

---

[4] Entry 28 Apr. 1917, diary of Edward M. House, in *Wilson Papers*, vol. XLII, p. 157.
[5] Sidney Mezes, David Hunter Miller, and Walter Lippmann, *The Present Situation: The War Aims and Peace Terms It Suggests*, 4 Jan. 1918, in *Wilson Papers*, vol. XLV, p. 471; entry, House diary, 9 Jan. 1918, in *Wilson Papers*, vol. XLV, p. 553; Wilson speech of 8 Jan. 1918, in *Wilson Papers*, vol. XLV, p. 538.

displayed an acute sense of the limitations on what America or the Allies could do to help the Armenians. In June, he told the former Ambassador to Turkey, Henry Morgenthau, "There is nothing practical that we can do for the time being in the matter of the Armenian massacres." A month later, the President instructed his secretary, Joseph Tumulty, to clarify a statement that he had supposedly given to Miran Sevasly, an Armenian-American leader. Sevasly had, Wilson contended,

> stated more confidently than I had any right to state the expectation that the hopes of the Armenians 'will be crowned.' . . . I have no doubt that I did express my own resolution to do all that I could to see that the hopes of the Armenians were satisfied and that no question of essential justice involved in the present European situation should be left unsettled in the general reckoning of the war.[6]

What these references show is that Wilson continued to be informed about Armenia and wanted to do something to help the Armenians. But they also show that his new role as a war leader made him acutely aware of the complications that surrounded the Armenian Question and the limitations of American power.

The third index to the *Wilson Papers* is to the sixteen volumes that cover the period from the end of the First World War until Wilson's death. Actually, none of the entries refers to anything after Wilson left office in March 1921. Under "Armenia and the Armenians" there are sixty-seven references, and under "Paris Peace Conference: Mandates: Armenia and Armenians" there are eighty-seven references. Nearly all of these references involve discussions of the fate of the defeated Ottoman Empire and the part that a possibly independent or semi-autonomous Armenia might play in the post-war settlement. As the number of references shows, the area of greatest concentration, for Wilson and nearly everybody else at the conference, was the ultimately abortive project for a League of Nations mandate over Armenia and the subsidiary suggestion that the United States assume the mandatory power there. Linked to that suggestion was another mandatory trial balloon, namely that the United States also assume a mandate over Constantinople and the Straits.

What these references show is that, at the peace conference even more than during the war, Armenia had become for Wilson, as it had for all the Allied leaders, part of that larger and more complicated international picture. Others have written at great length about the peace conference and the treaties that emerged from it. Among all these documents and the events that produced them, three are most revealing about Wilson's attitudes towards Armenia. One of these incidents involves statements

---

[6] Wilson to Morgenthau, 14 June 1918, in *Wilson Papers*, vol. XLVIII, p. 311.

that Wilson gave in Paris on successive days in May 1919. The second is the mention Wilson made of Armenia in his ill-fated speaking tour in the western United States on behalf of the Treaty of Versailles and the League of Nations in September 1919. The third is a belated attempt by him to do something for Armenia in May 1920.

The first statement is one Wilson made on 21 May 1919, at a long meeting of the Council of Four – Clemenceau, Lloyd George, Orlando, and himself, the real shapers of the settlement. According to Sir Maurice Hankey's notes,

> He could only say that at this stage, that he feared it was impossible for the United States to take a mandate for Asia Minor. It was difficult for her to take a mandate even in Armenia, where she had permanent interests of long standing, and where a good deal of money had been spent by Americans for the relief of the Armenian people. As regards Constantinople, he thought that even some of the public men who were opposed to him politically would support him in taking a mandate. He did not, however, think that he could persuade them to accept a mandate for Asia Minor.

By "public men who were opposed to him politically," Wilson almost certainly meant Senator Henry Cabot Lodge of Massachusetts and other Republicans who were fighting him over proposed American membership in the League of Nations.[7]

The following day Wilson met with two junior staff members of the American delegation, David Magie and William Westermann. Both men were professors of classics, Magie at Princeton and Westermann at the University of Wisconsin. They were two of the "bright young men" who had joined Colonel House's Inquiry and then come to the conference to offer their knowledge about and advice on what was then called the Near East. It was a measure of the underdeveloped state in American colleges and universities of what are now called "area studies" that scholars of Ancient Greece and Rome such as Magie and Westermann – neither of whom was really all that conversant with current affairs in the region – held the positions that they did. Still, inexpert as they were, Magie and Westermann had strong views about what was happening in their area, and they had wangled an interview with the top man to unburden themselves and see where he stood.

Westermann was keeping a diary of the conference, which gives a nice view of the second and third tier of activities in Paris and contains much interesting observation and gossip about both the former Ottoman Empire and such personages as Emir Faisal and T. E. Lawrence. Although Westermann was present at some open meetings of the plenipotentiaries,

---

[7] Hankey minutes of Council of Four, 21 May 1919, in *Wilson Papers*, vol. LIX, p. 335.

this was the only time that he met face-to-face with the President or discussed policy with him.

In the entry from his diary for 22 May 1919, Westermann notes,

The President began by saying that the chief problem was the disposition of Anatolia. He was prepared to propose to the American people that the United States take mandates for Armenia and Constantinople, saying that American sympathy for Armenia pointed to the adoption by Congress of this burden in the case of the former, but that the acceptance of a Constantinopolitan mandate was doubtful.

Later in the interview, Wilson reiterated those views and added that if the United States did hold both mandates it "would be in a strategic position to control that portion of the world," and thereby oversee the actions of any other mandatory powers. Westermann concludes the entry: "Throughout the interview, the President declared himself as strongly opposed to the secret agreements. We think that he will still fight them."[8]

Those seem to be two poles of Wilson's thinking about Armenia at the peace conference. He wanted to assume the mandate there and in Constantinople, but he was doubtful of support at home. Again, for him these questions were parts – and relatively small parts – in the overall peace settlement.

The second incident occurred on Wilson's speaking tour. What is surprising here is how little he mentioned Armenia. This was what later generations would call a "hot button" issue, and it worked in favor of his position on the League. Curiously, however, he mentioned Armenia only twice in the forty speeches he packed into this uncompleted three-week tour. Early in the tour, speaking at Kansas City, he called the Armenians:

a Christian people, helpless, at the mercy of a Turkish government which thought it the service of God to destroy them. And at this moment, my fellow citizens, it is an open question whether the Armenian people will not, while we sit here and debate, be absolutely destroyed. When I think of words piled upon words, of debate following debate, when these unspeakable things are happening in these pitiful parts of the world, I wonder that men do not wake up to the moral responsibility of what they are doing.[9]

Then, on what turned out to be only two days before the end of the tour, Wilson spoke in the same vein about Armenia. The place made the appeal almost inescapable. Wilson was speaking in Salt Lake City, in the Mormon Tabernacle. The Mormon Church had taken perhaps the strongest stand of any American denomination in favor of the Armenians,

[8] "Interview of Magie and Westermann with President Wilson on 22 May 1919," in *Wilson Papers*, vol. LIX, pp. 374– 6.
[9] Wilson speech at Kansas City, 6 Sept. 1919, in *Wilson Papers*, vol. LXIII, p. 71.

and Utah's Democratic senator, William King, who was a Mormon, was one of the most outspoken advocates of the Armenian cause on Capitol Hill.

Wilson obliged his audience by calling the Armenians "those people infinitely terrified, infinitely persecuted" and by excoriating the Turkish government for saying "that it was unable to restrain the horrible massacres which have made that country a graveyard." But that was now going to be changed because:

> Armenia is one of the regions that is to be under trust of the League of Nations. Armenia is to be redeemed . . . So that at last this great people, struggling through night after night of terror, knowing not when they would see their land stained with blood, are now given a promise of safety, a promise of justice, a possibility that they may come out into a time when they can enjoy their rights as free people that they never dreamed they would be able to exercise.[10]

That is a nice sample of Wilsonian oratory on his speaking tour. Wilson is usually thought of as a rather cerebral speaker, and most of the time he did strive in his public persuasion to play the educator rather than the evangelist. Wilson, however, could tug at the heartstrings – as he was doing increasingly in those speeches in September 1919. Still, the important point about Armenia is how rarely he used this issue. On this speaking tour, as at the peace conference, Armenia was on his mind only occasionally and in a secondary way.

Finally, there is a last sour note to the place of Armenia in the struggle over the peace settlement. In May 1920 – after Wilson had suffered a crippling, debilitating stroke and after the Senate had twice failed to consent to the Treaty of Versailles – Armenia became a pawn in a transparently partisan struggle between Wilson and the Republican-controlled Congress. On 13 May, Senator Warren Harding of Ohio, who was a candidate for his party's presidential nomination, introduced a resolution expressing sympathy for the Armenians' "deplorable conditions of insecurity, starvation, and misery." Harding's resolution also affirmed support for Armenian independence and called for the dispatch of a warship and marines to protect the lives and property of American citizens in the area.[11]

Wilson responded to this resolution by upping the ante. He urged:

> that the Congress grant the Executive the power to accept for the United States a mandate over Armenia . . . *At their hearts this great and generous people have made the cause of Armenia their own.* It is to *this* people and to their Government that the hopes and earnest expectations of the struggling people of Armenia turn as

[10] Wilson speech at Salt Lake City, 23 Sept. 1919, in *Wilson Papers*, vol. LXII, p. 458.
[11] *Congressional Record*, 66th. Congress, 2nd. Session, 6978–9 (13 May 1920).

they now emerge from a period of indescribable suffering and peril, and I hope that the Congress will think it wise to meet this hope and expectation with the utmost liberality.

Wilson succeeded in calling his opponents' bluff. On 1 June, the Senate adopted a resolution to reject his request for a mandate by a vote of 52 to 23. The resolution's author was Senator Philander Knox of Pennsylvania, a former Secretary of State, and it gained the votes of 13 Democrats, as well as all of the Senate Republicans, including another of the Armenians' erstwhile champions, Henry Cabot Lodge of Massachusetts.[12]

For all practical purposes, that was the end of American engagement with the Armenian Question. It was also a sad end to Woodrow Wilson's engagement with Armenia. By then, Wilson was a broken man, only partially recovered from his stroke, subject to mood swings, and harboring delusions about running for a third term as President. The only thing that can be said to his credit here is that, unlike Harding and the Republican senators, he was not engaging in a mere political ploy. Wilson really did think that there was a chance to have the United States assume a mandate over Armenia. The response of the Senate showed how out of tune he was with political reality.

This is, in sketchy form, a measure of how Armenia figured in Wilson's mind and actions. Clearly, this indisputably idealistic President, the man who coined the term "human rights," cared about the plight of Armenia. But he really did prefigure Franklin Roosevelt two decades later in responding to the destruction of European Jewry. He was the commander-in-chief and peacemaker-in-chief of the most powerful member of the winning coalition in a world war. He kept his mind focused on what is now called the "big picture." During the war, he was concerned about how best to use American military power and how to retain the greatest freedom of diplomatic maneuver. The major consequence of Wilson's approach was not to widen the war, not to declare war against Bulgaria and Turkey. That restraint, he believed, could give him leverage over the Allies and curb their imperialistic appetites in the Near East.

Unquestionably, Wilson's choice limited and possibly ruled out American military intervention on behalf of the Armenians, at least during the war. But was Wilson's choice all that was involved? How much latitude in contemplating action to help the Armenians did he really enjoy? Was there ever a real chance of such intervention in any event?

There seems to have been only one conceivable scenario under which American military forces might have gone into Turkey in 1917 or 1918,

---

[12] Wilson message to Congress, 24 May 1920, in *Wilson Papers*, vol. LXV, pp. 320–3; *Cong. Rec.*, 66th. Cong., 2nd. Sess., 8073 (1 June 1920).

in time to make a difference in the magnitude of the genocide. That would have been if Theodore Roosevelt had been President when the United States entered the First World War. This Roosevelt indeed did favor declaring war on all of the Central Powers, including Turkey. An expeditionary force to save the Armenians would seem to be just the kind of enterprise that would appeal to Roosevelt's militant moralism.

But was this a realistic alternative? Theodore Roosevelt out of power, in full fulmination against what he saw as the weakness and pusillanimity of Wilson, was one thing. Roosevelt in power, with full knowledge of the delicacies and complexities and limitations of waging war and coalition diplomacy, would necessarily have been something else. Moreover, the prospect of invading Turkey was not appetizing to anyone, as the Allies had learned so painfully at Gallipoli. Furthermore, any savvy politician had to be sensitive to American opinion, especially the reluctance to get involved in distant and, to Americans, exotic places.

The best evidence of such sensitivity comes from the behavior of Henry Cabot Lodge. This man, who was Roosevelt's closest friend and political legatee, simply abandoned the Armenians. Lodge believed that he had a handy way out by blaming Wilson, as he did to Lord Bryce in April 1920:

The fact is, the protracted debate on the League both inside and outside the Senate has wrought a great change in public opinion and the feeling is growing constantly stronger against the United States involving itself in the quarrels of Europe at all. For this reason it will be impossible to get a mandate accepted by the United States and I doubt very much if we could secure a loan from the Government for any political or military purpose.

This was coming from a senator who was responsive to his active Armenian-American constituency in Massachusetts and who had earlier spoken out loudly against the massacres. From the Armenians' standpoint, with a friend like that they did not need enemies in the United States.[13]

Should the same thing be said about Wilson? The answer must be "no." Wilson never minimized the plight of the Armenians or doubted where the responsibility for the genocide lay. It is true that he did not take timely action on their behalf. He made choices as a war leader and peacemaker that may have prevented more vigorous action to aid Armenia. Still, the case for the defense ought to be highlighted. His design for world order, his vision of a powerful, vigorous League of Nations led by a fully participating United States, offered the best guarantee against continuation or expansion of this genocide. The hard fact remains that Wilson had the

---

[13] Lodge to Bryce, 20 Apr. 1920, Henry Cabot Lodge Papers, Massachusetts Historical Society.

best program available for restoring peace to the world and protecting peoples such as the Armenians; that program came too late to stop the genocide, and, after the Armistice, it was rejected by the United States Senate. The fault lay in others, not in Woodrow Wilson; the obstacles to effective action both during and after the Great War were embedded in a political and strategic situation that worked inexorably against Armenia. That is one definition of tragedy.

5   Wilsonian diplomacy and Armenia: the limits of power and ideology

Lloyd E. Ambrosius

Armenia emerged as a new nation during the First World War, joining the world order that was taking shape in the wake of collapsing empires. President Woodrow Wilson, in his wartime addresses, proclaimed the principles that should guide the peacemaking for this new world. His decision to attend the 1919 Paris Peace Conference increased the expectations that all peoples, including the Armenians, would have a better future. Wilsonian ideology promised peace and justice for all nations, both old and new. American power, greater than that of any other empire, would presumably enable the United States to help others fulfill Wilson's ideals in the post-war world. Contrary to these hopes, however, Armenia failed as a new nation, revealing not only its own limits but also those of Wilsonianism. The realities of international politics prevented the Armenian people, who had suffered so much in the past, from achieving the Wilsonian promise after the Great War. The limits of American power and ideology resulted in an outcome very different from what the Armenians wanted and what the US President had heralded.

Armenia possessed assets that made it attractive to American leaders. Its people were white – literally Caucasian – and Christian, at least culturally, as a result of the Armenian Orthodox Church's role since the fourth century CE in shaping and preserving national traditions.[1] It also enjoyed bipartisan support from the American political elite. Not only the Democratic President but also the Republican leader, Senator Henry Cabot Lodge, favored the new nation. Lodge joined the American Committee for the Independence of Armenia, which Wilson's former Ambassador to Germany, James W. Gerard, organized in 1918. This lobby of prominent Americans, from Democrats William Jennings Bryan and Cleveland H. Dodge to Republicans Charles Evans Hughes and Elihu Root, worked

---

[1] Ronald Grigor Suny, *Looking Toward Ararat: Armenia in Modern History* (Bloomington: Indiana University Press, 1993).

closely with the Wilson administration and the Republican-controlled Congress to promote the Armenian cause.[2]

With this broad range of bipartisan support, Armenia apparently enjoyed a real advantage in the peacemaking after the First World War. No other new nation could claim such a prominent lobby in the United States. Moreover, the Armenian cause ranked second only to that of French security against renewed German aggression in the willingness of leading Republicans such as Lodge and Root to approve long-term commitments by the United States in the Old World.[3] The question for pro-Armenian Americans was how to translate this amorphous bipartisan support into effective action that would actually assist Armenia. The answer would depend not only on the pro-Armenian inclinations of President Wilson and Congress, or the State Department and US diplomats, but also on the capability of the United States to project its influence into the crossroads region of the Near East under the prevailing wartime and post-war conditions. This would test the limits of US power and ideology.

Among the Americans most actively promoting US support for Armenia were two former Ambassadors: James W. Gerard and Henry Morgenthau. Gerard organized and led the American Committee for the Independence of Armenia. Morgenthau, who had represented the United States in Constantinople from 1913 to 1916, exposed the Ottoman Empire's connections with Imperial Germany and its cruel treatment of the Armenians. He informed not only the Wilson administration but also the American people about the Armenian Genocide. After returning home, he published a potent account of his years in Turkey, *Ambassador Morgenthau's Story* (1918).[4]

Morgenthau wanted to expose the anti-Armenian behavior of the Young Turks and their ally, imperial Germany. In his book he reported that "the Turkish Government was determined to keep the news, as long as possible, from the outside world. It was clearly the intention that Europe and America should hear of the annihilation of the Armenian race only after the annihilation had been accomplished."[5] The former Ambassador sought, contrary to Turkey's preference, to disclose

[2] Richard G. Hovannisian, *The Republic of Armenia*, vol. I: *The First Years, 1918–1919* (Berkeley: University of California Press, 1971), pp. 261–5, 293–5, 309–12.
[3] Lloyd E. Ambrosius, "Wilson, Republicans, and French Security after World War I," *Journal of American History* 59 (September 1972), pp. 341–52.
[4] Henry Morgenthau, *Ambassador Morgenthau's Story* (Garden City: Doubleday, Page, & Company, 1918). For Morgenthau's reports to Lansing in 1915, see US Department of State, *Papers Relating to the Foreign Relations of the United States: The Lansing Papers, 1914–1920*, vol. I (Washington: US Government Printing Office, 1939), pp. 762–75.
[5] Morgenthau, *Ambassador Morgenthau's Story*, p. 326.

Armenia's plight and Germany's involvement in it. In 1918, before the book appeared, he published the chapters of *Ambassador Morgenthau's Story* as articles in *World's Work*. Sending the first three installments to Wilson, he sought the President's opinion about the idea of turning the book into a motion picture. Playing up Germany's alliance with Turkey, and thus its complicity with the Armenian massacres, seemed to Morgenthau's publishers an ideal way to disseminate "anti-German propaganda" in the United States. "I myself think," he told Wilson, "that nothing could so completely bring before the American people the true nature of the German aggression as a picture showing the Armenian massacres and the responsibility of Germany for them."[6]

Wilson opposed Morgenthau's idea. The President noted that he was "very much distressed" that Gerard had allowed his book, *My Four Years in Germany* (1917), to be turned into a motion picture. "Movies I have seen recently," Wilson explained,

have portrayed so many horrors that I think their effect is far from stimulating, and that it does not, as a matter of fact, suggest the right attitude of mind or the right national action. There is nothing practical that we can do for the time being in the matter of the Armenian massacres, for example, and the attitude of the country toward Turkey is already fixed.[7]

Recognizing the limits of American power to assist Armenia, Wilson did not welcome Morgenthau's proposal for anti-German and anti-Turkish propaganda.

This response was consistent with Wilson's decision not to recommend an American declaration of war against the Ottoman Empire. In December 1917, he had asked Congress to declare war against the Habsburg Empire, but not against Turkey or Bulgaria. The President had observed that "the government of Austria-Hungary is not acting upon its own initiative or in response to the wishes and feelings of its own peoples but as the instrument of another nation. We must meet its force with our own and regard the Central Powers as but one." He acknowledged that "the same logic would lead also to a declaration of war against Turkey and Bulgaria. They also are the tools of Germany." For practical reasons, however, Wilson did not call upon Congress to declare war against them, noting that "they are mere tools and do not yet stand in the direct path of our necessary action. We shall go wherever the necessities of this war

---

[6] Morgenthau to Wilson, 11 June 1918, in Arthur S. Link, ed., *The Papers of Woodrow Wilson* (hereinafter *PWW*), vol. XLVIII (Princeton: Princeton University Press, 1985), p. 284.
[7] Wilson to Morgenthau, 14 June 1918, in *PWW*, vol. XLVIII, p. 311.

carry us, but it seems to me that we should go only where immediate and practical considerations lead us and not heed any others."[8]

Congress, while accepting Wilson's recommendation and voting for war against the Austro-Hungarian Empire, wanted clarification of the President's reluctance to take the same action against Bulgaria and Turkey. Secretary of State Robert Lansing gave the Senate Foreign Relations Committee a list of practical reasons for this decision. He acknowledged that the United States did not have a military force to commit on the eastern front. It would instead concentrate on fighting the war on the western front in 1918. Lansing emphasized, moreover, that a declaration of war against Turkey would jeopardize American missionary and educational interests in that country and would likely provoke the Turks into retaliation with new massacres of Christians and Jews.[9] In short, the limits of American power in this region made it prudent for the United States to ignore ideological consistency in favor of practical considerations. It was more realistic not to declare war against Turkey, or even Bulgaria.

Wilson's analysis of Germany's global threat provided the framework in which US diplomats, particularly Felix Willoughby Smith in Tiflis, endeavored to assist the Armenians. As an obstacle to the German bid for hegemony from Berlin to Baghdad, Armenia became strategically significant for the United States during the last year of the Great War. Although rejecting open warfare against Germany or Turkey on the eastern front, Wilson and Lansing sanctioned covert financial assistance to the British and French governments to support their operations designed to defeat the German–Turkish alliance and, incidentally, to support the Armenians. As US Consul, Smith promoted this activity in the Transcaucasian region of the disintegrating Russian Empire.[10]

Following the Russian Revolution in March 1917, Smith had urged the Wilson administration to resist the combined efforts by Germany and Turkey to gain control over Transcaucasia. Aware of the inadequacies of Russia's provisional government, he urged the State Department to encourage the various nationalities in the region to continue the war against the Central Powers. Smith wanted to exploit the separate national identities of the Caucasian peoples to reinforce their war effort against the German–Turkish alliance. He advocated, for example, the transfer of Armenian and Georgian troops from the collapsing eastern front to

---

[8] Woodrow Wilson, *The Public Papers of Woodrow Wilson* (hereinafter *PPWW*), ed. Ray Stannard Baker and William E. Dodd, vol. V (New York: Harper & Brothers Publishers, 1927), pp. 135–6.

[9] Laurence Evans, *United States Policy and the Partition of Turkey, 1914–1924* (Baltimore: Johns Hopkins University Press, 1965), pp. 32–42.

[10] Hovannisian, *Republic of Armenia*, vol. I, p. 179.

their homelands, where they could continue fighting against the Central Powers.

Since July 1917 Smith had lost confidence in the provisional government's capability, although he still favored a united and democratic Russia. "There seems to be a total lack of patriotism and national spirit towards this country as a whole," Smith reported to Lansing in October. He complained that

> the Provisional Government has heretofore tended to discourage the local national spirit, considering it as a disruptive force, but recent events have shown that practically the only hope of union and peace lies in the encouragement of this racial or national spirit and the utilization of this force towards the formation of units which in turn would inevitably unite in the formation of a Russian federation . . . These racial feelings if encouraged and wisely guided would save Russia and would be of particular and lasting benefit to this district.[11]

Smith's eagerness to encourage nationalist sentiments in Transcaucasia as a way of mobilizing its peoples against Germany and Turkey worried Lansing. After receiving the consul's repeated requests for assistance to Armenians and others, the Secretary of State demanded an explanation of how "the financial support you propose will not tend to encourage sectionalism or disruption of Russia or civil war." He stressed that the "Department cannot encourage tendencies in any of these directions."[12] Lansing's concerns about too much national self-determination reflected Wilson's as well. The President, having long ago adopted a pro-Union interpretation of the American Civil War, did not favor the breakup of existing nation-states. He saw Russia as a whole nation, and thus hesitated to endorse any action that might foster secession by any section.[13]

Lansing informed Edward M. House, Wilson's personal envoy in Paris for a meeting with Allied leaders, that the State Department would not allow Smith to recognize any separatist nation in Transcaucasia. In late November 1917, the Secretary of State explained that Smith "will not be given authority to recognize de facto government until it is evident that such action will not tend to foster sectionalism or disruption of Russia or

---

[11] Smith to Lansing, 19 Oct. 1917, US Department of State, *Papers Relating to the Foreign Relations of the United States, 1918: Russia* (hereinafter *FRUS: Russia*), vol. II (Washington: US Government Printing Office, 1932), pp. 578–80.

[12] Smith to Lansing, 23 Nov. 1917 and Lansing to Smith, 26 Nov. 1917, in *FRUS: Russia*, vol. II, p. 582.

[13] Lloyd E. Ambrosius, "Dilemmas of National Self-Determination: Woodrow Wilson's Legacy," in Christian Baechler and Carole Fink, eds., *The Establishment of European Frontiers after the Two World Wars* (Bern: Peter Lang, 1996), p. 25; Thomas J. Pressly, *Americans Interpret Their Civil War* (New York: The Free Press, 1962), pp. 196–226.

civil war."[14] By this time the Bolsheviks had seized power in Petrograd and Moscow. Nevertheless, US policy continued to favor a united and democratic Russia as foreseen by the provisional government. This enduring commitment to Russia not only prevented the United States from recognizing the new Soviet government but also restricted the ways it might sustain the Armenians and other Caucasian peoples.[15]

The Wilson administration worked with the Allies, particularly the British and the French, to channel financial assistance to these separate peoples within the former Russian Empire. This form of indirect assistance was Lansing's alternative to Smith's earlier proposal for direct US aid to the Armenians and others in Transcaucasia. In December 1917, after the Bolsheviks concluded an armistice with Germany, Wilson approved the covert plan that the State Department then arranged with the Allies.[16]

Multiple purposes shaped American involvement in Transcaucasia. Assistance for the Caucasian peoples obviously involved intervention in the Russian civil war. Wilson and Lansing pursued anti-Bolshevik as well as anti-German purposes. However, US aid, albeit indirect, was also anti-Turkish and pro-Armenian.[17] This was a key feature of Smith's proposal for financial assistance. In response to Lansing's concerns about fostering sectionalism and disrupting Russia, Smith noted the importance of Armenia, while assuring him that "the Allies would be supporting both Russian union and democracy against absolute dependence of Russia on Germany." If, however, they failed to provide critical financial assistance to Transcaucasia, "this would involve [the] loss of Armenia and render most likely the concentration of Turkish–German forces against [the] British in Bagdad."[18] Lansing and Wilson agreed. Because the United States lacked the means to deliver substantial quantities of direct aid to Armenia or elsewhere in the Caucasus region, expediency led them

[14] Lansing to Sharp, 28 Nov. 1917, in *FRUS: Russia*, vol. II, pp. 582–3.
[15] Lansing to Wilson, 10 Jan. 1918, US Department of State, in *Papers Relating to the Foreign Relations of the United States: Lansing Papers* (hereinafter *FRUS: Lansing*), vol. II (Washington: US Government Printing Office, 1940), pp. 349–51.
[16] Lansing to Wilson, 10 and 12 Dec. 1917, in *FRUS: Lansing Papers*, vol. II, pp. 343–6; Page to Lansing, 18 Dec. 1917 and Sharp to Lansing, 23 and 27 Dec. 1917, in *FRUS: Russia*, vol. II, pp. 591–2, 596–600; Wilson to Lansing, 1 Jan. 1918, in *PWW*, vol. XLV (Princeton: Princeton University Press, 1984), pp. 417–19.
[17] Other scholars have neglected anti-Turkish or pro-Armenian dimensions, while focusing on anti-German or anti-Bolshevik features of US intervention in the Russian civil war. See, for example, George F. Kennan, *Soviet–American Relations, 1917–1920: Russia Leaves the War* (Princeton: Princeton University Press, 1956), vol. I, pp. 167–88, and David S. Fogelsong, *America's Secret War Against Bolshevism: US Intervention in the Russian Civil War* (Chapel Hill: University of North Carolina Press, 1995), pp. 76–105.
[18] Smith to Lansing, 4 Dec. 1917, in *FRUS: Russia*, vol. II, pp. 584–5.

to adopt a collaborative plan with the Allies. Accordingly, Lansing instructed Smith to cooperate with British and French representatives in the region and to keep the State Department informed.[19]

Before the Bolshevik seizure of power in November 1917, Smith had begun to advocate US help for the Caucasian peoples as the most effective way to protect them from Germany and Turkey, and thus to help defeat the Central Powers. This timing indicated that anti-Bolshevism was not Smith's primary motivation at the outset. The anti-German strategic rationale for assisting Armenians, Smith's initial priority, ended with the German Armistice on 11 November 1918. Humanitarian concern for protecting Armenians against the Turks, also important to Smith, persisted into the post-war era. Pro-Armenian and anti-Turkish considerations, not merely anti-Bolshevism, remained important factors in the US involvement in Transcaucasia after Germany's defeat. In the mixture of strategic, humanitarian, and ethnic agendas, the Wilson administration pursued a complex foreign policy in the Near East.[20]

In Washington, neither Wilson nor Lansing, nor any other American leader, was willing to make costly commitments to the Armenians. Even while authorizing some covert assistance via the Allies to the region, the President did not plan to recognize Armenia or any other new nation in Transcaucasia. In his Fourteen Points on 8 January 1918, he called for preserving Russia's territorial integrity and respecting its right of self-determination. Accordingly, he did not favor independence for Russian Armenia. Nor did he favor independence for Turkish Armenia. Wilson's peace plan would leave Turkish portions of the Ottoman Empire under Turkish sovereignty, but he thought that "the other nationalities which are now under Turkish rule should be assured an undoubted security of life and an absolutely unmolested opportunity of autonomous development, and the Dardanelles should be permanently opened as a free passage to the ships and commerce of all nations under international guarantees."[21] Wilson had given some consideration to making point 12, which dealt with the Ottoman Empire, more specific by naming Armenia and other nationalities, but acquiesced in House's advice not to bother.[22] Thus he cautiously applied his principles, calling for the Open Door and collective

---

[19] Lansing to Smith, 28 Dec. 1917, in *FRUS: Russia*, vol. II, pp. 600–1.

[20] For the Armenian dimension, see especially Richard G. Hovannisian, *Armenia on the Road to Independence, 1918* (Berkeley: University of California Press, 1967), pp. 80–2, 117–19.

[21] An Address to a Joint Session of Congress, 8 Jan. 1918, in *PWW*, vol. XLV, pp. 537–8; Address of the President, 8 Jan. 1918, in *FRUS, 1918: The World War*, vol. I (Washington: US Government Printing Office, 1933), pp. 15–16.

[22] Diary of Colonel House, 9 Jan. 1918, in *PWW*, vol. XLV, p. 553.

security in the Turkish Straits and for national self-determination in the Russian and Turkish territories.

After Germany imposed the Treaty of Brest-Litovsk on the Bolshevik government on 3 March 1918, forcing the Soviets to cede some of Russian Armenia to Turkey, the plight of Armenians worsened.[23] Nevertheless, Wilson still ruled out both US and Allied military intervention in this region. In late March and early April, Lord Reading, the British Ambassador to the United States, presented the Allied case for military intervention in Russia. Among other arguments, he noted that "it is in the East that the German Government are now taking steps to overcome the effects of the blockade, to upset the security of British India, and to carry the war down to Afghanistan and Persia, incidentally giving the Turks a free hand in Armenia." Wilson was not convinced by Reading's case. "I must say," he informed Lansing, "that none of these memoranda has anything in it that is at all persuasive with me."[24] The President wanted no further American or Allied involvement in the Russian civil war regardless of the consequences for Armenia.

During the spring of 1918, Smith continued to inform the State Department about Armenia's worsening situation and urged more assistance. He reported that the Turks were still advancing, placing the "Armenians in real danger of extermination." He requested more British assistance to the Armenians, noting that they "possess great potential military force." Given "the inactivity of the Allies," the Armenians were not achieving their full potential. They were, however, generally able to hold their villages against the "armed Moslems." In early April, Smith warned that the Turks might occupy even more Caucasian territory unless the Armenians and Georgians received instant financial aid and future British military assistance. Turkish conquest of Armenia, he forecast, would mean the "massacre of Armenians." He hoped the State Department would arrange with London to transfer money to Tiflis "to provide for safety of [the] Armenian people and prevent [their] total extermination."[25]

Lansing relayed Smith's concerns to the US Ambassador in London, Walter Hines Page, seeking clarification from the British government. However, neither Washington nor London ever provided as much financial and military assistance as Smith requested. Only later, during the summer of 1918, did Wilson finally approve American and Allied military intervention in Russia, which resulted in the sending of

[23] Summers to Lansing, 22 Apr. 1918, in *FRUS: Russia*, vol. I (Washington: US Government Printing Office, 1931), pp. 471–5.

[24] Wilson to Lansing, 4 Apr. 1918, in *PWW*, vol. XLVII (Princeton: Princeton University Press, 1984), pp. 241–6.

[25] Lansing to Page, 3 Apr. 1918, in *FRUS: Russia*, vol. II, pp. 623–5.

some British troops to Armenia. Despite the Consul's best efforts, the Armenians received only minimal help during the Great War.[26]

Caught in the midst of the many conflicts that overwhelmed their homelands during the First World War, the Armenians sought to survive. By the end of May 1918, all efforts by the Caucasian peoples to work together against their common external enemies had ended in failure. The Germans and the Turks extended their dominance over much of formerly Russian Transcaucasia. In collaboration with these Central Powers, the Georgians and the Azerbaijanis established independent republics. The Armenians, left with no other alternative, also proclaimed their own separate republic in Russian Armenia on 28 May. They did not, however, use the word "independence" to describe it. They kept open the possibility of federation with either a White or Soviet Russia, which might help protect them against the Turks.[27]

For the moment, the Wilson administration saw no way to give more assistance to the Armenians. It did not grant even de facto diplomatic recognition to the Armenian Republic. Nor did the United States declare war against Turkey, although the Allies had recommended this action.[28] Looking beyond the war, however, the President pledged to be more helpful to Armenia at the future peace conference. On 4 July 1918, he uttered this promise to Miran Sevasly, Chairman of the Armenian National Union of America, who published it in an Armenian journal in Boston. Wilson later recounted that "I did express my own resolution to do all that I could to see that the hopes of the Armenians were satisfied and that no question of essential justice involved in the present European situation should be left unsettled in the general reckoning after the war."[29] He professed his desire to help the Armenians, but eschewed more US involvement at that time.

For both the United States and the Allies, Armenia in 1918 was an important interest, although not the highest priority. In response to a State Department inquiry, General Tasker H. Bliss, who represented the United States at the Allied Supreme War Council in Paris, summarized the American stakes in the Caucasus region, particularly in Armenia. He noted the traditional concern for "the moral and educational welfare of the Christians" in the Ottoman Empire. The Turkish massacres of Armenians since 1915 had made this humanitarian interest even more

---

[26] Lansing to Wilson, 15 March 1918, in *PWW*, vol. XLVII, pp. 44–5. For the plight of Armenians in 1917–18 and the inadequacies of American and Allied support, see Hovannisian, *Armenia on the Road to Independence*, pp. 94–185.

[27] Hovannisian, *Armenia on the Road to Independence*, pp. 157–215; Hovannisian, *Republic of Armenia*, vol. I, pp. 1–38.

[28] Lansing to Wilson, 20 May 1918, in *PWW*, vol. XLVIII, pp. 79–80.

[29] Wilson to Tumulty, c. 19 July 1918, in *PWW*, vol. XLIX (Princeton: Princeton University Press, 1985), p. 20.

urgent for the United States. Bliss also emphasized the strategic importance of supporting Armenia in order to curb Germany's drive from Berlin to Baghdad. "After the Russian Revolution," he observed, "Germany improved her position first in European Russia, then in Transcaucasia." The Germans had helped the Turks recapture Turkish Armenia and also parts of Russian Armenia, which the Treaty of Brest-Litovsk granted to Turkey. Beyond these territorial gains, the German–Turkish alliance threatened to invade Persia.

General Bliss clearly understood that Consul Smith's efforts on behalf of the Transcaucasian nationalities had been designed to serve American and Allied strategic interests in the Great War, although the results might incidentally assist these peoples for their own sake. He explained that

Smith's aim, however, was not solely to help the Georgians and Armenians. He was anxious to warn the Allies of the danger in the Near East, and to induce them, in the interest of the Entente itself, to utilize these Christian peoples and their potential military force by properly leading and financing them in order to prevent the Central Powers from further improving their position in the Near East and in Asia.

When Acting Secretary of State Frank L. Polk forwarded the Bliss report to London, he instructed Ambassador Page to ask the British government for its assessment of the state of affairs in the Caucasus and the measures "to preserve the cooperation of the Armenians in the Allied cause."[30] US officials thus viewed the Armenians more as an asset in winning the war than as a people worthy of support for their own sake.

Wilson continued to express sympathy for Armenians after the United States and the Allies finally defeated the Central Powers in the autumn of 1918, although Armenia now lost its strategic value for the United States. Germany's drive for hegemony from Berlin to Baghdad had failed. Pope Benedict XV asked the President to help small and oppressed Christian nationalities, particularly the Armenians, at the peace conference. On the day before Christmas 1918, after arriving in Paris, Wilson assured the Catholic Pope that

I am speaking not only for myself but also I am sure for the whole body of the American people when I say that the sufferings of no other people have appealed to them more deeply than those of the Armenians. It will certainly be one of my most cherished desires to play any part that I can in securing for that wronged and distressed people the protection of right and the complete deliverance from unjust subjection.[31]

[30] Polk to Page, 31 July 1918, in *FRUS: World War*, vol. I, pp. 891–3.
[31] Diary of Dr. Grayson, 18 Dec. 1918 and Wilson to Benedict XV, 24 Dec. 1918, in *PWW*, vol. LIII (Princeton: Princeton University Press, 1986), pp. 420, 489.

Whether Wilson and US diplomats could achieve more for Armenia at the Paris Peace Conference than they had during the war would become the next challenge for Wilsonianism. Peacemaking in 1919 would again test the limits of American power and ideology.

While expressing a favorable attitude towards Armenia, Wilson avoided any specific commitments. Various advocates of the Armenian cause wanted the United States to take on a larger responsibility. Shortly before the President's departure for Europe, Lansing forwarded an appeal to him from some Americans with missionary interests in Turkey. They urged him to support the merger of Turkish Armenia and Russian Armenia into an independent new nation.[32] In London before the opening of the peace conference, evangelical church leaders, including Baptists and Methodists, told Wilson about both their support for the League of Nations and their concern for Armenian Christians. He gave them no promises, but did reveal his own anxiety about the immense task ahead. He affirmed the importance of religion for himself "in these times of perplexity with matters so large to settle that no man can feel that his mind can compass them." Professing his dependence on God, the President said: "I think one would go crazy if he did not believe in Providence. It would be a maze without a clue. Unless there were some supreme guidance we would despair of the results of human counsel."[33]

More down to earth, British Prime Minister David Lloyd George encouraged Wilson to accept a mandate for Armenia, and possibly for Constantinople, under the League of Nations, which they both hoped to create at the peace conference. Rather than depending upon divine intercession, he thought US troops might be more useful. This would obviously allow the British to shift the burden of assisting Armenians to the Americans. Wilson, however, was reluctant to entangle the United States in territorial questions in the Old World, fearing that such intervention would tarnish America's reputation as a disinterested outsider.[34]

At the peace conference the British Prime Minister and the American President vied with each other to place the burden of assisting Armenia on someone else. Lloyd George wanted the victors to proceed with the assignment of future mandates under the League of Nations. The peacemakers anticipated the end of Turkish control in Armenia, Syria, Mesopotamia, Palestine, and Arabia. Although Lloyd George favored British mandates for vast areas of the former Ottoman Empire, he continued to look for a way to withdraw from Armenia. He did not want British

[32] Lansing to Tumulty, 22 Nov. 1918, in *PWW*, vol. LIII, p. 180.
[33] Remarks to Free Church Leaders, 28 Dec. 1918, in *PWW*, vol. LIII, p. 530.
[34] Memorandum [30 Dec. 1918], in *PWW*, vol. LIII, pp. 561–2.

troops to stay in Russian Armenia or move into Turkish Armenia. Wilson, noting that the United States had not declared war against the Ottoman Empire, thought the Allies should agree among themselves about which of them would keep troops in those parts of the former Empire that the Turks should no longer control. He did not absolutely rule out an Armenian mandate for the United States, but wanted at least to postpone this question.[35]

Armenians looked to the peace conference from the outside. American and Allied leaders refused to seat Armenian delegates, in contrast to those from several other new nations. Neither of the two Armenian delegations, one headed by Avetis Aharonian representing the Armenian Republic and the other by Boghos Nubar representing Turkish Armenians, gained official recognition in Paris. Wilson explained to Nubar that the peace conference could not accept any delegation from Armenia because it had not yet joined the family of nations as a recognized state. He insisted, however, that "this will not mean the slightest neglect of the interests of Armenia."[36]

Wilson quickly learned what Armenians wanted from the peace conference. Reminding him of their status as Christian martyrs who had suffered greatly from Turkish misrule, Nubar requested liberation for all the Armenian provinces of the former Ottoman Empire. He defined this territory generously to include a vast area from Mount Ararat to the Mediterranean, including historically Armenian Cilicia on the coast. He advocated union between these liberated areas of Turkish Armenia and the Armenian Republic to create a new nation. Before it became a fully independent democracy, he wanted the League of Nations to give a temporary mandate for the new Armenian state to one of the Great Powers. Appealing to Wilson, Nubar told him that "the great American democracy, by granting her assistance to our new State, can of all Nations, by her disinterestedness, give confidence to the Armenians about the future of their Motherland. That would be an act worthy of the great American people who joined this War for the sake of their ideals."[37] Aharonian and Nubar later presented their joint requests on behalf of Armenia to the peace conference.[38]

During the drafting of the League of Nations Covenant early in 1919, Wilson began to give more serious consideration to accepting greater

---

[35] Meetings of Council of Ten, 28 and 30 Jan. 1919, in *PWW*, vol. LIII, pp. 329–30, 369–71.

[36] Wilson to Nubar, 23 Jan. 1919, in *PWW*, vol. LIII, p. 226.

[37] Nubar to Wilson, 29 Jan. and 6 Feb. 1919, in *PWW*, vol. LIII, pp. 346, 516–18.

[38] Minutes of Council of Ten, 26 Feb. 1919, in *FRUS: The Paris Peace Conference, 1919* (Washington: US Government Printing Office, 1943), vol. III, pp. 147–57.

US responsibility for Armenia. He asked Secretary of War Newton D. Baker about the legality and wisdom of sending American troops to Constantinople and Armenia. Noting the US interest in Robert College in Constantinople and "the pitiful fortunes of the Armenians," the President expected the American people to approve the sending of a small force, which presumably would be welcomed in the occupied areas.[39] Baker discouraged this idea. As an alternative, he suggested that the United States might relieve Great Britain of some of its duties on the western front so that British troops could go to Turkey. If Wilson decided to send US troops, however, Baker wanted to restrict their mission to Turkey and Armenia, where they might protect Christians, a mission which American public opinion would most likely approve. Revealing his ignorance about the harsh conditions in those countries, especially in the mountains of Armenia, the secretary added that "they would have a pleasanter climate than is possible in the winter and spring months in France."[40]

Both Republicans and Democrats in the United States urged Wilson to support Armenia in Paris. On behalf of the American Committee for the Independence of Armenia, James Gerard and Senators Henry Cabot Lodge and John Sharp Williams sent him a resolution adopted at a New York meeting after hearing Charles Evans Hughes and William Jennings Bryan voice their concerns for the welfare of Armenia. The resolution called for "a separate and independent state" encompassing not only Russian Armenia and all of Turkish Armenia, including Cilicia, but also Persian Armenia. The resolution did not, however, indicate what means beyond diplomacy the United States should employ on Armenia's behalf. Aware of the potential costs and the difficulties involved, Wilson hesitated to make any specific American commitment to Armenia in Paris.[41]

After returning home in late February 1919, Wilson increased his rhetorical support for Armenia. Upon his arrival in Boston, he advocated the League of Nations Covenant, which he and Allied leaders had just finished drafting in Paris. He defended this new plan for collective security to preserve world peace. Alluding to Armenians, the President told his audience: "You poured out your money to help succor Armenians after they suffered. Now set up your strength so that they shall never suffer again." The League of Nations, he announced, should protect new nations such as Armenia: "Arrangements of the present peace cannot stand a generation unless they are guaranteed by the united forces of the

---

[39] Wilson to Baker, 8 Feb. 1919, in *PWW*, vol. LV (Princeton: Princeton University Press, 1986), pp. 27–8.
[40] Baker to Wilson, 11 Feb. 1919, in *PWW*, vol. LV, pp. 81–2.
[41] Gerard, Lodge, and Williams to Wilson [c. 10 Feb. 1919], Dodge to Wilson, 25 Feb. 1919, Gerard to Wilson [5 March 1919], in *PWW*, vol. LV, pp. 65–6, 265, 446.

civilized world."[42] Wilson repeated this view at a White House meeting with the Senate and House committees responsible for dealing with foreign relations.[43] Thus he used the Armenian cause to win approval for the League. He was also signaling his inclination to make a greater US commitment to post-war Armenia.

In even more explicit terms Wilson shared his emerging views about American involvement in the former Ottoman Empire at a meeting with the Democratic National Committee. He noted that the German, Austro-Hungarian, and Turkish Empires had disintegrated at the end of the war. Because not all peoples in the German colonies or in the Habsburg and Ottoman Empires were ready for self-rule, he expected the League of Nations to become the "trustee for these great areas of dismembered empires." The President now believed that the United States should accept its share of responsibility as a mandatory for Armenia and possibly Constantinople. "The whole heart of America has been engaged for Armenia," he observed. Referring to fellow Americans, he stated that "they know more about Armenia and its sufferings than they know about any other European area; we have colleges out there; we have great missionary enterprises, just as we have had Robert College in Constantinople. That is a part of the world where already American influence extends – a saving influence and an educating and an uplifting influence." Given this historic American interest, Wilson concluded that:

I am not without hope that the people of the United States would find it acceptable to go in and be the trustees of the interests of the Armenian people and see to it that the unspeakable Turk and the almost equally difficult Kurd had their necks sat on long enough to teach them manners and give the industrious and earnest people of Armenia time to develop a country which is naturally rich with possibilities.[44]

After returning to the peace conference in Paris, Wilson faced the question of mandates for Armenia and other parts of the former Ottoman Empire. Bryan, identifying himself as a member of the American Committee for the Independence of Armenia, appealed to the President to fight for justice for the Christian Armenians. Bryan thought that Armenia should encompass Cilicia, which would give the new state access to the Mediterranean. Wilson agreed, immediately responding that "my interest in Armenia is identical with your own."[45] This kind of affirmation increased the expectations that the United States would substantially

---

[42] Address in Boston, 24 Feb. 1919, in *PWW*, vol. LV, pp. 238–45.
[43] News Report [26 Feb. 1919], in *PWW*, vol. LV, pp. 268–76.
[44] Remarks to Democratic Committee, 28 Feb. 1919, in *PWW*, vol. LV, pp. 309–24.
[45] Bryan to Wilson, 19 March 1919 and Wilson to Bryan, 19 March 1919, in *PWW*, vol. LVI (Princeton: Princeton University Press, 1987), pp. 95–6.

assist the new nation. So, too, did House's statement to French Premier Georges Clemenceau and British Prime Minister Lloyd George while sitting in for the President at the peace conference. Shortly before Wilson's return, House had affirmed his belief that the United States would accept mandates for Armenia and Constantinople.[46]

Wilson and Allied leaders agreed that much of the former Ottoman empire should be severed from Turkey and placed under mandates, but found it more difficult to divide those areas among themselves. He told the Allies that he would attempt to get the American people to accept mandates for Armenia and Constantinople. Before proceeding with the division of territory and assignment of mandates, however, he wanted to send an inter-allied commission to the Near East "to find the most scientific basis possible for a settlement." Neither the British nor the French wanted this commission. They welcomed the prospect that the United States might become the mandatory for Armenia, and perhaps for other areas of Turkey, but did not want to jeopardize their own claims in the former Ottoman Empire.[47]

Clemenceau, seeking to preserve cooperation among the three Great Powers against post-war Germany, showed his willingness to make concessions on the Armenian mandate and other issues. On 14 April, he informed House that France would accept the compromise regarding the Rhineland occupation and the Anglo-American guarantee of French security. The peacemakers had negotiated this deal over the past month since Wilson had returned to Paris. In the same conversation Clemenceau also told House that if the United States became the mandatory for Armenia, France would give up its claim to Cilicia, allowing it to be included in the Armenian mandate. Clemenceau offered this concession to the United States although earlier Anglo-French agreements, which had provided for British and French spheres of influence in the Ottoman Empire, had promised Cilicia to France as part of Syria in exchange for British dominance in Mesopotamia, Palestine, and Arabia.[48] The French Premier's top priority was to keep the United States involved in maintaining the peace settlement, whether in Europe as the guarantor of French security against Germany or in the Near East as the mandatory for Armenia.

[46] House to Wilson [7 March 1919], in *PWW*, vol. LV, pp. 458–9.
[47] Diary of Dr. Grayson, 20 March 1919, Meeting of Council of Four, 20 March 1919, Diary of Vance McCormick, 22 March 1919, Memorandum of Arthur James Balfour, 23 March 1919, Memorandum, 25 March 1919, in *PWW*, vol. LVI, pp. 102–3, 116–18, 180, 203–4, 272–5.
[48] Diary of Colonel House, 14 Apr. 1919, in *PWW*, vol. LVII (Princeton: Princeton University Press, 1987), pp. 334–5.

Negotiations in Paris delayed assistance for Armenia from either the United States or the Allies. In May 1919, while the peacemakers discussed sending an inter-allied commission to the Near East, they postponed the establishment of mandates. Lloyd George urged Wilson meanwhile to send US troops into Turkish Armenia and Constantinople. The President declined, observing that "the British troops were the only ones accustomed to this kind of business, although the French had some experience. United States officers would be quite unaccustomed to it." He doubted whether any American troops were available for the assignment.[49] Even as he was anticipating US acceptance of the Armenian mandate, Wilson did not plan for costly involvement in the Near East either now or in the future. His reluctance to send a military force to Armenia revealed the limits of American power and ideology in the peacemaking.

Despite his own reservations, Wilson expected the US Senate to approve and the Turks to acquiesce in the eventual role that the United States might play in the former Ottoman Empire. He assured Clemenceau that the Senate would accept new responsibility for the United States as the mandatory for Armenia. He also thought the Turks would submit to guidance even in Turkey itself. He expressed the opinion that the Turks were "really docile people. They were all right so long as they were not put in authority. Under the guidance of a friendly power, they might prove a docile people." Clemenceau tried to warn him to anticipate a difficult task in Armenia. The President acknowledged that reports from Armenia were so appalling that he found it hard to read them. "At this very moment," he said, "the Turks are interning a great number of Armenians, many of whom are dying of hunger. I have been given some horrible details." Lloyd George urged him to publish these reports to shape American public opinion in favor of accepting the Armenian mandate. Despite Wilson's attempts to reassure them, Allied leaders obviously doubted whether the United States would undertake this potentially costly mandate, or even whether Wilson understood post-war realities in Armenia.[50]

While refusing to send US troops to Armenia and postponing a decision on the establishment of mandates, the President attempted to assure the Armenians of his good intentions. "In common with all thoughtful and humane persons," he wrote to Avetis Aharonian on 13 May,

---

[49] Meeting of Council of Four, 5 May 1919, in *PWW*, vol. LVIII (Princeton: Princeton University Press, 1987), pp. 436–8.
[50] Meeting of Council of Four, 13 May 1919, in *PWW*, vol. LIX (Princeton: Princeton University Press, 1988), pp. 87–103; Paul Mantoux, *The Deliberations of the Council of Four (March 24 – June 28, 1919)*, ed. Arthur S. Link with Manfred F. Boemeke (Princeton: Princeton University Press, 1992), vol. II, pp. 49–60.

I have learned of the sufferings of the Armenian people with the most poignant distress, and beg to assure you that if any practicable means of assisting them in their distress presented themselves at the moment, I for one would rejoice to make use of them. It adds to the tragical distress of the whole situation that for the present there seems to be no way which is not already being as far as possible followed in which to relieve the suffering which is exciting the sympathy of the whole world. I can only hope that as the processes of peace are hastened and a settlement is arrived at which can be insisted upon, that an opportunity may then promptly arise for taking effective steps to better the conditions and eventually assure the security of the people of Armenia.[51]

Wilson apparently hoped to convince the head of the Armenian Republic's delegation in Paris that he genuinely cared for the Armenian people, but that there were no "practicable means" to give them any assistance at that time. At most he offered a vague prospect of future help after an eventual peace settlement had been reached. Unless the President was being totally disingenuous, he was recognizing the inability of the United States to fulfill the Wilsonian promise. Acknowledging the limits of American power in Armenia, he also revealed the irrelevance of Wilsonianism in that country. Wilson could find no way to transform his principles into reality for that new nation during the peace conference. In this instance his ideology was inadequate for the new world order that was emerging after the Great War. Wilsonianism was not a universal solution for the world's problems.

As the American and Allied leaders considered the disposition of the former Ottoman Empire, Wilson made a qualified commitment to Armenia. On 14 May 1919, at a meeting of the Council of Four, he agreed to accept League of Nations mandates for Armenia and Constantinople, subject to approval by the Senate. He also joined with Lloyd George and Clemenceau in a tentative agreement giving the Smyrna region of Asia Minor to Greece and placing the remainder of Turkish Anatolia under mandates assigned to Italy and France. The boundaries were not yet drawn for any of these mandates. Pending that division of territory, Lloyd George and Clemenceau agreed to determine the respective British and French spheres of military occupation in the former Ottoman Empire. They assigned this task to two subordinates, Sir Henry Wilson and André Tardieu.[52]

Within a week, even these provisional understandings among the peacemakers collapsed. Anglo-French tensions erupted in the Council of Four

---

[51] Wilson to Aharonian, 13 May 1919, in *PWW*, vol. LIX, pp. 103–4.
[52] Minutes of Council of Four, 14 May 1919, in *FRUS: The Paris Peace Conference, 1919*, vol. V (Washington: US Government Printing Office, 1944), pp. 614–23; Hankey's and Mantoux's Notes, 14 May 1919, in *PWW*, vol. LIX, pp. 136–47; Mantoux, *Deliberations*, vol. II, pp. 60–73.

on 21 May. Lloyd George now proposed that the mandate for Turkish Anatolia should go to the United States, not to Italy and France. Arguing that post-war Turkey should not be divided among several Great Powers, he proposed that the mandate for all of Turkey, including Constantinople, be given to the United States, as well as the one for Armenia. This British attempt to use the United States as a wedge to reduce French influence in the Near East evoked a strong response from Clemenceau. Wilson, too, rejected the idea. Although he agreed with Lloyd George that it would be best to place Turkey under a single mandate, the President did not want it. "I must say without further delay," he asserted, "that it will be very difficult for the United States to assume the mission which you propose to it. It has no direct interests in Anatolia; it has not invested capital there. We could only accept the role that you offer us as a burden and against bitter opposition from American opinion. We desire absolutely nothing in Asia Minor. We desire only two things: agreement among the great powers and the peace of the world."[53]

Wilson eschewed additional involvement in the Near East. Apparently now more aware of the potential costs of trying to control the "docile" Turks, he preferred not to place Turkey under a mandate rather than to accept this responsibility for the United States. Yet he reaffirmed his commitment to the Armenian mandate, which he regarded as a humanitarian mission. "Americans," he explained, "have already sent missionaries, money, and relief societies to Armenia. American opinion is interested in Armenia." While Congress might approve the Armenian mandate, he doubted that it would approve one for Turkish Anatolia. Henry White, the only Republican in the American Commission to Negotiate Peace in Paris, afterward reinforced this point, warning him that Congress would probably reject a mandate for Turkey, and perhaps even for Constantinople.[54]

Lloyd George's willingness to sacrifice French interests, reneging on his own previous commitments, prevented any agreement at this time. Clemenceau felt betrayed not only over mandates for Turkey but also over spheres for British and French military occupation. The Tardieu–Wilson negotiations had failed to resolve this issue. Tardieu had attempted to get the British troops to withdraw from Syria, so that French troops could replace them, but Henry Wilson had endeavored first to alter the earlier Anglo-French division of the Ottoman Empire. The British wanted to

---

[53] Mantoux's Notes, 21 May 1919, in *PWW*, vol. LIX, p. 345; Mantoux, *Deliberations*, vol. II, p. 137.
[54] Mantoux's Notes, 21 May 1919, White to Wilson, 22 May 1919, in *PWW*, vol. LIX, pp. 345, 395–6; Mantoux, *Deliberations*, vol. II, p. 137.

reduce the French area of Syria and to enlarge their own mandate for
Mesopotamia and Palestine. Tardieu refused to negotiate boundaries,
which he regarded as the prerogative of the peace conference. An an-
gry Clemenceau brought this issue back to the Council of Four. "My
constant policy," he said, "has been to preserve the union of France
with Great Britain and with America. In order to do that I have made
greater concessions than I first would have thought possible." The French
Premier resisted any more compromises with Lloyd George, however.
President Wilson sought to deal with this territorial dispute by relegating
it to the inter-allied commission that he had earlier proposed. Under the
circumstances, Clemenceau refused to appoint French representatives
to the commission. Lloyd George also declined. The President nevertheless decided to send American representatives, Henry C. King and
Charles R. Crane, on their own to the Near East. Wilson's decision to
proceed with the King–Crane commission, along with the Anglo-French
impasse, again postponed peacemaking for the former Ottoman Empire,
and consequently for Armenia.[55]

Shortly before Wilson left Paris, he and Allied leaders briefly discussed
the future peace treaty for Turkey and the fate of Armenia. In the Council
of Four on 25 June, he told them that the US delegates who would remain in Paris could deal with these questions. He had given his views to
Lansing, House, Bliss, and White. The President wanted to sever from
Turkey the parts of the Ottoman Empire that would be placed under
League of Nations mandates, while leaving the Turks their sovereignty
in Anatolia. The treaty could require Turkey to surrender all other areas of the former Ottoman Empire. He expected Armenia, which should
include part of Cilicia, to become a separate state. Having not yet recognized the Armenian Republic, Wilson remained noncommital on the
question of whether Russian Armenia should join Turkish Armenia in
a single new nation. Nor did he know where the boundaries should be
drawn between Armenia and Turkey. Despite Wilson's expressed desire
to avoid long delay, all of these unresolved issues would postpone the
peace treaty for Turkey.[56]

[55] Meeting of Council of Four, 21 May 1919, Diary of Edith Benham, 21 May 1919,
Diary of Dr. Grayson, 22 May 1919, Diary of William Linn Westermann, 22 May 1919,
in *PWW*, vol. LIX, pp. 326–46, 369–72, 374–6; Minutes of Council of Four, 21 and
22 May 1919, in *FRUS: Paris Peace Conference*, vol. V, pp. 756–71, 807–12; Mantoux,
Deliberations, vol. II, pp. 128–40.
[56] Close to Lansing, 24 June 1919, Meeting of Council of Four, 25 June 1919, in *PWW*,
vol. LXI (Princeton: Princeton University Press, 1989), pp. 127–9, 156–7; Council
of Four Minutes, 25 June 1919, in *FRUS: The Paris Peace Conference, 1919*, vol. VI
(Washington: US Government Printing Office, 1946), pp. 675–7; Mantoux, *Deliberations*, vol. II, pp. 552–4.

As the United States and the Allies failed to resolve their own differences regarding the former Ottoman Empire, the future of Armenia remained problematic. Just before returning home from Paris, Wilson told newspaper correspondents that he personally favored American mandatories for Armenia and Constantinople. He emphasized, however, that Congress must decide whether to accept these new responsibilities. He explained that he had promised only to present this decision to the American people and Congress.[57]

After arriving in the United States, Wilson revealed his own decision to postpone the Armenian mandate. On 10 July 1919, the day he presented the Versailles treaty to the Senate, he held a press conference. One reporter asked him: "Do you expect to ask that the United States act as mandatory for Armenia?" The President answered: "Let us not go too fast. Let's get the treaty first."[58] Until the Senate approved the Versailles treaty, including the League of Nations Covenant, he did not intend to proceed with the Armenian mandate. Thus he made acceptance of this mandate conditional upon the outcome of the treaty fight. Meanwhile, Armenians could expect little assistance from the United States.

Wilson's decision to postpone consideration of the Armenian mandate, making it dependent upon the Senate's approval of the League of Nations, created a potential political problem for him. Oddly enough, he was not certain whether he could restrain the public demands for immediate US assistance to Armenia. Gerard and others in the American Committee for the Independence of Armenia urged him to take quick action to stop Turkish aggression against Armenia. Wilson assured Senator John Sharp Williams, who had joined Gerard in expressing his concern, that he would transmit their request to the peace conference. However, the President sent a very different message to Paris. Confessing his anxiety, Wilson told Lansing:

I fear that it would be most unwise to put before Congress just at this stage of its discussion of the Covenant either a proposal to promise to assume the Mandate for Armenia or a proposal to send American troops there to replace the British and assume the temporary protection of the population; and yet will our own public opinion tolerate our doing, at least our attempting, nothing?[59]

Despite pressures to act quickly, Wilson rejected US military intervention to protect the Armenians from the Turks at this time. Pending ratification of the Versailles treaty, he left them to their own fate.

---

[57] Diary of Dr. Grayson, 27 June 1919, Notes of Walter Weyl, 27 June 1919, Report by Charles Thompson, 27 June 1919, Diary of Ray Stannard Baker, 27 June 1919, in *PWW*, vol. LXI, pp. 238, 240, 246, 253.

[58] Report of a Press Conference, 10 July 1919, in *PWW*, vol. LXI, p. 424.

[59] Wilson to Williams, 2 Aug. 1919 and Wilson to Lansing, 4 Aug. 1919, in *PWW*, vol. LXII (Princeton: Princeton University Press, 1990), pp. 116, 149.

As Wilson considered what to do about Armenia, he adopted an increasingly negative view of international politics. His pessimism reflected his sensitivity to the limits of power and ideology. It was easier to proclaim principles than to implement them. While advocating American membership in the League of Nations in the future, Wilson privately expressed his growing doubts about involving the United States in any arrangement for collective security in the Old World. His reluctance to help Armenia was part of his larger reconsideration of American foreign relations. He questioned whether the United States should ever risk entanglement abroad either through the League of Nations or the French security treaty. He liked the idea of collective security better than the practice.

Wilson expressed his new doubts about American involvement in international politics with reference to the formation of League of Nations mandates. House, who represented the United States in London on the Commission on Mandates, reported to him and Lansing that the French had refused to proceed with the establishment of mandates. Although aimed at the British because of the Anglo-French impasse over the division of the former Ottoman Empire into mandates, Wilson reacted negatively against what he perceived to be a French attack on the League itself and on the new world order that it symbolized. Rather than blaming the British, he condemned the French and other Europeans who were apparently resorting to traditional diplomacy. "I will tolerate no such suggestion as this message conveys," Wilson informed Lansing with reference to House's telegram; "I will withdraw the French treaty rather than consent to see the Turkish Empire divided as spoils!" He threatened, moreover, to jettison the Versailles treaty unless Clemenceau changed his position: "I shall not press the treaty with Germany upon the Senate if this is to be the course pursued about the other treaties. The United States will certainly not enter the League of Nations to guarantee any such settlements, or any such intolerable bargains as the Greeks and Italians seem to be attempting."[60]

Wilson vented his anger primarily against France over the breakdown in the peacemaking, but other nations such as Armenia would also suffer as a consequence. Frustrated by the limits of American power and ideology, he gyrated between the extremes of advocating the principles of Wilsonianism and withdrawing the United States from the Old World. He sought either to control or to abandon international politics. Wilson did not like the compromises or the costs inherent in relations among nations. He ordered Lansing to instruct Frank L. Polk, who now headed the US delegation in Paris, to threaten Clemenceau with American rejection of

---

[60] House to Wilson and Lansing, 6 Aug. 1919 and Wilson to Lansing, 8 Aug. 1919, in *PWW*, vol. LXII, pp. 187–9, 235.

the entire peace settlement unless he agreed to proceed with the creation of mandates. The President also informed House of this important decision. When Polk raised the issue in Paris, the French Premier immediately offered to comply with Wilson's request to continue with the consideration of mandates, carefully explaining that his previous action had been directed at the British, not the Americans.[61] This resolved the immediate crisis, but not the underlying problem of sorting out the competing interests in the Near East.

While Wilson was attempting to win votes in the Senate for the Versailles treaty, which embodied his principles for the new world order, he told Lansing that he was not at all certain he wanted the United States to be involved any longer. Wilsonianism in theory and in practice were two altogether different things. In view of the continuing conflicts in Europe and the Near East, the President vehemently denounced the Old World in a statement to the Secretary of State on 20 August 1919. "When I see such conduct as this," he asserted,

when I learn of the secret treaty of Great Britain with Persia, when I find Italy and Greece arranging between themselves as to the division of western Asia Minor, and when I think of the greed and utter selfishness of it all, I am almost inclined to refuse to permit this country to be a member of the League of Nations when it is composed of such intriguers and robbers. I am disposed to throw up the whole business and get out.

Lansing noted that the President expressed these words with "considerable heat" and that "he never before spoke so emphatically."[62] Wilson was obviously frustrated by the ongoing practice of traditional politics. Experiencing the limits of American power and ideology to create a new world order, he now sensed failure. If Wilsonianism could not transform international relations, as he had promised, he seriously considered escaping from the ordeal of peacemaking.

Wilson's route of escape led him increasingly to emphasize ideals over reality. He reiterated his concern for Armenia, but rejected any type of costly US involvement in the country. The British were preparing to withdraw their troops from Transcaucasia, starting in mid-August 1919, making the question of American help a matter of urgency. He knew that the only effective way to protect the Armenians was to send US troops to the region, even before formally accepting the mandate. Yet he refused

---

[61] Wilson to Lansing, 8 Aug. 1919, Lansing to Polk, 9 Aug. 1919, Wilson to Lansing and House, 11 Aug. 1919, Polk to Wilson and Lansing, 11 Aug. 1919, in *PWW*, vol. LXII, pp. 235, 242, 256–8.
[62] Memorandum by Robert Lansing, 20 Aug. 1919, in *PWW*, vol. LXII, pp. 428–9.

to consider that option. "In the present situation of things out there," Wilson explained to Senator Williams,

it does look as if the only effectual assistance would be the assistance of an armed force to subdue those who are committing outrages more terrible, I believe, than history ever before witnessed, so heartbreaking indeed that I have found it impossible to hold my spirits steady enough to read the accounts of them. I wish with all my heart that Congress and the country could assent to our assuming the trusteeship for Armenia and going to the help of those suffering people in an effective way.[63]

The President expressed his hope that Congress might approve a significant US role in Armenia, but he had not recommended any such action. Nor was he intending to do so now. He held to his earlier decision to postpone the Armenian mandate until after the Senate approved the Versailles treaty, which he knew was problematic.[64] Pending that unlikely outcome, he refused to consider dispatching US troops to Armenia.

Wilson sought to shift responsibility for inaction to the Congress and the British, knowing that new Armenian massacres might follow the withdrawal of British troops. "It is manifestly impossible for us," he told his old friend Cleveland Dodge, a prominent member of the American Committee for the Independence of Armenia,

at any rate in the present temper of Congress, to send American troops there, much as I should like to do so, and I am making every effort, both at London and at Paris, to induce the British to change their military plans in that quarter, but I must say the outlook is not hopeful, and we are at our wits' ends what to do.[65]

This misleading statement vastly overstated the minimal efforts that Wilson and Lansing were actually making to keep British troops in Transcaucasia where they might help protect Armenians pending the establishment of an American mandatory for Armenia. They did not want even to pay the British to stay temporarily, much less to take on any direct US military role. The Secretary, moreover, privately encouraged the President never to accept the Armenian mandate, suggesting the possibility of attaching it to some other profitable mandate in the region.[66] They were obviously more concerned about shifting the responsibility for protecting Armenia to the Allies, and blaming Congress for inaction, than with actually helping the Armenians.

[63] Wilson to Williams, 12 Aug. 1919, in *PWW*, vol. LXII, pp. 259–60.
[64] For the struggle over the League of Nations, see Lloyd E. Ambrosius, *Woodrow Wilson and the American Diplomatic Tradition: The Treaty Fight in Perspective* (Cambridge: Cambridge University Press, 1987).
[65] Wilson to Dodge, 14 Aug. 1919, in *PWW*, vol. LXII, pp. 285–6.
[66] Desk Diary of Robert Lansing, 21 Aug. 1919, in *PWW*, vol. LXII, pp. 453–4.

Going through the motions of appearing to advocate immediate action to protect the Armenians, Wilson continued to postpone any US
involvement that might exact a price. When the King–Crane commission completed its trip through the Near East and submitted its report
in late August, he did not use its recommendations as the occasion for
any diplomatic initiative. While in Paris, he had postponed peacemaking
for the former Ottoman Empire to await the return of the King–Crane
commission, but did not now attach any urgency to its report.[67]

Wilson did encourage Senator Williams to seek authorization from
Congress for US troops to be sent to Armenia, but this was a charade.
The President instructed Assistant Secretary of State William Phillips to
contact the Senator about passage of such a resolution, but refrained from
a formal request to Congress. Despite Wilson's informal intervention,
Williams deleted from his draft resolution the provision approving the use
of US armed forces in Armenia. He did so, the Senator explained, because
the Senate Foreign Relations Committee was reluctant to authorize this
deployment, especially since the French seemed ready to send their own
troops to Armenia. In fact, the French were not preparing to dispatch
their troops to Russian Armenia, from which the British were evacuating.
On 23 September, Wilson expressed his disappointment to Phillips that
"Senator Williams has concluded to omit the authorization for sending
troops to Armenia. I believe that it is of the immediate humane necessity
to take energetic action and that the very existence of the Armenian people
depends upon it. I would greatly appreciate his urgent assistance in this
matter."[68] This request was exceedingly disingenuous within the context
of Wilson's earlier decision not to deploy US troops to Armenia until the
Senate had approved both the Versailles treaty and the Armenia mandate,
and of his public statements, including his speech on that very day.

On his western tour, Wilson pointed to Armenia as a prime example
of the reason for the United States to join the League of Nations. He
endeavored to exploit pro-Armenian public opinion to secure the Senate's
approval of the Versailles treaty. On 6 September, he explained what the
peacemakers in Paris had attempted to accomplish. "We wanted to see
that helpless peoples were nowhere in the world put at the mercy of
unscrupulous enemies and masters," the President said:

[67] Crane to Wilson, 31 Aug. 1919, in *PWW*, vol. LXII, pp. 607–9; Report by Crane and
King, 28 Aug. 1919, in *FRUS: The Paris Peace Conference, 1919*, vol. XII (Washington: US
Government Printing Office, 1947), pp. 751–863. See also Richard G. Hovannisian, *The
Republic of Armenia*, vol. II: *From Versailles to London, 1919–1920* (Berkeley: University
of California Press, 1982), pp. 322–34.
[68] Wilson to Phillips, 16 and 23 Sept. 1919, Phillips to Wilson, 20 and 23 Sept. 1919, in
PWW, vol. LXIII (Princeton: Princeton University Press, 1990), pp. 304–5, 423, 464.

There is one pitiful example which is in the hearts of all of us. I mean the example of Armenia. There was a Christian people, helpless, at the mercy of a Turkish government which thought it the service of God to destroy them. And at this moment, my fellow citizens, it is an open question whether the Armenian people will not, while we sit here and debate, be absolutely destroyed . . . When shall we wake up to the moral responsibility of this great occasion?

While sounding this note of urgency, Wilson qualified his own commitment to Armenia. He reiterated that "these unspeakable things [in Armenia] . . . cannot be handled until the debate is over" and the United States had ratified the peace treaty.[69] At best, this would postpone any US action to defend the Armenians to the distant future.

During his western tour, Wilson elaborated the principle of collective security, emphasizing his expectation that US involvement in the League of Nations would not be costly. In Salt Lake City on 23 September, he emphatically rejected reservations to the Versailles treaty, and particularly one that would qualify the mutual obligation of League members under Article 10 of the Covenant to defend each other against external aggression. Wilson's uncompromising stance against reservations would actually guarantee the treaty's eventual defeat in the Senate. Even if that had not been the outcome of the treaty fight, he emphasized that the United States would not be obliged by Article 10 or any other provision in the Covenant to defend other nations in the Old World. "If you want to put out a fire in Utah," the President assured his audience,

you don't send to Oklahoma for the fire engine. If you want to put out a fire in the Balkans, if you want to stamp out the smoldering flames in some part of Central Europe, you don't send to the United States for troops. The Council of the League selects the powers which are most ready, most available, most suitable, and selects them at their own consent, so that the United States would in no such circumstance conceivable be drawn in unless the flames spread to the world.

Wilson closed his Salt Lake City address, moreover, with the assurance that the United States could participate in the League of Nations to liberate foreign nations from the dangers of external aggression without the costs of bloodshed. "Are you willing to go into the great adventure of liberating hundreds of millions of human beings from a threat of foreign power?" he asked. "If you are timid, I can assure you [that] you can do it without a drop of human blood. If you are squeamish about fighting, I will tell you that you won't have to fight." Wilson's public statements, which expressed at once his own growing reluctance to involve the United States in the Old World and his global promise of collective security

---

[69] Address in Kansas City, 6 Sept. 1919, in *PWW*, vol. LXIII, p. 71; Wilson, *PPWW*, vol. VI, pp. 7–8.

without sacrifice, clearly belied his private message to Senator Williams on this same day. Although the President publicly described the plight of Armenians as an example of the importance of ratifying the peace treaty and joining the League, his Salt Lake City address called into question the sincerity of his meager private efforts to encourage Congress to initiate and pass a resolution authorizing the use of US troops in Armenia.[70]

No longer engaged in serious peacemaking, Wilson was practicing the politics of escape. Still championing the League in theory, he avoided immediate or costly US military involvement in the Near East. Even before his major stroke a few days later, he had already sacrificed any real possibility of assisting Armenia. He did not act on his own presidential authority. Nor did he attempt to reach bipartisan agreement with Republicans that might have enabled the United States to help the Armenians. Except for France, Armenia offered better prospects for bipartisan consensus than any other nation. Several Republican leaders, including Senator Lodge, had shown genuine interest in guaranteeing French security against German aggression. They also favored Armenia. Wilson, however, had steadfastly refused to seek agreement with them on behalf of either nation, subordinating specific US commitments to France or Armenia to his ideal League. Until the Republican-controlled Senate accepted the Versailles treaty exactly as he had negotiated it, he delayed consideration of both the French security treaty and the Armenian mandate. He postponed and thereby destroyed any real prospect for US action to defend either France or Armenia. He liked the idea of global collective security better than the practice.

Wilsonianism offered the universal promise of a new world order, but could not deliver it to Armenia. On 19 November 1919, the Senate rejected the Versailles treaty, thereby keeping the United States from joining the League of Nations. Anticipating that outcome, Lansing understood that an American mandatory for Armenia was also dead. "As for assuming a mandate over anything or anybody," he informed Polk, "the present state of the public mind makes the idea almost out of the question."[71] The time for effective US action had long since passed.

Wilson's failure to win the Senate's approval for the Versailles treaty, along with his poor health following his major stroke in early October, removed the United States from active participation in the peacemaking. The Allies proceeded on their own with the peace treaty for Turkey. At conferences in London and San Remo from February through April 1920, Allied Premiers and Foreign Ministers negotiated the conditions of

[70] Address in Salt Lake City, 23 Sept. 1919, in *PWW*, vol. LXIII, pp. 449–63; Wilson, *PPWW*, vol. VI, pp. 346–65.
[71] Lansing to Polk, 17 Nov. 1919, in *PWW*, vol. LXIV (Princeton: Princeton University Press, 1991), pp.54–7.

peace for the former Ottoman Empire. Meanwhile, Turkish Nationalists under Mustafa Kemal created a counter government in Ankara, asserting their dominance in Anatolia and challenging the established Turkish government, the neighboring countries, and the Allies. This resurgence of Turkish nationalism threatened the Armenians, who now experienced more massacres, and demonstrated that the Allies could not easily impose their terms on Turkey. In this context, British Prime Minister Lloyd George and French Premier Alexandre Millerand, who had replaced Clemenceau, sought to reduce their nations' obligations towards Armenia. They did not want the Armenian mandate. Nor did they want to extend the border of Turkish Armenia so far into Anatolia that the Turks would never accept it, thereby jeopardizing the new Armenian state's very existence from the outset. If the Allies could induce the United States to accept the Armenian mandate and guarantee the new Armenian–Turkish boundary, this would be the ideal solution for them as well as the Armenians.[72]

Wilson monitored the peacemaking from the sidelines, occasionally injecting himself into the process. Acting Secretary of State Frank L. Polk, who had recently returned from Paris, informed him about the London conference. He noted that US experts agreed with the Europeans that Armenia should receive less territory than its delegates had previously claimed. None of them wanted to include Cilicia in the new nation. Even within more restricted boundaries, Armenia could not protect itself from the Tartars, Kurds, and Turks. "The various races are so mixed up in North Eastern Asia Minor," Polk observed, "that it was the unanimous opinion of the experts that without an international police there would be no peace in that part of the world." If the United States were to accept the Armenian mandate, this would require a large military force. "It is obvious that the British and French cannot and will not supply the troops necessary to maintain order, and I fear there is no hope of our people feeling this obligation so strongly as to compel Congress to consent to a mandate, and appropriate the necessary money."[73] In other words, given the problems and the costs, Polk acknowledged the difficulty of fulfilling the Wilsonian promise of collective security and national self-determination for Armenia.

In March 1920, notwithstanding the complications, Wilson reaffirmed his belief that the United States should accept the Armenian mandate. He authorized Polk to convey this message to Paris. The President did not want either Great Britain or France to become the mandatory for

---

[72] Richard G. Hovannisian, *The Republic of Armenia*, vol. III: *From London to Sevres, February–August, 1920* (Berkeley: University of California Press, 1996), pp. 20–112.

[73] Polk to Wilson, 21 Feb. 1920, in *PWW*, vol. LXIV, pp. 448–50.

Armenia, or France to hold Cilicia. Instead, he asserted, "it is our clear duty to assume that mandate and I want to be left as free as possible to urge such an assumption of responsibility at the opportune time." He was not actually planning to make this request to Congress at this time, but wanted to keep open the possibility in the future.[74]

Wilson's apparent openness to accepting the Armenian mandate gave the Allies a way to resolve their difficulties at San Remo. In late April, seeking to shift the burden for protecting Armenia from themselves, they formally requested the United States to accept the Armenian mandate. The Allies also wanted Wilson to arbitrate the western boundaries of Armenia with Turkey. In effect, the President could determine the extent of territory that he wanted the United States to protect as the mandatory for Armenia. A month later Wilson finally took action on these requests. Secretary of State Bainbridge Colby, who had replaced Lansing, now advised Wilson to ask Congress to approve the Armenian mandate, noting that the Russian Bolsheviks and the Turkish Nationalists were cooperating together against the Armenians. "At the present time," Colby stressed, "when the Allied Powers admit their inability to render any assistance and solemnly appeal to us, a refusal on our part might involve further bloodshed, the ruin of the present Armenian Republic, and the opening of the way to further Bolshevism, pan-Turanism and pan-Islamism in Turkey and in Asia."[75]

Before Wilson acted in late May, James Gerard pleaded with him to help Armenia directly. The Bolsheviks were threatening the Armenian Republic, Gerard emphasized, creating the "most grave crisis in Armenian history." Without prompt US assistance for Armenia, he warned, "she will be wiped out by massacre and starvation." More was needed than the de facto diplomatic recognition that the United States had extended to the Armenian Republic on 23 April 1920. Gerard reminded Wilson, moreover, that in August 1919 several leading Republicans, including Senator Lodge, Elihu Root, and Charles Evans Hughes, had informed him that he had the authority as President to send US armed forces to Armenia. He could help Armenia without awaiting Congressional approval of a mandate.[76]

Republicans took the initiative to register their concern for Armenia. Senator Warren G. Harding, as Chairman of a subcommittee of the

---

[74] Polk to Wilson, 6, 10 and 22 March 1920 and Wilson to Polk, 8 and 17 March 1920, in *PWW*, vol. LXV (Princeton: Princeton University Press, 1992), pp. 64–5, 72–7, 91, 111–15.

[75] Swem to Colby, 20 May 1920 and Colby to Wilson, 20 May 1920, in *PWW*, vol. LXV, pp. 299, 305–12.

[76] Gerard to Wilson, 14 and 18 May 1920, in *PWW*, vol. LXV, pp. 287–8, 298.

Senate Foreign Relations Committee, prepared a resolution that the Senate passed on 13 May. This resolution expressed the hope that the Armenians would fully realize their national aspirations for freedom, endorsed the President's decision to recognize the Armenian Republic, and requested him to dispatch a warship with marines to the port of Batum for the purpose of protecting American lives and property. It articulated the Republican Senators' approval for limited American commitments overseas.[77]

When Wilson finally submitted the Armenian mandate to Congress on 24 May it was already too late. He made an eloquent appeal on behalf of Armenia, but no one expected it to affect the outcome. He saw it as "providential" that the Senate was expressing its concern for Armenia in the Harding resolution at about the same time that the San Remo conference was asking the United States to accept the Armenian mandate. "The sympathy for Armenia among our people," the President said,

has sprung from untainted conscience, pure Christian faith, and an earnest desire to see Christian people everywhere succored in their time of suffering, and lifted from their abject subjection and distress and enabled to stand upon their feet and take their place among the free nations of the world. Our recognition of the independence of Armenia will mean genuine liberty and assured happiness for her people, if we fearlessly undertake the duties of guidance and assistance in the functions of a mandatory.[78]

Wilson succeeded only in shifting the blame for inaction to Congress. On 19 March 1920, the Senate had again defeated the Versailles treaty, keeping the United States out of the League of Nations. There was no prospect that the Republican-controlled Senate would now accept a League mandate, not even for Armenia. In the politics of escape, the Allies had transferred the responsibility for protecting Armenia to the United States, and the President now shifted the burden to Congress. Senator Philander C. Knox prepared a resolution for the Foreign Relations Committee, which declined to accept a mandate. On 1 June, the Senate passed this resolution. Eleven Democrats joined the Republicans to provide a decisive margin of 52 to 23 votes for the resolution. They rejected the mandate as too costly and too entangling, despite their avowed desire to assist Armenia. This was the expected outcome in the charade of Wilsonian peacemaking.[79]

[77] Ambrosius, *Woodrow Wilson and the American Diplomatic Tradition*, pp. 257–8.
[78] Wilson, *PPWW*, vol. VI, pp. 487–91; Message, 24 May 1920, in *PWW*, vol. LXV, pp. 320–3.
[79] Ambrosius, *Woodrow Wilson and the American Diplomatic Tradition*, p. 258; Richard G. Hovannisian, *The Republic of Armenia*, vol. IV: *Between Crescent and Sickle – Partition and Sovietization* (Berkeley: University of California Press, 1996), pp. 10–28.

Wilson left the delineation of the Armenian-Turkish boundary to the experts whom Secretary Colby appointed for the task, but their actions made no difference in reality. Professor William Westermann, who had worked in 1919 as the Western Asia specialist in the American Commission to Negotiate Peace, now headed the group of experts to draw the lines. Westermann submitted their report to the State Department on 28 September 1920, outlining the proposed boundaries of "Wilsonian Armenia." On 22 November, the President belatedly approved the report and submitted it to the Allies in Paris. It changed nothing, however, because Mustafa Kemal's Nationalists had by this time conquered nearly all of Turkish Armenia.[80]

Wilson's position on the Armenian-Russian boundary also gave no real support to Armenia. On 9 August 1920, Colby submitted his famous note summarizing US policy towards the Russian Revolution. In it he reaffirmed that the Wilson administration would not recognize the Bolshevik regime. Pending the creation of a democratic government, the United States also declined to approve the dismemberment of Russia. For this reason, unlike the Allies, it had refrained from recognizing the republics of Georgia and Azerbaijan. "Finally," Colby added,

> while gladly giving recognition to the independence of Armenia, the Government of the United States has taken the position that the final determination of its boundaries must not be made without Russia's cooperation and agreement. Not only is Russia concerned because a considerable part of the territory of the new State of Armenia, when it shall be defined, formerly belonged to the Russian Empire: equally important is the fact that Armenia must have the good will and the protective friendship of Russia if it is to remain independent and free.[81]

The Russian Bolsheviks, however, were no more friendly towards Russian Armenia than the Turkish Nationalists were towards Turkish Armenia.

At this late stage in the peacemaking, US diplomats could do nothing more for Armenia than to participate in the politics of escape. The Allies wanted to place the burden on the United States, while Wilson sought to shift it either back to them or to Congress. On 22 November, the League of Nations Assembly adopted a resolution, which Paul Hymans, President of the League Council, sent to the State Department, requesting the United States to undertake the humanitarian task of stopping the hostilities in Armenia. Concerned that total inaction would leave Wilson

---

[80] Wilson to Davis, 4 July 1920 and Colby to Wilson, 20 July 1920, in *PWW*, vol. LXV, pp. 496–7, 532; Colby to Wilson, 26 Aug. and 11 Nov. 1920, Wilson to Colby, 10 Sept. and 13 Nov. 1920, in *PWW*, vol. LXVI (Princeton: Princeton University Press, 1992), pp. 65, 110, 349–50, 357. See also Hovannisian, *Republic of Armenia*, vol. IV, pp. 28–44.
[81] Colby to Wilson, 9 Aug. 1920, in *PWW*, vol. LXVI, pp. 19–25.

vulnerable to criticism, Colby advised him to offer the good offices of mediation by a personal representative. "The situation comes upon the Western nations at a time when they are distracted and almost helpless in the post-war reaction," Colby explained; "The possibilities of organizing an effective force are almost nil, and unless you exercise your moral authority it would almost seem that there is no way to avert the fate that hangs over the Armenians." The Secretary of State recommended the appointment of Henry Morgenthau as the President's personal representative. Colby was obviously more interested in appearances than results: "You might be rebuffed, and your representative might fail, but I think it would be an action on your part which the world would welcome and history approve." Wilson agreed, naming Morgenthau for this role and informing Hymans of the decision.[82]

This charade of Wilsonian peacemaking made no difference in Armenia. By the end of 1920, all of Armenia had fallen under foreign control. The Turkish Nationalists had conquered "Wilsonian Armenia" and the Russian Bolsheviks had established their dominance in the Armenian Republic. Armenia's enemies were not at all interested in Wilson's mediation when it was clear that diplomacy would not be backed by military force. When the Allies in the League once more requested US intervention, the Wilson administration again practiced the politics of escape, believing that "the responsibility and blame should be thrown back on them." Wilson's official response, on 18 January 1921, reiterated his willingness to instruct Morgenthau to proceed with his mission, but only if the Allies helped create favorable conditions for success. The message admitted that "the President has no control, and any measures which he might take or recommend in this direction would be dependent upon the hearty cooperation and support of the Allied Powers." Wilson acknowledged, moreover, a fundamental problem with the concept of collective security: "The great impediment to peaceful reconstruction in these troubled border territories, the imminent danger of new hostilities, is caused by the utter confusion between offense and defense. Unless this distinction can be clearly defined, there is not only small hope of peace, but no hope of a clear perception of who is responsible for new wars." These words were crafted as a public exoneration for Wilson's inability to help the Armenians.[83] Armenia was beyond the control of the United States,

[82] Colby to Wilson, 26, 27, 28, and 29 Nov. 1920, Davis to Wilson, 6 Dec. 1920, Davis to Hymans, 15 Dec. 1920, in *PWW*, vol. LXVI, pp. 421–3, 426–8, 436–7, 443–4, 480, 517–18.
[83] Davis to Wilson, 15 and 21 Jan. 1920, in *PWW*, vol. LXVII (Princeton: Princeton University Press, 1992), pp. 63–7, 79.

revealing the limits of American power and ideology. Wilsonianism had failed.

Arnold J. Toynbee placed this failure in the larger context of international affairs after the Great War with particular reference to Armenia, Georgia, and Azerbaijan. "In writing the epitaph of these short-lived 'successor states' of the Russian Empire in the Middle East," he observed,

it would not be wholly correct to describe the cause of death as either suicide or murder . . . In this part of the world the Supreme Council in Paris . . . were not in a position to exercise effective power, and by attempting nevertheless to make a show of authority they committed both a moral and a political blunder. By supporting the 'Whites' against the 'Reds' in Russia and the Greeks against the Turkish Nationalists in Anatolia, they aroused a fury of opposition which they could not control; and by encouraging the inexperienced and unorganized Transcaucasian Republics to look to them for a guidance and a protection which they had no intention of giving at any sacrifice to themselves, they deterred them from coming to terms before it was too late with the two locally dominant Powers, and merely exposed them to reprisals as satellites of Turkey's and Russia's most dangerous enemies.[84]

Felix Willoughby Smith had recognized this crucial point earlier. While deeply involved in seeking to convince the Wilson administration to give more help to the Armenians and other peoples in Transcaucasia during the war, he had understood that meager assistance would not suffice and might actually convey the wrong message. On 7 January 1918, the US Consul in Tiflis had candidly advised officials in the State Department: "If we are not to give aid to the Caucasus, we should clear out, giving local Christians notice, so that they can come to an understanding with the Ottomans."[85]

Richard G. Hovannisian appreciated this insight, notwithstanding the virtual impossibility for the Armenians to pursue the unthinkable alternative to dependence on the Allies and the United States – i.e. accommodation with Turkey. "In retrospect," he concluded,

it is clear that Armenia should have probed every available avenue for an understanding with her bruised neighbor to the west; but in reality the obstacles were too many and too great. Not only was the Turk despised as the historic oppressor and of late the butcher of half the nation, but on a more objective plane, the Armenian question had become an international issue, its solution seemingly dependent more on decisions reached in Europe than in either Constantinople or Erevan.[86]

[84] Arnold J. Toynbee, *Survey of International Affairs, 1920–1923* (London: Oxford University Press, 1925), pp. 373–4.
[85] Hovannisian, *Armenia on the Road to Independence*, p. 118.
[86] Hovannisian, *Republic of Armenia*, vol. I, p. 417.

Tragically, Armenia was caught between its nearby enemies who were intent on destroying it and its distant friends who were equally intent on avoiding the costs of defending it.

Scholars who have touted Wilsonianism as the universal ideology for a new world order have missed this important point about the limits of American power. It is perhaps significant that Tony Smith, Amos Perlmutter, and Frank Ninkovich[87] left Armenia out of their triumphalist accounts of the Wilsonian century, for it would not fit well. The Armenian experience after the First World War offers a different perspective on power and ideology in American diplomatic history, questioning the triumphalism of some recent interpretations. Wilson's inability to implement his own principles in Armenia suggests that Wilsonianism cannot provide the universal foundation for a new world order. With limited power, the United States cannot fulfill the Wilsonian promise everywhere.

---

[87] Tony Smith, *America's Mission: The United States and the Worldwide Struggle for Democracy in the Twentieth Century* (Princeton: Princeton University Press, 1994); Amos Perlmutter, *Making the World Safe for Democracy: A Century of Wilsonianism and Its Totalitarian Challengers* (Chapel Hill: University of North Carolina Press, 1997); and Frank Ninkovich, *The Wilsonian Century: US Foreign Policy since 1900* (Chicago: University of Chicago Press, 1999).

6 American diplomatic correspondence in the age of mass murder: the Armenian Genocide in the US archives

Rouben Paul Adalian

The world conflict ignited in August 1914 did not see the immediate departure of the French, British, and Russian Ambassadors in Constantinople. The Triple Entente was at war only against Germany and Austria-Hungary. Its envoys vigorously appealed to the Ottoman Empire to remain neutral. Secretly allied with Germany, the Young Turk government waited to enter the conflict until the end of October. Whether the fate of the Armenians in the Ottoman Empire was sealed in those intervening three months is still debated.[1] What is indisputable is the fact that in November 1914 only one major Western country not aligned with Germany remained with representation at the Sublime Porte, namely the United States of America.

Unlike the European powers, each a colonial empire vying for greater influence in Turkey, the United States had not vested political capital in the Armenian Question. If anything, the United States had stood on the sidelines of the Armenian issue and been engaged only with matters related to humanitarian assistance in response to earlier crises. The United States entertained no territorial ambitions in the Near East. Compared to the level of European involvement in the commercial and financial affairs of the Turkish Empire, US business interests were modest. The US government viewed the entire region as one vast economic space open for American commerce. This too contrasted with European economic

---

[1] See Rouben Paul Adalian, "Comparative Policy and Differential Practice in the Treatment of Minorities in Wartime: the United States Archival Evidence on the Armenians and Greeks in the Ottoman Empire," *Journal of Genocide Research* 3:1 (2001), pp. 31–48; Vahakn N. Dadrian, "The Secret Young-Turk Ittihadist Conference and the Decision for the World War I Genocide of the Armenians," *Holocaust and Genocide Studies* 7:2 (1993), pp. 173–201; Stephan H. Astourian, "Genocide Process in Perspective: Reflections on the Armeno-Turkish Polarization," in Richard G. Hovannisian, ed., *The Armenian Genocide in Perspective: History, Politics, Ethics* (New York: St. Martin's Press, 1992), pp. 53–79; Gerard Libaridian, "The Ultimate Repression: The Genocide of the Armenians, 1915–1917," in Isidor Wallimann and Michael N. Dobkowski, eds., *Genocide and the Modern Age: Etiology and Case Studies of Mass Death* (Westport, Conn.: Greenwood Press, 1987), pp. 203–35; Robert Melson, *Revolution and Genocide: On the Origins of the Armenian Genocide and the Holocaust* (Chicago and London: The University of Chicago Press, 1992).

policies and practices in the Ottoman Empire with investments concentrated in certain geographic areas or specific fields of commercial endeavor. European countries required government concessions and treaty relations, through so-called Capitulations, in order to maintain positions of advantage acquired over the course of the nineteenth and earlier centuries. In comparison the United States enjoyed no special privileges.[2]

The Capitulations shaped the Ottoman state's external trade relations, a vestige of the older imperial order when Ottoman might held greater sway over maritime commerce. The tectonic shift of economic power in favor of Western Europe in the age of industrial capital, however, had resulted in a form of financial bondage. A characteristic of the modern relations between lending and borrowing economies, the introduction of such an unfavorable imbalance threatened notions of sovereignty. Breaking out of this dependency constituted one of the central tenets of the Young Turk program. Doing so involved more than redefining economic and trade policy, for the Ottoman social structure that had been constructed to accommodate a multi-ethnic population broadly interfaced with Western economic interests. A reversal of course in the financial flows of the Ottoman economy, therefore, also required the dismantling of the domestic agencies that perpetuated and benefited from the pre-existing system. Such agencies primarily were represented by minorities. The global conflict, most particularly the manner in which it aligned the antagonists, created a window of opportunity to address this issue. At a time of increasing political tensions in the relations between the Young Turk government and various minorities, notably the Armenians, the chance to forge ahead created the framework to consider the application of the wealth of minorities whose continued inclusion in the constitution of the Ottoman state was under reconsideration by those in power. The exigencies of war and the urgencies of financial infusions are constants on the minds of policy-makers. The convergence of these extreme demands during the First World War prepared the ground for the adoption of radical solutions. The seizure of assets construed as wartime necessity paired with revolutionary fervor aiming to overturn some, if not all, parts of the prevailing order revealed how far the Young Turks were prepared to go in the implementation of wholesale measures.

The specific nature of American relations with the Ottoman Empire extended to the United States Embassy in Constantinople the advantage of speaking on behalf of a country whose policies presented no

---

[2] See Joseph L. Grabill, *Protestant Diplomacy and the Near East: Missionary Influence on American Policy, 1810–1927* (Minneapolis: University of Minnesota Press, 1971), pp. 35–105.

threat to the sovereignty and the territorial integrity of the Turkish state. The remoteness of the United States and its absence of involvement in European balance-of-power contests explain this state of affairs. Therefore, United States neutrality in the world conflict guaranteed the continuance of an American diplomatic presence in the Ottoman Empire, at least until April 1917. This presence also meant that US officials enjoyed access to Ottoman authorities and exercised functions protected by immunities that kept them informed of internal developments in the Turkish state.[3]

The Great War made England, France, and Russia external and hostile observers of the Ottoman state. Only Germany, Austria-Hungary, and the United States remained as the main internal observers.[4] Of the three, the first two were bound by military considerations that diminished compunctions concerning the lawful treatment of civil society. The overriding objectives of total mobilization and combat advantage had already induced early in the war an attitude licensing the unfettered treatment of civilian populations.[5] The attitude of American diplomatic officials remained the single point of contrast where the consideration of a government's treatment of its citizenry continued to define the central viewpoint. Accordingly, while the German and Austrian records of the period provide considerable factual information about the condition of the Armenians in the Ottoman Empire during the First World War, the American record of the period presents a collective concern with the human disaster that began to unfold soon after the Ottomans entered the conflict.

The vast portion of the US archival documentation on the Armenians resides in the Department of State files.[6] That the Armenians were

[3] For narrative accounts of the US envoy's meetings with state officials, see Henry Morgenthau, *Ambassador Morgenthau's Story* (Garden City, N.Y.: Doubleday, Page, & Company, 1918).
[4] Vahakn N. Dadrian, "Documentation of the Armenian Genocide in German and Austrian Sources," in Israel W. Charny, ed., *Genocide: A Critical Bibliographic Review*, vol. III (New Brunswick: Transaction Publishers, 1994), pp. 77–125; Artem Ohandjanian, ed., *The Armenian Genocide: Documentation*, vol. II (Munich: Institut für Armenische Fragen, 1988), and *Österreich-Armenien 1872–1936: Faksimilesammlung Diplomatischer Aktenstücke*, 12 vols. (Vienna: Ohandjanian Ergenverlag 1995); Richard G. Hovannisian, *The Armenian Holocaust: A Bibliography Relating to the Deportations, Massacres, and Dispersion of the Armenian People, 1915–1923* (Cambridge, Mass.: Armenian Heritage Press, 1978);
[5] Jay Winter and Blaine Baggett, *The Great War and the Shaping of the 20th Century* (New York: Penguin Books, 1996); see section on "The Cultivation of Hatred: Total War and Genocide," pp. 144–53.
[6] Rouben Paul Adalian, compiler and ed., *The Armenian Genocide in the US Archives, 1915–1918* (microfiche publication) (Alexandria, Va.: Chadwyck-Healey Inc., 1991–3), and *Guide to the Armenian Genocide in the US Archives, 1915–1918* (Alexandria, Va.: Chadwyck-Healey Inc., 1994). The microfiche collection contains 37,000 pages of material from the

residents of a foreign country is only a partial explanation for the location of these files. A century of contacts between Armenians and Americans due to missionary activities at first, and commercial relations later, as well as Armenian emigration to the United States also explains why the Department of State was well informed about the Armenians in Turkey. The restrictions of wartime communication were an additional explanation, when delivery of correspondence ceased being a private concern handled by the postal office and the services expected from an embassy increased to include the transmission of mail.[7]

Ambassador Henry Morgenthau

All these administrative reasons, however, do not entirely explain why the Department of State came to receive such a significant body of information on the Armenians. The real explanation lies elsewhere. Mainly it has to do with the diplomatic personnel assigned to Turkey. Among them, the US Ambassador by far exercised the most crucial role, constrained also to the degree that the circumstances of war, and American neutrality, placed the American emissary in an especially delicate position. Another Ambassador might have construed a strict definition of neutrality as a form of disinterest and a reason to maintain distance. That did not turn out to be the case, as the individual happened to be a personality in his own right who had been designated by the President as Ambassador for his role as a major supporter in the 1911 presidential election. The close relationship between Ambassador Henry Morgenthau and President Woodrow Wilson, therefore, is a much more important explanation for the conduct of the Ambassador and of the liberties he took to express his views on matters of policy and diplomacy, with both his hosts and his employers. Lastly, the character of the Ambassador must be given consideration as well, as he rarely refrained from forcefully communicating

United States National Archives and the Library of Congress spanning the years 1910 to 1929. The documents referenced in this chapter constitute part of the collection. See also the special issue of the *Armenian Review* 37:1 (1984), "The Genocide of the Armenian People," especially "Documents: the State Department File," pp. 60–145, and "Documents: the US Inquiry," pp. 164–202. On the subject of documentation, see Rouben Adalian, "Source, Evidence, and Authority: Documenting the Armenian Genocide Against the Background of Denial," in Roger W. Smith, ed., *Genocide: Essays Toward Understanding, Early-Warning, and Prevention* (Williamsburg: Association of Genocide Scholars, 1999), pp. 67–77.

[7] For a brief study of the stratigraphy of the American documentation, see Rouben Paul Adalian, "Le Génocide des Arméniens dans les archives américains," in Jack Lang, preface to Hrayr Henry Ayvazian *et al.*, eds., *Actualité du génocide des Arméniens* (Paris: Edipol, 1999), 93–107.

the message required by the circumstances and obligations of the day.[8] His cables to the State Department reveal his growing sense of alarm with the rapid deterioration of the status and welfare of the Armenians. His succinct summations of the Armenian situation stressed the gravity of the policies being implemented.

In one of his first critical dispatches to the Department of State, dated 30 April 1915, Morgenthau wrote: "Continued report of persecutions, plunder and massacres of Armenians in certain parts of empire had been received."[9] This was followed by an 18 June dispatch reporting back to the Department the Ottoman response to his delivery of the 24 May joint note issued by England, France, and Russia, accusing the Young Turk government of "crimes against civilization and humanity," which Morgenthau stated that he "communicated on June third to the Grand Vizier who expressed regret at being held personally responsible and resentment at attempted interference by foreign governments with the sovereign rights of the Turkish government over their Armenian subjects."[10] He concluded the message by saying: "Meanwhile persecution against Armenians increasing in severity."[11] On 10 July, he reported: "Persecution of Armenians assuming unprecedented proportions. Reports from widely scattered districts indicate systematic attempt to uproot peaceful Armenian populations and through arbitrary arrests, terrible tortures, wholesale expulsions and deportations from one end of the Empire to the other accompanied by frequent instances of rape, pillage, and murder, turning into massacres, to bring destruction and destitution [upon] them."[12]

A week later, on 16 July, Morgenthau communicated his personal indictment: "Deportation of an excess against peaceful Armenians is increasing and from harrowing reports of eye witnesses it appears that a campaign of race extermination is in progress under a pretext of reprisal against rebellion."[13] By 3 September, Morgenthau no longer spoke of persecution, as even the question of what appeared to be a policy of wholesale decimation was resolved in his mind and only the pace of implementation was news: "Destruction of Armenian race in Turkey is progressing rapidly."[14] Even the end result had become predictable as described in his dispatch of 24 September: "Hundreds of thousands many of whom were prosperous graduates stripped of all their belongings some even of the clothing they were wearing and are in the fields without shelter and

[8] For biographical information on the Ambassador, see Henry Morgenthau III, *Mostly Morgenthaus: A Family History* (New York: Ticknor and Fields, 1991), pp. 55–209.
[9] Record Group 59 (hereinafter "RG"), Records of the Department of State, 867.4016/59.
[10] RG59, 867.4016/70.   [11] Ibid.   [12] RG59, 867.4016/74.
[13] RG59, 867.4016/76.   [14] RG59, 867.4016/117.

will die of hunger, fatigue, exposure and disease unless help is immediately and systematically extended before they are exposed to the severity of winter."[15] By 4 October, he was more pessimistic: "Several hundred thousand Armenians have already been destroyed or so placed that their destruction is inevitable. Armenian quarters of towns and villages where they lived have been entirely evacuated . . . The injustice, grief, poverty, starvation, resulting therefrom are terrible."[16]

The evolution of Morgenthau's vocabulary in his cables to the Department of State captured the brutality of what effectively characterized the process of implementing a policy of genocide. The early descriptions relied on terminology reminiscent of the episodes of orchestrated violence that the diplomatic community in Constantinople had grown accustomed to reporting about the Armenians. In his 25 May cable Morgenthau had summarized for the Department the rapidly deteriorating situation "as a markedly unfavorable turn by reason of the War."[17] Speaking of the Armenians, he added that "the recollection of the Adana Massacre of 1909 is still fresh in their minds" and a contributive cause to the "mutual fear" between Armenians and the Young Turk government. The cables describing the persecutions, inclusive of massacre and plunder, bore the hallmarks of the seeming recurrence of behavior typified by the selective targeting of specific locales or groups of Armenians.

Morgenthau's 25 May cable also reported the early actions of the Ottoman government against places like Van and Zeitun with compact concentrations of Armenians. Taking into account their history of organized resistance, the Ambassador was prepared to give credence to official explanations of insurrection, evasion of the draft, and desertion as causes for reprisals. It was not long, however, before he lost confidence in the government's excuses for its violent conduct. By midsummer (26 July) he was certain that "the measures . . . are being enforced against the Armenian population in different parts of the Ottoman Empire."[18] On 11 August, he reported: "Armenian population is fast being swept from Ada Bazaar and Izmit. Bardizag, some fifty miles from Constantinople, has been lately threatened . . .";[19] on 3 September "massacre reported at Angora and Broussa."[20] By this point he regularly associated deportations with destruction and the host of mortifying hardships resulting from exposure, including starvation and disease. He also had abandoned explaining to the Department that the geography of the last-named cities could not in any shape or form be connected with the dangers of the warfront, or anything having to do with internal security, as they were

[15] RG59, 867.4016/145.   [16] RG59, 867.4016/159.   [17] RG59, 867.4016/71.
[18] RG59, 867.4016/105.   [19] RG59, 867.4016/90.   [20] RG59, 867.4016/117.

located in north-west Anatolia, the safest region of the Empire. The absence of connection between the government's anti-Armenian policies and the progress of the war became so thoroughly subsumed that it did not even receive mention. By August, the Allied landing at Gallipoli, started in April, was completely stalled, and the Russian army, after its initial advance in the first half of the year, had retreated pretty much to the pre-war borders in the face of an Ottoman counter-offensive.

Morgenthau no longer saw any relationship between war and genocide worth taking notice of. Once the engine of extermination was set in motion, the only question remaining was its timetable. In this context his choice of words was even more striking. Strict abidance with neutrality was abundantly evident by the absence in Morgenthau's cables of any discussion of the war and especially anything having to do with military matters at a time when the situation at the front was the only headline news for more than four years. A reading of the dispatches reveals his singular usage of the word "campaign" in relation to the expression "race extermination," which he coined. This example provides further insight into the deliberate and judicious usage of vocabulary across all the diplomatic correspondence carried out by US officials, accuracy of communication and information being all the more critical for the proper exercise of national policy and official responsibility during a time of global conflict.

Ambassador Abram I. Elkus

Henry Morgenthau commands the central portion of the US record on the reportage about the atrocities committed in the Ottoman Empire since the most ferocious phase of the anti-Armenian policies in the spring and summer of 1915 coincided with his tenure as US Ambassador. Yet the fact remains that two American Ambassadors were assigned to the Sublime Porte during the First World War and Abram Elkus succeeded Morgenthau in August 1916. His role in Armenian affairs has not received as much attention. Elkus served less than a year, and returned home in April 1917 as the Ottomans broke relations with the United States when it finally declared war on Germany; nor did he publish anything autobiographical. By the time Elkus arrived in Constantinople the deportations had run their course, and it may be thought that he would be shouldering a less strenuous assignment. As it happened, Elkus became, if anything, an even more caustic critic of the Young Turk government than Morgenthau. He was unreserved in his expressions of indignation at the constant interference of the government in the delivery of humanitarian assistance. Morgenthau's more frequently quoted disapprovals of the

Young Turk regime seem mild in comparison. Elkus's main task during his brief stay in Turkey turned out to be the administering of relief aid, a much more difficult proposition than he undoubtedly expected and one which regularly tested his patience as Turkish officials frequently impeded and complicated its delivery.

Elkus cabled on 23 November 1916 that it was only after "prolonged and difficult negotiation Embassy obtained consent of Turkish Government to the importation free of duty and requisition of food supplies to be consigned to our Consul General at Beirut and distributed conjointly by Beirut Chapter of American Red Cross and Red Crescent to the starving and destitute inhabitants of Syria and the Lebanon."[21] On 1 December, reporting on his personal interview with the Ottoman Minister for Foreign Affairs, he relayed to the Department that, apart from conveying his grievances to the government over its "unnecessary interference with . . . humane efforts," he "[s]tated that if Turkish officials do not wish aid to their starving and dying people who continuously beg Embassy for it, officials should frankly say so and then American Government could act upon such inhumane action as it saw fit."[22] He knew well enough the consequences of such policy as he makes mention on 5 December of "fifty thousand deported starving helplessly east, west, south of Aleppo," adding: "Pressure to embrace Islam continues in interior especially outside our relief centers."[23]

No piece of communication, however, captures Elkus's sense of outrage more forcefully than his 9 February 1917 cable, which encapsulated the full range of deceit and deadly obstruction practiced by Young Turk officials in the course of their exchanges with the American diplomats. It was triggered by false charges brought by the government against the American Consul stationed in Harput accusing him of having engaged in the improper conduct of purveying journalistic propaganda abroad:

This whole question could probably be allowed to gradually sink into oblivion were it not for the fact that the Ottoman military authorities have requested the Foreign Office to make representations to this Embassy censoring numerous telegrams which Mr. Davis forwards in replies to inquiries from Armenians in the United States, sent through the Department, about their relatives in the Harpoot district. The Foreign Office has presented this matter to the Embassy and has pointed out that such action on the part of the Consul at Harpoot is objectionable on the grounds that he is interfering with a purely domestic matter, and is acting on behalf of Ottoman subjects both in Turkey and in the United States without knowledge or consent of the Ottoman Government. It is further represented to the Embassy that should Ottoman subjects living in America desire to obtain news of their relatives in Turkey, they have only to apply to the Ottoman

[21] RG59, 867.48/475.   [22] RG59, 367.11/1480.   [23] RG59, 867.48/487.

Embassy in Washington or to the Ottoman consular offices in New York and elsewhere.

This latter claim is entirely specious as the said Ottoman officials in the United States experience very great difficulty in communicating with their home government, and presuming that they would really endeavor to comply with the requests made to them, which is doubtful, they could only forward inquiries regularly through the Department of State and this Embassy.

Besides, a large number of the Armenians in the United States, as well as their relatives and friends in Turkey about whom they inquire, are naturalized American citizens, and consequently entitled, from our point of view, to all possible assistance from the American representatives in Turkey, even although their acquired American citizenship is not recognized by the Ottoman Government. Furthermore, this attitude of the Sublime Porte is a clear indication of its desire that Ottoman subjects should in no way be aided directly by foreigners. Even if its consent to the extension of pecuniary or other relief to Ottoman subjects has in some cases been rather grudgingly granted, nevertheless, as has often been reported to the Department, the general official attitude of the Ottoman Government now is that such needy Ottoman subjects should rather go unrelieved than that they should look to outside sources of help, administered through channels which are not entirely under Turkish governmental control.[24]

The US consular corps in the Near East

As Ambassadors Morgenthau and Elkus were mostly confined to Constantinople during the war years, the question remains: how did they know so much about the Armenian situation in the Ottoman Empire? Also, why did they feel themselves sufficiently well informed to make the kind of unqualified assertions that they communicated to the Department of State and even to the Young Turk government?

There were fundamentally two reasons for this, or two avenues of knowledge. The network of consular offices located in key cities of the Ottoman Empire served as the Ambassadors' primary source of information. The American missionary stations in many of Turkey's larger urban centers provided the second source of information. The American public at the time was under the impression that missionaries constituted the main eyewitnesses to the atrocities, and historians too have worked under the same impression, for the reason that, as private citizens, the missionaries were at liberty to communicate their account of events, published in books, journals, and newspapers, which became the main source of knowledge on the Armenian Genocide.

The Department of State records (which remained classified until the 1960s), however, reveal the contrary. The missionaries' reports were only

[24] RG59, 867.4016/313.

supplementary to the flow of information developed by the Consuls. The cover letters attached by the Ambassadors to all the consular reports themselves document the influx. Morgenthau wrote to the Department on 11 August 1915: "Turkish anti-Armenian activities continue unabated reports of which you will receive copies are constantly received from our consuls and others of horrors to which large numbers of innocent and helpless people of this race are being subjected."[25]

A sampling of these cover letters gives ample proof of the method by which a mass of documentation accumulated in the Department of State files on the treatment of the Armenians in the Ottoman Empire. They outline the course of events from start to finish. On 21 July 1915, Morgenthau forwarded the earliest detailed account obtained by the embassy: "I have the honor to transmit herewith two copies of a report received from the American Consul General at Beirut relative to what has been going on in the Zeitoon region of Asiatic Turkey."[26] On 26 July, he transmitted "a copy of a despatch from the American Consul at Trebizond, dated June 18th, in which he gives an account of the commencement of the application at that place of the measures of deportation."[27] On 23 August, he informed Washington that "Jackson telegraphs massacres of Armenians at Ourfa. Edelman[,] who is there[,] telegraphs that belligerents[,] missionaries . . . are safe."[28] On 21 September, Morgenthau forwarded two separate reports from distant corners of the Empire. The first of these started: "I have the honor to enclose herewith for the information of the Department copy of a despatch dated September 1, 1915, from the American Consul at Bagdad, relative to the Armenian arrests and deportations of that place."[29] The second began: "I have the honor to enclose herewith for the information of the Department copy of a despatch, dated September 11, 1915, which this Embassy received from the American Consul at Mersine, relative to the deportation of the Armenians in that district."[30]

The frequency of the reports also alerted the Embassy and the Department of the sudden crisis, not to mention the rapidity with which the Young Turk government proceeded with its policies. The Consul in Trebizond wrote directly to the Secretary of State on 2 July, 1915: "I have the honor to enclose for the information of the Department copies of despatches sent to the Embassy dated June 28th, 30th, July 3rd, 7th,

[25] RG59, 867/4016/90.   [26] RG59, 867.4016/104.
[27] RG59, 867.4016/105.   [28] RG59, 367.11/712.   [29] RG59, 867.4016/192.
[30] RG59, 867.4016/193. Variant spellings of Mersin include Mersine and Mersina. Presently renamed İçel. The contemporary name of other consular cities include: Trebizond = Trabzon; Constantinople = Istanbul; Adrianople = Edirne; Smyrna = Izmir; Harput or Harpoot = Elazig; Alexandretta = Iskenderun.

and 10th regarding the deportation of the Armenian population of Trebizond and vicinity to the interior."[31]

The staff at the US Embassy in Constantinople may not have been
large. The consular corps assigned to Turkey, however, was composed
of a very respectable number of diplomats. They included: Gabriel
Bie Ravndal, Consul-General, Constantinople; George Horton, Consul-
General, Smyrna; Leland B. Morris, Vice-Consul, Smyrna; Charles E.
Allen, Consular Agent, Adrianople; Edward I. Nathan, Consul, Mersin;
Colden A. Brown, Consular Agent, Alexandretta; Oscar S. Heizer, Con-
sul, Trebizond; W. Peter, Consular Agent, Samsun; Leslie A. Davis,
Consul, Harput; Jesse B. Jackson, Consul, Aleppo; George W. Young,
Consular Agent, Damascus; W. Stanley Hollis, Consul-General, Beirut;
Ralph F. Chesbrough, Vice-Consul, Beirut; Otis A. Glazebrook, Consul,
Jerusalem; Theodore Struve, Consul, Haifa; Charles F. Brissel, Consul,
Baghdad; and Samuel Edelman, Vice-Consul, originally from the consulate in Jerusalem and re-assigned to Aleppo in May and June 1915,
apparently to further investigate and substantiate Jackson's reports on
the developing crisis, and whence he also ended up in Urfa. To the consular list, Hoffman Philip, Chargé d'Affaires at the American Embassy,
Constantinople, must be added, as he also maintained vigorous correspondence with the Department, especially in the months intervening
between Morgenthau's departure and Elkus's arrival.

This contingent in turn was supported by a penumbra of embassies and
consulates in countries adjacent to the Ottoman Empire. Although the
communications from the surrounding stations addressed mostly problems and challenges of relief work, nevertheless they augment the documentation on the fate of the Armenians. Among the Foreign Service officers and their locations were: Paul Knabenshue – American Diplomatic
Agency, Cairo, Egypt; Arthur Garrels – consulate in Alexandria, Egypt;
Jon E. Kehl – consulate in Salonika, Greece; John H. Roy – consulate
in Odessa, Russia; David R. Francis – consulate in Petrograd, Russia;
and Felix Willoughby Smith – consulate in Tiflis, Russia (current Tbilisi,
Georgia). It ought to be noted that among other US diplomatic commu-
nicants, in relation to Armenian matters, were Ambassadors William G.
Sharp in Paris, Peter A. Jay in Rome, and Walter Hines Page in London.
Lastly, the American Legations in Berne, Switzerland, and Teheran, Iran,
forwarded information on the Armenians as well.

After the break in relations with the Ottoman government, the State
Department reassigned to the region some of the Consuls from Turkey.
The decision contributed to preserving considerable continuity in the

---

[31] RG59, 867.4016/114.

American record as these career officers brought years of experience to their observation of ongoing events. George Horton was relocated to Salonika across the Aegean Sea, and returned to Smyrna after the end of the war only to witness the destruction of the city in 1922. Jesse Jackson returned to Aleppo after the end of the war and resumed his efforts to assist the Armenians. Oscar Heizer was in Baghdad during the British occupation.

A cartography of the consulates

The location of the American consulates also factored as an element in both the qualitative and quantitative growth of information obtained by the embassy in Constantinople. The consulates were situated in the principal trading ports of the Ottoman Empire. By virtue of their commercial importance, these towns and cities were also some of the major centers of Armenian demographic concentration. This combination of an Armenian population and an American presence signified that every Consul was in a position to gauge closely the political and the economic consequences of policies stemming from the center.

More specifically, the consulates dotted two distinct lines of contact with the Armenians. The first set of consulates – Trebizond, Samsun, Adrianople, Smyrna, Mersin, and Alexandretta – established an external perimeter encircling the Anatolian mainland from the Black Sea, to the Aegean, and the Mediterranean. With the exception of Adrianople, all were coastal cities, with Constantinople included among them. Adrianople was inland. Its location at the western extremity of the Ottoman state, at the farthest corner of its European quadrant, connected the entire northern perimeter.[32]

Constantinople was situated at the western reach of the Ottoman Empire, and was physically in Europe. The string of consulates along the perimeter actually placed it at the center of a circle. This geographical relationship, as much as organizational hierarchy, defined the directional delivery of information from the periphery to the center. The geographic equation bore two additional attributes of political importance. It provided the embassy a panoramic view of the Ottoman expanse, as well as independent confirmation on the course of domestic policies with

---

[32] For sample documents arranged from a geographic perspective see Viscount Bryce, ed., Arnold Toynbee, compiler, *The Treatment of Armenians in the Ottoman Empire, 1915–1916: Documents Presented to Viscount Grey of Fallodon, by Viscount Bryce* (London: His Majesty's Stationery Office; Miscellaneous no. 31, 1916); and Ara Sarafian, ed., *United States Official Documents on the Armenian Genocide*, 3 vols. (Watertown, Mass.: Armenian Review, 1993, 1994, 1995).

Empire-wide consequences. The consulates were too distant from each other to be in any meaningful contact and wartime restrictions further hampered communication. As a result, the reportage from the consulates had a distinctly independent character, each providing the embassy its own unique view of conditions within its respective district. Edward Nathan, Consul in Mersin, wrote on 7 August 1915:

"two days ago an order was received here for the immediate deportation of the entire Armenian population of Mersina consisting of about 1800 souls. Yesterday nearly three hundred persons were sent to Adana and to-day many more have been ordered to be ready to leave."[33]

US Consul Leslie Davis wrote to Morgenthau on 11 July 1915, from Harput:

On July 1st a great many people left and on July 3rd several thousand more started from here. Others left on subsequent days. There is no way of obtaining figures but many thousands have already left. The departure of those living in Harpout was postponed, however, and many women and children were allowed to remain temporarily. People began to hope that the worst was over and that those who remained might be left alone. Now it has been announced by the public crier that on Tuesday, July 13, every Armenian <u>without exception</u>, must go.[34]

US Consul Oscar Heizer submitted a report on 28 July 1915, from Trebizond, detailing the deportation of the Armenians from the city:

On Saturday, June 26th, the proclamation regarding the deportation of all Armenians was posted in the streets. On Thursday, July 1st, all the streets were guarded by gendarmes with fixed bayonets, and the work of driving the Armenians from their homes began. Groups of men, women and children with loads and bundles on their backs were collected in a short cross street near the Consulate and when a hundred or so had been gathered they were driven past the consulate on the road toward Gumushhane and Erzingan in the heat and dust by the gendarmes with fixed bayonets. They were held outside the city until a group of about 2000 were collected then sent on toward Gumushhane. Three such groups making about 6000 were sent from there during the first three days and the smaller groups from Trebizond and the vicinity sent later amounted to about 4000 more. The weeping and wailing of the women and children was most heartrending. Some of these people were from wealthy and refined circles. Some were accustomed to luxury and ease. There were clergymen, merchants, bankers, lawyers, mechanics, tailors and men from every walk of life.[35]

The net result for the embassy, therefore, went beyond the occasional, or even periodic, report of the Consuls. The announcements of the Ottoman authorities manifested in a flurry of correspondence from the consulates to the Ambassador alerting him of the comprehensive scale of the government's design and the catastrophic results of the actions taken.

[33] RG59, 867.4016/124.   [34] RG59, 867.4016/127.   [35] RG59, 867.4016/126.

The reportage from the perimeter would have been sufficient to raise serious suspicion as to the intent of the government's policies. The Embassy, however, did not have to engage in guesswork as to the results, for it also enjoyed the rueful advantage of obtaining reports from consulates situated along another geographic line of contact which coincided with the primary trunk line of the Empire's internal transportation network, and which also served as the main route of the Armenian deportations. This line extended south from Harput to Aleppo, Syria, forking from there towards Damascus and Jerusalem in one direction, and towards Baghdad in another. Both termini were too distant from the main relocation, concentration, and, ultimately, extermination centers in the Syrian wilderness, to view the Armenian population at its final destination.[36] Harput and Aleppo, therefore, emerged as the focal points of observation by the American officials witnessing the mass transfer of Armenians from Anatolia and Armenia to Syria.

The importance of the consular witnesses to the Armenian deportations may be emphasized by observing the junction of the perimeter, formed by the coastal consulates, with the transport trunk line. To further elaborate on this cartographic analysis of the location of the American consulates, Harput may be viewed as the final link in the chain of posts that completed the circle around Anatolia. From this viewpoint, the Harput consulate too constituted an observation post on the perimeter servicing the nexus in Constantinople.

Leslie A. Davis, American Consul in Harput

While this cartographic perspective establishes the thoroughness with which the embassy scanned the Armenian situation, it misses the other equally critical role of Harput's geographic location. All the other towns and cities on the perimeter were points of departure. Harput, too, as an Armenian population center, was a point of departure. However, by virtue of its position, as the egress portal of the Armenian highland, Harput also became a major point of transit through which countless Armenians from all across the province of Mamuret al-Aziz, or Harput, traveled to the bleaker lowlands. In the same 11 July report to Morgenthau, Davis wrote:

If it were simply a matter of being obliged to leave here to go somewhere else it would not be so bad, but everyone knows it is a case of going to one's

[36] See Raymond H. Kévorkian, "L'Extermination des déportés Arméniens Ottomans dans les camps de concentration de Syrie-Mesopotamie (1915–1916), la deuxième phase du génocide," *Revue d'histoire Arménienne Contemporaine* 2 (1998).

death. If there was any doubt about it, it has been removed by the arrival of
a number of parties, aggregating several thousand people, from Erzeroum and
Erzingan.[37]

In one other respect, therefore, Harput was indeed a place of departure:
a departure from this world.

Yet still, Harput was also a destination, its environs a place for mass
executions, hence its designation by the resident American Consul as the
"slaughterhouse province."[38] Davis also observed that a selection process
designed to eliminate the male population, especially persons of status,
preceded the deportations:

Not many men have been spared, however, to accompany those who are being sent
into exile, for a more prompt and sure method has been used to dispose of them.
Several thousand Armenian men have been arrested during the past few weeks.
These have been put in prison and each time several hundred had been gathered
up in that way they were sent away during the night. The first lot were sent away
during the night of June 23rd. Among them were some of the professors in the
American college and other prominent Armenians, including the Prelate of the
Armenian Gregorian Church of Harput. There have been frequent rumors that
all these were killed and there is little doubt that they were. All Armenian soldiers
have likewise been sent away in the same manner. They have been arrested and
confined in a building at one end of the town. No distinction has been made
between those who had paid their military exemption tax and those who had not.
Their money was accepted and then they were arrested and sent off with the
others. It was said that they were to go somewhere to work on the roads but no
one had heard of them and that is undoubtedly false.

The fate of all the others has been pretty well established by reliable reports
of a similar occurrence on Wednesday, July 7th. On Monday many men were
arrested both at Harput and Mezreh and put in prison. At daybreak Tuesday
morning they were taken out and made to march towards an almost uninhabited
mountain. There were about eight hundred in all and they were tied together in
groups of fourteen each. That afternoon they arrived in a small Kurdish village
where they were kept over night in the mosque and other buildings. During all this
time they were without food or water. All their money and much of their clothing
had been taken from them. On Wednesday morning they were taken to a valley
a few hours' distant where they were all made to sit down. Then the gendarmes
began shooting them until they had killed nearly all of them. Some who had not
been killed by bullets were then disposed of with knives and bayonets. A few
succeeded in breaking the rope with which they were tied to their companions
and running away, but most of these were pursued and killed. A few succeeded
in getting away, probably not more than two or three. Among those who were
killed was the Treasurer of the American College. Many other estimable men,

[37] RG59, 867.4016/127.
[38] See Leslie A. Davis, *The Slaughterhouse Province: An American Diplomat's Report on the Armenian Genocide, 1915–1917*, ed. Susan K. Blair (New Rochelle, N.Y.: Aristide Caratzas, Publisher, 1989).

were among the number. No charge of any kind had ever been made against any of these men. They were simply arrested and killed as part of the general plan to dispose of the Armenian race.[39]

One other aspect differentiated Harput from all the other consulates on the perimeter. While the view of the coastal consulates was unidirectional, from the shore to the interior, the view from Harput was multidirectional. Here people along the entire horizon were in motion.

Jesse B. Jackson and the American consulate in Aleppo

The Aleppo consulate shared this same vantage as the largest concentration and transit center of the entire operation, with one fundamental difference of its own. Aleppo was located outside the perimeter and beyond the circle of the cities of Asia Minor historically inhabited by Armenians. The perspective of the Aleppo consulate, therefore, was primarily dominated by its view as a destination, even as Armenians were shipped every which way from there. As Jackson wrote on 5 June 1915:

There is a living stream of Armenians pouring into Aleppo from the surrounding towns and villages, the principal ones being Marash, Zeitoun, Hassanbeyli, Osmania, Baghtche, Adana, Dortyol, Hadjin, etc. They all come under a heavily armed escort, usually from 300 to 500 at a time, and consist of old men, women, and children; all the middle aged and young men have been taken for military service.[40]

Aleppo, therefore, complemented the perspective of the perimeter, and thereby completed another type of circle, namely the narrative of events, thus furnishing the conclusive evidence of the intent and purpose of the Ottoman policy to remove the Armenians from their places of habitation and send them on the open road to places beyond Aleppo: "Travellers report meeting thousands in such localities as Anah on the Euphrates River, five or six days journey from Baghdad, where they are being scattered over the desert to starve or die of disease in the burning heat, accustomed as they were to the higher altitudes."[41]

All told, the consulates, without prior knowledge of the course of the events about to unfold, documented the deportation and decimation of the Armenians as a continuous process, and in so doing ascertained the fundamental difference between the atrocities of 1915 and preceding episodes of organized violence. Altogether they witnessed nearly every facet of the Young Turk policy of eradicating the Armenians.

[39] RG59, 867.4016/127.   [40] RG59, 867.4016/77.   [41] Ibid.

As for the town of Ana, or Anah, it was the farthest south on the Euphrates to which Armenians are known to have been deported past Deir el-Zor.

Oscar S. Heizer, Consul in Trebizond and Baghdad

The reassignment of Oscar Heizer from Trebizond to Baghdad placed this American Consul in the extraordinary position of having witnessed and reported both the departure of Armenians from the northernmost consular post and the arrival of survivors at the southernmost consular post of the entire eastern region of the Ottoman Empire. He may have covered more territory than any of the other US consuls. On Morgenthau's instructions he had even traveled from Trebizond to Erzerum. As he wrote on 25 September 1915, in his report entitled "Trip to Erzerum": "I . . . left Trebizond on horseback August 12th . . . I returned to Trebizond September 19th having been absent 39 days, but not outside of this Consular district."[42] On 30 November 1917 he forwarded a copy of the "Second Report of the Armenian Relief Work in Bagdad and Mesopotamia" signed by E. E. Lavy of the Church Missionary Society. The report talked of the rescue of surviving children and women and included a section on "Male Refugees." They had a story to tell about the last great killing center in the heart of the Syrian desert.

Nearly two months ago a party of fifty refugees came in, of these thirty-seven were men, the rest women and children and their story was most interesting. Last winter they were in an Armenian Camp at Deir Ez-Zor. At various intervals batches of these prisoners were taken out into the desert and slaughtered. One method of killing the women was as follows: A large deep pit was dug, a few Arabs were stationed at the bottom and the women thrown in one by one, those who were not killed by the fall, were dispatched by the slayers below. The party above mentioned were in turn taken out into the desert, some managed to escape and apparently two or three days out the rest were left to starve. They reached the Jebel Sinjar to the N.W. of Mosul and there with a number of other refugees lived with the Yezidees or devil worshippers who treated them kindly. After six or seven months the fifty who reached us persuaded some Arab Sheikh to lead them through desert ways to Rumadi, which the British had just taken.[43]

This scarce piece of communication from the Baghdad consulate captured the moment of rescue of a handful of bedraggled survivors walking out of the desert; a snapshot of the final moments of the Armenian Genocide for those fortunate few who reached Allied protection. For a picture of the months leading up to the war, the dispatches of the Beirut

[42] RG59, 367.116/412.   [43] RG59, 867.48/728.

consulate probably provide the broadest evidence of the beginnings of the policies, which, in their later full fury, undermined the entire Armenian community of the Ottoman Empire.

W. Stanley Hollis and the Beirut consulate: requisition and the Capitulations

Morgenthau's report to the State Department on 6 August 1914, just days after war broke out in Europe relayed: "Feverish haste and high-handed method employed to complete mobilization here. Consuls of Mersine, Aleppo, Smyrna, Beirut send similar [reports]. Entire empire under martial law."[44] The lack of preparation and, at the same time, the sense that opportunity knocked as the Young Turk government sealed its secret alliance with Germany explains the haste in mobilization. The high-handedness, of which the Consuls repeatedly informed the Ambassador, however, attested to a second set of domestic objectives that the Consuls also registered.

Stanley Hollis, a professional in the diplomatic services, provided the embassy with detailed accounts of the economic consequences of the process of requisition implemented by the authorities to support the rapid mobilization of the Ottoman forces. He wrote on 10 August 1914, in reference to the Governor-General of Beirut:

Yesterday the police were searching all the stables in town, while commandeering parties, led by the Vali himself in person, visited many of the shops in town from which they took by force scores of bales of textiles as well as many other articles, giving in return, not cash, but vouchers which probably will never be honored.

The Vali has orders to send North to Constantinople, if possible, all recruits, as well as animals, food stuffs, textiles, clothing, et cetera, which he may commande[e]r here; and as he is carrying on this commandeering (looting would almost be the more proper designation) in a very high-handed manner, he is causing a great deal of excitement as well as a lot of hardship in the town. He has avowed to some of his friends, who have afterwards been rather talkative, that a general mobilization of the Turkish forces is being carried on; that they expect to have completed their mobilization in about a month, and that they will attack Russia.[45]

Writing on behalf of Hollis, Vice-Consul Ralph Chesbrough added on 19 August: "Last night all the Consuls General here received from the Vali of Beirut identical letters informing them that by decision of the Council of Ministers at Constantinople requisitions in general, commandeering of goods and animals, will be made directly upon all foreigners

---

[44] RG59, 867.00/784.   [45] RG59, 867.00/6119.

and without consular intervention."[46] Chesbrough followed up the same day with a cover letter forwarding a report from another consulate on the Mediterranean coast south of Beirut: "Consular Agent Struve of Haifa, wherein he gives an account of the high handed methods practiced by the Ottoman military authorities at that point in requisitioning and confiscating the property both of natives and foreigners."[47]

Four days earlier, on 15 August, Edward I. Nathan reported similar activity from Mersin, also on the Mediterranean north of Beirut on the Cilician coast. Mersin's non-Muslim population consisted of Armenians and Greeks.

Requisitions of all kinds of goods that may be needed for military purposes are being made. Christian merchants have been the worst sufferers in regard to requisitions and the military exemption tax has been taken from them in some cases unnecessarily.

Foreign subjects liable to military duty in their respective countries have been departing in large numbers. Most of these were engaged in the construction of the Baghdad railroad all work on which has now been suspended.[48]

The consequences of mobilization and requisition were quite apparent. The Christians were bearing the initial brunt of the financial cost of mobilization. The requisition process presented an occasion to extract resources from them at rates, or by methods, that verged on looting and confiscation. Manpower shortages, especially in the professions and specializations previously filled by Europeans working under contract, became immediately apparent. In the case of a strategic asset such as the railroads and the still-unfinished Baghdad line, the shortages of construction workers created a demand for labor, when the male conscripts of military age were at the frontlines. The condition of the army also explains the excessive demands made on the civilian population.

Leslie Davis, who had left Beirut a short time earlier on his way to Harput, and who had been held up in Aleppo for want of horses to ride the rest of the journey, wrote to Hollis on 19 September:

The constant stream of ragged, dirty, hungry recruits all along the way, the deserted fields except for a few women and children at work, the almost complete devastation of these fields by the soldiers, the big fire at Diarbekr which is said by all to have been of incendiary origin, all these and more made it a trip that will not soon be forgotten. Then almost immediately after my arrival here the announcement of the abrogation of the capitulations has naturally caused more or less excitement among the natives and speculation among the Americans as to what will be done about it.[49]

[46] RG59, 867.00/656.   [47] RG59, 867.00/657.
[48] RG59, 867.00/652.   [49] RG59, 867.00/698.

Hollis had already forwarded to the embassy and the State Department the translation of an announcement regarding the abrogation of the Capitulations transmitted with the following descriptor: "Copy of the telegram received from the general headquarters of the Committee of Union and Progress, under date of August 27th (September 9, 1914)."[50]

Perhaps more so than any other document generated during the First World War, or any statement attributed to any one of the Young Turk leaders, this proclamation emanating from CUP headquarters best summarized the party's ideology. Nor were its objectives kept circumspect as once again the European conflict, with the Great Powers diverted by their mutual struggle, appeared an occasion when the colonial shackles on the Ottoman government could be discarded. Proceeding with the expectation that an alliance with German military and industrial might would relieve them of past encumbrances and limitations, the CUP subscribed to the belief that it stood better than a chance to prevail against Turkey's foes.[51] The decree on the unilateral abolition of the Capitulations, issued a month after sealing the secret alliance with Germany, was a message delineating a new foreign policy, a radical departure from Ottoman practices, and a public rupture with past alignments and balance-of-power arrangements. The revocation of the Capitulations fundamentally redefined political and economic relations with the principal concessionaries, namely France and England.[52]

---

[50] RG59, 867.00/672. The abolition of the Capitulations was announced on 7 September 1914, effective 1 October 1914. Morgenthau devoted attention to this matter in his memoir, writing: "Despite the protests of all the ambassadors, the Cabinet issued its notification that the capitulations would be abrogated on October 1st. This abrogation was all a part of the Young Turks' plan to free themselves from foreign tutelage and to create a new country on the basis of 'Turkey for the Turks' ": p. 116. While he opposed the elimination of the judicial rights attendant to the Capitulations, Morgenthau was not against abandoning the economic provisions of the treaties. "These were treaty rights which for centuries had regulated the position of foreigners in the Turkish Empire. Turkey had never been admitted to a complete equality with European nations, and in reality she had never been an independent sovereignty. The Sultan's laws and customs differed so radically from those of Europe and America that no non–Moslem country could think of submitting its citizens in Turkey to them. In many matters, therefore, the principle of ex-territoriality had always prevailed in favour of all citizens or subjects of countries enjoying capitulatory rights": p. 112.

[51] On Ottoman–German economic relations during the First World War, see Ulrich Trumpener, *Germany and the Ottoman Empire 1914–1918* (Princeton, N.J.: Princeton University Press, 1968), pp. 271–84.

[52] For a close analysis of the economic policies and conduct of the CUP, see Çağlar Keyder, *State & Class in Turkey: A Study in Capitalist Development* (London and New York: Verso, 1987), pp. 49–90; also, Erich J. Zürcher, *Turkey: A Modern History* (London and New York: I. B. Tauris, 1993), pp. 127–37.

The commercial practices associated with the Capitulations also had a domestic constituency that, over the course of the preceding decades, had benefited from the penetration of the Near East by European capital. They were mainly the Christian minorities. The decree, therefore, complicated, if not severed, this relationship. Given that the urban Armenian population was in large measure engaged in commerce, the cumulative economic effect of mobilization (which conscripted the Armenian adult male population), the requisitions (which are reported to have been onerously imposed on Christians), and the abolition of the Capitulations (which disrupted the established channels of finance and transaction) was quite significant. Moreover, the rapidity with which the government proceeded only contributed to greater economic hardship and the evident breakdown of commerce. In some parts, as observed by Davis, even agriculture was already in disarray; all this at the end of September 1914, a month before the Ottomans even entered the war and engaged in military action.

This raises the question, why would a government, about to plunge into war, knowingly jeopardize the economy of the country and risk its supplies and supply lines? How exactly did a country, already deeply indebted, expect to finance a war when its economic policies were ruining various sectors of the merchant class? Pragmatic considerations of the like ordinarily drive policy and the options selected are determined by motivations seeking advantage, particularly in the military sphere, where territorial and political objectives were to be settled. If practical and rational judgment is suspended, however, and crisis in one sphere of human affairs is relied upon to generate crisis in another, the case needs to be examined whether both crises, military and economic, were propelled by considerations exceeding the normative calculus of war, namely a contest of arms. From the onset the First World War was far more than a conflict over the apportionment of disputed territory. The explanation for the overriding motivations in such a context must accordingly be located in the sphere of excessive security criteria. Or else, it is embedded in the domain of ideological justification. The 9 September 1914 CUP declaration on the abolition of the Capitulations furnished that very framework:

At the time the Ottoman Government enjoyed the plenitude of its force and power and was at the apogee of its glory, it granted to the foreigners, living in Turkey, in a manner of pure generosity and courtesy and most willingly, certain administrative, judicial and economical privileges.

However, at a time when the Ottoman Government, as the result of certain events, became powerless and weak, these privileges were turned out into the form of forced rights and obligations; thus the Government not only lost its liberty of action, but also a great part of its political and economical independence.

We, therefore, were left to suffer from the oppressive yoke of these heavy obli-gations which effected the national sentiment, dignity, and honor of the Empire. So our Government in order to be enabled to safeguard its interior indepen-dence, to regain its national political rights, to become a true free government, to administer its own finances in accordance with economical laws, to regain the right of existence, to become the proper judge of its destiny, and, last of all, to be enabled to free the empire from the yoke of these bonds, our government consid-ered the abolishment of these despotic obligations and had recourse to repeated diplomatic efforts, which, however, did not yield any successful results, but on the contrary these obligations took a form extremely dangerous and vexatious, bound the country in iron ties and placed it in a very difficult situation.

So in order to put an end, for good and all, to this state of things, our Imperial Government, dependent upon the help of God and the support of the nation, which is full of patriotic sentiments, decide definitely to abolish these privileges and to free the nation from the yoke of these bonds.

Now, Ottomans we congratulate ourselves upon this most happy event, which opened a new chapter in our national history and a white page in the new era of welfare and prosperity, after a series of events full of misfortune, and we invite our people to extend their thanks to the Government for having set us free from this dishonorable bondage, and to prove our grand happiness by means of brilliant manifestations.[53]

Besides the historical logic by which the case was argued, and the re-versal of fortunes the declaration proposed and anticipated by starting a "new chapter" in Turkish history, the central operative ideological po-sitions were made abundantly clear. In this respect the declaration was really tantamount to a revolutionary manifesto, relieving the Ottoman government of past burdens and unfettering its resources. The predom-inant objectives were freedom of action, sought by the CUP on behalf of the Ottoman government in all matters, political, economical, financial, and internal, and to become masters of their own destiny. The declaration cast the impending military contest as a war of liberation taking the most militant page out of the journal of nationalism and sanctioning it with revolutionary fervor. Against this backdrop, the subsequent measures of the Young Turk government unfold with predictability, for the oncoming war is welcomed as an opportunity to readjust external relations, as well as rearrange the internal structure of state and society, with the objective of enhancing freedom and honor dressed in nationalist terms.

Stanley Hollis, who so anxiously observed the process of requisitioning and measured its consequences in the context of the government's other activities, prognosticated the covert objective of the economic policies coming into effect. Just as the shooting was starting along the Black Sea as Ottoman naval vessels bombarded the Russian coast and the Caucasian

[53] RG59, 867.00/672.

front was opened, Hollis predicted the domestic goals of the oncoming war in his 2 November 1914 cable writing:

For about a week or so after my above-mentioned despatch was written, Beirut and the surrounding country continued in a state of moribund inactivity, although from many quarters, I saw indications that the Turkish authorities were maturing plans to put all foreigners and foreign institutions under the iron heel of the despotic regime which the present Ottoman government is striving to impose upon this unhappy country in order to thoroughly Turkishize it.[54]

Fourteen months later, after the Armenian population had been methodically and thoroughly plundered of its possessions, Morgenthau realized the connection between all the various measures introduced by the Young Turk regime with regard to the question of the property of the Armenians in the Ottoman Empire, especially "the law of September 26, 1915, relative to the disposition to be made of the property left behind by 'deported persons,' i.e. the Armenians who have been exiled and killed in various parts of the Turkish Empire."[55] On the final day of that savage year, 31 December 1915, he wrote:

As may be seen from a perusal of the supplementary law on the subject, the Commissions instituted to settle the intricate questions of ownership, claims, debts, etc. in connection with the estates of these Armenians, are given far-reaching and arbitrary powers. Considering the general state of the administration of justice in Turkey, especially since the attempted abolition of the Capitulations, it is to be feared that in the unspeakable confusion created by the wholesale deportations and massacres most of the property in question will be confiscated by the State or squandered and lost in the process of settlement.[56]

Morgenthau was wrong on one thing. Lives are lost. Property is merely transferred. In this case, the expropriator was the state. The state declared war, the war propelled the genocide, and the genocide financed the war.

The consulates in Mersin and Alexandretta: the demise of commerce and class

The deleterious effect of the deportations on US interests quickly registered with the Consuls, many of whose stations represented the outposts of American commerce. The appeals filed by US company representatives also revealed the extent to which international trade in the Ottoman Empire depended on the intermediary services of the Armenians. If the consular reports on the effects of the requisitions process shed light on the macroeconomic consequences of rapidly depleting the domestic

---

[54] RG59, 867.00/715.   [55] RG59, 367.11/1054.   [56] Ibid.

inventory, especially of manufactured and imported goods, the reportage on the process of depleting the skilled and specialized labor pool captured the microeconomic consequences of deportation as American companies notified the consulates regarding individual employees, specific contractual obligations, and the status of financial transactions – all abruptly suspended with the wholesale eviction of the Armenians from their homes and businesses.

The physical hardships of homelessness and exposure have dominated the depiction of the deportations.[57] Far less has been said about the sudden unemployment of hundreds of thousands of productive individuals. The dramatic drop in production and productivity would have been a shock to any economic system, and for one undergoing the stresses and strains of war, the results would have rippled all across the country. In this environment, the one-time compensatory contribution of requisition, plunder, and expropriation might have played a temporary ameliorative role. Any government, however, would have had to contemplate the rationality of a decision that deliberately undermined a country's economic capacity under circumstances of pre-existing duress. Once again, it may be argued that only an overarching consideration, disregarding the detriment to the state's annual revenue and the economy's productivity, could license such a measure. From this viewpoint, the powerful motivating factors of national ideology and wartime opportunity rise again as the plausible causes. The real economic effects of the deportations, however, were not located in the rapid material destitution of the Armenian population as the wealth of their community precipitously decreased. The other side of the coin, after all, was the hasty accumulation of the same wealth by the Turkish and Kurdish population of the Ottoman Empire through methods of forcible transfer. More critical than the fixed sum of wealth seized from the Armenians and handed over to the Turkish authorities and the Muslim populace were the services provided by the Armenian population. By managing a sizable sector of the commerce of the Ottoman state, Armenians played a vital mediatory role shaped by centuries of functional assignment by the Ottoman system, and selection by, and association with, international networks of exchange.

By reducing the Armenian population, the Young Turk regime erased the fixed class of merchants and demolished its emergent role as an economically influential segment of society at a time of increasing European and American penetration of the Ottoman Empire. Just a couple of years

---

[57] See Rouben Paul Adalian, "A Conceptual Method for Examining the Consequences of the Armenian Genocide," in Levon Chorbajian and George Shirinian, eds., *Studies in Comparative Genocide* (London: Macmillan Press Ltd.; New York: St. Martin's Press, Inc., 1999), pp. 47–59.

earlier, as a result of the Balkan Wars, the coincidence of European economic expansion with the territorial diminution of the Ottoman state had resulted in the seeming delivery of a disproportionate share of the wealth of the country to groups disposed towards professional and commercial specializations, which in the Turkish state historically had been relinquished to minorities. At the intersection of these economic realities, political possibilities, ideological objectives, and wartime exigencies, the widely dispersed Armenians were particularly exposed socially, and vulnerable physically.[58]

The US consular communications invariably recorded this vast process of economic reduction and social reorganization as reflected in the sudden disengagement of the Armenian professional and commercial class from the existing Ottoman system. To this effect, for example, Colden A. Brown, US Consular Agent in Alexandretta, Syria, notified Consul Jackson in Aleppo on 5 July 1915, of a "letter from the local office of the Standard Oil Company of New York . . . advising that their Agent at Deurt-Yol, a certain Mr. Chukri Chekmeyan, is to be deported to the interior, and asks the intervention of the good offices of this and your Consulate in behalf of the said Agent of this American Company."[59] To stress the seriousness of the embedded message, he underlined a word in his communication: "I am informed that orders have been issued that all Armenians including women and children of the towns of Deurt-Yol, Hadjin and Hassan Beyli, were to be immediately sent to the interior."[60] On 2 August 1915, Brown was notified by another firm, MacAndrews & Forbes Company, about a similar dilemma, which reconfirmed the information about the deportations and their effect on local American enterprises:

> We are today informed that a party of twenty seven Armenian families are being sent away from Alexandretta tomorrow, by order of the Ottoman Government.
> It is also rumored that such deportations will take place every few days until all the Armenians here have been sent to the interior.
> We have in our employ an Armenian by the name of Haji Agop Garabetian, a man of fifty seven years of age, and who has been in our service for the past thirty years. He is at present our head mechanic, and we would suffer very much indeed if he was sent away, especially so just now, as we have during the past two weeks begun transport of licorice root from outside stations of Alexandretta, and

---

[58] See Vahakn N. Dadrian, *The History of the Armenian Genocide: Ethnic Conflict from the Balkans to Anatolia to the Caucasus* (Providence and Oxford: Berghahn Books, 1995), specially ch. 2, "The Eviction of the Turks from the Balkan Peninsula: A New Sense of Peril for Anatolia," pp. 185–99.

[59] RG84, Department of State Consular Post Records, US Consulate in Aleppo, Syria, General Correspondence, 1915, Box 2/6 300S.

[60] Ibid.

we are in hopes of commencing baling operations here very shortly, & should our mechanic be sent away, we would be placed in a very awkward position. We, therefore, beg of you to take the necessary steps to prevent this employee's departure, on the grounds that he is an employee of an American Company, and his absence would greatly affect us, in fact there is no one to be found here at present who could take his place, as all mechanics and others in Alexandretta have been drafted for Government service.[61]

Brown forwarded the notice the same day to Jackson under cover and raised a separate matter of direct concern to himself with regard to a member of his staff. He stated plainly: "I kindly request that you also intercede on behalf of our Dragoman, Mr. Ashdjian and family."[62]

The State Department in Washington also forwarded inquiries from company headquarters in the United States. One sample response dated 2 November 1915, from American Consul Edward I. Nathan, sheds considerable light on the procedures by which Armenian-owned enterprises in Turkey were being liquidated. Nathan explained:

that in consequence of measures taken in accordance with the new law regarding deported persons (principally Armenians) the firm of Avedissian and Kechichian established in Adana, Turkey was dissolved and the various goods which remained in their store were taken possession of by the authorities and their creditors. As this firm represented a number of American exporters it is desirable that the above fact be brought to their attention with a view to recovering any possible outstanding indebtedness. The following firms should in any case be advised:

> The International Harvester Company, Chicago, Ill.
> The Goulds Manufacturing Company, Seneca Falls, N.Y.
> Messrs. Rumsey and Company, Ltd., Seneca Falls, N.Y.[63]

In the mistaken belief that recourse to judicial or diplomatic procedure might resolve the matter of an outstanding debt, one of the companies, Goulds Manufacturing Company, had gone to the trouble of filing a claim against Avedissian and Kechichian of Adana, Turkey. Asked to respond nearly two years after his initial communication, and after having returned to the United States with the rupture of relations with the Ottoman Empire, Nathan could barely restrain his ire. Once again he outlined the legal mechanisms, introduced by the Turkish government for that sole purpose, by which Armenian property was confiscated, at the same time implying the Imperial Ottoman Bank was guilty of dereliction, if not outright complicity, in the matter. In this instance, it just so happened that, while the firm in question was Armenian-owned, the goods belonged to

---

[61] RG84, Department of State Consular Post Records, US Consulate in Aleppo, Syria, General Correspondence, 1915, Box 2/6 300.
[62] Ibid.   [63] RG59, 367.11/1002.

US manufacturers. Writing from Washington, D.C., on 22 September 1917, on "Mersina, Turkey, American Consulate" stationery, Nathan stated:

The letter therein referred to for the Imperial Ottoman Bank was duly transmitted and the bank replied that it was not in a position to state when the claim would be settled. I may add that inasmuch as the entire stock of the Adana firm was seized by the Turkish Commission for Transported Persons (Messrs. Avedissian and Kechichian having been exiled with the rest of the Armenian population of Adana), and said stock sold at a great sacrifice despite my official protest I fear there will not be much remaining for creditors. I have also reason to believe that if the bank had been more energetic in securing goods to cover the claim the Goulds company would not have suffered any loss.[64]

In a final example, on 16 October 1915, Jackson notified George Horton, American Consul-General in Smyrna, of information from one scrupulous associate of another major American industrial firm who, after having been deported hundreds of miles from his hometown on the Aegean coast just north of Smyrna, had gone to the trouble of notifying the Consul in Aleppo of the company's inventory left in storage unattended.

Stephan Messeldjian from Dikily, Smyrna Vilayet, who represented International Harvester Co., selling "McCormick" binders etc., has been deported to Aleppo. He says he left in his depot about 16 binders, 2 mowers, 2 hay rakes, 1 farming mill, 2 tool grinders, 45 bales of binder twine, and many machine parts and accessories.

Please notify the Company's representative in Smyrna, Mr. Garabet Artinian, or the Company's General Offices in Constantinople, so the necessary precautions can be taken, to safeguard their interests.[65]

The deportations, in their total effect, concluded the intent of abrogating the Capitulations, for the declaration alone would not have disengaged the existing mechanisms of commerce. With the excision of a significant segment of the social class supporting the pre-existing Ottoman system, the disruption of economic order, coincident with the state's bold intrusion into the economy because of the war, materially advanced the Young Turk policy of fermenting a national economy disentangled from a previous subsidiary and concessionary disposition. The destruction of the Ottoman commercial middle class, as defined by ethnic minorities, proceeded with rapid steps, and, in the span of less than a year, the larger portion of the Armenian urban element which contributed so much to the cosmopolitanism of many an Ottoman city had disappeared. In those

[64] RG59, 867.11/2241.
[65] RG84, Department of State Consular Post Records, US Consulate in Aleppo, Syria, General Correspondence, 1915, Box 2/6 300.

parts of the country where the Armenian element previously dominated trade, the net effect was a social leveling, leaving in its train a society consisting mostly of peasantry and state authority, an ideal combination for strengthening government control and fostering ideological conformity.

As to the matter of the future livelihood of the forcibly unemployed multitudes, any government would have had to concern itself with their care and feeding, unless, of course, the point of the policy was to ignore addressing the calamitous conditions created that threatened their very survival. The most dramatic consequences of the government's policy, however, registered the following year, when the exhaustion of the already expropriated stock and the absence of a vast portion of the labor pool resulted in the spread of famine even among segments of the Ottoman population untouched by deportation and expropriation since they did not constitute part of the targeted population. It is a telling commentary of the extremes the CUP was prepared to inflict upon the entire Ottoman population in order to extract from the disintegration of its historic imperial construct the new political consensus it hoped to achieve. Leslie Davis described the extent of the economic ruin of the countryside in places never even disturbed by frontline military operations in a report written in October 1917 upon his return home to Port Jefferson, New York:

Economic conditions in Turkey, and especially in the interior of Asia Minor, are decidedly bad. The principal industry there is agriculture and as much of it had formerly been carried on by Armenians, nearly all of whom were killed or deported, including even the women who did much of the work in the fields, there were few persons left to cultivate the lands. Then, as most of the Moslem men were taken for military service, that left the country with hardly any farming population. The result is that most of the lands are abandoned and the agricultural products are wholly insufficient for the needs of the people. The supply of wheat in the spring of this year was so limited that oftentimes no flour or bread could be found in the market and the masses of the population, both Mohammedan and Christian, were literally starving. Barley was likewise almost unobtainable. Meat was so scarce that none except the high officials and the very rich could have it at all and much of the time they could find none.

Trade and commerce of every kind has been at a standstill, of course, since the beginning of the war. Nearly all the merchants and business men in the Harput consular district were Armenians. More than ninety per cent. of the deposits in the banks in Harput were those of Armenians. It naturally follows that in exterminating the Armenians the Turks practically destroyed all the business of the country, and, as they are not business men themselves, there is not much opportunity for it to be revived in the near future. What is true of the Harput consular district is probably true to a large extent in many other parts of Turkey.[66]

---

[66] RG59, 867.00/803.

The Armenian dragomen: interpreters for the Consuls

The Consuls were quite powerless to do anything on behalf of the Armenian employees of American companies by virtue of the fact the individuals in question were Ottoman citizens. There were, however, a handful
of men, Armenians in the service of the consulates, who enjoyed inter-
mediate jurisdiction as employees of the US government. They rendered
a critical service to the Consuls as native interpreters of the languages
spoken and written in the Ottoman Empire. All were highly educated
individuals, who, in the case of the Armenians, brought facilities in languages beyond the official ones. At a minimum they spoke and wrote
English, they spoke Turkish, wrote Ottoman, and spoke and wrote Armenian. French was a common fourth language, and some, from Syrian
parts, would have knowledge of Arabic, if not other indigenous or European tongues. Known as a "dragoman," the interpreter employed in a
diplomatic representation in the Ottoman Empire enjoyed special status
and foreign protection.[67] Even so, only strenuous efforts spared the lives
of these individuals. The Consuls remained solicitous of the welfare of
their former employees for years after their departure from Turkey as the
fate awaiting them continued to be a matter of deep concern. While still
in Turkey, the Consuls saw to it that the protections afforded their employees were duly recorded. One such communiqué, from Mersin dated
15 July 1915, on the subject of "Protection of alien employees of Consulate," which listed all employees, gave a representative picture of the
composition of a typical consulate in the Ottoman Empire, inclusive of a
Vice-Consul, three interpreters, two clerks, and two guards.[68]

In the course of the destruction that ravaged Anatolia, the dragoman Nichan Zelveian lost all his possessions. He would have lost his
employment record too if Consul Nathan had not interceded on his behalf, seven and a half years after his July 1915 registration with the Department of State, by issuing Zelveian new identity papers on 8 February
1923, to the following effect:

---

[67] On Armenian dragomen in the Ottoman Empire, see Rouben Paul Adalian, "The
Armenian Colony of Egypt during the Reign of Muhammad Ali (1804–1848),"
Armenian Review 33:2 (1980), pp. 126–33.

[68] RG59, 125.5973/20:
    John Debbas, Merchant, Greek subject, Vice Consul.
    Elie Naccache, Shipping Agent, Ottoman subject, Interpreter.
    Aristides Simeonoglou, Manufacturer, Ottoman subject,[Interpreter].
    Nichan Zelveian, Merchant, Ottoman subject, Interpreter.
    Bechara Naccache, Ottoman subject, Clerk of Consulate.
    Shamoon Bano, Ottoman subject, Guard.
    Mahmoud Ben Suleiman, Ottoman subject, Guard.
    Marius Dellalian, Ottoman subject, extra clerk.

I hereby certify that sometime in or about 1912 while I was Consul of the United States of America at Mersina, Turkey, Mr. Nichan M. Zelveian was appointed Dragoman (Interpreter) of the American Consulate at Mersina, Turkey, with the approval of the Department of State, Washington, D.C. and recognized as such by the Ottoman authorities; that he exercised his functions as dragoman until the rupture of relations between the United States and the Ottoman Empire in April, 1917; that after such rupture he was attached as dragoman to the Spanish Consulate at Mersina which was charged with the protection of American citizens.[69]

Nathan, who was stationed at the time in Palermo, Italy, prepared the certificate at the request of G. Bie Ravndal, the American Consul-General in Constantinople, "in lieu of a certificate issued by me while Consul at Mersina, which certificate was destroyed during the recent fire at Smyrna, Turkey."[70] Nathan forwarded the document to Ravndal with the urging that the Zelveian case be given attention and payment of salary considered in view of services rendered.[71]

Earlier, the American Consul in Harput had thought of another avenue to justify keeping his dragoman on payroll. Writing on consulate stationery posted Port Jefferson, New York, 12 October 1917, Leslie A. Davis urged the Secretary of State:

to continue the salaries of two employees of the American Consulate at Harput, Turkey . . . The employees are Mr. Haroutune Pekmezian, who was my clerk, and Ahmed Tahiroghloo, a cavass . . . Both have been in the service of the Consulate for several years and have been faithful employees. They remained with me until I left, instead of attempting to escape from the country, as they might easily have done prior to that time. Since then escape from Harput has been impossible and both of these men remain there without any resources of any kind. I feel that, in view of their faithful services, it will be no more than just if some provision can now be made for them for their necessary subsistence and earnestly request that they continue to be paid either all or part of their former salaries from July 1, 1917.

I am now in receipt of some recent letters from Harput which change the situation somewhat and seem to furnish the necessary justification from a practical standpoint for continuing the salary of at least one, and I think of both, of these men. When I was in Constantinople there were a considerable number of remittances for Harput which had been received too late to be sent to me. I found a way to send this money to Harput, with the names of the payees, and am pleased to learn that it was received and paid to the proper parties. This was done very largely through the help of my former employees, and especially Mr. Pekmezian.

[69] RG59, 125.5973/62.   [70] Ibid.
[71] RG 59, 125.5973/63: "Mr. Zelveian was paid his salary by me until I left Mersina in May, 1917. I believe he was entitled to salary from that time as an employee of the Spanish Consulate in charge of our interests until the State Department finally dispensed with his services in 1921. As Mr. Zelveian is now in very straitened circumstances any balance due him for salaries should, I submit, be paid and charged to the Department."

As there is still a way to send money to Harput, and as in meeting the Armenians in America, in accordance with Department's Instruction of September 20, 1917, to me, I find many who wish to send money to their relatives there, it seems that there will continue to be need of Mr. Pekmezian's services for the same kind of work he was doing while I was there, and that his services will be of great value in this connection.[72]

The most dramatic case by far was that of the dragoman of the Alexandretta consulate about whom Consular Agent Colden A. Brown had first notified Consul Jackson in Aleppo in July 1915. Like Nichan Zelveian and Haroutune Pekmezian, Moses Ashdjian too was left destitute. He appears, however, to have been a man of some substance, and attempted to file a claim. Jackson forwarded the claim to the Department in a document dated 24 August 1922, outlining Ashdjian's employment history with the Alexandretta consulate with the following introduction: "The writer is conversant with the details of the circumstances surrounding Mr. Ashdjian's forcible departure by the Turkish authorities and which was accomplished in a most brutal and atrocious manner, and it was only through herculean efforts on the part of this Consulate that his life was not lost during those events."[73] Jackson's summary cover does not even hint at the ordeal endured by Moses Ashdjian, who in the attachment to his appeal sketched one man's trials condensed into a single paragraph written on 5 January 1922, in Aleppo, Syria. What his fate would have been without Consul Jackson's vigorous interventions need hardly be speculated.

Nov. 6th 1915, I have been ordered by the governor Kaimmakam Fatin Bey to leave the city Alexandretta at once, and he sent me with nine members of my family and one servant to Aleppo. After a week the Vali Aleppo imprisoned me, then exiled to Mousool with three gendarms on Nov. 28th 1915. My family also were deported from Aleppo to Jerusalem on August 18th 1916. I have been imprisoned at Mousool thirty five days, then on 27 Sep. 1917 I was sent to Konia accompanied by the gendarms. After eight months I was imprisoned 25 days at Konia. Then the Turkish Government sent me again to Mousool on

---

[72] RG59, 125.4633/22.

[73] RG59, 467.67As3: "He was appointed Dragoman at the Consular Agency in 1908, and the Department approved the same by its instruction No. 9, dated November 7, 1908 (File No. 2597/39–43), addressed to this Consulate. He was continually in performance of his duties from that date until the time of his departure from Alexandretta on November 6, 1915, and his appointment as Dragoman has never been revoked by the Department. The action of the Turkish authorities completely ruined Mr. Ashdjian financially and it is hoped that everything possible will be done for the reimbursement of his losses, especially in view of the fact that his treatment at the hands of the Turks was primarily because of his official position as Dragoman and his required activities on behalf of American citizens and the belligerent subjects of the Allied powers whose interests were in charge of the American Consulate."

22 July 1918. When I arrived at Mousool, caring not that I was 52 years old, the Turkish Government forced me to go the Labour Regiment four days distance from Mousool at Zakho near Diarbekir. I worked there three months, having daily very hard work and at night laying on the ground. Then I was sent back to Mousool. After many dangers whose description would take much time, I arrived at Alexandretta on 18 Dec. 1918. I found that all my properties, household goods, merchandise, and effects had been seized and sold by the Turkish Authorities at public auction, as confirmed by the attached legalized certificate. Hence I assert that (1) The Turkish Government is responsible for the losses and damages caused to me, because I am one who is under the protection of the Government of USA. That (2) the circumstances being very extraordinary and my deportation unawares, it was impossible to have by me the documentary evidences concerning my losses and damages; but the attached legalized certificates show that I am the very owner and proprietor of the said losses and damages occurred.

There is no reason or guilt which the Turkish Government could attribute to me. I was never tried nor questioned.[74]

George Horton and the Smyrna consulate

The dragomen epitomized the services function provided by the Armenians of the Ottoman Empire. In a very literal sense they were intermediaries or middlemen, and in this respect their profession was entirely consistent with the specializations and adaptations that had made the Armenians a sizable segment of the Ottoman middle class. By this too they constituted part of the resented entrepreneurial and commercial class that was targeted by the Young Turk regime. On the other hand, much as the ethnic specialization in commerce was the result of the structure and nature of the Ottoman system, so too was the office of the dragoman. By eliminating these constituents, physically or professionally, the Young Turk program effectively sought to dismantle this aspect of the Ottoman system. From this standpoint, the generation and exploitation of ethnic animus by the CUP created justification and obtained popular sanction. In so doing, a competitive and skilled component of the system deemed now undesirable was removed from the field of commerce, labor, and ownership, therein freeing up the resources they previously controlled for the benefit of segments of Ottoman society patronized by the CUP ultra-nationalists.

Much as Hollis in Beirut theorized about the ultimate objective of the Young Turk ideology, so too did another of the old hands in the US diplomatic service. Moreover, George Horton had the advantage of having witnessed recent history and the conduct of Young Turk officials in the Smyrna region during, and immediately after, the Balkan Wars when

[74] Ibid.

a portion of the Greek population of the Aegean coast was expelled in response to the seizure of nearby islands and part of Thrace by Greece. A small-scale involuntary population exchange had occurred. Horton and the other European Consuls in Smyrna at the time had gone so far as to investigate the reported cases of atrocity committed in the district. As a result he had formed strong views about the honesty, or dishonesty, of the Ottoman government and its manipulation of the Turkish populace.[75]

Smyrna also equipped Horton with a perspective quite different from that of the other US Consuls to the degree that Smyrna was largely a Christian city with a very sizable Greek, Armenian, and European presence. Moreover, the core of the so-called Levantine community, namely Europeans settled in the Near East on a permanent basis, resided in Smyrna. To the keen observer, conditions in Smyrna, therefore, were a good barometer of the course of policy in the Ottoman Empire, since ideologically motivated changes in attitude and conduct could only be directed from the center. The thriving commerce of the region also made it the most developed part of the country. Therefore, someone in Smyrna, like Horton, would have been even better placed to perceive the effects of policy on the local economy. For the very same reasons, the one place in Turkey the Germans prevented deportation of the Armenians was also Smyrna.[76] That did not, however, contradict in Horton's view the larger objective of the gradual reduction of the Armenian population.

Writing from Salonika on 15 August 1918, where Horton had been reassigned upon entry of the United States into war, he felt at greater liberty to express his views and to offer his theory on the causes of the mistreatment of minorities in the Ottoman Empire and their intended objective:

The Christians of Turkey, Greeks, Armenians and the others who have settled there, are the industrial backbone of the country – the merchants, cultivators, carpenters, builders, doctors, mechanics, electricians, etc. The elimination of this element means the ruin of the country, its economic and industrial prostration. And there is no doubt that there has been for some time now a consistent and methodical policy being carried out with this end in view.

That the Turks are incapable of carrying out such a consistent plan of extermination seems also incredible to those who know them well. Their history has proved them rather the leaders of the world in savage outbreaks and massacres. Every portion of the Turkish Empire has its story of one or more massacres.

[75] See Adalian, "Comparative Policy."
[76] Trumpener, *Germany and the Ottoman Empire 1914–1918*, pp. 244–5; Marjorie Housepian, *Smyrna 1922: The Destruction of a City* (London: Faber and Faber, 1972), p. 46. General Otto Liman von Sanders, as Fifth Army commander with troops in the region, intervened to prevent deportations. He had arrived in Ottoman Turkey in 1913 as head of the German military mission.

The consistent and long drawn-out policy of extermination or crushing of the Christian elements of Turkey has been directed by the leaders of the Young Turk party, who are mere tools of Germany. If successful and carried out to the bitter end, that country will have no local competition when she starts in to develop the country and exploit the Turk.[77]

Smyrna may have been insulated from the full effect of the deportation of the Armenians, but Horton was by no means uninformed. If anything, he was quite well advised, for the very reason that the city was the base of operations for many European and American firms with branches in the Ottoman Empire, and therefore travel to and fro the city was a requirement for conducting business in the interior. Horton had reported such on 8 November 1915, with a communiqué to the State Department that contained some demographic calculations that revealed the scope and scale of the policies being implemented against the Armenians.

From what all these people worthy of the highest credence tell me, from 800,000 to 1,000,000 human beings are now going through this process of slow and hideous torture, and the movement instead of waning is increasing in ferocity, so that before it is finally over, in the neighborhood of 2,000,000 people will be affected, a very large percentage of whom will certainly perish as they are driven along for weeks and months without food or shelter and without the means of procuring these.[78]

On 16 December 1918, Horton, still in Salonika, transmitted to the Department a copy of a report that had come into his hands prepared by Luther Fowle, who was attached to the embassy in Constantinople. The report was prepared for the benefit of Lewis Heck, appointed US Commissioner to post-war Turkey, who was at the moment in Berne, Switzerland. Fowle estimated that, "exclusive of the Armenians of Constantinople and Smyrna, there are about 300,000 souls, of this race." Another memorandum obtained by Horton and transmitted to the Department, from Smyrna on 8 November 1915, contained a different kind of estimation: "Some idea of the decimation of their numbers may be obtained when one learns that of an expedition of 2,500 which left a village in the vicinity of Harput, only 600 arrived in Deir-El-Zor."[79] The best demographic tabulations were probably made by Consul Jackson who had direct access to the refugees and witnessed the mass exodus of the Armenians through Aleppo in 1915 and who remained at his post until 1917. It is evident from his reports sent to the State Department, subsequent to his return to Aleppo after the war, that he continued to be concerned with the well-being of the Armenian refugees. His figures

[77] RG59, 867.4016/388.   [78] RG59, 867.4016/243.   [79] Ibid.

too support the estimation that 80 percent or more of the deportees perished. The identification of Talaat, the Young Turk triumvir held most responsible for the mass murder of Armenians, in his hiding place in Germany by an Armenian who gunned him down, prompted the following communication from Aleppo, Syria, on September 7, 1921:

> The attention of the Department is respectfully drawn to the substance of the various telegraphic instructions from Talaat Pasha to the different Turkish officials, especially in Aleppo, the character of the said instructions being such as would indicate that few if any of the victims should have survived. But notwithstanding the severity thereof, 146,924 deported Armenians were found in Syria and Mesopotamia in 1919, as reported in my despatch No. 395 dated August 23, 1919 (File No. 840.1) their existence being due principally to the activities of this Consulate.[80]

The death of an American witness

On 16 November 1915, Horton sent a particularly startling message to the State Department. It involved the death of an American, neither an official nor a missionary, who had witnessed the massive scale of the deportations and been specially affected by the suffering he had seen of the tens of thousands of homeless Armenians. He had dictated a detailed account at the consulate in Smyrna where he had returned some days earlier. Few reports filed at the time captured so graphically the utter degradation of the Armenian population and the full terror of their brutalization. It appears he was unable to continue living with the imagery of the horrific scenes he traveled through, and so Horton found himself bearing the responsibility of notifying the Department of the death of Walter M. Geddes, reporting:

> Mr. Geddes committed suicide by shooting himself through the head with a revolver at his room in the Kraemer Hotel of this city early on the morning of the 7th November 1915. He was seen by myself and others on the preceding afternoon and was perfectly sane and natural in his behaviour and manner of talking giving no indication that he contemplated taking away his life. It is the opinion of those who knew him best here that certain experiences which he has passed through since he has been in Turkey preyed heavily upon his mind. He was dragged from his horse at Alexandretta in the month of October 1914 by Turkish soldiers, beaten and otherwise maltreated and thrown into prison. Just recently in returning from Aleppo, he passed for days through the scenes which are resulting

---

[80] RG59, 860j.4016/84. Jackson identified Talaat as Minister of Foreign Affairs in this communication. Talaat served as Minister of the Interior and Prime Minister during the war years. For a brief biography, see the entry by Rouben Paul Adalian, "Talaat, Mehmet," in Israel W. Charny, ed., *Encyclopedia of Genocide* (Santa Barbara, Denver, and Oxford: ABC-Clio, 1999), vol. II, pp. 531–2.

from the measures which are being taken against the Armenians by the Turkish Authorities. It was noticed that he was greatly changed and saddened on his return from Aleppo. In dictating to the stenographer of the Consulate General an account of what he saw, he broke down several times. He was particularly affected in speaking of the sufferings and deaths of the children who were perishing in thousands.[81]

Among the Armenian children in Turkey, there happened to be a small group fully entitled to American protection by virtue of the fact that their fathers were naturalized citizens of the United States. The Ottoman government did not recognize changes of citizenship, but these children were American-born and thereby US citizens. Even by the norms of international law in the early twentieth century, these children fully qualified for American protection, especially, Davis testifies, since they held valid documents. Technically, the legal guarantees for their safety were stronger than those of the dragomen. Consul Davis of Harput brought this matter to the attention of the Department in October 1917 upon his return to the United States:

In speaking of the facilities accorded to me and to the American missionaries at Harput by the officials there and elsewhere, I should call attention to the fact that no persons of Armenian origin were permitted to leave with us. There were a number of women whose husbands are naturalized American citizens living in America and who had been in America themselves. Some of them had children who were born in America. I made every effort to bring these women and children out with me and was given to understand at first that they could come, but when formal permission for their departure was asked it was refused in every case, even to those who had passports in good order. I feel that this is a matter that should be taken up vigorously with the Turkish Government when it is possible to do so.[82]

It is not clear whether any action was taken.

Conclusion

This analysis traced one strand of the evidence on the Armenian Genocide accumulated in the National Archives of the United States. Even from as narrow a prism as the practical operation of the American consulates in the Ottoman Empire and their attention to US interests during the course of the First World War, there emerges a clear picture of the true intentions of the Young Turk regime in its mistreatment of the Armenians. An examination of aspects of the economic consequences of the deportations,

---

[81] RG59, 367.113/32.   [82] RG59, 867.00/803.

as reported by the Consuls, reveals a process of state intervention in the economy of the country, whose objectives exceeded purely acquisitive ends. The occasion of global warfare facilitated the social reorganization of the Ottoman economy and initiated the nationalization of the domestic economy by liquidating an ethnically defined class intervening between, and, in the view of the CUP, impeding, a state-managed order and a free economic system, which delivered a disproportionate share of the gross domestic revenue into the hands of elements whose political outlook was inconsistent with the ideological conformities required of a national order whose stability was presumably derived from ethnic homogeneity. From this standpoint, the radical wing of the Young Turk revolutionary movement, consolidated as the CUP, shares characteristics of the Bolshevik wing of the Russian Social Democratic movement, which espoused the violence of a vanguard willingly waging class warfare against targeted sectors of society. While the CUP's policy fell short of the full program of state ownership of property, it did rapidly proceed towards defined types of ownership, which in the longer course of the country's development markedly enlarged the state sector in the economy. The absence of social resistance to that type of economic development and the political determination of that necessity was in part based on the fact that reliance on an entrepreneurial approach was not a readily available option, itself the result of a situation, however, created with the deliberate destruction and methodical decimation of a class capable of its delivery.[83]

The individual consular reports represent highly particularized views of conditions in the Ottoman Empire. As a collection, however, they contain the outlines of numerous courses of policy and action introduced by the Turkish government. As steady observers and recorders of the events affecting the Armenians, a good portion of which they witnessed, the Consuls, in due course, each on his own, came to the realization that the full mechanism of the Ottoman state was bearing down on the Armenian population and that the persecutions were so widespread that they went beyond the scope of reprisal, mob action, social explosion, or vengeful reaction. The scale and method of the total operation pointed to an unnamed scheme to dismantle a facet of Ottoman society by systematically extricating a distinct ethnic group from its historically established points of habitation and depriving them en masse of the routines that sustain community and life. The American envoys did not miss the larger picture.

---

[83] On the subject of accelerated nation-building and genocide, see Mark Levene, "Why is the Twentieth Century the Century of Genocide?" *Journal of World History* 2:2 (2000), pp. 305–36. By Levene, see also, "Creating a Modern 'Zone of Genocide': The Impact of Nation and State-Formation on Eastern Anatolia, 1878–1923," *Holocaust and Genocide Studies* 12:3 (1998), pp. 393–433. See also Robert Melson, *Revolution and Genocide*.

Walter M. Geddes had confided in his memorandum: "Several Turks[,] whom I interviewed, told me that the motive of this exile was to exterminate the race."[84] In his own cover letter of 16 November 1915, to Geddes's memorandum, George Horton wrote: "I have also other statements from eye-witnesses, not natives of this country, of the highest standing in the religious and educational world, which leads me to believe that what is now taking place in Armenian Turkey, surpasses in deliberate and long-protracted horror and in extent anything that has hitherto happened in the history of the world."[85] As early as 21 July 1915, Stanley Hollis had forwarded an unsigned report from Beirut predicting the outcome: "If a means is not found to aid them through the next few months, until they get established in their new surroundings, two thirds or three fourths of them will die of starvation and disease."[86] Hollis was not even aware of the extent of the atrocities being committed in the interior. Leslie Davis had preceded him with a harsher and grimmer assessment and advised Morgenthau on 11 July 1915 that: "There seems to be a definite plan to dispose of all the Armenian men."[87] He had reason to think at the moment that the women and children might be spared, but Jesse Jackson had seen the worst in Aleppo, and even before either Hollis or Davis he had written Morgenthau on 5 June 1915: "It is without doubt a carefully planned scheme to thoroughly extinguish the Armenian race."[88] Jackson, who maintained an unflappable fortitude through it all while submitting one clinical report after another, finally sent a message on 3 August 1915, sharing his own sense of shock: "The situation is becoming more critical daily as there is no telling where this thing will end. The Germans are being blamed on every hand, for if they have not ordered this wholesale slaughter (for it is nothing less than the extermination of the Armenian race) they at least condone it."[89] Almost a year later, at the other end of the Ottoman Empire, Charles Allen wrote from Adrianople on 18 March 1916: "The Germans and Austrians therefore may or may not be guilty of complicity in the plot to secure the disappearance of the Armenian nation."[90] Lastly, Morgenthau's successor as American envoy to the Sublime Porte, Ambassador Abram I. Elkus wrote on 17 October 1916:

From report by eyewitness sent by Consul Jackson and from other reliable sources it appears that deportations accompanied by studied cruelties continue. Families are separated and scattered among Moslems. Clergy separated from their people, forced conversions to Islam perseveringly pushed, children and girls from

[84] RG59, 867.4016/243, attached memorandum, p. 4.   [85] Ibid.
[86] RG59, 867.4016/104.   [87] RG59, 867.4016/127.   [88] Ibid.
[89] RG59, 867.4016/126.   [90] RG59, 867.00/786.

deported families kidnapped. In order to avoid opprobrium of the civilized world, which the continuation of massacres would arouse, Turkish officials have now adopted and are executing the unchecked policy of extermination through starvation, exhaustion, and brutality of treatment hardly surpassed even in Turkish history.[91]

In the concluding chapters of his account of the time he spent in Turkey, Henry Morgenthau sketched out the events of 1915. By the time *Ambassador Morgenthau's Story* appeared in 1918, the former envoy had had time to reflect and organize his experiences into a coherent narrative, the thrust of which was to demonstrate the criminal conduct of the Young Turk regime and the complicity of the German government. In the chapter entitled "The Murder of a Nation," he made a bold assertion meant to place the atrocities committed against the Armenians in historic context, comparing them with previous disasters of the like and finding that in its dimensions the Armenian catastrophe exceeded any suffered by humankind up to that time. It is one of the most frequently invoked quotations from his book: "I am confident that the whole history of the human race contains no such horrible episode as this. The great massacres and persecutions of the past seem almost insignificant when compared with the suffering of the Armenians in 1915."[92]

It would be difficult to compose a more forceful statement on the Armenian Genocide, and anyone less certain of the facts would have hesitated making an outsized claim of the like on the record of human history. Throughout the months of reporting on the deportations and massacres, Morgenthau had coined some powerful and moving statements. All these were for official consumption alone. His autobiographical work was directed to a wider audience and intended to communicate in more literary prose the meaning of the events that transpired during the years he was stationed in Constantinople. Of all the things he might have said about the Armenian Genocide, this particular remark may raise in the mind of the later student of the same events the thought that surely this assertion was made by Morgenthau as a means of persuasion rather than evidence of fact. Like so much else that the US archival record demonstrates, the truth of the matter was quite the contrary. Morgenthau had every reason to be confident of his assertion, for, of all the things that he did say and write, this, it turns out, was his least original observation.

[91] RG59, 867. 4016/299.
[92] Morgenthau, *Ambassador Morgenthau's Story*, pp. 321–2.

7   The Armenian Genocide and American missionary relief efforts

Suzanne E. Moranian

In 1920, an American peace negotiator declared that it was "no exaggeration to say that the Armenians would have disappeared as a nation" had it not been for the relief efforts initiated by the American missionaries.[1] From 1915 to 1927, they were swept into the violence of revolution, war, and annihilation. They saw firsthand the Armenian Genocide and the efforts of the Turkish government to exterminate Turkish Armenians. Numerous missionaries in the field protected countless Armenians and saved their lives, sometimes sacrificing their own. The largest American missionary organization operating in Turkey at that time was the American Board of Commissioners for Foreign Missions, headquartered in Boston. Based on reports it received from its missionaries in the Turkish field, the American Board launched a relief drive that broke new ground in the history of American philanthropy. The American missionaries were the most critical figures in the relationship between the United States and the Armenians during the genocide era. They were unmatched in exerting influence and expertise in the Turkish field and on the American home front, as well as in American policy, intellectual, and cultural circles.

The Protestant missionary movement in the United States derived its fire and zeal from the intellectual and religious atmosphere in early nineteenth-century New England. Impressed with Samuel Hopkins, the prominent Revolutionary War-era religious leader and his doctrine of "disinterested benevolence," the missionaries followed the call of unabashed devotion to the active service of God. They believed that it was their moral duty to redeem an errant mankind through active intervention. Throughout the nineteenth century, this led the Protestant missionaries to bear the cross for abolition, temperance, and world peace.

The material in this chapter originally appeared in Suzanne E. Moranian's "The American Missionaries and the American Question: 1915–1917," Ph.D. diss., University of Wisconsin–Madison, 1994.
[1] Benjamin Burges Moore, "Some Facts About Armenia," *New York Times Current History* 12 (June 1920), p. 508.

This spirit inspired evangelists for generations in the immodest attempt to convert all non-Christians around the globe.[2]

In this setting, the American Board became a legal corporation in Massachusetts in 1812. It was the premier missionary organization of its time. Its founders were Congregationalists, though until the late 1800s it included a Presbyterian and Dutch Reformed membership. Based in Boston, the American Board was a galvanizing force in the American evangelical Protestant movement. Its earliest missions were to India and Ceylon in 1812 and 1816, but only a few years later its Prudential Committee became intrigued with the idea of evangelizing the Holy Land. By the early 1830s, the American Board opened a station in Constantinople, the first in Turkey. In rapid succession, it then opened additional stations in Smyrna, Brusa, Trebizond, and Erzurum. By 1863, its evangelical missions dotted the map all across Asia Minor, Northern Syria, and Mesopotamia.

At the beginning of the twentieth century, the American Board operated 12 stations and 270 outstations in Asiatic Turkey. Nearly 145 missionaries and over 800 native workers managed these enterprises. By then, the Board had established 114 organized churches with over 13,000 converts. Their evangelists taught over 60,000 students in their 132 high-grade and over 1,100 lower-grade schools.[3]

In addition, the American Board ran the American College for Girls in Constantinople – founded only ten years after Vassar College, the first college for women in the United States, opened its doors; Euphrates College in Harput; Anatolia College in Marsovan; American College in Van; Central Turkey College for men and women in Aintab; International College in Smyrna; as well as various theological seminaries, several industrial schools, and two schools for the deaf and the blind.[4] A former American Board missionary, Cyrus Hamlin, founded Robert College, which operated independently of the American Board. It was, however, an active and prestigious participant in the Yankee Protestant education that swept Turkey. Opened in 1863 on the shores of the Bosporus, it was the first American college established outside of the United States.[5]

---

[2] Clifton Jackson Phillips, *Protestant America and the Pagan World: The First Half Century of the American Board of Commissioners for Foreign Missions, 1810–1860*, Harvard East Asian Monographs (Cambridge, Mass.: East Asian Research Center, Harvard University, 1969), pp. 2–6.
[3] Edwin Munsell Bliss, Henry Otis Dwight, H. Allen Tupper, eds., *The Encyclopedia of Missions* (2nd edn., 1904; reprint edn., Detroit: Gale Research Co., 1975), pp. 29–31.
[4] Ibid., p. 31.
[5] For more information on these schools, see: Robert L. Daniel, *American Philanthropy in the Near East* (Athens, Ohio: Ohio University Press, 1970); Joseph L. Grabill, *Protestant Diplomacy and the Near East: Missionary Influence on American Policy, 1810–1927* (Minneapolis: University of Minnesota Press, 1971).

In 1870, the Presbyterians peeled off and formed their own Board of Foreign Missions, serving in Persia, Syria, and Lebanon. Other American groups sponsored missions in the Near East, including the Methodist Episcopal church (North) and the American Baptist Missionary Union. Missionaries from other countries also operated in Turkey, notably French Catholics as well as German, English and Scotch Protestants. However, the American Board reigned there, effectively cornering the market in Turkey.

In AD 301, the Armenians became the first people in the world to adopt Christianity as the national religion. The missionaries believed that the Armenians were spiritually corrupt, pursued Christianity incorrectly, and were candidates for reform. Thus, the missionaries attempted to transform the Armenian church into a glittering example to the Muslims of what Christianity could be if practiced properly – that is, like Yankee Congregationalism. The Armenians would then act as a lure to the Turks, who would renounce their Islamic faith and convert. Even into the twentieth century, the missionaries did not abandon their hope of converting the Turks.

Satisfied with their own religion and culture, the Turks did not show the slightest tendency to accept the Christian Gospel and saw no benefit in abandoning the Koran. The Turkish authorities punished any Muslim who did show an interest. Except for seeking medical assistance from the American Christians, the Turks dismissed the missionaries as useless religiously and dangerous politically as threats to the rule of the mullahs and sultan.

When the American missionaries arrived in Turkey, there was already underway an effort to reform the Armenian Apostolic Church from within. The native reformers challenged the "theology, rites, and rituals of the Armenian church," explained church historian Vahan H. Tootikian, "to the extent that they accused her of losing her original New Testament simplicity and purity and insisted that the Church ought to be cleansed of her corruption and the Gospel be substituted for 'human inventions.' " Unfortunately, both the reformers and the Apostolic church leadership proved to be inflexible and uncompromising.[6] Initially, the missionaries hoped to reform the Apostolic Church; they did not set out to rupture the Armenian community by encouraging a separate evangelical church to be established.

From the start, the Apostolic clergy persecuted the evangelical Armenians, who – with the support of the American Board – sought change, freedom from clerical and intellectual repression, education and literacy

---

[6] Vahan H. Tootikian, *The Armenian Evangelical Church* (Detroit: Armenian Heritage Committee, 1982), pp. 15–19.

for all, and greater equality in the church, especially between clergy and laity as well as for women. Unyielding and intolerant of reform, the Armenian patriarch feared the collapse of his religious and civil jurisdiction over this growing minority. He forbade all marriages and business with the reformers. Finally, in 1846, he excommunicated all Armenian evangelicals. This forced the reluctant creation of the new and separate Armenian Evangelical church as a last resort. When the Armenian Protestants established their church, they enlisted the guidance and financial support of the American Board. By 1850, spurred on by the British Ambassador at Constantinople, Lord Henry Wellesley Cowley, the Turkish government officially recognized the Armenian Protestants as a distinct political community in Turkey with its own civil representative. Missionary money, organization, and support allowed the Armenian Evangelical church to grow and flourish.

The American missionaries met the concerns and demands of the growing evangelical movement in Turkey. They were the catalysts for establishing the Armenian Protestants as a separate entity spiritually and politically. Yet, in so doing, they fractured the ancient Armenian Apostolic church. Turkish Armenians had withstood insults of all sorts for almost a millennium. The Apostolic church had held the nation together, ensuring the survival of its people throughout centuries of countless onslaughts. Within twenty years of the arrival of the preachers from New England, the Armenians turned on one another. In an atmosphere of rancor and disdain, they split in two. The division, though far more cordial, remains today.

The typical American Board missionary was an Anglo-Saxon Protestant. Before the Civil War, he most often came from New England or upstate New York. Usually they were graduates of either elite private colleges or large state universities. By the turn of the century, though, the recruits mostly hailed from the Midwest. These came from middle-class families residing in small towns, not farms or cities. The early twentieth-century Board missionary was a married, ordained minister. He was likely to be a graduate of such smaller denominational colleges as Beloit, Grinnell, or Oberlin.[7]

Women missionaries accounted for about half of those in foreign service. They never attained the same status as did the men, primarily because they could not become ministers. The women labored abroad no less ardently, though, claiming the higher mortality rate. They had fewer opportunities to preach than did the men. Frequently college graduates,

---

[7] Valentin H. Rabe, "Evangelical Logistics: Mission Support and Resources to 1920," in John K. Fairbank, ed., *The Missionary Enterprise in China and America* (Cambridge, Mass.: Harvard University Press, 1974), pp. 70–5.

they represented the minority of American women who attended college at that time. The married women were teachers and nurses, assisting their husbands and raising their families overseas in usually primitive surroundings. However, some of the female evangelists were single and served as teachers. Most were graduates of such women's colleges as Mt. Holyoke, whose founder, Mary Lyon, was a staunch proponent of female mission work.[8] As missionaries, the unmarried women worked in locales where eligible bachelors were rare. Service in foreign fields for these women was tantamount to taking a vow of celibacy.[9]

When the American evangelists first arrived in Turkey in the early 1830s, they believed that they had come to bear witness to a peaceful and loving Christ. Little did they imagine that their successors were to bear witness to genocide. "From 1915–1918 came that series of atrocities such as the world of our day had hardly the emotions and conscience to comprehend," reflected missionary S. Ralph Harlow, "even amid the horror of the cruelties of those years." "Those of us who were in the land at the time, who saw these things with our own eyes," he revealed, "have never told half the truth of the terror of those dark hours."[10]

After the Young Turks seized power in 1908, they gradually adopted an ideology of pan-Turkism. This ideology became a deadly tool of power in the hands of the driven Young Turk junta. The Young Turks wanted to move beyond their boundaries. Having lost their European possessions, they now wanted to crush Russia and combine Ottoman Turkey with Turkish Caucasia and Central Asia. Their ambition was to create an invincible pan-Turkish empire. They would emancipate the Turkish-speaking Islamic world from infidel oppressors. They had redefined Turkish identity and decided to cast out the ethnic minorities. It would be nothing less than a Turkey for the Turks.

The Armenians, then, were in the way. They were the largest non-Turkish minority in Turkey. The Young Turks considered the Armenians to be a principal impediment to their expansionist plans. The Armenians and their ancient lands physically interfered with any attempt to unify the Turks. In fact, most Armenians inhabited Eastern Anatolia. The Young Turks considered these provinces to be the very heart of their nation.

A substantial number of Armenians also lived in Russia, near the Turkish border. The Young Turks promoted the notion that the Armenians were disloyal as Turkey headed towards war with Russia.

[8] Phillips, *Protestant America*, p. 311.   [9] Rabe, "Evangelical Logistics," pp. 72–7.
[10] S. Ralph Harlow, ABC 16.5, vol. 5, no. 179, from the American Board of Commissioners for Foreign Missions archives, hereinafter referred to as the "ABCFM archives." All ABCFM material quoted in this chapter is published by permission of the Houghton Library, Harvard University, as well as Wider Church Ministries, United Church of Christ.

The government portrayed the Armenians, traditionally Turkey's most loyal minority, as frightening agents of its sworn enemy. Accusing the Armenians of treacherously attempting to endanger the security of the Turkish people endangered the security of the Armenian position in Turkey. The Young Turks knew this.

Moreover, the Young Turks regarded the emerging Armenian nationalism and ethnic renaissance, as well as habitual demands for political reforms, as insufferable hindrances to the pan-Turanian quest. Armenian prosperity challenged Turkish superiority as Muslims. In addition, these matters kept Turkey under foreign scrutiny and invited unwanted intervention.

Thus, the Armenians posed a political problem to which the Young Turks responded with a biological solution: kill them. The elimination of the Armenians became essential to the achievement of Turkish nationalism. The extermination of the Armenians was violence executed for the sake of power. The Young Turk's "Little Napoleon," Enver Paşa, declared in the presence of the Papal Envoy in Constantinople that he "would not rest so long as a single Armenian remained alive."[11]

The Young Turk leadership decided to rid Turkey of the Armenians, if they could, not as a consequence of the First World War, but, rather, prior to its outbreak. The Armenian persecution, a domestic affair, was not a result of the war. Instead, it derived from problems deeply embedded in Turkish history. The Young Turks planned the killings and deportations carefully before the war started. They defined the Armenians as powerful, while in reality the Armenians were politically powerless. Alleging that the Armenians were in nationwide revolt, the Young Turks cited wartime national security as the reason for exiling them. Any deaths, the Young Turks argued, that resulted from these preventative measures were casualties of the war.

However, numerous American missionaries serving in Turkey received warnings that the Armenians were in danger before Turkey entered the war in November 1914. In September of that year, a German army Colonel visited American evangelist Mary L. Graffam in Turkey. "He was a Christian, although a German," Graffam explained, "and he tried to warn us of things which might take place in the coming summer; this showing that the deportations were planned as early as this." The Colonel told her that "a certain fate was in store for all Armenians, but if the Germans were in the country, there would be no massacres."[12]

---

[11] Martin Niepage, *The Horrors of Aleppo: Seen by a German Eyewitness* (1917; reprint edn., Plandome, N.Y.: New Age Publishers, 1975), p. 15.

[12] Mary L. Graffam, "Miss Graffam's Own Story," 28 June 1919, ABC 16.5, vol. 6, no. 262, ABCFM archives.

Susan Billington Harper has drawn attention in the next chapter of this book to Graffam's testimony. American missionary Geneveive DuVal Irwin noted a similar warning in her journal. A year prior to the onset of the Armenian atrocities, a German officer, Major Lange, visited the missionaries in Sivas. He told them, she wrote, "under oath of secrecy as to <u>what</u> it was, that something terrible of which they never dreamed would happen to the Armenian people" in 1915.[13]

To launch mass murder, the Young Turks used propaganda, and, specifically, a contrived argument of Armenian treachery. This was not unlike the propaganda blitz that the Nazis were to wage against their victims only a few decades later. The issue of Armenian loyalty was important because it was the cornerstone of the Young Turks' propaganda program. Even today, it is the central point underlying the continuing Turkish denial of the predetermined persecution of the Armenians. Many missionaries observed firsthand the propaganda campaign depicting the Armenians as traitors, which laid the groundwork for the ensuing deportations. American Boarder Henry Harrison Riggs, for example, recalled that once Turkey entered the war, "the Turkish authorities began a systematic build-up of hostility to the Armenians," dispensing "a great deal of fiction to prove that the Armenians were a disloyal element menacing the safety of the Turks." Riggs explained that on a large scale, the Turks spread the idea that all of the Armenians were arming for revolt. At widely scattered points, the Turks would announce the discovery of hidden arms, and then arrest thousands of Armenians for owning them. "The arms thus discovered," wrote Riggs, "were put on exhibition to arouse public indignation, and accomplished that purpose in spite of the fact that the number and character of the 'arms' were nowhere important enough to bother a local sheriff, and many were obviously 'planted.'" Riggs complained that a case was thereby built up against the Armenians "in the minds of the common Turkish people, in preparation of the atrocities which were to follow." "In fairness to both the Armenians and to the ignorant Turks," Riggs declared, "it should be known that the situation was artificial and the accusations false."[14]

From the start of the genocide, the missionaries became intensely engaged in protecting the Armenians. The American evangelists in Turkey not only observed the killing of the Armenian people, but, frequently at the risk of losing their own lives, tried to save countless Armenians from

[13] Geneveive DuVal Irwin, November 1914 – March 1917, ABC 16.5, vol. 6, no. 262, ABCFM archives.
[14] Henry Harrison Riggs, "Turkey, 1910–1942," ABC Ms. History, vol. 31a, ch. III, pp. 3–5, ABCFM archives.

their tormentors. These reports are amply documented in the missionary archives.

One such missionary woman, Tacy Atkinson, and her husband, Henry, a doctor, helped many Armenians escape. It began one night after they heard, she explained, that a Kurdish patriarch whom they knew from the Dersim would be at their gate after dark. For 40 Turkish pounds, she noted, he would take any one who wished to go to the Dersim. She rounded up a professor and several other Armenians, and sent them off dressed as Kurds. "Then began sort of an underground railway," she wrote, "for which our back porch was a station sending people to Dersim." The Atkinsons kept this system going, inspired by America's abolition movement, for one and a half years, assisting hundreds of Armenians to safety.[15]

Indeed, the American missionaries who served in Turkey during the war years suffered personally as witnesses to a crime they felt helpless to stop. One missionary, Theodore Elmer, wrote after he returned to the United States that he carried with him the memories of the "sight of tens of thousands of innocent women and little children . . . packed in cattle trucks, or languishing in the open fields, or crowded at the stations along the Anatolian Railway, waiting in herds like sheep for the slaughter for transportation to unknown places of death by starvation or violence and outrage." These scenes, he said, are "to me still like a nightmare which I cannot banish from my mind."[16]

Only a few weeks after the genocide officially began on 24 April, 1915, America's Ambassador to Turkey, Henry Morgenthau, urgently cabled Secretary of State William Jennings Bryan that the American mission stations in Turkey were begging for relief funds. "Some say starvation threatens," he warned; "Please help quickly."[17] Bryan immediately forwarded this cable to James L. Barton, the prominent Foreign Secretary of the American Board in Boston. Thus were wedded the United States government and missionaries in Near East pursuits. It was the problem of relief that brought piety into overt partnership with the political, and elevated the missionaries to a position of influence in Washington. In only a few years, through sophisticated fund-raising techniques, the American Protestants eventually created a multimillion-dollar business of Near-East aid.

[15] Tacy W. Atkinson, 23 September 1916, ABC 16.9.7, vol. 25b, no. 156A, ABCFM archives.
[16] Theodore A. Elmer to William E. Strong, 5 October 1916, ABC 16.9.3, vol. 42, no. 30, ABCFM archives.
[17] William Jennings Bryan to James L. Barton, 17 May 1915, ABC 16.9.3, vol. 40, no. 26, ABCFM archives.

Within war-stricken Anatolia, the missionaries tried to relieve what one American, Dr. Wilfred M. Post, described from Konia as "this constant stream of misery we have before us."[18] The missionaries could not assist the Armenians sent out on the death marches. As Barton, America's premier missionary statesman, explained, "it was almost impossible to aid in any way the unfortunate people as they were corralled and marched out of the cities and towns, or as they passed under heavy guard through the places where Americans were living. The caravans were isolated by soldiers and forced to move on continually."[19] In 1916, however, relief activities increased, with funds being dispersed to the Turkish interior, Syria, and the Caucasus. Relief work fell into four categories: general relief, which supplied the needy with a daily ration of bread; special relief for those considered only mildly or temporarily destitute, such as transient exiles or sick Armenian soldiers; medical work, which reached thousands monthly; and, most important to the missionaries, help for orphans, who were supplied with food, clothing, bedding, shelter, and, when possible, basic education.

Beyond the interior of wartime Turkey, the missionaries worked in concert with the American Consuls. Together they helped over 150,000 surviving Turkish Armenians in Syria and the several hundred thousand more who fled over the frontier to the Russian Caucasus. A confidential 1916 telegram from the American embassy in Constantinople to the State Department reported that in Aleppo, for example, relief work supported 1,350 orphans. However, this served only a portion of the destitute children there. "So insufficient are the funds," read the message, "that many . . . have only grass to eat, and they are dying of starvation by the hundreds."[20]

Dr. William Chambers of the American Board described the situation in Beirut during the war, where the Presbyterian missionaries and the local Syrian people assisted their relief activities. "Out of a camp of 5–6000 not more than 1500 are in extreme destitution. The others are able to live. In spite of the crowded unsanitary conditions of the camp," Chambers wrote, "the health condition has been remarkably good."[21]

Another American Boarder, E. St. John Ward, spent the war years stationed in Jerusalem and worked with the American Red Cross

---

[18] E. D. Cushman and Wilfred M. Post, "Armenian Relief Work in Konia," October 1916, ABC 16.5, vol. 6, no. 4, ABCFM archives.

[19] James L. Barton, *Story of Near East Relief (1915–1930): an Interpretation* (1930; reprint edn., Astoria, N.Y.: J. C. & A. L. Fawcett, Inc., 1991), p. 62.

[20] Alvey A. Adee to James L. Barton, 11 May 1916, ABC 16.5, vol. 6, nos. 167–8, ABCFM archives.

[21] "Missionary Work among the Armenian Refugees in Syria," ABC 16.9.2, vol. 5, no. 65, ABCFM archives.

Commission to Palestine. Ward reported that there were about 30,000 Armenians each in Damascus and Aleppo, and another 30,000 scattered throughout Syria, Palestine, and Egypt. He estimated that there were about "90,000 Armenians left of the nearly 400,000 deported down through Aleppo south and southeast. Many of them are quite self-supporting, but there are probably 10,000 destitute and many more who are without work and will be in distress before long if relief does not come."[22]

Even when the United States entered the war in 1917, most American relief workers remained at their stations and carried on. Many were then made attachés of the Swedish legation, which was charged with the care of American interests in Turkey. Often isolated and confined in the Turkish interior, and lacking most basic supplies, these workers risked death from typhus, little food, hostile conditions, and the strain of trying to alleviate the horrors around them. More than a few gave their lives in this service.

Following the defeat of Turkey and the signing of the armistice in Mudros that ended the fighting in the area in October 1918, relief operations blossomed. Communication was open and the terrain accessible. New American personnel were sent to replace the beleaguered relief workers who had endured the war. Supplies of every sort and all types of medical equipment were desperately needed to begin feeding and rehabilitating the ravaged population.

Appalled at the start by the overwhelming need for assistance, leading American philanthropists joined the American Board, and other mission and religious societies, in founding numerous relief organizations. These included the formation in 1915 of the American Committee for Armenian and Syrian Relief (ACASR), which briefly became the American Committee for Relief in the Near East (ACRNE), and then evolved into the Near East Relief (NER). The United States Congress granted the NER a charter in 1919, thereby infusing it with political prestige.

Naively, the early relief organizers believed that $100,000 would be an adequate amount. In 1915, they raised almost $177,000, all of which was sent overseas for immediate use. However, the American Committee quickly realized that it had not comprehended the magnitude of the need, and renewed appeals were made across the United States.[23] The following year, 1916, donations rose to about $2,404,000, after which the American Committee's promotional genius, Charles Vickrey,

---

[22] E. St. John Ward to James L. Barton, December 1918, ABC 16.5, vol. 6, no. 117, ABCFM archives.

[23] Barton, *Story of Near East Relief*, p. 409.

spearheaded a vigorous fund-raising campaign. In 1917, receipts dou-
bled as the public understood better the desperate conditions of the
Armenians. In 1918, they doubled again to the amount of $7 million.
This was especially impressive considering the wide variety of war-related
appeals. Americans were being asked to give money to such causes as
Billion Dollar Liberty Loans, Belgian and French Reliefs, the Red Cross,
United War Work, and many more. Yet, as Barton observed, "In spite of
this the people found room in their hearts for the needy people of the Near
East."[24]

After the armistice, the opportunity for widespread relief work neces-
sitated the launching of a new, special fund-raising campaign. Under the
direction of the Laymen's Missionary Movement, which utilized the latest
business-world methods of organization and financial management, and
with the cooperation of the talented Vickrey, in 1919 they took in the unprecedented amount of almost $19.5 million. In the ensuing years, as the
crisis diminished, so, too, did the receipts. By 1929, public campaigning
stopped.[25]

The Rockefeller Foundation made early and large contributions, which
it increased as the needs mounted. The unfailing support of the American
Red Cross during the war years made it possible to increase greatly Near
East relief work. By January 1918, the Red Cross donated $1,800,000,
and, with subsequent appropriations, its total gift amounted to $6 million.
The Armenian-American community also worked hard to raise money for
the relief of their fellow Armenians. The Armenian Benevolent Union,
for example, collected over $1.5 million, which the NER transmitted
overseas.[26]

Over the years, the United States government would donate $25 million
to the NER in supplies, services, and cash. Herbert Hoover, Franklin D.
Roosevelt, and William Howard Taft each served as trustees of the NER.
Over fifteen years, the missionary-based NER spent a staggering $116
million in assistance. It helped well over 1, if not 2, million refugees –
two-thirds of whom were women and children. More than 132,000 orphans graduated from the Near East Relief orphanage schools. It trained
200 nurses. Of its volunteers, 30 lost their lives, succumbing to illness and
the sometimes dangerous environment. Foreshadowing the work of the
Peace Corps, the NER built hundreds of miles of roads and well-paved
streets. Through irrigation it reclaimed thousands of acres of arable land.
It erected permanent buildings and repaired old ones. The NER established new industries. It imported new breeds of cattle and poultry. It
planted better seeds of corn, cotton, wheat, other grains, and vegetables.

---

[24] Ibid., p. 410.   [25] Ibid., p. 409.   [26] Ibid., pp. 395, 409–10.

The NER also demonstrated the advantages of such equipment as the modern tractor.[27]

During its fifteen years of allocating relief funds, the NER spent, as examples, about $28 million in the Caucasus; about $30 million in Turkey; over $12 million in Syria and Palestine; nearly $8 million in Persia and Mesopotamia; almost $6 million in Greece; and $667,000 went to other areas. Expenses for freight, personnel, warehousing, and general relief were about $7.5 million. Costs for administration were nearly $7 million.[28]

Certainly, because of the missionaries, America had assumed the moral mandate of the Near East. "The Armenians will never forget this debt of gratitude," declared the eminent Armenian, Boghos Nubar, in 1918.[29] It was true, as Woodrow Wilson remarked, that "the fate of Armenia has always been of special interest to the American people."[30]

However, America's philanthropy abroad hardly began with the Armenians, as it can be traced to the beginnings of the new nation. Historian Merle Curti noted that "the seeds of the idea that if charity begins at home, it does not end at home, had been planted and had begun to grow" in America's earliest years.[31] America's tradition of donating relief abroad built on such experiences as rallying aid for the Greek struggle for freedom in the 1820s, the widespread American giving during the Great Famine in Ireland in the 1840s, saving thousands of starving and sick Cubans following their 1890s fight for independence from Spain, and even raising nationwide contributions of $300,000 for the Armenian victims of the 1895–6 massacres in Turkey. As the twentieth century dawned, America "now had the habit of giving," observed Curti, "and organizations with which to meet new emergencies such as those brought by the Great War."[32]

When the Germans marched through Belgium en route to Paris, in August 1914, the Belgian people rose up to resist the occupation. Soon cut off by the Allied blockade from their food resources, mostly imported, the 9 million desperate Belgians quickly earned the sympathy of the world. In short order, international relief efforts commenced with the future American President, Herbert Hoover, at the helm. Appointed Director of the Commission for Belgian Relief, Hoover appealed especially to the

[27] Ibid., p. 341.   [28] Ibid., p. 411.
[29] Boghos Nubar to James L. Barton, 7 July 1918, ABC Personal: Barton papers, 5:11, ABCFM archives.
[30] Woodrow Wilson to M. Paul Hymans, 30 November 1920, ABC 16.9.1, vol. 2, no. 174, ABCFM archives.
[31] Merle Curti, *American Philanthropy Abroad: A History* (New Brunswick, N.J.: Rutgers University Press, 1963), p. 21.
[32] Ibid., pp. 125, 223.

United States for help. With the cooperation of the American press, the Commission waged a successful propaganda campaign at home to enlist the American people in the cause. In fact, during the period of American neutrality, the largest and most professional relief program conducted was that for Belgium, which expanded in 1915 to include relief for 2 million people in northern France. Of the $52 million the Commission raised, the United States donated over $34 million, including cash contributions of about $6 million, and clothing and provisions totaling over $28 million. However, unlike charity efforts on behalf of the Armenians, the United States was not the principal donor towards the Belgians on a per capita basis. Hoover was chagrined that citizens of Australia gave more per capita than did Americans.[33] Actually, Canada, Great Britain, Australia, and New Zealand all gave more per capita than did the United States. While it is true that the Hoover team's skillful management of relief saved Belgium, Belgian participation played a significant role in the success of the mission. Unlike the homeless Turkish Armenians scattered throughout the diaspora after the war, the Belgian people were able to recover economically and help themselves – by Hoover's design. Moreover, unlike the Armenian Republic, which lacked power and resources, the exiled Belgian government was able to assume much of the cost of relief.[34]

As the war got underway, a variety of American relief committees was organized to help desperate people in Serbia, Rumania, Russia, and Poland. In addition, the plight of the Jews in Palestine, as well as the millions of Jews suffering under German and Austrian occupation in Poland, the Baltic provinces, and Russia, instantly captured the sympathy of American Jewish relief organizations. In the end, a remarkable $63 million was raised by American Jews and Gentiles together to assist the Jews overseas.[35]

During the armistice, the Wilson administration named Hoover Director General of the American Relief Administration, created in February 1919. Hoover was to deliver food, clothing, medical supplies, and other items needed in the post-war recovery of Europe. The money came from the United States government, as well as private donations solicited through well-organized fund-raising campaigns, in partnership with numerous charitable organizations. In total, the United States delivered about $5 billion. Much was in the form of government loans, although a substantial amount derived from private and government sources.[36] It

[33] David Burner, *Herbert Hoover: A Public Life* (New York: Alfred A. Knopf, 1979), p. 91.
[34] Curti, *American Philanthropy*, p. 235.
[35] Ibid., p. 244.　[36] Burner, *Herbert Hoover*, p. 130.

is widely recognized that, together with Great Britain, the United States rescued millions of Europeans from starvation and deprivation in the aftermath of the war.

However, it was in Russia that the largest and most complicated relief problem emerged. In 1921, famine and drought had struck, threatening the lives of up to 25 million people. Once again, Hoover met the crisis head on. Insisting that the Soviets contribute nearly $18 million of their gold reserves, and almost $14 million in local money, Hoover persuaded the United States Congress to act in cooperation with voluntary agencies. Within months, Hoover's team began shipping over 740 tons of food, medical supplies, and clothes to Russia, with a value of over $80 million. In 1922, at its peak in Russia, the American Relief Administration, with the help of other American philanthropic groups, fed over 10 million people at 18,000 feeding stations. Critics saw this in part as an anti-Bolshevik move, yet nonetheless, American generosity once again sought to relieve human suffering.[37]

While Russia presented the most enormous post-war relief challenge, Hoover plainly stated that reports from Armenia in 1919 were "shocking enough": in some locales, deaths were at the rate of 3,000 a month; typhus was rampant; women were stripping flesh from dead horses with their bare hands; and in larger towns, "the dead and dying were everywhere in the streets, children wandering about like dogs looking through the offal."[38] Indeed, as Barton noted, it was in the Caucasus that the "most critical situation in the whole Near East following the armistice was found."[39]

Hoover assessed the urgent need in Armenia. According to his reports, he estimated that at least 1 million people lived in the Armenian Republic. An additional 500,000 Armenian refugees flooded in from Turkey – fleeing the genocide there only to face death by famine or disease in Armenia. "At least 250,000 were at the absolute point of death and all would be out of food in twenty days," he explained.[40] The masses of refugees, who could not return home, burdened an already impoverished Armenia, reducing the entire population to starvation rations. Moreover, the local government had no funds and unstable currency, and rested their authority on shaky grounds.[41]

At the urging of Howard Heinz, his representative in the Near East, Hoover decided that the American Relief Administration would take charge of Armenia with its own personnel sent in from Paris. First, Hoover

---

[37] Curti, *American Philanthropy*, pp. 280–9.
[38] Herbert Hoover, *The Memoirs of Herbert Hoover: Years of Adventure, 1874–1920* (New York: The Macmillan Company, 1951), p. 386.
[39] Barton, *Story of Near East Relief*, p. 122.   [40] Hoover, *Memoirs*, p. 387.
[41] Barton, *Story of Near East Relief*, p. 120.

sent Major Joseph C. Green, who immediately made improvements. By American law, though, American operations had to end on 1 July 1920. Fearful of abandoning Armenia, Hoover arranged that Colonel William N. Haskell, the American Relief Director in Rumania, be appointed by the "Big Four" as High Commissioner for Armenia to represent the power of the Allied and Associated governments. Haskell was to preserve order, protect Armenia, and oversee the relief operations.

With the arrival of Haskell, the Near East Relief agreed to pay all administrative, orphanage, and transportation costs involved, which amounted to $500,000 per month. The Near East Relief also furnished almost 30 per cent of the supplies used. Haskell allocated assignments to the NER workers, especially care for children and the orphanages.[42]

Haskell served in Armenia for one year, but unfortunately the Colonel turned out to be a treacherous profiteer. Based on the records of the Lord Mayor's Fund, the primary British relief charity, Haskell regularly sold to the Azerbaijani government the relief materials which were intended for the Armenians. These supplies enabled Azerbaijan to advance its campaign against Armenia. The Colonel and his crew hastily departed Tiflis upon news that the Allied investigators and auditors were due to arrive. He hurriedly disposed of the goods and ordered the records destroyed in Tiflis and Yerevan upon fleeing in May 1920.[43]

In late July of that year, Hoover informed the State Department in Washington that Haskell would present his resignation to the Council of Ambassadors in Paris on 1 August. Hoover also announced that along with "Colonel Haskell's resignation my intervention in the management of this branch of European Relief will also come to an end."[44]

Haskell's behavior notwithstanding, during his tenure the United States delivered to Armenia over 119,000 tons of food and milk as well as over 16,000 tons of clothing, soap, and medical supplies. The United States also financed Armenia with about $15.5 million in loans; and from Great Britain, Armenia received a transportation loan of over $630,000.[45] In addition, the NER donated over $11 million, and the American Red Cross contributed a special gift of $500,000. Combining loans and gifts, between January 1919 and July 1920, the total relief distributed in Armenia and the Caucasus amounted to nearly $29 million.[46]

---

[42] Ibid., p. 124.
[43] Christopher J. Walker, *Armenia: The Survival of a Nation* (New York: St. Martin's Press, 1980), p. 287.
[44] Herbert Hoover to Bainbridge Colby, 26 July 1920, in *Papers Relating to the Foreign Relations of the United States, 1920* (Washington: US Government Printing Office, 1932–40), vol. III, p. 785.
[45] Hoover, *Memoirs*, p. 389.   [46] Barton, *Story of Near East Relief*, p. 124.

During this time, 338 villages and towns received flour, and daily an average of over 332,000 people were fed. Public bakeries in the cities were requisitioned, and bread rations were distributed rather than flour. Food and medical treatment were dispensed through such facilities as orphanages – housing over 30,000 children – soup kitchens, milk stations, and hospitals and clinics. Almost the entire population depended on the NER's hospitals, which were supervised by American doctors and nurses, and staffed by native personnel. In addition, where possible, the Armenians were encouraged to prepare a harvest and thereby become self-supporting.[47]

The United States was the only government to appropriate relief funds for Armenia at that time, although, as Barton noted, it was understood that the "British army, during the months of occupation, generously distributed relief supplies from their army stores, and also assisted in the matter of transportation of relief supplies."[48]

Nearly thirty years later, a reflective but proud Hoover wrote that the American relief operation overall "saved the Allies millions of human lives; it saved the peace-making; it saved larger parts of Europe from Communism; it saved millions from starvation, and restored at least 15,000,000 children to health."[49]

The most distinguishing characteristic of American charitable giving throughout the First World War era was, as Curti remarked, "the increasing reliance on large-scale, highly organized, businesslike approaches to the problem."[50] The fund-raising missionaries were visionary in their adoption of the sophisticated fund-raising and mass-marketing techniques of big business. They were exceeded in dollar amounts collected only by the American Relief Administration and the American Red Cross. They broke new ground, however, by expanding the foundation of support of American philanthropy in the Near East. "The magnitude of the disasters in the Near East attracted the attention of the general public," explained historian Robert L. Daniel, "and this in turn enabled the founders of the Near East Relief to create a broadly based committee in support of relief work."[51] The extended nature of the crises forced the missionary-based relief organizers to exceed earlier parameters and solicit funds from well outside the usual circle of missionary donors. The repeated campaigns produced a list of regular contributors from all corners of the United States, whose successive gifts gave them a sense of proprietorship in the settlement of these overseas disorders.[52]

[47] Ibid., pp. 126–8.   [48] Ibid., p. 125.   [49] Hoover, *Memoirs*, p. 427.
[50] Curti, *American Philanthropy*, p. 258.
[51] Daniel, *American Philanthropy in Near East*, p. 169.   [52] Ibid.

Nothing was left to chance or to unworldly church volunteers. The agile Protestants quickly learned that their faraway missions abroad – revolutionary in native settings – could enhance their religious and political base in the mainstream at home. Paradoxically, they used a radical approach overseas to promote a traditional, if not conservative, domestic goal. While the missionaries depended on their outreach ministries to recreate Christianity globally, they simultaneously used these foreign programs to enhance their role in an increasingly secular and politically changing United States. The missionary-led relief efforts were part of the larger move by the Protestant progressives towards the mainstream of an urban-industrial America.

Early on, the Protestants understood that in the new urban, ethnically mixed, and industrial America, power was organized differently than before. American Protestantism had to reinvent itself, as the homogenous climate of the nineteenth century gave way to the cultural diversity of the next. The Protestant churches faced a difficult question. What role were they to play? The Social Gospel was the first Protestant movement to address these profound changes in the United States.

Protestants saw that they could reshape the lives of others in large and sweeping ways. The ethos of social participation and social duty came alive as they looked to the Social Gospel as the religious expression of progressivism. The believers felt obligated to assume responsibility for the welfare of the world, with themselves at the helm. When the Social Gospelers seized on the fact that a modernizing America had a changing power base, they revitalized and restructured the early twentieth-century foreign mission movement.

Many Social Gospelers discovered that mission and relief outreach energized the role of religion in society, and, especially important to Barton and his colleagues, in politics. Their crusade helped to move the Social Gospel in step with progressivism. It was an avenue of opportunity for them and Protestantism to command power and position. The foreign missionary movement was useful to the Protestants as they sought rank and leverage in an industrial, urban America. Ironically, the Protestants' search for power at home would come to depend, in part, on their evangelical and humanitarian programs abroad.

Thus, because "the new order promised them release," as historian Robert H. Wiebe commented,[53] the Social Gospelers drew upon the dynamic, twentieth-century ideas of bureaucracy and rationalization. They adopted the rhetoric and meaning of system and efficiency. The American missionary leadership turned fund raising into a modern science.

---

[53] Robert H. Wiebe, *The Search for Order* (New York: Hill and Wang, 1967), p. 112.

Commenting on its multimillion-dollar budgets, historian Valentin H. Rabe described the missionary agitation for funds as "less of a spontaneous movement than of a giant service industry."[54]

Fund raising for Armenian relief mirrored the methods of a business conglomerate. Indeed, the Near East Relief campaign in the decade following 1918 raised more than four times the total annual income of the foreign boards of the eleven largest American Christian denominations.[55] Furthermore, the American Board, which dominated the relief committee, was the country's first multinational enterprise, and from its inception tackled government-level tasks.[56] By the early twentieth century, organization, calculated pragmatism, as well as the art of selling, all joined to serve the holy doctrine of stewardship.

The relief organizers, from the beginning, held strategy meetings, developed and executed lines of promotional attack, maintained local, state, national, and international levels of organization, intensely pursued government lobbying, and coordinated local and national media outreach. They established and supervised an international network of relief agents. They expertly transferred money, food, clothing, and supplies overseas, while overcoming wartime blockades, and delivered them to the remotest corners of the Middle East. Their progressive, philanthropic efforts incorporated state-of-the-art organizational skills with the ancient zealousness of the Gospel. That is what made them so potent.

The administrators learned from previous experience that linking mission work to worldly crises, especially those in exotic places, brought in donations: the bigger the crisis, the more contributions. "Missions had to be justified in secular terms," explained Rabe, "because support simply for the evangelization of non-Christians was not forthcoming."[57] The missionaries suffered enormously themselves from the devastation of persecution and war. The fact remained, however, that the Armenians' plight boosted missionary business.

Paradoxically, while the Armenian Genocide nearly destroyed the Turkish mission field, the missionary organizations, at the same time, profited from this catastrophe. The Armenian crisis overseas created an opportunity for the missionaries at home. Their budgets increased with the surge in donations. So, too, did their presence and prestige in the United States as well as abroad. Although unintentional, a direct result

[54] Rabe, "Evangelical Logistics," p. 61.

[55] Valentin H. Rabe, *The Home Base of American China Missions, 1880–1920* (Cambridge, Mass.: Council on East Asian Studies, Harvard University, 1978), p. 166.

[56] James A. Field, Jr., "Near East Notes and Far East Queries," in Fairbank, ed., *Missionary Enterprise*, p. 39.

[57] Rabe, "Evangelical Logistics," p. 86.

of the missionary fund-raising activities was their prestige and influence in Washington and in negotiating the post-war reconstruction of a peaceful world. With little competition, it made them important. Both church and secular circles held them in high esteem. If American Protestants were looking for a way to assert themselves in the early decades of the twentieth century, the relief crusade provided a unique opportunity.

This occurred in conjunction with the fact that something of an inbred community existed among the missionary leadership, politicians, and journalists. Often they were friends or relatives. For example, Cleveland H. Dodge, one of the prominent leaders of the Armenian relief effort, was Woodrow Wilson's closest and truest friend. Dodge's daughter was married to a professor at Robert College in Turkey – an institution closely allied with the American missionaries. Her brother was the son-in-law of Howard Bliss, President of the missionaries' Syrian Protestant College, which the Dodges long supported. One of Wilson's classmates at Princeton was a missionary in Turkey. Albert Shaw, the writer, editor, and an incorporator of the Near East Relief was friend to both Wilson and the premier missionary leader Barton. A prominent New York journalist, Talcott Williams, was raised in Turkey, the son of missionaries. Secretary of State Robert Lansing's Private Secretary was the son of the industrialist Charles Crane, who was instrumental in the Armenian relief effort. Edwin Bliss, a son of the well-known missionary family, was the assistant magazine editor of the *Independent*. Colonel Edward House, Wilson's one-time friend and confidant, was friendly with various missionaries, including his summer neighbor Dr. George Washburn, the son of the President of Robert College, who was a cousin of the former Secretary of State John M. Hay. In other words, the missionaries were clearly established in the elite world of influence both in policy circles and in the media.

The American public regarded the missionaries as the most trustworthy experts on the Armenian Question. This was no accident. The missionaries were unique as global couriers of knowledge. They served as unrivaled experts and teachers in mission locales usually devoid of other Americans. In so doing, they became the main sources of their native charges' perception of the outside world. Importantly, however, the missionaries were also unmatched in creating America's understanding of the world beyond her own shores. The missionaries interpreted the world for many Americans. They were unchallenged in their grasp of people and places abroad. The evangelists wielded pervasive influence at home and in distant lands, communicating information and shaping opinion.

Barton reflected on the fact that missionaries become deeply involved in all aspects of the lives and communities of those they serve. Inevitably,

veteran missionaries became extremely knowledgeable regarding the local peoples "with whom they had been so intimately identified," he explained. Because many missionaries lived for years in often isolated and
interior stations, far removed from any American diplomatic or consular
office, they were regularly asked by American government officials to report on conditions with which they were familiar. "This is especially emphasized," Barton commented, "when unusual disturbances take place,
such as the conflicts between Turks and Armenians in the Near East and
the Boxer uprising in China." All information was sent to the home base
back in the United States. "In fact," boasted Barton, "no secretary of a
large foreign missionary society can fail to be in touch with many important questions of an international character and have in his files important
information bearing upon them."[58]

The missionaries took very seriously the effort to educate their supporting constituencies back home. Evangelists in the United States
visiting on furlough crisscrossed the country giving speeches and addresses. So did the mission society secretaries, such as Barton, who was
tirelessly peripatetic. They propagated knowledge and developed their
reputations as experts at the same time. Indeed, Barton was considered the ranking authority above all others. An editor of *The Boston
Herald* declared of Barton that "there is no man in this community in
whom I have more confidence or whose leadership" he accepted "more
unhesitatingly."[59]

The missionary organizations had in-house periodicals and regularly
contributed to many others. They also published nondenominational
textbooks for readers of all ages describing the geography, history, and
political problems of the foreign lands being served. Many Americans
received their only understanding of other peoples and places because
of missionary education. Missionaries introduced the idea of thinking
internationally to many Americans. As Albert Howe Lybyer, Professor
of Near Eastern History at the University of Illinois remarked in 1924,
the missionaries' visits to the American churches, combined with their
publications, "have made a large proportion of our people familiar with
events and conditions in the Near East."[60]

Further, the missionaries served repeatedly as advisors to governments. Samuel Capen, President of the American Board, explained that

[58] James L. Barton, "Relations with Governments," ABC Personal: Barton papers, 12:2, ABCFM archives.
[59] Robert L. O'Brien to James L. Barton, 15 May 1923, ABC 14.2, vol. 6, no. 220, ABCFM archives.
[60] Albert Howe Lybyer, "America's Missionary Record in Turkey," *The Current History Magazine*, 19:5 (February 1924), p. 808.

diplomats and Consuls were apt to change every few years and often did not speak the local language. The missionary, however, lived in "the same community twenty, thirty, and sometimes forty years. He knows the people, their language, their modes of thought, their traditions, their history," he stated. The missionary, Capen proclaimed, "has a mass of information of inestimable value that he can communicate to any government official."[61]

Historian Arthur Schlesinger, Jr., observed that the "missionary impact on the American mind may have been more profound than its impact on the non-Western mind."[62] Even Herbert Hoover recalled in his memoirs that the "association of Mount Ararat and Noah, the staunch Christians who were massacred periodically by the Mohammedan Turks, and the Sunday School collections for over fifty years for alleviating their miseries – all cumulate to impress the name Armenia on the front of the American mind."[63]

Certainly, the missionaries determined almost everything that the American people knew about the Armenians. From their years in the Anatolian field, the missionaries knew more about the Armenians than did any other Americans. No one else could fill this void of ignorance. The public knew this and trusted the evangelists.

The missionary interests ran an information network and purposely attempted to control public opinion. They did this partly out of a lofty sense of sharing and teaching. They also did this to build a nationwide constituency of support for their programs and concerns. The missionary endeavor to inform the home base paved the way for their world-acclaimed relief fund-raising program. Collecting money depended on stirring the public sentiment and drawing people together. Laymen with commerce backgrounds came to replace those who traditionally raised money, such as untrained volunteers or clergy, who were less experienced in business. Since public image was important, these sleek and professional missionary and relief administrators were adept at not just religious but also promotional awakenings. Soliciting money would not depend on children saving up pennies.

From the beginning, the relief organization included appeals to wealthy individuals for donations, community campaigns, gifts from churches, and public information and collection meetings. The relief administrators encouraged the press to give publicity to these activities.

[61] Samuel B. Capen, *Foreign Missions and World Peace*, no. 7, part 3 (Boston: World Peace Foundation, October 1912), pp. 12–13.
[62] Arthur Schlesinger, Jr., "The Missionary Enterprise and Theories of Imperialism," in Fairbank, ed., *Missionary Enterprise*, p. 372.
[63] Hoover, *Memoirs*, p. 385.

Appeals to individuals were based on a system, like everything else. Lists were compiled of potential donors who might be interested in the Middle East. Detailed records were kept of each gift. The prominent donors received special information packets with significant news from overseas. This kept the contributors up to date, apprised them of the results of their gifts, and made them feel important. The committee continuously sought out new givers, who were cultivated with personal letters and printed literature.

However, the rapid growth of the relief organization made it necessary to develop "branch offices," as Barton called them, to run more efficiently. Thus were established state committees with their own local offices in every state; larger states had two offices.[64] Divisions included the bureau of speakers, bureau of public information, and the bureau of public and organizational relations. The foreign department coordinated the relief operations. National campaign directors supervised the state-level staff. They all worked together to prepare printed material, local and national publicity, and in the control and selection of speakers.[65]

Thus, they were able to shape public opinion, educate the country, and serve as close advisors to those in the government. Held in high esteem in both church and secular circles, this unusual perch made the missionaries powerful and prestigious in the early decades of the twentieth century.

Vickrey was prodigious and aggressive as administrator of the relief committee, although he was "on loan" from the Layman's Missionary Movement. He made sure, for example, in the fall of 1916, when the proceeds of the much-anticipated Harvard–Yale football game were to be donated to Armenian relief, a carefully designed publicity blitz would accompany the event. In October 1916 President Wilson had set aside special days of remembrance for the suffering of the Armenians. However, by early September, the White House had not yet issued a public proclamation. It was Vickrey who ensured that two missionary leaders, Barton and Samuel Dutton, went to Washington and delivered to Wilson a prepared proclamation for the President's "convenience."[66]

Vickrey's touch also included the display posters disseminated across America that yearly conveyed new pictures and slogans. Some of the nation's most renowned artists donated their talents. One poster, designed after the armistice, showed the unsettled refugees; a picture of desolation was highlighted by the phrase "Hunger Knows No Armistice." Another

---

[64] James L. Barton, "Near East Relief 1915–1925 – A Brief History," ABC Personal: Barton papers, 13:12, ABCFM archives.
[65] Barton, *Story of Near East Relief*, p. 375.
[66] Charles V. Vickrey to James L. Barton, 6 September 1916, ABC 16.5, vol. 6, no. 128F, ABCFM archives.

showed a small child alone and asleep on the bare ground. The caption read: "A Cry in the Night. Would you pass by? Can you turn away?" Countrywide, agencies gave advertising space for free on subways, street cars, fences, and in commercial areas.[67]

The posters, along with other relief promotions, stressed certain themes and spoke to specific motives. They appealed to America's national pride and historic sense of mission globally. They highlighted the nation's special responsibility to the Armenians as well as America's interests in the Middle East. They played on the emotion of guilt and asked, "How can you eat when others are starving?" The appeals also expressed the religious and secular values of charity, altruism, and brotherhood. They reminded the public of the responsibility to help the unfortunate. The promotions also embodied the Social Gospel message that one attains salvation by saving others.

Because so few pictures from the Middle East were available in America during the war, visual publicity did not flourish until after the armistice. Then newsreels of the Middle East became popular. The relief committee gave the photographers unique access to unusual material in the field. In turn, the motion picture companies took special pictures of the relief conditions and the children for the committee's exclusive use. Relief workers also took many photographs. The committee showed these films in schools, churches, public gatherings, and as "fillers" in movie theatres. Titles included *Alice in Hungerland*, *One of These Little Ones*, and *Stand by Them a Little Longer*. These movie reels replaced the illustrated lectures and colored slides the committee speakers used during the war years when pictures were unavailable.[68]

In 1924, the child movie star, Jackie Coogan, donated his services to the cause. The Near East Relief organized a nationwide milk campaign, collecting from the patrons cans of condensed or evaporated milk in movie theaters featuring Coogan movies. The milk was sent to New York and then abroad. During the 1920s, the NER distributed almost 2 million cans of milk. Coogan led the children's crusade and even accompanied a shipment to Greece. The NER showed films of Coogan's visit with Near Eastern orphans to the boys and girls across America.[69] It was powerful imagery not soon to be forgotten.

In 1923, Vickrey toured the Middle East and was haunted by his walks through the orphanages and refugee camps – which he called "the land of stalking death." Once home, he got the idea to initiate the observance

[67] Barton, *Story of Near East Relief*, p. 390; "Advertising the Campaign," *News Bulletin, American Committee for Armenian and Syrian Relief*, 2:7 (December 1918).
[68] Barton, *Story of Near East Relief*, pp. 390–1.   [69] Ibid., p. 391.

of Golden Rule Sundays. They were to become the hallmark of the Near East Relief. A special sub-committee managed the promotion. The first Sunday in December from 1923 through 1929 became a special day to focus on the suffering Middle Eastern children. An advertiser underwrote the costs of an ad flashing on a huge electric sign in New York's Times Square. It said: "Do you believe in the Golden Rule? Then practice it on Golden Rule Sunday." It asked for contributions for "the destitute orphans of the Near East. They ask that you do unto others as you would that others should do unto you."[70]

Families were to eat a simple orphanage meal and donate the cost of an average American dinner. Golden Rule Sunday inspired organizations and the press unlike any previous promotion. Local groups ran special campaigns holding community Golden Rule luncheons and dinners serving orphanage fare. Hotels donated the use of banquet rooms. Local merchants provided the food. Local committees or schools administered the program. Frequently, over 1,000 people attended these gatherings, during which the NER arranged for the showing of their films and featured guest speakers from abroad.[71]

In 1923, fourteen nations observed Golden Rule Sunday. The next year, the number rose to twenty-three. In 1925, fifty countries participated, with the largest contribution of about $1 million coming from the United States. In 1924, an American journalist, Mabell S. C. Smith, observed that Golden Rule Sunday "swept the country in a remarkable way. No part was more surprising than the cooperation of the city officials and civic bodies." She expected the plan to be popular with the "church people and with folk accustomed to giving to philanthropic causes," which it was. However, as Smith noted, "it also hit the fancy of a myriad of people unused to introspection or to the making of donations to foreign needs. Of the thousands upon thousands of contributors to the Golden Rule fund of the Near East Relief, 75 percent were new subscribers."[72]

Across America, everyone seemed to join in. New donors received a letter of appreciation from President Calvin Coolidge, former President Woodrow Wilson, Cabinet members, United States Senators, and Governors. Editors, heads of Granges, bank presidents, the Kiwanis, Rotary, Lions, and Civitan clubs all encouraged participation from coast to coast. America's Mayors were devoted to Golden Rule Sunday. The Mayor of

---

[70] Charles V. Vickrey, "Golden Rule Sunday: Earthquakes and Orphans in Armenia; A Thanksgiving Season in America," *American Review of Reviews* 74 (December 1926), p. 592.

[71] Barton, *Story of Near East Relief*, p. 392.

[72] Mabell S. C. Smith, "Civic Cooperation in the International Golden Rule Campaign," *The American City Magazine* 31 (November 1924), p. 483.

Charleston, South Carolina, held a tea at his house. The Mayor of Albany, New York, was the Chairman of the Golden Rule Committee there, as were the Mayors of Troy, New York, San Francisco, and Salt Lake City, to name a few. Many other Mayors were active helpers at the events, setting examples for the citizenry. "But underneath the gayety," commented Smith, "lay a profound sympathy for the little children whose housing and daily food depend upon the application of the Golden Rule."[73] The innovative Near East Relief had systematically mobilized the nation – and many other countries – to save these children. In building such broad-based support, they became trend setters in American philanthropy.

The relief committee members had voted not to use relief funds to pay for advertising, deciding that expensive advertising would be injurious to the cause. Instead, they depended on the goodwill of the American press. Melville Stone of the Associated Press served as their media consultant. Barton later praised the press, convinced that "no other relief organization, except the Red Cross, has ever received so great and widespread sympathetic cooperation from the secular press."[74]

The committee released facts of conditions in the Middle East, which usually originated from the missionaries or Consuls living in the field, "as rapidly as they were obtained and verified," Barton explained. They made contacts with the editorial staff of all of America's leading journals. They furnished special material for editorial purposes regarding the countries, people, and conditions to the press. The committee published a pamphlet on these subjects, under the supervision of Professor William W. Rockwell of the Union Theological Seminary. They placed this booklet in "the hands of the editors," according to Barton. On a weekly basis, the relief organization asked recognized authorities to prepare articles which appeared widely in papers and magazines. "These served to enlighten the general public," Barton noted, "upon subjects bearing upon the Near East peoples and conditions, and provided a substantial background for the items which appeared in the daily papers." It was a masterful propaganda blitz. The relief committee soon became, as Barton boasted, "the chief source of information regarding economic and social conditions in Turkey and the Near East."[75]

Thus, the missionaries worked hand-in-glove with American newspapers and magazines. Between 1915 and 1928, over twenty different American magazines ran hundreds of stories on the Armenians, which

[73] Smith, "Civic Cooperation," pp. 483–4; Mabell S. C. Smith, "The Mayors and Golden Rule Day," *The American City Magazine* 33 (November 1925), p. 513.
[74] James L. Barton, "Relief in the Near East," ABC Personal: Barton papers, 8:6, ABCFM archives.
[75] Barton, *Story of Near East Relief*, pp. 14–15.

by the relief committee's design, were central to raising money. Many of the writers, and often editors, were missionaries, friends of the missionary interests, or relied on missionary information as sources.

Among the many publications that covered the Armenian story, reinforcing the relief publicity machine, were *The New York Times Current History Magazine* with thirty-five articles; *The Missionary Review of the World* with eighteen; *The Outlook* with nineteen; *The Survey* with twelve; *National Geographic* with seven; *The Independent* with nineteen; *Contemporary Review* with fifteen; *The New Republic* with thirteen; and *The Literary Digest* with forty-two. Sample titles include "Armenians Killed with Axes by Turks"; "Rescue of Armenia"; "Armenian Appeal to America for Help"; "Armenia: Worst Sufferer of the War"; and "America's Duty in Turkey."

Major American newspapers gave comprehensive coverage to the Armenian Question, also enhancing the relief effort. Because the American missionaries were usually the only Americans living in the Turkish interior, the news reported often originated with them. *The New York Times* ran 146 pieces in 1915 alone. A sampling of titles from that one year includes "Talaat Bey Declares That There is Room Only for Turks in Turkey"; "Armenian Women Put Up at Auction"; "Armenians Thank Wilson"; "Aid for Armenians Blocked by Turkey"; and "Millions of Armenians Killed Or Are In Exile: Policy of Extermination."

Certain themes ran through the articles appearing in the United States concerning the Armenians dating back to the 1895–6 massacres. These motifs had a profound bearing on American understanding of and feelings towards both the Armenians and the Turks. The pieces combined facts with emotion. Even the most straightforward story could become lurid simply by its documentary contents. The reports and commentaries were gripping. They seized the heart and were high human drama. The plot repeated in the American media for years was a basic one: good versus evil. The press championed the underdog fighting the oppressor, who naturally hated his prey. The Armenians were portrayed as the innocent, martyred Christians whom the barbaric Muslim Turks victimized. Americans identified with the Christian Armenians. The Armenians were considered the advanced race and invited the sympathies of all Social Darwinists. To Americans, the Turks were backward and sadistic.

Even intellectuals wrote in these terms. Albert Bushnell Hart of Harvard University, for example, declared in a scholarly journal in 1923 that the "Turk is a Near Eastern Ku Klux Klan." He condemned the Turks, stating that they "exterminated a race far superior to themselves in culture, in religion, in history, and in all that goes to make up a nation."

"Everybody," he added, "has now been massacred who was in the way of the Turk!"[76]

Many educational leaders, convinced of the need to assist the Armenians, often lobbied Washington, and used the media, to promote the Armenian cause. These included, among many others, the Presidents of Vassar College, University of Maryland, University of Chicago, Western Reserve University, Lafayette College, University of Pennsylvania, Smith College, and Catholic University of America. Such academic notables as J. H. T. Main of the Congregational Grinnell College, Sidney Mezes of the City College of New York, and John Grier Hibben of Princeton University took up the Armenian banner. Scholars like Charles W. Eliot of Harvard University and Herbert Adams Gibbons of Princeton joined Hart by writing articles as well as participating in public forums to speak out on behalf of the Armenians.

From the very first relief committee meeting in 1915, the members worked in partnership with the federal government. The State Department routinely provided crucial dispatches and documents regarding conditions in the disturbed areas to the missionary leadership. This information immediately entered the relief committee publicity machine, with the purpose of bringing in more donations. It was a twentieth-century public awareness bureaucracy. The system of spreading the fresh information across America worked fast and efficiently. Implementing a professional process, the relief committee got its message out – frequently spread on the front pages of every prominent paper in America within days.

For instance, Barton first reviewed State Department materials regarding Turkey on 21 September 1915. He described them as a vast collection concerning "regimented and designedly inhuman deportations of an entire race." After he finished, he immediately left for New York by train. "It was important," he said, "that the material I had secured in Washington be in the hands of [the committee's] Secretary Dutton for delivery to the press the next day." He rushed to the Hotel Roosevelt and by midnight had copied the press reports regarding the desperate situation in Turkey. According to Barton, these dispatches "made four columns in the daily papers" and were "spread upon the first pages of practically every journal in America."[77]

In addition, the State Department, both during and after the war, interceded with the Turkish and Allied governments on behalf of the relief

---

[76] Albert Bushnell Hart, "Reservations as to the Near Eastern Question," *Annals of the Academy of Political and Social Science* 108 (July 1923), p. 122.

[77] James L. Barton, "Relations with Governments," ABC Personal: Barton papers, 12:2, p. 252, ABCFM archives.

committee to enable them to ship supplies to the Middle East. Moreover, the State Department assisted the relief organizers in asking the United States Navy to transport these relief materials.

Indeed, the United States led the world in a massive outpouring of giving towards the Armenians, spearheaded and then delivered on site by the missionaries, with funds raised through the missionary-led NER. "Never since the Civil War has the country been so sympathetically unified in a particular enterprise of Christian fellowship," declared American editor Albert Shaw in 1930. "I do not forget, of course, Red Cross campaigns," he affirmed, "but still I am sure that the special appeal of the Near East Relief transcended anything in the way of a nationalizing movement of charity and brotherhood that we have ever known."[78]

In October 1922, President Warren G. Harding sent a telegram to Barton concerning the Armenians. There is, Harding affirmed, a "great call which has come out of the Near East to the heart of the American people. More than half a million suffering human beings, the majority women and children, are dependant on the benevolence of America."[79] It was not a coincidence that the Armenian refugees turned to the United States. The missionaries encouraged the Armenians to believe that America was their salvation. One relief worker serving the Armenian refugees in Syria proclaimed, "Everywhere these people look to Americans as their heaven on earth."[80] "We have taught them to look to us. Can we leave them to the fate from which we have thus far saved them?" entreated another.[81]

The Armenian Patriarch of Constantinople, Zaven Der Yeghiayan, remarked with great emotion on Armenian gratitude to an NER representative in Constantinople. "The Armenians can never forget what the Near East Relief has done for them. The children would all be dead had it not been for you. We owe everything to the Americans," he declared.[82]

Forging new ground in the history of American philanthropy, the missionary-based relief efforts led the world in feeding, housing, clothing, and educating the refugee Armenian population. It is hard to imagine that any organization at that time could have been more dedicated or done more in the face of such human catastrophe. Countless were

[78] Albert Shaw to James L. Barton, 12 February 1930, ABC Personal: Barton papers, 6:2, ABCFM archives.
[79] Warren G. Harding to James L. Barton, 23 October 1922, ABC 16.9.1, vol. 2, no. 140, ABCFM archives.
[80] "Missionary Work among the Armenian Refugees in Syria," ABC 16.9.2, vol. 5, no. 65, ABCFM archives.
[81] W. W. Peet to James L. Barton, 10 July 1917, ABC 16.9.3, vol. 48, no. 468, ABCFM archives.
[82] "The Pleas of the Patriarchs," ABC 16.9.1, vol. 2, no. 280, ABCFM archives.

still left destitute, and countless perished. That any were rescued at all made the American missionaries valiant as a moral force, because at least they tried. Speculating whether any other organization could have done more for the Armenians hardly mattered, because none did. That the missionaries helped between 1 and 2 million Armenians testified to their commitment and ability to deliver a stricken people from deprivation and death.

The missionaries' humanitarian relief program showed the effect of practical humanitarian politics, which, paradoxically, the horror of war and genocide prompted. The evangelists also taught many Americans to think internationally, beyond their borders to faraway shores. They carried knowledge of the Middle East back home to Americans who knew very little of such an exotic place. Missionary relief propaganda left a lasting imprint on the American perception of the Armenians as innocent victims of the "terrible" Turks. These stereotypes shaped American public opinion for generations.

Americans became the world leaders in the foreign missionary movement by 1920. Activism and donations peaked in the first two decades of the twentieth century. Contributions connected to the secular crisis of the Armenians' plight figured largely in that accomplishment.

The First World War, however, raised in the minds of many American Protestants the issue of just who might be the pagans in need of the Gospel. The spectacle of Christian nations involved in such bloody conflict drew outraged criticisms of hypocrisy. It nullified the optimistic pledge to evangelize the world in one's generation. Among its many consequences, the First World War initially expanded and then hastened the decline of the foreign mission movement. It robbed the mission message of its spirit and legitimacy. The lesson that civilization and Christianity were not one and the same was graphic. This revelation coincided with events in Anatolia which were disastrous to the once-flourishing missionary operations there. After the First World War, the missionaries' opportunities in Turkey drastically diminished, as, eventually, did their political influence.

The paradox presented here has many contemporary echoes. Altruism expanded to meet the demands of a humanitarian crisis of terrifying proportions. The terms of that crisis, however, and the war which encapsulated it, were devastating. The activities of the people who stayed the course can tell us much about the dilemmas they faced, dilemmas still painfully alive in our own day.

8   Mary Louise Graffam: witness to genocide

Susan Billington Harper

Introduction

On 14 August 1901, Mary Louise Graffam, a shy teacher from the National Cathedral School for Girls in Washington, D.C., left Boston for a new life as an educational missionary for the American Board of Commissioners for Foreign Missions (ABCFM) in Ottoman Turkey. She embarked on what promised to be a fairly conventional missionary career as the head of Female Education in the Near Eastern mission post of Sivas, an established American mission station. Little did she know that she would be thrust, instead, into the horrors of twentieth-century warfare and would become a first-hand witness to genocide conducted by a government against a portion of its own people.

The story of Mary Louise Graffam deserves to be told at the beginning of a new century replete with possibilities for the development of new forms of evil. As the only American to stay with Armenians at her mission in eastern Turkey throughout the First World War, Graffam occupies a unique position in history. Her commentary provides a direct and powerful testimony about the history of modern genocide. Surprisingly, no serious account, let alone major biography, of Graffam has ever appeared, despite the existence of numerous unpublished documents, oral and written histories in Armenian, scattered primary source materials as well as general works on the Armenian Genocide and missionary history that mention her heroic resistance to the massacres.[1]

---

[1] In addition to the major primary and secondary sources given below, evidence is available in: *Patmagirk' hushamatean Sebastioy ew gawaṛi Hayut'ean* (History and Memorial Book of the Armenians of Sebastia and of the Region) [prepared by Aṛak'el N. Patrik] Publication of the Hamasebastahay Verashinats' Miut'iwn-New York, vol. I (Beirut: Tparan Mshak, 1974), pp. 547–65, 744–51; vol. II (New Jersey: Tparan Rōzgir, 1983), pp. 20, 31, 41, 231, 265, 474, 516; M. Graffam, "Sebastioy hayut'ean patmagrut'iwně" (History of the Armenians of Sebastia), *Lusaber* 2 (January 1938), p. 516; Haykaz Kazarean, "Sebastioy hargank' ě Mis Měri Krefěmi hishatakin" (Sebastia's Respect in Memory of Miss Mary Graffam), *Lusaber* 2 (May 1946), p. 519; Haykazn G. Ghazarean, "Ov ěr Mis Mayn Lowiz Krěfěm. Ir keank'n u gortsě. 20 erkar tariner tsaṛayets' an Sebastahayerun" (Who was Miss Mary Louise Graffam? Her Life and Work. For 20 Years she served the Armenians

---

This neglect is particularly startling since she was a celebrated figure in the United States during and after the First World War, not only among missionaries but also among government officials and the general public. At the time of her death in 1921, the glowing title of the *Boston Evening Transcript*'s tribute to Graffam captured something of the respect with which her contemporaries viewed her services in Turkey: "A Lone Sentinel of the Near East Mustered Out: The Thrilling Story of Mary Louise Graffam, the Heroine of Sivas, Dead at Her Post After Adventure, Sufferings, Accomplishments Which Words Fail Adequately to Portray."[2]

Other Americans in Turkey gave testimony of her heroism at the time, including both missionaries and government officials such as Henry Morgenthau, Ambassador to Turkey from 1913 to 1916.[3] A leader of no less importance than Major General James Harbord, Chief of Staff under General Pershing and Head of President Wilson's Commission to investigate conditions in Anatolia after the war, wrote of Graffam in 1920: "It is no disparagement of other zealous and efficient missionaries to say that Miss Mary Graffam is the outstanding missionary figure in this part of Asia . . . [She has played] a part in the stirring events of the last six years which has probably never been equaled by any other woman in the chronicles of missionary effort."[4]

of Sebastia) *Alis* 10: 3 (November 1929 – January 1930), pp. 3–4. I am indebted to Levon Avdoyan of the Library of Congress, to Dr. Osgan Kechian, of the Pan Sebastia Rehabilitation Union, Inc., and to Dr. Ara Sarafian of the University of Michigan for assistance with sources.

Armenians of Sebastia who survived the genocide have provided some oral and written testimonies of Graffam's work informally to this author as well. For instance, the leader of the New-York-based Pan-Sebastia Rehabilitation Union, Inc., recalled: "When I was a child in Turkey, my mother used to talk about the Armenian deportation. She always mentioned how Miss Graffam accompanied them on their march. The Armenians entrusted all their valuables to her to prevent the Turkish government from confiscating them" (Dr. Osgan Kechian to author, 25 March 1994). Mention is also made of her work in missionary histories such as Fred Field Goodsell, *They Lived Their Faith: An Almanac of Faith, Hope and Love* (Boston: ABCFM, 1961), pp. 156–8. See also Rouben Paul Adalian, ed., *The Armenian Genocide in the US Archives, 1915–1918* (Microform; Alexandria, Va.: Chadwyck-Healey, 1991), fiche 95.

[2] 3 September 1921. Copy in: "Missionaries of the ABCFM," vol. 2 (Vinton), 226–7, ABCFM archives, Houghton Library, Harvard University, Cambridge, Mass. (hereafter: ABCFM). The author is grateful to Houghton Library and to the Wider Church Ministries of the United Church of Christ for permission to use material from these archives.

[3] Valuable information may be found in the Papers of Henry Morgenthau, Library of Congress, Manuscript Division, Reel 22: Armenia, Documentary file. Also: United States Department of State, Records Relating to Turkey, 1910–29, Record Group 59, file nos. 867.4016/187 and 867.4016/288. See also Henry Morgenthau, *Ambassador Morgenthau's Story* (Garden City, N.Y.: Doubleday, 1918), chs. 22–7.

[4] Major-General James G. Harbord, "Investigating Turkey and Trans-Caucasia," in *The World's Work: A History of Our Time* (Garden City, N.Y.: Doubleday, 1920), vol. XL (May–Oct. 1920), p. 189.

Despite such accolades from the highest ranks of the American establishment, Graffam's fame was short-lived, the victim not only of her own untimely death from cancer in 1921 but also of the decline of American interest in the Armenian Genocide after the First World War. The plight of the "starving Armenians," whose stories of deportation and massacre were widely publicized via newspapers, journals, and eyewitness accounts between 1915 and 1918, faded precipitously after the cessation of hostilities. As the Armenian tragedy became a "forgotten genocide," American memory of important figures such as Mary Louise Graffam faded as well. Today, she appears briefly, if at all, in general studies of genocide. Her unpublished letters in the ABCFM archives of Houghton Library at Harvard University, the principal source for her biography, remain largely unread.[5] A full account of Graffam's life remains to be written and, one would hope, to be recreated for film. This chapter seeks only to provide a preliminary reconstruction and description of Graffam's experience in Sivas during the First World War, focusing on her contributions to our understanding of the Armenian Genocide and the role of American missionaries in working to counteract the tragedy.

Early career

ABCFM missionaries had operated in Turkey for almost a century before Graffam's arrival in 1901. Established in 1810 by Congregationalists of Massachusetts at the request of a group of students from Andover Seminary who had been inspired by an evangelical revival to dedicate themselves to the evangelization of the world, the ABCFM was the first American foreign missionary society. Although mainly Congregational in identity, it drew roughly half of its missionaries from other reformed denominations, such as Presbyterians. The society aimed to spread the Gospel in foreign lands, to translate the Bible and to found schools and hospitals. During Mary Graffam's lifetime, the ABCFM was in its heyday, having grown from 375 missionaries in 1877 to its peak of 724 missionaries in 1920.

---

[5] ABCFM Individual Biographies, Mary L. Graffam, 24:33, contains two particularly important sources: (1) "Miss Graffam's Own Story, taken stenographically by Dr. Richards' Secretary, June 28, 1919," ts. (hereafter: Miss Graffam's Own Story), and (2) Ernest and Winona Graffam Partridge, "Mary Louise Graffam: A Missionary Heroine," ts. (hereafter: Partridge). See also: ABCFM Papers of Candidates Accepted, 1900–9, G, vol. 1, ABC New Series 6, C. T. Riggs, "Near East Memorial Biographies to 1953," ts., 3 fols.: 6–8, ABC New Series 6, Western Turkey Mission, vols. 39, 40, 42, 48, 50, fo. 431, ABC: 16.9.3; Western Turkey Mission, Women's Board, 1909–14, vol. 3, and 1915–20, vol. 6, ABC: 16.9.4, ABCFM. Another archive that contains information on Graffam is the Andover Historical Society, Andover, Massachusetts.

Forbidden by law from open evangelization among Muslims in Turkey, the ABCFM had earlier adopted an indirect strategy that focused primarily on the education of Armenian and Greek Christian populations. The implicit longer-term goal was to increase the faith and witness of indigenous Christian populations so that they would become motivated themselves to spread the faith to Muslims. Graffam's colleague in Sivas, Henry Holbrook, expressed the views of many new ABCFM missionaries when he wrote, shortly after his arrival in 1913:

It is almost maddening to be actually here in the heart of the Moslem world – to whose crying appeal we consecrated our lives . . . – and yet be forced to realize that there is at present practically nothing we can do directly for these young Turks. In the present condition of the country anything like active anti-Moslem propaganda would be a dreadful blunder – the Moslem world will never be won by militant methods but only by infinite patience and love.[6]

The ABCFM missionary to Turkey was not to be "a tall man in a long, black coat preaching to naked savages on a cannibal island" but rather a far less adventurous teacher of indigenous Christian schoolchildren. For enthusiasts such as Holbrook, it was hard to abandon such evangelistic dreams. He admitted, "the longing to grapple at once with the Moslem problem dies hard. It seems far less heroic and splendid to go quietly to work to educate a few hundred Armenian and Greek children." Yet, he remained confident that the ABCFM's educational work would "quicken the native Christianity of this land into a life worthy of the name it bears, a vitality and power that can command the respect of those who now despise and hate it."[7]

Graffam shared these common frustrations and hopes, having first attempted in 1895 to gain a post in Japan doing "direct evangelistic or missionary work rather than teaching in a school" before accepting her station in 1901 as an educational missionary in Turkey.[8] She, like Henry Holbrook, resigned herself to the necessity of working only indirectly as an evangelist to Muslims. However, neither her career nor the career of Holbrook ended the way they would have predicted or hoped. In Holbrook's case, his expectation of a long and peaceful career as an educator of young Armenian and Greek children was dashed when he was brutally and mysteriously murdered in 1913 by Turkish bandits. In Graffam's case, her educational ministry was completely overtaken shortly thereafter by genocide and war.

[6] C. Henry Holbrook, Turkey Letter No. 3, Western Turkey Mission, Women's Board, 1915–20, docs., reports, letters A–L, ABC: 16.9.4, vol. 6, ABCFM.
[7] Ibid.
[8] Mary Louise Graffam (hereafter: MLG) to C. H. Daniels, 4 March 1895, ABCFM Papers of Candidates Accepted, 1900–9, G, vol. 1, ABCFM.

Mary Louise Graffam was born in the small town of Monson, Maine, and moved to Andover, Massachusetts, at the age of five. She was raised with a younger sister, Winona, in a Christian home – probably Congregational. Her father was a farmer and her mother, who was sickly, died at the age of forty-one shortly after Graffam graduated from high school. A spiritual awakening at the age of fourteen prompted Mary to join a new local church and to take part in a revival meeting.[9] She decided to become a foreign missionary during her freshman year at Oberlin College, recalling years later that: "From my childhood my friends had predicted that I would go to the foreign field, but I never thought seriously of the matter until some of my friends from Oberlin were in Andover and tried to persuade me to go there to college."[10]

Oberlin was known widely as a missionary training college although, at first, Graffam was determined not to become a missionary herself. After her mother's death, she changed her mind. "That," she remembered, "was the turning point and before I had been in college a term I was a member of the Missionary Volunteer Band," a college branch of the popular Student Volunteer Movement which was recruiting missionaries from college campuses across the country at the time. These bands organized meetings, study groups, and lectures on the subject of foreign missions and served as both recruiting and training organizations for the missionary cause.

After her college graduation in 1894, Graffam's dream of becoming a missionary to Japan was postponed for six years while she worked as a high-school teacher to pay off her college debts. This experience seemed only to strengthen her resolve. "We were educated with great sacrifice on the part of my father and with a great deal of hard work on our own part and I want to make it count for as much good in the world as possible," she wrote to her mission board.[11] Interestingly, Graffam's sister, Winona, also attended Oberlin College where she met her future husband, Ernest Partridge. The Partridges would also become missionaries to Sivas where they served together with Mary – known to them as "Polly" – until the outbreak of the First World War when they returned to America.

When Graffam accepted an offer from the ABCFM in 1901 to take charge of Female Education in its Near Eastern mission post in Sivas, Turkey, she was thirty-years old, 5 feet 7 inches tall. She weighed 127 pounds and was in good health. Before leaving, she wrote: "I never worry and never passed but one sleepless night."[12] Those who had

---

[9] Ibid.   [10] Ibid.
[11] MLG to C. H. Daniels, Washington D.C., n.d. (c. 1901), ABCFM Papers of Candidates Accepted, 1900–9, G., vol. 1, ABCFM.
[12] Health Questionnaire, 28 January 1901, ABCFM Papers of Candidates Accepted, 1900–9, G, vol. 1, ABCFM.

recommended her to the post described her as a hard-working, generous, and self-sacrificing young woman, although one warned that "She might well be cautioned not to overwork herself, and wear herself out early."[13] Graffam displayed a combination of realism, determination, and faith on departure that suggested one key to her future resiliency: "I know it to be a fact that hardship and suffering come to people in this world and possibly more in foreign missionary work than any other, but I shall trust the same Providence that leads me into this work to take care of me while I am doing it."[14]

Graffam spent the remaining twenty years of her life in Sivas, a city on the upper reaches of the River Halys (Kizil Irmak) that empties into the Black Sea. Its impressive stone bridge dating back to the Roman era provided passage for the ancient caravan route from Baghdad to the Bosporus. At the time of Graffam's ministry, the city of Sivas was composed of roughly 30,000 Armenians within a total population of 75,000 that also included Turks, Kizilbash, Circassians, Kurds, Khalds, Afshars, Chechens, and Greeks. The Turkish population was well represented in government service; the Armenian population was predominant in business, crafts, and manufacturing where they served as shopkeepers, craftsmen, and grocers. Graffam quickly immersed herself in the life and culture of Sivas, returning again to America only once briefly in 1909–10.

Graffam immediately proved a competent and dedicated educational missionary. Shortly after her arrival, a teacher in the ABCFM mission school fell ill and retired, forcing Graffam to complete most of her language training "on the job" while teaching full-time. Fortunately, she learned languages easily and, before long, was fluent in Armenian, Turkish, and German (in addition to French and classical languages) and had been promoted to Principal of the ABCFM girls' schools of the city and district. Graffam taught algebra, geometry, and trigonometry and was described as "an inspiring teacher" who "chafed under the routine of every day classes."[15] She also taught music, domestic science, and gymnastics and organized social, literary, and musical events, such as a bilingual school performance of Handel's *Messiah* in English and Armenian.

This was a time of rapid growth and productivity for the Sivas mission. The missionary staff doubled in size, a hospital was built and new buildings for the mission College and Girls' School were initiated. Graffam's roles in this expanding mission ranged from church organist to Mission Treasurer, a post that would become unexpectedly important when the mission became a conduit for wartime relief efforts. Although her early

[13] Elizabeth P. Pratt to C. H. Daniels, 7 March 1895, ABCFM Papers of Candidates Accepted, 1900–9, G, vol. 1, ABCFM.
[14] Health Questionnaire.   [15] Partridge.

career seems uneventful by comparison with her later wartime career, it was not without difficulties. Graffam contracted a serious case of typhoid in 1903, from which she recovered in Switzerland, and the mission school struggled from 1909 to cope with declining enrollments caused by a serious famine and, later, an outbreak of typhus. Mary responded to these needs by helping locally and fund raising internationally. To help the girls (some "as young as five") who were forced by poverty to leave school and to work in local rug factories, Graffam established a special Sunday School. To raise funds, she returned to America in 1909 where she gave speeches about famine in Turkey, and assisted newly arrived Armenian immigrants on Ellis Island in New York. This work, which demanded considerable resilience, helped to prepare her for the much more difficult work during the war. Writing with good humor in 1913 about her busy schedule and cramped living conditions, she claimed to look forward to having the opportunity someday to "be a little sick if I want to. This year I have been perfectly well because there is no place for me to even indulge in a slight headache."[16] Unfortunately, her hopes for future amelioration of conditions in the Sivas mission were never realized.

Wartime career

Graffam was thrust into the horrible chain of events that followed the outbreak of the First World War, partly by virtue of circumstance – she happened to be in Sivas at the time – and partly by choice – she decided to stay and to fight rather than to return to America. As the only American to accompany the Armenians of Sivas on a deportation and to witness many of the horrors they faced, Graffam occupies a unique position in the history of the Armenian Genocide.

Graffam responded to the outbreak of hostilities with heroic efforts to relieve the suffering of friends, colleagues, and also, when needed, of enemies. She served as a nurse on the Russian Front and as a relief and rescue worker during the Armenian deportations and throughout the war from her base in Sivas. In the end, she also became a victim of this violent period's hardships and persecutions. Graffam died shortly after the war at the age of fifty, of a heart attack following emergency cancer surgery, having refused to travel to Europe or America for specialized care. Like other ABCFM colleagues in Turkey, such as Dr. Clarence Ussher and George P. Knapp who died prematurely during the war, Graffam was thrust into unexpected and extraordinary wartime roles which entailed years of

---

[16] MLG to Miss Lamson, 24 March 1913, Sivas, Western Turkey Mission, Women's Board, 1909–14, vol. 3, ABC: 16.9.4, ABCFM.

exposure to hardship, disease, and suffering and likely contributed to her own early demise.

The American missionaries in Sivas learned of potential danger to the Armenian community shortly after the outbreak of war, from a visiting German officer whose message provoked "grave forebodings of the future of the Armenians." Graffam related to a stenographer in 1919:

Late in the Fall of 1914 we had a visit from a colonel in the German Army. He was a Christian, although a German, and he tried to warn us of things which might take place in the coming summer; this showing that the deportations were planned as early as this. He said that a certain fate was in store for all Armenians, but if the Germans were in the country, there would be no massacres.[17]

Graffam did not have much time to reflect on this dire warning. Fighting had erupted 200 miles away on the Russian Front and a typhus epidemic was raging in the town of Erzerum. The Sivas mission offered to send a Red Cross unit to assist in caring for the sick and wounded until reinforcements arrived from greater distances. Thus, Graffam left Sivas for Erzerum with a small party consisting of the mission's doctor, two nurses, and a pharmacist, to volunteer as a nurse for a Red Crescent Hospital on the frozen Russian Front. "I did not go to help the Turks particularly," she recalled in 1919, "I went to work with the Turks, thinking that possibly I could get on the good side of some of the pashas, and it might help us later on, for I felt the time was coming when we would need such help."[18]

They had a long, cold journey to the Russian Front, taking twenty days instead of the normal ten to cross the mountains separating Sivas from Erzerum. At least four horses fell off snowy hillsides, and one dropped dead just three hours before they reached their destination. On arrival, Graffam and a nurse continued immediately to the battle lines to attempt to save another missionary doctor who was dying of typhus. Graffam's sister and brother-in-law described that part of the trip as follows:

Roar of cannon, flashes of gunfire directed their course, they forded rivers in the darkness of night, plodded in deep snow, and reached the bedside in a deserted village, attended only by a stupid soldier. The doctor died within a few hours, and improvising a coffin out of the door of the cabin, they transported the body back to Erzroom on horseback.[19]

Back in Erzerum, Graffam found the city crowded with ill, frozen, and wounded soldiers. During the next four months in the cold winter of 1914–15, she worked in the central hospital for Turkish officers. Here, she succeeded in her objective of winning the gratitude of these men,

[17] Miss Graffam's Own Story.   [18] Ibid.   [19] Partridge, p. 7.

many of whom were hospitalized with frozen feet, through acts of kindness and courage reminiscent of Florence Nightingale. The Partridges remembered:

She gradually took things into her own hands until her authority was absolute. If the cook protested against giving milk to the patients, she got the visiting doctor to write milk on every chart, so she could give it at her discretion. If she thought a meat meal was necessary for tired and hungry newcomers from the front, and the cook objected, she would go into the kitchen and cook it herself. A most remarkable situation, an unsalaried unofficial foreign woman at the head of a Turkish military institution, an absolute autocrat [*sic*], yet respected and trusted by her staff.[20]

Turkish officers apparently never forgot Graffam's hospital services during this early phase of the war. They continued to send her letters of appreciation until the time of her death, she received the decoration of the Red Crescent by Imperial Grade from the Turkish government in 1917, and it appears likely that Turkish officers extended practical favors to her during the remainder of the war that helped her to accomplish more difficult and subversive missions that still lay ahead.

Early in 1915, after the military campaign had subsided, she and one of the nurses, Marie Zenger, started back to Sivas. The inns were full of soldiers dying of typhus and the roads were lined with dead and dying men and horses. Her companion contracted a malignant case of typhus and died within a few days on the road. Graffam hired a wagon, driver, and guard to continue her trip shortly after the funeral. The army had requisitioned all healthy horses, so the best she could find were sick and dying. "Some days she rode in an open wagon in the rain, and walked a good deal to spare the horses," her sister remembered. Exhausted and concerned about the danger of typhus, she wired her sister in Sivas to say that, if she should become ill on the road, she would be conscious for two days and would wire for help.

When her telegram arrived in Sivas, two college professors volunteered to go out to meet her with a wagon sent by the Sivas Vali. As the Partridges recalled afterwards:

These were two of the finest men on the College staff, Michael Frengulian and Rupen Racubian, both degree men from American colleges. This was a wonderfully brave thing for them to do, as they were both marked men, and would be in constant danger . . . Both were later murdered, one in the deportation, the other was taken out of prison, in a systematic murder scheme, by which two [*sic*] men a day were taken out of jail, escorted outside the city by police, compelled to dig

20 Ibid., p. 8.

trenches, knocked in the head, stripped and buried. These men were the picked leaders of the Armenian residents.[21]

Graffam survived her trip home from the Russian Front thanks to the heroic efforts of these men. Sadly, she was not able to save their lives, in turn, during the next, more horrible phase of the war. On returning to Sivas in March, she found that conditions in the city had deteriorated. The army was returning from the Russian Front. Typhus was rampant throughout north-eastern Turkey and sick and hungry deportees had begun to arrive from the Black Sea coast. Although she tried to resume routine educational work in preparation for the final weeks of school, final exams never took place in 1915. Instead, arrest and deportation orders arrived and the Armenian community was shattered forever. Graffam was in her fourteenth year of missionary service. She was forty-four years old.

Deportations of Armenians

Graffam's accounts of what followed bear similarities to reports by other witnesses to deportations elsewhere in Turkey: first, a call for arms, then arrests of men and rumors of massacres in neighboring villages, followed by full-scale deportation orders, the chaos of departure, and the agonies of transport and death in the wilderness. When the Armenians of Sivas were ordered to give up their arms, Graffam remembered:

A photographer in Sivas was called to the Government House to photograph the collection of arms, but as they did not make an impressive showing he was asked to return the next day when he noticed that a great many pieces of Turkish ammunition had been added, and his photograph of this last collection was used as official evidence that the Armenians were armed against the Turks.[22]

On the basis of this falsified photograph, officials began to arrest and imprison the male population, beginning with merchants, the wealthiest men, and one of the mission teachers: "The Turks told us that if the men were not given up the houses would be burned and the families would be hung in front of them." Although she wanted to hide the mission's teacher, he protested that "it would be useless." Graffam's account continues:

Three times they came to us and took away our men. Finally I became desperate and I decided to visit the prison, if possible. I went to the Chief of Police (one of the ringleaders) and I was permitted to visit the men, and this I did several times

---

[21] Ibid., p. 9. Other sources suggest it was 200 men per day.
[22] Miss Graffam's Own Story.

after that. This went for several weeks and when all the men of importance were in prison, then the Vali called two or three of the remaining men and the Armenian bishop, saying that on the following Monday (this was Friday) the deportations would begin. The men were to go by one road and their families by another. I was at the bank when I heard the news and went at once to the Vali, commander, etc., trying to do something and was told that the Armenians were going to the Euphrates valley; that was all.[23]

Evidence of what happened next is clearly demonstrated by Graffam's letters, reports, and later recollections, and from accounts by other missionary colleagues. As the Turkish government censored many of the most important documents authored at the time, these primary sources must be read collectively in order to gain a complete picture of breaking events. Indeed, a word about these censored sources, and the codes necessary to decipher them, is appropriate before delving into the story of the Armenian deportations.

With the outbreak of war, Graffam's letters were censored, either directly through erasures made by the censors themselves or indirectly through Graffam's defensive self-censorship. By 1 February 1915, she wrote to her mission from Erezrum: "I cannot, of course, write freely of all we see and hear. I feel as if I were a different person from the one that left Sivas not two months ago. I do not feel that I have done much . . . Pray for this poor country."[24] In this letter, government officers tried to censor her request to "pray for this poor country," but were strangely unsuccessful. The historian can still today read the letters beneath the censor's marks. The censors were more successful, however, in defacing large portions of the next letter in this collection. Indeed, defacement by censorship mars much of the most valuable missionary documentation from this wartime period and constrained Graffam from writing freely about her experiences at the time. In May of 1915, Graffam explained to members of her mission board, with double meaning, "that the experience of these months were never to be forgotten, but impossible to write in letters."[25]

To subvert the constraints of censorship, Graffam devised several strategies to improve communication with the outside world. First, she utilized a code that would be recognizable to other members of her

[23] Ibid.
[24] MLG to Dr. Barton, 1 Feb. 1915, Erezrum, Western Turkey Mission, 1910–19, vol. 40, ABC: 16.9.3, ABCFM.
[25] MLG to Miss Lamson, 6 May 1915, Sivas, Western Turkey Mission: Women's Board, 1915–20, vol. 6, ABC: 16.9.4, ABCFM.

missionary community but not to the censors.[26] The ABCFM Treasurer in Constantinople explained that, in order to evade censorship, "We are learning to write a new language and to express ourselves in ways, the full meaning of which is known to those who are bound together in the bonds of sympathetic comradeship."[27] Like her colleagues, Graffam used references to past experiences and to commonly recognized biblical and literary figures in order to pass news of death to worried friends outside. In letters to her sister penned in September 1915 after the Armenian deportations, she resurrected the figure of Henry Holbrook, her recently murdered missionary colleague, to communicate news of other murders to the outside world. Thus, Henry Holbrook, who was killed in 1913, made a ghostly appearance in a letter of 9 September 1915: "The other members of the staff do not write to us. We have heard nothing from Mr. Holbrook either. From what we can gather they must be together." In a typewritten copy of quotations from her September 1915 letters, her missionary colleagues interpreted Graffam's code in parenthesis as follows:

The other members of our staff do not write to us. *(Our deported teachers)*. We have heard nothing from Mr. Holbrook either. *(This means we think that they have received no definite news of the death of these teachers)*. From what we can gather they must be together, I think. The last I saw of Mike *(Mr. Frengulian, I think)*, he was planning to join them the next day. *(This we take to mean that they believe he has been killed, though they have no definite word)*.[28]

Missionaries were able to get letters with sensitive information past the censors quickly by the use of such coded language understandable to the smaller community aware of Holbrook's earlier assassination. Graffam also resurrected in her letters her colleague, Marie Zenger, who had died of typhus on the road home from Erezrum, writing on 16 September 1915:

I am having a new suit made by our old tailor. He and our teacher are employed in the same big shop *(military)* [adds the ABCFM interpreter]. Men of that stamp are all well at present. Mr. Holbrook and Miss Zenger are interested in seeing some of them, but they are too busy at present to go near them. Our other pupils come and play the phonograph when they have time. They, like the others, are

---

[26] The complexity of codes used by Americans to communicate with the outside world at this time is suggested by communication from John E. Merrill of Aintab to Ambassador Henry Morgenthau, in Papers of Henry Morgenthau, Library of Congress.

[27] Mr. W. W. Peet to Dr. James Barton, 17 August 1915, Western Turkey Mission, 1910–19, vol. 42, ABC: 16.9.3, ABCFM.

[28] Extracts of Letters to Mrs. Partridge, Sivas, September 1915, Western Turkey Mission, 1910–19, vol. 42, ABC: 16.9.3, ABCFM. Italics added.

well at present. If after the Fall work is over, they should see Mr. Holbrook they would be able to tell much about the pleasure his phonograph has given them. Dr. Maksud has tonsillitis and has gone to the hospital for a few days, not hours. The Doctors are in great demand and Mr. Holbrook could not even see them, much as he wanted to.[29]

Thus, Graffam's cryptic language conveyed news of death and possible death through the reminiscences of missionary colleagues who had already perished of violence and disease. Her letters from this period are also filled with evasive references to people whose names are not given except in general terms (viz. "our fellow travelers") to avoid identification by the Turks. Graffam began one letter to her sister on 26 November 1915, with the following clever decoy: "My dear Winona, I do not like type-written letters but I want this to be sure to get through for a Christmas letter and so I am making it easy for the censor to read."[30] The letter proceeded to communicate the means of death of "Mrs. Harris's three sons" as follows: "The Harrises are said to have had the same thing as Mr. Holbrook." By this, her readers understood that they, too, had been shot.

She evaded the censors by giving an account of the Sivas deportations using exaggerated and contradictory images about the weather to suggest what was happening to the people:

The weather was hot with more or less showers. Just before Hekim Khan we had a regular blizzard that made us just scatter. The women were protected by their charsoor and toros and – (two of the college teachers) took refuge with them and the other children, but it was pretty hard on those who were exposed to the full force of it . . . I am afraid the climate of Oorfa will be too hot for me and that I shall perhaps go back home."[31]

Graffam also employed biblical references whose significance, she calculated correctly, would evade the notice of the censors but not her missionary colleagues. She concluded a letter dated 31 October 1916 asking her mission Board for more relief money by writing: "The hundreds whom I am <u>obliged</u> to help are the remnants of the events of four months ago who find ways to communicate with me which are trustworthy Heb. 11:38."[32] This refers to the passage from the New Testament book of

---

[29] "Quotations from Sivas Letters," ts., extract of letter to Mrs. Partridge, 16 September 1915, Sivas, Western Turkey Mission, 1910–19, vol. 40, ABC: 16.9.3, ABCFM.

[30] MLG to Mrs. Partridge, 26 Nov. 1915, Sivas, Western Turkey Mission, 1910–19, vol. 40, ABC: 16.9.3, ABCFM.

[31] MLG to Mrs. Partridge, Malatia, ? August 1915 (handwritten copy of letter, date obscured by check mark on mss.), Western Turkey Mission, 1910–19, vol. 40, ABC: 16.9.3, ABCFM.

[32] MLG to Mr. Peet, 31 October 1916, Sivas, Western Turkey Mission, 1910–19, vol. 42, ABC: 16.9.3. ABCFM.

Hebrews which describes the persecution of the faithful: "the world was not worthy of them. They wandered in deserts and mountains, and in caves and holes in the ground." With this reference, she communicated to the outside world that she was assisting refugees hiding in the wilderness outside Sivas.

Fortunately, Graffam and her missionary colleagues also managed to send uncensored descriptions of the events of 1915 through consular and diplomatic channels. These serve as invaluable supplements to the more cryptic letters sent through the censors' offices. Graffam's verbatim and uncensored first-hand report of the Sivas deportation, written from Malatia on 7 August 1915, was sent to the American Board Secretary in Constantinople. On the basis of this report, he concluded that "it appears to be the purpose of the (Turkish) government to deport into the desert or to scatter among purely Turkish villages, the entire Armenian population."

On 13 September 1915, Ambassador Henry Morgenthau forwarded Graffam's uncensored deportation report directly from the American Embassy in Constantinople to the Secretary of State in Washington in order to inform him of "the situation as it at present exists in the Interior with respect to the deportation of Armenians."[33]

The larger story of Graffam's role as a valuable source of information to the American government, and of America's response to her reports and to the reports of other missionaries, lies outside the scope of this particular investigation.[34] The focus of this study is, rather, to reconstruct the basic horror of this missionary account based on an amalgamation of her letters and reports, authored both during the events and afterwards within the constraints posed by censorship and other limitations on sources.

When arrest and deportation orders were issued in Sivas, Graffam rushed to the Chief of Police and used her fluent Turkish to persuade him to let her visit arrested Armenian men in prison. She then tried unsuccessfully to persuade the Sivas Vali, Mora Bey, to release the men and to abandon deportation orders. When these efforts failed, she simply announced to the Vali that she would accompany the Armenians on the deportation, to see if they would really be as safely cared for as he had claimed. "The Vali was very much surprised, but said nothing," she wrote

---

[33] File no. 867.4016/187, reel 44, Record Group 59, United States Department of State, Records Relating to Turkey, 1910–29.

[34] It remains an open question as to whether Graffam was operating as an intelligence officer for the United States during the war years. I was unable to unravel this issue, but further research may do so.

afterwards. Taking this as his consent, she began frantically to prepare for departure with her students and teachers.

In the chaotic days leading up to the deportation, the Armenians made desperate efforts to protect their property. Graffam remembered afterwards:

> Before starting the Armenians brought us their jewels and other possessions to care for. They were so excited that they were almost crazy, and we had to shake some of them in order to get them to tell us their name. One man was caught bringing us his possessions and he was killed. One teacher was taken out and was going to be killed but his wife hurried to a Turkish official who had been friendly to them, and he was saved.[35]

Graffam was allowed to proceed on a deportation with 3,000 of her Armenian friends and college colleagues for five days, going as far as the town of Malatia. As the government provided no ox-carts for her pupils or teachers, the mission bought ten ox-carts, two house *arabas*, and five or six donkeys for the journey. She recalled: "It was as a special favor to the Sivas people who had not done anything revolutionary, that the Vali announced that the men who were not yet in prison should go with their families."[36] Donning the largest straw hat she could find, Graffam joined the section of deportees from the mission college and set off on the road with them. Her sister last saw her encouraging a reluctant woman as they began walking together.

During the next five days, Graffam observed and partly experienced all the early stages of genocide: robberies, deprivations of water and food, beatings, kidnappings. The first day, her company from Sivas was not permitted to stop walking until after dark when, she recalled, "we were so tired that we just ate a piece of bread and slept on the ground wherever we could find a place to spread a *yorgan*."[37] As they were still near home, she believed that gendarmes protected them and "no special harm was done." However, by the second night, "we began to see what was before us":

> The gendarmes would go ahead and have long conversations with the villagers and then stand back and let them rob and trouble the people until we all began to scream, and then they would come and drive them away. Yorgans and rugs and all such things disappeared by the dozens, and donkeys were sure to be lost. Many had brought cows, but from the first day those were carried off one by one until not a single one remained.[38]

[35] Miss Graffam's Own Story.
[36] MLG to Mr. Peet, 7 August 1915, Malatia, Western Turkey Mission, 1910–19, vol. 42, fo. 216, ABC: 16.9.3, ABCFM.
[37] Ibid.   [38] Ibid.

On the third day, she wrote, "a new fear took possession of us, and that was that the men were to be separated from us at Kangal." However, when nothing happened when they passed that village at noon, the Sivas deportees became preoccupied with other concerns. By now, the caravan was encountering escapees from nearby massacres and refugees from other deportations. First, they encountered a mission teacher and his family from Manjaluk who had escaped slaughter, been recaptured by police and were then permitted to join the Sivas deportation at Kangal due to Graffam's direct intervention with the local Kaimakam. Next, they began to meet exiles from Tocat whose condition, Graffam remembered, "was one to strike horror to any heart":

They were a company of old women who had been robbed of absolutely everything . . . For three days they had been without food and after that lived on the Sivas company who had not yet lost much. When we looked at them we could not imagine that even the sprinkling of men that were with us would be allowed to remain.[39]

These fears were well justified as the men of Sivas were separated from their families the next day. Graffam wrote that "we heard that a special Kaimakam had come to Hassan Chalebe to separate the men, and it was with terror in our hearts that we passed through that village about noon." After a meal and rest, the company began to wonder if the men would be spared when, Graffam recalled:

the Mudir, a regular scamp came around with gendarmes and began to collect the men saying that the Kaimakam wanted to write their names and that they would be back soon, but the night passed and only one man came back from those who were taken, to tell the story of how every man was compelled to give up all his money and were taken to prison. The next morning they collected the men who had escaped the night before.[40]

Writing shortly thereafter from Malatia, Graffam withheld judgment about the fate of these men. She wrote: "The Mudir said they had gone back to Sivas. The villagers whom we saw all declared that all those men were killed at once. The question of what becomes of the men who are taken out of the prisons and those who are taken from the caravans is a profound mystery. I have talked with many Islams and I cannot make up my mind what to believe."[41] It was not until later, when the men never returned to Sivas, that Graffam concluded the villagers had been correct. Her later account added important details to the story:

That night while we sat in the fields they came and took the men, saying that the Kaimakam wanted to see them and talk over matters with them. Turks armed

[39] Ibid.   [40] Ibid.   [41] Ibid.

with rifles threatened those who were skeptical. And all the men were taken into the village. The last person I saw disappearing over the hill was the old deacon of our church. They took the men and put them into a stable for the night; there were over 200 of them. When morning came six of them had died of suffocation; the rest were taken into a valley and killed with every kind of implement and in every sort of way.[42]

Meanwhile, on the dusty road from Hassan Chalebe, Graffam and the other "broken hearted" women and children continued their journey. Although officials at Hassan Chalebe extorted 45 liras from the Sivas company – now numbering by Graffam's estimation perhaps 2,000 people – in return for the promise of protection from 5 or 6 gendarmes, no protection materialized. "As soon as the men left us," Graffam recalled:

the Turkish Arabajis began to rob the women saying "you are all going to be thrown into the Tokma Su [River], so you might as well give your things to us and then we will stay by you and try to protect you." Every Turkish woman that we met said the same thing. The worst were the gendarmes who really did more or less bad things. One of our school girls was carried off by the Kurds twice but her companions made so much fuss that she was brought back.[43]

In a later account of the deportation, Graffam gave further information about how persecutions of exiles intensified after the massacre of the men:

At noontime the gendarmes came and took us on and there were only one or two men left; very old or very young. Everyone who lagged behind was killed and when I returned, I saw hundreds of them. Some died with thirst; others went crazy. I saw fifty drop in one day, and there were many others I did not see.[44]

By now, Graffam was becoming truly exhausted in her efforts to plead with persecutors. "I was on the run all the time from one end of the company to the other," she wrote. Sometimes the slightest mercies from Turkish and Kurdish persecutors produced in her an almost pathetic gratitude and even admiration, similar to the apologetic and sympathetic feelings sometimes developed by hostages for their hostage-takers. Graffam wrote grudgingly of her Kurdish persecutors shortly after she was ordered to leave the deportation that "My hat was very big and the Kurds always made friends with me . . . These robbing murdering Kurds are certainly the best looking men I have seen in this country. They steal your goods but not everything. They do not take your bread nor your stick."[45]

In the next and, for Graffam, last leg of the journey, robberies and bullying by Turkish and Kurdish drivers intensified. As they approached the place near Malatia, whose name she translated as "the Bridge of Forty

[42] Miss Graffam's Own Story.   [43] MLG to Mr. Peet, 7 August 1915.
[44] Miss Graffam's Own Story.   [45] MLG to Mr. Peet, 7 August 1915.

Eyes," she also began to witness the magnitude of the disaster that awaited the "thousands and thousands" of deportees camping here:

When we approached the bridge of the Tokmu Su it was certainly a fearful sight. As far as the eye could see over the plain was this slow moving line of oxcarts. For hours not a drop of water on the road and the sun pouring down its very hottest. As we went on we began to see the dead from yesterday's company and the weak began to fall by the way. The Kurds working in the fields made attacks continually and we were half distracted. I piled as many as I could on our wagons and our pupils both boys and girls worked like heroes. One girl took a baby from its dead mother and carried it until evening. Another carried a dying woman until she died. We bought water from the Kurds not minding the beating that the boys were sure to get with it. I counted forty-nine such deaths but there must have been many more. One naked body of a woman was covered with bruises. I saw the Kurds robbing the bodies of those not yet entirely dead. I walked or rather ran back and forth until we could see the bridge.[46]

In the midst of this chaos, Graffam attempted to continue in her role as foreign advocate for the Armenian exiles:

The hills on each side of the bridge were white with Kurds who were throwing stones on the Armenians who were slowly wending their way to the bridge. I ran ahead and stood on the bridge in the midst of a crowd of Kurds until I was used up. I did not see anyone thrown into the water, but they said and I believe that an Elmas that has done handwork for me for years was thrown over the bridge by a Kurd. Our Bodville's wife was riding on a horse with a baby in her arms and a Kurd took hold of her to throw her over when another Kurd said "She has a baby in her arms" and they let her go.[47]

In a later account, Graffam remembered further details of this scene: "The last day before reaching the river the people were crazy for water. The Kurds would sell water to them and if they liked the looks of any of the young girls, they would carry them off; if they did not like them they killed them."[48]

Strangely, the business of murder seemed not to have completely interrupted local agriculture. "Those of our people who went near the river to drink were shot. I saw one woman with four daughters who was saved by helping the Kurds harvest their grain."[49]

Although Graffam did not admit fear for her own safety during this leg of the journey, the strain of trying to protect her friends was becoming almost unbearable and she was not immune from deprivation despite her obviously privileged status as the only foreigner present: "Every time anything happened I was immediately told and asked to save them. The nervous strain was tremendous, and like the rest, I was all in rags."[50]

---

[46] Ibid.   [47] Ibid.   [48] Miss Graffam's Own Story.   [49] Ibid.   [50] Ibid.

On the other side of the bridge, Graffam's company joined several other groups of deportees waiting by the river. Some had come earlier from Sivas and others, Graffam learned, had arrived from "Samsoun, Amasia and other places." Here, the police began "to interfere" with Graffam's activities for the first time and, she recounted, "it was evident that something was decided about me."

> The next morning after we arrived at this bridge they wanted me to go to Malatia, but I insisted that I had permission to stay with the Armenians. The next day however they said that the Mutessarif had ordered me to come to Malatia and that the others were going to Kyakta. Soon after we heard that these are going to Ourfa there to build villages and cities etc.[51]

Forced onto a wagon, "with an old woman for my servant," Graffam was compelled to leave her Armenian friends. She gave no details in her accounts of the pain of this separation but, rather, seemed focused on obtaining permission to rejoin the deportees. In Malatia, she went immediately to "the Commander a captain who they say has made a fortune out of these exiles" and requested that she be allowed to return to them. She appealed to his good will by describing her previous work for Turkish officers in Erzroom and said that she "pitied these women and children and wished to help them." He was not impressed and merely referred her to the local Mutessarif. Graffam was not successful with him either. When she suggested that the government telegraph Sivas to confirm her permission to go "all the way" with the deportees, "the answer is said to have come from Sivas that I am not to go beyond here."[52] Instead, she was given residence with fellow missionaries associated with a German-run orphanage, the Bauernfeinds, who were, themselves, "nearly crazy with the horrors they have been through here." Graffam soon understood more fully the reasons for their distress:

> The next day I could only look out from the German Orphanage and see my girls and people file by. The sights that I saw were frightful. I remember one little boy who came to me and his throat had been cut all around, but not deeply enough to kill him at once. In this village everyone was killed but him.[53]

Keeping records of "only what I have seen and know to be true," Graffam mounted an aggressive letter-writing campaign from Malatia to furnish information to the mission board and to appeal for help. "Money will be needed in unlimited amounts, but little money with care and advice will do much," she wrote ABCFM colleagues.[54] She also continued to campaign for Turkish government permission to proceed to Ourfa to

---

[51] MLG to Mr. Peet, 7 August 1915.   [52] Ibid.
[53] Miss Graffam's Own Story.   [54] MLG to Mr. Peet, 7 August 1915.

organize relief work for survivors, but Turkish officials repelled her efforts repeatedly.

> The Mutessarif and other officials here and [in] Sivas have read me orders from Constantinople again and again to the effect that the lives of all these exiles is [*sic*] to be protected . . . , but they certainly have murdered a great many in every city. Here there were great trenches dug by the soldiers for drilling purposes. Now these trenches are all filled up and the Bauernfeinds saw carts going back from the city by night and Mr. B. when he was out to inspect some work he was having done, saw a dead body which had evidently been pulled out of these trenches probably by dogs.[55]

Despite increasing evidence of Turkish government officials' complicity in the massacres occurring around her, when Graffam was writing from Malatia on 7 August 1915, she was reluctant to accuse them openly of murder. It is possible that she felt constrained simply by the possibility of interception by censors. However, it is also likely (and perhaps understandable) that she was finding it impossible to believe that a government would willingly order the extermination of a portion of its own people. Graffam was, after all, witnessing a disaster of unprecedented proportions. It was the first large-scale modern genocide. In describing the Sivas Vali's decision not to allow her to complete the journey to Ourfa with the Armenian exiles, she wrote on 7 August 1915: "That seemed to me a very great mistake on the part of the government, for although the horrors of the present situation among the Armenians are sufficient, the false reports are so many, that a report of an eyewitness would have been of value if I could have continued the whole way."[56]

At this early date, Graffam still apparently believed that eyewitness reports of the deportations would benefit the government by undermining "false reports" and she seemed almost reluctant to draw the dire conclusions suggested by the orders from Constantinople that forbade her to proceed to Ourfa. As she recognized the complexity of local Turkish and Kurdish involvement in the crimes, noting that some seemed fully to support actions against the Armenians while others were reluctant or even resistant to the actions, she was also still hesitant to issue general condemnations against the Turkish government. She had little way of determining the reliability of explanations and reassurances being offered by local government officials with whom she interacted during these desperate days. In August 1915, Graffam wrote (perhaps with censors in mind, but perhaps also with some sincerity): "I am not in any way criticizing the government. Most of the higher officials are at their wits end to stop these abuses and carry out the orders which they have received, but

[55] Ibid.   [56] Ibid.

this is a flood and it carries all before it."[57] From her limited perspective in the midst of the first tragedy of this sort in history, and in response to repeated denials of wrongdoing on the part of the many local officials with whom she spoke, she was still at least partly willing to believe that the government was not behind the crimes unfolding before her eyes.

Graffam's later accounts of the events of 1915 are less charitable. The Sivas deportees did not return as promised: "Out of 30,000 people there are about 3,000 left," she wrote in 1919.[58] Furthermore, refugees returned with sickening tales of cruelty:

For instance [she recounted in 1919] there was a very deep ravine where the Turks used to cast the people and they were killed, but the number of people who suffered this particular form of death was very great so that finally the ravine became very full, and I know of two women who were thrown in after this ravine was full and they were not killed. When they regained consciousness they had to crawl through the dead bodies to get out.[59]

Only with the benefit of hindsight was Graffam able more accurately to assess both the full scope and meaning of the events she had herself witnessed only in part. By 1919, her descriptions of Malatia no longer allow much ambiguity as to the genocidal plan and purpose behind the deportations:

If anything could be a counterpart of the worst description of hell, that place was Malatia. During the time of all these killings in Malatia we kept carbolic acid on the window sills in order to keep the odor of dead bodies from coming in. The sky was black with birds and there were hosts of dogs, feeding on the bodies. You could tell where a massacre had taken place by the migration of birds and dogs. I went to the market one day but the sights I saw were so terrible that I never went again. At first they killed them in the streets, but there was so much blood that they strangled them with ropes and the bodies were taken out during the night. Sometimes they were buried and sometimes they were not. The place where they were taken was directly opposite our house, and every afternoon at two you could see two or three thousand Armenians file past us; sometimes it took an hour for them to pass.[60]

In 1915, from her confinement in the German orphanage, Graffam agonized about the fate of Armenian exiles from Sivas and elsewhere, but still hoped that their worst possible fates would not materialize and that she would be able to help them in Ourfa.

As to the road beyond here there is every kind of conjecture. Here the general opinion is that all are to be killed in a valley five or six hours from here, but my opinion is that the journey from Sivas here is a sample of what it will be farther on as far as protection is concerned . . . after this the way is very narrow and steep,

----

[57] Ibid.   [58] Miss Graffam's Own Story.   [59] Ibid.   [60] Ibid.

and whereas so far they have had oxcarts, after this they will have nothing but what they can carry on their backs, for beyond here the government furnishes no transportation whatever, not a donkey nor anything. The aged are not allowed to remain behind, and will most of them fall on the way . . . It is evident that many will die on their way, but many thousand will arrive on the Ourfa plain absolutely destitute, and unless aid can be sent at once they will certainly starve.[61]

Graffam continued for three weeks to petition for permission to provide relief to survivors in Ourfa. However, she finally gave up hope and returned to Sivas, writing despondently, "the longer I stay and the more I see, the less hope I have of seeing any of my friends again."[62] Once she realized that she would not be permitted to rejoin the deportees, she concluded: "Now the explanation of the refusal to let me go farther is that the massacres are to be beyond here and whatever is said cannot be denied."[63]

The trip home to Sivas turned out to be as personally terrifying for Graffam as the deportation itself. "When I was with the Armenians I was too busy to be afraid; then death would have been welcome," she remembered afterwards.[64] However, on the death-saturated road home to Sivas she experienced a new kind of terror.

I was passing through a village which was one of the prescribed points where the Armenians were to be massacred. I had the old woman with me and an Armenian driver ["Muggerdich of Khanzar" who had taken a Greek name and spoke village Turkish as well, the Partridges explained later]. There are regular places along the road where the official records of those who were killed were kept. Accurate records were saved and when the Kurds killed the Armenians they kept a record, and then went to these officially designated places to collect their money which the government had promised. There were two Germans traveling with me and two or three wagon loads of gendarmes returning to Constantinople. We got ready to start again when the Mudirs came and took my driver away very impatient at the delay. [He was taken away and killed because a Turk had recognized his true identity, the Partridges add.] They finally went off without me, as did the gendarmes too, leaving me alone. The Turk who was to be my driver walked off and so did the officials, and I was left in the midst of a great crowd of Kurds ["mocking and jeering" say the Partridges]. Then I was afraid for I did not know what might happen. I told the old woman to get into the wagon, and jumping into the driver's seat I struck the horses and they started off quickly. The Kurds yelled after me but did not attempt to stop me.[65]

Abandoned on the roadside in the midst of a hostile crowd of strangers and horrible evidence of death, this was the only time Graffam acknowledged personal fear during the entire deportation.

[61] MLG to Mr Peet, 7 August 1915.   [62] Ibid.
[63] Ibid.   [64] Miss Graffam's Own Story.
[65] Ibid. See also Partridge for supplementary information about this incident.

Back in Sivas, local government officials presented her with a cruel ultimatum: either she stay in Sivas to care for remaining orphans in the Swiss Orphanage, or the orphans would also be deported. Graffam opted to stay. Her sister and brother-in-law, who had since returned to America, believed that "the underlying motive" for this government offer "was the unwillingness to have her come back to America, and tell the story of the deportations as she saw them."[66]

Graffam immediately took charge of several hundred orphans. She also obtained permission to begin visiting Armenian men in prison condemned to death by edict without trial. These numbered between 1,000 and 2,000 (estimates vary). Every night, between 100 and 200 of them were taken to a spot a few miles from the city where they were "compelled to dig trenches, disrobe, knocked in the head, [and] thrown into the trenches and buried."[67] Graffam wrote: "I went to the prison every night to say good-bye to them."[68] In the case of imprisoned Michael Frengulian, the graduate of Oberlin College and Professor of Mathematics who had earlier rescued her on the road from Erezrum, she shared his agonized deliberations about whether to accept his captors' offer to save his life by converting to Islam and teaching in a government school. Frengulian refused the offer and Graffam returned the next morning to find an empty prison cell and a Greek carriage driver returning from the countryside with a wagon containing only prisoners' clothing.

"At this time," Graffam remembered in 1919, "I was like a skeleton and looked like a refugee myself. I was half crazed; I could not be left alone, and yet I could not give in . . . because refugees were beginning to come from Marsovan and other places."[69] The needs of refugees being so much greater than her own, Graffam once again became fully absorbed in providing assistance, first to orphans and prisoners, and then also to the many Armenian soldiers who had not yet been killed.

They were not killed at first and we had regiments of Armenian soldiers to care for. I knew every man in every regiment and they used to come and see me until finally the Turks posted a notice outside my yard and then caught and killed twenty Armenians who tried to get to me. We were able to help them a little through the doctors.[70]

On the fate of these regiments, Graffam continued:

After a year and a half all the soldiers were put into prison. I got the German consul to telegraph to Constantinople about it and answer [*sic*] came back that these men were to go to a certain place where they were needed. They went there

---

[66] Partridge.   [67] Ibid.   [68] Miss Graffam's Own Story.   [69] Ibid.   [70] Ibid.

and one day I met a German returning from Constantinople and learned that these soldiers were killed all along the road. They killed 2000 Armenian soldiers, the rest turned Islam. Some of the soldiers hid in the mountains, in caves, and it was part of our relief work to try and get food to them.[71]

To illustrate one of the ways she and other survivors in Sivas funneled assistance to refugees in the mountains, Graffam related one particularly compelling story:

One day a woman came to see me and told me about some men in the mountains who were starving. She pretended to be crazy and as the Turks never harm anyone who is insane, she was able to wander about at will. They called her the crazy bride and as they did not watch her she was able to take food to the men in the mountains. She did this throughout the war and after the Armistice was signed she thought she was safe and did not act crazy. When the Turks realized that she had deceived them for all that time, the Kaimakam and the people in the village beat her until they thought she was dead, but she was not and her daughter was able to nurse her back to health.[72]

Graffam was the only American to remain in Sivas throughout the remainder of the war. Her sister and brother-in-law departed at the time of the deportation and her last missionary companion, Mary Fowle, died of typhus two years before the Armistice, leaving her to fend alone in enemy territory. However, she continued to provide a safe channel for relief efforts. After the war, she thanked mission donors at home who had sent money in support of wartime Armenian relief: "I wish the people who gave so many times during the war could know how far a few cents went. Their money has saved hundreds of lives."[73]

Although accounts of her remaining wartime relief work are filled with gripping tales of bravery and tragedy, they lie somewhat outside the scope of a study of genocide more narrowly defined.[74] Graffam risked her life many times in underground efforts to assist surviving refugees and prisoners. She watched friends and soldiers die of typhus, was evicted from her home five times, was tried for treason and narrowly missed death by execution. She organized efforts not only to smuggle food to Armenian soldiers hiding in mountain caves, but also to rescue Armenian girls and women from Turkish and Kurdish homes and to save refugees from starvation through public and clandestine factory work. She hid from the police jewelry, valuables, and accounts that had been left in her care before the deportations by burying them and re-burying them in every portion of the town.

---

[71] Ibid.   [72] Ibid.   [73] Ibid.
[74] A vivid description of her relief work is given in Partridge.

Graffam's contemporaries marveled at her courage. She had admitted to fear only once during the deportation and, despite continuing persecutions throughout the war, her bravery seemed to grow rather than diminish. Her sister and brother-in-law recounted:

After Miss Fowle's death, she decided that she would surely, sooner or later, suffer death at the hands of the Turks for she was continually persecuted and interfered with in her relief work. She determined to call her life as dearly as possible. Having reached this conclusion deliberately, she lost all fear and pursued her plans, disregarding all the obstacles put in her way. She constantly appealed to the officials citing their own religion, "What will you say at the Day of Judgment?" The Turks could not understand her and became afraid of her.[75]

By the end of the war, Graffam's bravery had become legendary. Yet today, the effectiveness of her relief efforts has still not been fully documented or appreciated despite the fact that existing sources and numerous testimonies of survivors suggest that she was responsible, single-handedly, for saving and ameliorating the lives of thousands of Armenians and others in the Sivas area during the war and afterwards.

Post-war dénoument

After the war, Graffam was well placed to assume leadership of the Sivas Unit of the Near East Relief, which had been incorporated by an act of the United States Congress. Eventually, Graffam directed a staff of twenty Americans in bringing supplies and assistance by railroad to returning deportees and other victims of the war. Rumors of her influence became widespread in the region. When a representative of an Armenian relief organization was approaching Sivas early in 1919, he struck up a conversation with a refugee:

"How are the Armenians in Sivas," he asked?
"Oh they are safe," was the reply.
"How so," asked the American?
"Miss Graffam is in Sivas, and the Turks are all afraid of her," was the reply.[76]

Graffam integrated general post-war relief efforts with the work of the mission's large orphanages, schools, industrial shops, a farm, and a hospital, thereby creating a system to deliver assistance more efficiently. She declined requests to return to America for a rest. "This relief work is better for me than a vacation," she wrote; "I feel as if the trials of the past are in a way being balanced by this enormous pleasure of distributing this

[75] Ibid.   [76] Ibid.

relief." It is, however, not surprising that she would die shortly thereafter in Sivas, exhausted from her participation in this chapter of history. In a tribute to Graffam, the Partridges wrote:

The war years of stress and strain, of work and worry, had taken their toll until finally she needed a major operation. This was performed by an Armenian surgeon, one of the best in whom she had complete confidence. The operation was successful, but the great heart which had sustained her during war years was unable to bring her back to recovery and she died on August 23, 1922 [*sic*], mourned by the thousands whose lives she had saved and for whom she gave her own.[77]

The story of Mary Louise Graffam is more than a story of an American who responded to the Armenian Genocide. It is the story of an American who experienced the Armenian Genocide and was, in a very real way, also a victim of it. Her means of communication were limited by wartime conditions and Turkish government censorship, creating several levels of documentary evidence from which to reconstruct her experience today. However, despite these obstacles, her story informed both the American Ambassador in Constantinople and the Secretary of State in Washington, D.C., as early as September 1915. As such, she became a crucial human link between the Armenians and the outside world during this severe trial, and continues to serve today as an important, objective eyewitness to the first genocide in modern history.

[77] Ibid. Her date of death is given as 17 August 1921 in Riggs, "Near East Memorial Biographies to 1953." Given the appearance of Graffam obituaries in the United States by September 1921, the Riggs date seems the more reliable.

9   From Ezra Pound to Theodore Roosevelt: American intellectual and cultural responses to the Armenian Genocide

Peter Balakian

The response of American intellectuals and cultural leaders to the Armenian Genocide of 1915 can be seen as a landmark in American modernity and a prologue to twentieth-century American engagement in human rights disasters in the international arena. But that outpouring of social and political opinion was not without its antecedents: for the American narrative concerning the Armenian atrocities committed by the Ottoman Turks began in 1894, at the start of Sultan Abdul-Hamid's massacres, which took the lives of about 200,000 Armenians in 1894–6.

During those years Americans from all classes and walks of life spoke out against the Hamidian Massacres. In 1896, the US House and Senate passed the Cullom Resolution, condemning the Sultan and his government for wholesale massacres of innocent Armenians. Women's groups, churches, synagogues, and civic organizations around the country organized to protest the treatment of the Armenians and to raise money for relief. The National Armenian Relief Committee, headed by American industrialists including Spencer Task and Jacob Schiff and supported by John D. Rockefeller, raised more than $300,000 in 1896–7. Clara Barton organised the first international Red Cross relief mission to the killing fields of the Armenian provinces in eastern Turkey in 1896. The Armenian atrocities were covered regularly by the nation's major newspapers and magazines throughout the nineties. In some cities, such as Minneapolis and St. Paul, Americans even boycotted Thanksgiving dinner in November of 1896 on behalf of fund raising for relief of "the starving Armenians."[1]

American intellectuals made historically and morally significant statements about what was happening to the Armenians at the hands of the Ottoman Turkish government. Mark Twain, Stephen Crane, Julia Ward Howe, Isabel Barrows, William Lloyd Garrison, Jr., and William James were among America's intellectuals who wrote or spoke out against the

[1] Peter Balakian, *The Burning Tigris: the Armenian Genocide and America's Response* (New York: HarperCollins, 2003), see ch. 6, "Humanity on Trial."

Turkish policy of oppression and massacre. By the second decade of the twentieth century, public intellectuals as varied as Theodore Roosevelt, Ezra Pound, H. L. Mencken, William Jennings Bryan, and President Woodrow Wilson were speaking out about what was evolving into the century's first genocide. The Americans who became voices of conscience about the Armenian massacres in the 1890s and later the genocide of 1915 had come of age, like Howe, Garrison, and James, amidst the fervor of abolitionism at mid century, or like Roosevelt, Bryan, and Wilson, after the Civil War, in a cultural climate in which moral issues were inseparable from political discourse.

Much of this moral sentiment was deeply Protestant and was an emanation of the near-century of Protestant missionary presence in the Ottoman Empire. By the middle of the nineteenth century, American missionaries had set up a network of missions, colleges, and schools throughout Turkey for the Armenians, Greeks, and Assyrians. Although the missionaries were interested in converting the Turkish Muslim population, they found that any Turks who were interested in the Protestant message were ostracized by their families and communities, and sometimes even killed. Through their immersion in the cultures of the Christian minorities of the Empire, American missionaries became witnesses of the Turkish atrocities against the Armenians; often they became rescuers and aiders of the survivors. Through the missionaries, the events of the Armenian exterminations became headline news in the United States.

Protestants like Julia Ward Howe, Isabel Barrows, and William Jennings Bryan were impassioned and articulate to be sure. From the podium at Boston's Faneuil Hall in November 1894, at a mass meeting to protest the Armenian massacres, Howe defined a Christian moral sentiment: "I throw down the glove which challenges the Turkish Government to its dread account." She exclaimed, "What have we for us in this contest? The spirit of civilization, the sense of Christendom, the heart of humanity. All of these plead for justice."[2] The cultural response to the Armenian massacres and then the genocide, however, was not defined solely by denominational perspective.

American Catholics and Jews, as well as secular intellectuals, all articulated their concerns about the Armenian crisis. The priest R. M. Ryan, in an essay for the *Catholic World*, "Why We Catholics Sympathize With Armenia," depicts the Armenians as the martyred Christian bulwark of the crossroads between East and West. In what sounds like a late-nineteenth-century version of "how the Irish saved civilization," Ryan

---

[2] Laura E. Richard and Maud Howe Elliott, *Julia Ward Howe 1819–1910* (Boston: Houghton Mifflin, Co., 1916), p.190.

asserts that while Europe was in its dark ages, "contending against hordes of barbarians . . . the Armenians were cultivating the arts and creating literary treasures . . . He who wishes for the civilization of Asia," the Irish-American priest asserted, "must sympathize with downtrodden Armenia."[3]

American Jewish opinion was led by Rabbi Stephen Wise, a Zionist who spoke out and worked for Armenian relief from the 1890s through the 1920s, and by Ambassador Henry Morgenthau, who was the first high-ranking government official to witness the Young Turk government's plan to exterminate the Armenians. The sentiment of American Jews was so broadly based that the Central Conference of American Rabbis went so far as to pass a proclamation in 1909 in the wake of continued killings of Armenians "urging the governments of the civilized world, particularly the signatory Powers of the Berlin Treaty, to take vigorous and perse-vering action for the protection of the Armenian Christians in Turkey, and for the protection of and granting of rights of citizenship to Jews in Roumania."[4]

Less than a decade after the Hamidian Massacres, the feminist writer and social critic Charlotte Perkins Gilman wrote in the journal *Armenia* – on which she served as an editorial board member, along with Julia Ward Howe and William Lloyd Garrison, Jr. – that the Armenian crisis was the primary symbol for what she hoped would be America's new age of global leadership:

The most important fact in this new century is the rapid kindling of the social consciousness; and among the shocks of pain which force that wakening the archetype is to be found in the sorrows of Armenia . . . The word "Armenian" has a connotation of horror; we are accustomed to see it followed by "atrocities," "massacre," "outrage"; it has become an adjective of incredible suffering.

In a decade that saw the continued growth of various peace movements, as well as the second Hague Conference, Gilman's vista was broadly framed and her appeal to international ethics was adamant. "America has heard and responded to a certain degree," she wrote, and "individ-ual sympathy and help have been given: but no amount of individual sympathy and help prevails on the Turkish government to desist from its criminal conduct." She went on, "National crimes demand international law, to restrain, prohibit, punish, best of all, to prevent."

---

[3] R. M. Ryan, "Why We Catholics Sympathize With Armenia,"*Catholic World* 62: 367–72 (October 1895 – March 1896), pp.181–5.
[4] *Central Conference of American Rabbis Yearbook XIX (1909)*, 162 (Central Conference for American Rabbis, 1909).

As it would be a disgrace to a civilized city to have within it any citizens living in filth, disease, vice and poverty – as it is such a disgrace, so it is a disgrace to a civilized world to have within it any nation committing such revolting crimes as those of Turkey.

If a nation is bankrupt, it should be put in the hands of a receiver and forcibly improved. If it is frankly criminal, it should be restrained. If it is simply ignorant, it should have compulsory education, and if it has senile dementia it should be confined under treatment, and the estate administered in the interests of the heirs.

"Who is to do it?" she asked, sounding a little like Walt Whitman trumpeting America's promise. "Who will usher in the new age of global social consciousness? . . . America," she answered, "with the blended blood of all peoples in her veins, with interests in every land, and duties with the interests; America, who leads in so many things, can well afford to lead in this: not only allowing human liberty here, but using her great strength to protect it everywhere."[5]

In 1915 as the World War entered its second year, the Armenian Genocide had become for Americans both an international human rights crisis and an issue that was entangled with the controversial and thorny issue of US entry into the First World War. The very idea that an entire defenseless civilian population could be wiped out under the cover of war was something new and profoundly alarming in most corners of the West. As Jay Winter has put it, the First World War "created the military, political and cultural space" in which the ruling Turkish political party, the Committee of Union and Progress, could engage in the act of genocide. The American sense of this unprecedented catastrophe was acute. From the American consulate in Kharpert, on the central Anatolian plateau, Consul Leslie Davis sent a dispatch to Ambassador Morgenthau on 30 June 1915, describing the beginning of the Armenian Genocide in his region: "Sir: I have the honor to report to the Embassy about one of the severest measures ever taken by a government and one of the greatest tragedies in all history."[6]

By 15 August, Consul Jesse Jackson in Aleppo reported that practically all the Armenians from the provinces of "Van, Erzeroum, Bitlis, Diarbekir, Mamouret ul-Aziz, Angora and Sivas have already been practically exterminated, and even conservative estimates already place the death toll well over 500,000."[7] A month later, Jackson informed

[5] Charlotte Perkins Gilman, "International Duties," US State Department Record Group 59, 867, 401.
[6] Leslie Davis to Henry Morgenthau, 30 June 1915, US State Department Record Group 59, 867.4016/269.
[7] Jesse Jackson to Morgenthau, Aleppo, Syria, August 1915, US State Department Record Group 59, 867.4016/148.

Morgenthau that the survival rate of the deportation marches was about 15 percent and this put the toll of vanished Armenians at about 1,000,000.[8] Recording the vivid scenes of horror, Jackson wrote:

One of the most terrible sights ever seen in Aleppo was the arrival early in August, 1915, of some 5,000 terribly emaciated, dirty, ragged and sick women and children, 3,000 in one day and 2,000 the following day. These people were the only survivors of the thrifty and well to do Armenian population of the province of Sivas, where the Armenian population had once been over 300,000.

They told Jackson that they had traveled about 1,000 miles on foot since before Easter, and thousands of the women had been carried off into harems, or raped, and robbed, and left naked.[9]

The reports of Jackson and Davis were echoed by dozens of reports and eyewitness accounts from other Armenian diplomats and missionaries. It is not surprising, then, that Ambassador Henry Morgenthau in his memoir *Ambassador Morgenthau's Story* titled the seminal chapter about the Armenian Genocide "The Murder of a Nation." He wrote:

The Central Government now announced its intention of gathering the two million or more Armenians living in the several sections of the empire and transporting them to this desolate and inhospitable region [the Syrian desert] . . . The real purpose of the deportation was robbery and destruction; it really represented a new method of massacre. When the Turkish authorities gave the orders for these deportations, they were merely giving the death warrant to a whole race; they understood this well, and in their conversations with me, they made no particular attempt to conceal the fact . . . I do not believe that the darkest ages ever presented scenes more horrible than those which now took place all over Turkey.[10]

By the fall of 1915, the Armenian Massacres had caused a shock-wave in the already traumatized minds of Americans who were wrestling with the First World War. The situation generated strong opinions from cultural elites, politicians, and statesmen. The chorus of American voices now included avant-garde poets as well as imperialistic former Presidents; leftist intellectuals and popular journalists. Ezra Pound, the new "genius" of literary modernism, wrote in *New Age* in October 1915 that the United States could no longer maintain its neutrality because the "broader interests of humanity" were at stake, interests that were at the heart of American history from its Enlightenment foundations to the abolition of

---

[8] Jackson to Morgenthau, Aleppo, Syria, 29 September 1915, US State Department Record Group 59, 867.4016/219.
[9] Jesse Jackson to US Department of State, Report "Armenian Atrocities," US Department Record Group 59, 867.4016/373.
[10] Henry Morgenthau, *Ambassador Morgenthau's Story* (New York: Doubleday and Doran, 1918), pp. 305, 307, 309.

slavery. America, Pound argued, was being called to extend that tradition in the global arena; "tyranny in the modern world is most visible," he wrote, "in German militarism and the Armenian massacres."[11]

H. L. Mencken, perhaps the most famous wit, social critic, and journalist of the era, expressed in his inimitable way his reaction to the Armenian situation: "The same Armenians who were being exterminated in 1896 are being exterminated again. The only difference is that in the present case the accommodating Secretary Lansing has given the atrocity-mongers a life by addressing a moral note to the Turkish Government." If he treated the liberal philanthropists with a touch of irony, he is also acerbic about hollow, bureaucratic gestures from government officials, and he went on: "the circulation of such notes now constitutes one of the chief duties of the State Department."[12]

The war also gave a sense of political realism to the Armenian Massacres that peacetime did not afford during Abdul-Hamid's Massacres in the 1890s. Although Congress had passed a resolution in 1896 calling for President Cleveland to denounce the Sultan's massacres, and some Senators like Wilkinson Call of Florida had even called for intervention and an independent Armenia, there was no urgent political circumstance drawing the United States into Turkish affairs in the 1890s. The First World War changed that, and now with Turkey as Germany's ally, the call for US involvement became more pressing each month as the intransigent trench war continued. Wilson's policy of neutrality grew increasingly controversial, and the debate over American entry into the war preoccupied the country. Part of that cultural and political moment was inseparable from the evolving response to the Armenian Genocide and the debate about the politics and ethics of intervention in Turkey on behalf of the Armenians.

Theodore Roosevelt discarded his earlier ambivalence about entry into the World War and became a passionate advocate. For him, the Armenian massacres, which he called "the greatest crime of the war," were an on-going part of this thinking about the American character, foreign policy, and international ethics. Writing to Samuel Dutton, Secretary of the Committee on Armenian Atrocities, the former President refused an invitation to a meeting because he disapproved of what he considered the Committee's too-passive response towards the Armenian Massacres. In responding to Dutton, he expounded on not only the Armenian

---

[11] Ezra Pound, *New Age* (October 1915); also Walter Kalaidjian, "The Edge of Modernism: Genocide and the Poetics of Traumatic Memory,"in *Modernism inc.* (New York: New York University Press, 2001).

[12] H. L. Mencken, "Who Can Save Armenia?" *Literary Digest* 51 (30 October 1915).

Massacres, but the problem of American neutrality, as well as some of his lifetime convictions about American culture.

My Dear Mr. Dutton:
Even to nerves dulled and jaded by the heaped-up horrors of the past year and a half, the news of the terrible fate that has befallen the Armenians must give a fresh shock of sympathy and indignation. Let me emphatically point out that the sympathy is useless unless it is accompanied with indignation, and that the indignation is useless if it exhausts itself in words instead of taking shape in deeds.
If this people through its government had not . . . shirked its duty in connection with the world war for the last sixteen months, we would now be able to take effective action on behalf of Armenia. Mass meetings on behalf of the Armenians amount to nothing whatever if they are mere methods of giving a sentimental but ineffective and safe outlet to the emotion of those engaged in them. Indeed they amount to less than nothing . . . Until we put honor and duty first, and are willing to risk something in order to achieve righteousness both for ourselves and for others, we shall accomplish nothing; and we shall earn and deserve the contempt of the strong nations of mankind.[13]

For Roosevelt, honor and duty meant going to war to bring about justice for the Armenians. Roosevelt was enraged by pacifist sentiment, which he believed was holding sway over Wilson's policy; his passion for entry into the war was equal to his hatred of Wilson, whom he called an "abject coward" and the "worst President since Buchanan."[14]Roosevelt went on in his letter to Dutton:

The American professional pacifists, the American men and women of the peace-at-any-price type, who join in meetings to "denounce war" or with empty words "protest" on behalf of the Armenians or other tortured and ruined peoples carry precisely the weight that an equal number of Chinese pacifists would carry if at a similar meeting they went through similar antics in Peking . . . They accomplish nothing for peace; and they accomplish something against justice. They do harm instead of good; and they deeply discredit the nation to which they belong.
All of the terrible iniquities of the past year and a half, including this crowning iniquity of the wholesale slaughter of the Armenians, can be traced directly to the initial wrong committed on Belgium by her invasion and subjugation; and the criminal responsibility of Germany must be shared by the neutral powers, headed by the United States, for their failure to protest when this initial wrong was committed.[15]

Thinking about justice for Armenia was not something new for Roosevelt. As President during the first decade of the century, he corresponded regularly with prominent Americans about the issue of

---

[13] Theodore Roosevelt, *Fear God and Take Your Own Part* (New York: T. R. Doran Co., 1916), pp. 377–83 (Theodore Roosevelt to Samuel Dutton, 24 November 1915).
[14] Henry F. Pringle, *Theodore Roosevelt* (Harcourt, Brace, and World, 1956), pp. 408–16.
[15] Theodore Roosevelt, *Fear God and Take Your Own Part* (New York: George H. Doran, 1916), pp. 377–83.

intervention on behalf of Armenia. In letters to Lymon Abbott, Andrew Carnegie, Jacob Schiff, Oscar Straus, and others, the President meditated on the suffering of the Armenians. For the most part, he concluded that there were no opportune political conditions for United States intervention at that time. Writing in 1907 to his friend Lymon Abbott, the Progressivist clergyman, he said, "I put righteousness above peace, and should be entirely satisfied to head a crusade for the Armenians . . . but it would be simple nonsense to start such a crusade unless the country were prepared to back it up; and the country has not the remotest intention of fighting on such an issue."[16]

And to Andrew Carnegie he wrote in 1906 about the upcoming Hague Conference on international peace that he was skeptical about a plan for international disarmament, because he believed that "it would only be safe to do so if there were some system of international police; but there is now no such system; if there were, Turkey for instance would be abolished forthwith unless it showed itself capable of working real reform." While Roosevelt saw certain colonial arrangements such as Russia in Turkestan, France in Algeria, and England in Egypt as positive for the peace and order they created, he told Carnegie that conversely, "it would be an advantage to justice if we were able to effectively interfere for the Armenians in Turkey, and for the Jews in Russia . . . and in the Congo Free State."[17]

But it was the war that gave Roosevelt another vantage point on the Armenian atrocities. In a letter to Cleveland Dodge, the primary benefactor of the American Committee for Armenian and Syrian Relief and later for the Near East Relief, in May 1918, more than a year after the United States entered the war and only about six months before Armistice, Roosevelt made what is perhaps his most eloquent summation of the failure of American policy towards Turkey in the wake of the Armenian Genocide. Disappointed with his old friend Cleveland Dodge for putting the missionaries' self-interest ahead of the call to duty that the Armenian Massacres demanded, Roosevelt urged Dodge to stop evading the reality in Turkey with euphemisms and evasions.

The fact was, Roosevelt wrote:

in Turkey public opinion is nil and the people always obey any effective executive force, and obey nothing else. The surest way to strengthen the German hold on Turkey is to give the impression that the Allies are in any way divided. The perpetuation of Turkish rule is the perpetuation of infamy, and to perpetuate it on the theory that there are large numbers of Turks who have fine feelings but who never make those feelings in any way manifest, is an absurdity. If Robert and

---

[16] Elting Morison, ed., *The Letters of Theodore Roosevelt* (Cambridge, Mass.: Harvard University Press, 1952), vol. V, pp. 536–8.

[17] Ibid., p. 345.

Beirut Colleges [American missionary-run schools in Constantinople and Beirut]
are used as props for the Turkish infamy and if they exert directly or indirectly any
influence to keep this country from going to war with Turkey, they will more than
counterbalance the good they have done in the past, and will make themselves
bywords of derision for the future.

Moreover, I feel that we are guilty of a peculiarly odious form of hypocrisy
when we profess friendship for Armenia and the downtrodden races of Turkey,
but don't go to war with Turkey. To allow the Turks to massacre the Armenians
and then solicit permission to help the survivors, and then to allege the fact that
we are helping the survivors as a reason why we should not follow the only policy
that will permanently put a stop to such massacres is both foolish and odious.

In concluding, Roosevelt continued to point to the hypocrisy of it all.
"The arguments advanced against our going to war with Turkey are on a
par with those formerly advanced against our going to war with Germany
and then with Austria; only they are not quite as good. The Armenian
horror," Roosevelt exclaimed,

is an accomplished fact . . . We should go to war because not to do so is really to
show bad faith towards our allies, and to help Germany; because the Armenian
massacre was the greatest crime of the war, and failure to act against Turkey is to
condone it; because the failure to deal radically with the Turkish horror means that
all talk of guaranteeing the future peace of the world is mischievous nonsense; and
because when we now refuse war with Turkey we show that our announcement
that we meant "to make the world safe for democracy" was insincere claptrap.[18]

It is ironic but indicative of the breadth of the response to the Armenian
Genocide that the British philosopher and social critic Bertrand Russell –
one of those pacifists Roosevelt detested – spoke out as vigorously against
his country's policy on the Armenians as Roosevelt spoke out against
Wilson. Having taught at Harvard in 1914, Russell was no stranger to
the new wave of American pacifism, but his perspective on the Armenian
Question went back to the 1890s, when Gladstone spoke out dramatically against the Sultan. For Russell, his government's inability to sustain
a moral stance against the Armenian Massacres was an important issue in
the evolution of British foreign policy. He even attributed the erosion of
democratic dissent in his country's foreign policy to Gladstone's successor, Lord Rosebery, who "dramatically dropped the agitation against the
Armenian massacres."[19] In doing so, Russell contended, Lord Rosebery
commenced a new drive for consensus in British foreign policy, one that
represented a further "closing of the ranks among the governing classes
against their common enemy, the people." [20]

[18] Ibid., vol. VIII, pp. 1316–18.
[19] Richard A. Rempel, ed., *Bertrand Russell, Prophecy and Dissent 1914–16* (London: Unwin
Hyman, 1988), p. 266.
[20] Ibid.

In assessing the power of empires and their abuse of small cultures and nations, Russell criticized what he called the "unbelievable barbarities of the Turks." "The fact that the Turks," he wrote, "had for ages displayed a supremacy in cruelty and barbarism by torturing and degrading the Christians under their rule was no reason why Germany should not, like England in former times, support their tottering despotism by military and financial assistance. All considerations of humanity and liberty were subordinated to the great game."[21]

As the news of what Consul Davis was calling "one of the greatest tragedies in all history," and what Ambassador Morgenthau would soon call "the murder of a nation," reached the United States, the media were more than responsive, as they had been in the 1890s. The *New York Times* alone ran 145 articles on the Armenian Genocide in 1915; it was not surprising to read in a front-page story in the *New York Times* on 4 October 1915: "Tell Of Horrors Done In Armenia: Report of Eminent Americans Says They Are Unequaled in a Thousand Years / A Policy of Extermination Put in Effect Against a Helpless People." Another *Times* headline later in the same week announced, " Rockefeller Foundation Leads Donations to American Committee With $30,000." Of the many philanthropic organizations that worked for Armenian relief at the outbreak of the genocide, the Rockefeller Foundation was among the most intensely engaged.

From the very beginning, the Rockefeller family expressed its sense of moral urgency over the Armenian massacres by giving generously to the Committee on Armenian Atrocities. John D. Rockefeller had supported Armenian Relief in 1896. Lady Henry Somerset, one of the leading British philanthropists supporting Armenian relief, had even cabled him for money in a moment of crisis in March 1896, when she was working with Armenian refugees in Marseilles. Now, as the whole process started up again, the Rockefeller Foundation took an even more vigorous role in trying to save Armenians. The Foundation – which had been set up in1913 "to promote the well-being of mankind throughout the world" – had developed a particularly international vision under the leadership of John D. Rockefeller, Jr. Armenian relief seemed like a natural cause for the Rockefellers, especially given John D. Jr.'s interest in the interfaith movement and world peace.

As early as August 1915, the Foundation was receiving detailed reports from its War Relief Commission about the plight of the Armenians; it relied on such reports in order to guide its philanthropic policy. In

[21] Richard A. Rempel, ed., *Bertrand Russell, Pacifism and Revolution, 1916–18* (London and New York: 1995), p. 89.

an extensive report of 1915–16, Eliot Wadsworth and Jeremiah Smith, Jr., of the Foundation noted that the Turkish government was hostile to foreigners investigating civilian conditions in their country, and that government censorship was severe and communication was difficult. To the horror of Wadsworth and Smith, the few Turkish officials they met tried to cajole them into giving Rockefeller Foundation money to their government, instead of to the dying Christians.

What Wadsworth and Smith reported about the devastation of the Armenians corroborated US and European consular reports, missionary reports, and accounts of survivors and other eyewitnesses. Wadsworth and Smith reported that the Armenians were being subjected to "torture" and a "policy" of "massacre," "wholesale deportation," and forced conversion to Islam. Their report contained a statement from a professor at the American college at Marsovan that was emblematic of the massacre process that was occurring all over the Ottoman Empire:

in the first week of July the Turkish troops arrested large numbers of Armenians, took some four hundred of the men, including some of the leading citizens, separated them from their wives and children and marched them out of town . . . As the guards in care of these men returned to town very shortly and some days afterwards a terrible stench arose from a nearby valley it is believed that most, if not all, of these men were killed outside the town. The wives and children of these men have been taken away by the Turks, no one knows where, and it is believed that the women will be given to the Turks for their wives.

The remaining Armenian population, threatened with the same fate, was urged to become Mohammedan in order to escape it, and we understand that about one thousand Armenians have been forced to sign petitions to become Mohammedans, thereby giving the matter the appearance of voluntary action on their part.

The Rockefeller Report called the "situation of the Armenians . . . a desperate one," and noted that "there is perhaps as much necessity for relief at the present time as in 1895 and 1909 when large relief funds . . . were raised by friends of Armenians in both England and the United States."[22] Before the War was over, US Ambassador Elkus (who had replaced Henry Morgenthau in the fall of 1916) sent his own message to the Rockefeller Foundation about the need for Armenian and Syrian relief.

In the first year of fund raising for Armenian relief, the Rockefeller Foundation gave $290,000, and by the end of 1917 the Foundation had poured about $610,000 into Armenian and Syrian relief. And John D. Rockefeller, Jr., whose interest in international peace and

[22] Wadsworth and Smith, "War Relief Report, 1915–16," Rockefeller Foundation, Record Group 1.1 Series 100N, Box 76, folder 719.

philanthropy grew during the war, wrote his own personal checks for Armenian relief, sometimes for as much as $10,000. That the American cultural response to the Armenian Genocide encompassed capitalist philanthropy was a harbinger of what was to come and also an emblem of the limits of US involvement.

By the time of the Armistice in November 1918, Americans had made significant cries for justice and had sent huge sums of money for Armenian relief. But the question remained: were the rhetoric and the relief efforts enough to affect foreign policy? Could public opinion and philanthropic aid yield an intervention from the US government? As early as 31 August 1916, President Wilson had issued a Presidential proclamation declaring 21 October and 22 October "joint days for Americans to make contributions for the Armenians and Syrians" who were perishing at the hands of the Turks.[23] Then, on his famous western tour in September 1919, in which he hoped to sell the Treaty of Versailles and the League of Nations to the American people, the President spoke for an American mandate for Armenia.

To a crowd of more than 15,000 in Kansas City's Convention Hall, Wilson appealed to America's responsibility to protect the Armenians who were being exterminated on their own homeland. The Treaty of Versailles, Wilson told the crowd, would protect the helpless people in the world "who were at the mercy of unscrupulous enemies and masters. There is one pitiful example, which is in the hearts of all of us," Wilson went on: "I mean the example of Armenia. A helpless people, the Armenians were and still are at the mercy of a Turkish government which thought it the service of God to destroy them. And, at this moment, my fellow citizens, it is an open question whether the Armenian people will not, while we sit here and debate, be absolutely destroyed." In some way, consciously or unconsciously, Wilson was acknowledging his own administration's failure to act against Turkey during the war. "When I think of words piled upon words, of debate following debate, when these unspeakable things are happening in these pitiful parts of the world, I wonder that men do not wake up to the moral responsibility of what they are doing."[24]

To an audience at the Mormon Tabernacle in Salt Lake City, on 23 September, Wilson once again brought up the issue of America's political responsibility for Armenia. "Armenia is to be redeemed," the President said, "so that at last this great people, struggling through night after night of terror, knowing not when they would see their land stained

---

[23] Woodrow Wilson, 66th. Congress, 2nd. Session, Senate Document 266.
[24] *New York Times*, Sunday, 7 September 1919.

with blood, are now given a promise of safety, a promise of justice, a possibility that they may come out into a time when they can enjoy their rights as free people."[25]

Yet Wilson had refused to make any military commitments that would have aided the Armenians during the genocide. And after the war Wilson proved to be similarly ineffective. As the Armenians in Turkey continued to suffer massacre, and the fledgeling Armenian Republic on the other side of the Turkish border in Transcaucasia was being battered by the Ottoman army in 1918 and then by Mustafa Kemal's army in 1920, Wilson refused to push for any military commitment to the region. When the Allies asked Wilson in April 1920 to draw the western boundary line for the new Armenian Republic, Wilson was unable to complete the task until late November, by which time the Turkish army had invaded and taken over the western part of what was to have been Armenia. The fact was that Wilson was incapable of implementing his idealism about small nation self-determination and his hope for a new Armenia. Not only was his failing health a serious impediment to his ability to act, but he faced a hostile, isolationist Republican Senate – led by his bitter foe, Henry Cabot Lodge – that opposed American political commitments abroad. To the post-war isolationists, the idea of aiding Armenia or making the new republic an American mandatory was unthinkable.

The only thing the Republicans were willing to commit themselves to in the post-war Near East was the pursuit of the vast oil fields of the now-defeated Ottoman Empire. By 1921, as the Harding administration succeeded the Wilson administration, Secretary of State Charles Evans Hughes launched his new "dollar diplomacy" in the Middle East with an open-door policy for oil, so that the United States would be able to compete with Great Britain, the Netherlands, and France in the new industrial age, which would be driven by fossil fuel. Given the new tone of American international interests, there was little political energy for Armenia.[26]

Perhaps Theodore Roosevelt crystallized the irony of American engagement when in 1915 he noted that there was something tragic about a US policy that would not risk military intervention to save the Armenians. Later, in 1918, he wrote to Cleveland Dodge that it was absurd and hypocritical "to profess friendship for Armenia," then allow Armenians to be massacred, and then raise money and engage in enormous efforts

[25] Ibid., Wednesday, 24 September 1919.
[26] Marjorie Housepian Dobkin, *Smyrna 1922: The Destruction of a City* (London: Faber & Faber, 1972), pp. 72–83. Dobkin discusses the turnabout in US policy towards Turkey which was driven by oil politics and dollar diplomacy.

to help the survivors, only to claim those efforts as reason to refrain from military intervention.

In the end, the American response to the Armenian Genocide was divided between a passionate popular appeal for aid and justice, and the limits of the federal government – the State Department, the White House, and a powerful segment of the Senate. Americans mobilized an extraordinary philanthropic response but not a state-sponsored political response. By the end of the 1920s, American philanthropy and humanitarian organizations driven by ordinary citizens, as well as the federal government would give an extraordinary $120 million to the Near East Relief (the offspring of what was once the American Committee on Armenian Atrocities) and established a landmark in the history of American international philanthropy. In some sense, this paradox would become a problem for the United States through the twentieth century and beyond, when it was faced with the challenge of genocide and other human rights atrocities being committed across the globe. Notwithstanding this conundrum, the foundation of an American consciousness about the Armenian Question and the genocide of 1915 had already taken shape in the powerful response to what former President Theodore Roosevelt called "the greatest crime of the war."

Part III

After the Catastrophe

10 The Armenian Genocide and US post-war commissions

Richard G. Hovannisian

The diplomatic and humanitarian measures of the United States to assist the victims of the genocide committed against the Armenian people during the First World War carried over into the post-war period. Although the country ultimately shied away from shouldering a part of the political and military responsibility for maintaining peace in the Near East, the Wilson administration did undertake extensive, detailed studies and made its views known to the Allied Powers as they were drafting the treaty of peace with the defeated Ottoman Empire. The reality of the Armenian Genocide and the plight of the Armenian survivors ran as a strong current in these investigations and recommendations. The voluminous materials on the subject deposited in the United States National Archives make it clear that the two American fact-finding missions sent to the Near East displayed a high degree of professionalism and completed their assignments with impressive thoroughness.

When these American missions set out in 1919 there was still the possibility that the United States would serve in one form or another as a protector and "big brother" of an emerging Armenian state and perhaps the surrounding territories as well. For a time, it seemed that the United States, however reluctantly drawn into the Great War, could not simply retreat to its own shores once the fighting was over. In fact, shortly after the country's entry into the war in April 1917, both the White House and the Department of State began to formulate general principles of peace, among which were certain propositions relating to the future of Armenia and the Armenian people. These were followed by the post-war field missions to report on the state of affairs and to make recommendations for a durable settlement. In the end, neither the reports nor the recommendations were used to good stead by the administration of Woodrow Wilson, but they remain as important contemporary documentation attesting to the indisputable reality of the Armenian Genocide and to the fact that the United States both recognized and condemned this calamity as a crime against humanity.

Soon after US involvement in the First World War, President Wilson entrusted the preparation of American guidelines and recommendations for the future peace settlement to a body of specialists organized as the "Inquiry."[1] As early as December 1917, the Inquiry advised: "It is necessary to free the subject races of the Turkish Empire from oppression and misrule. This implies at the very least autonomy for Armenia and the protection of Palestine, Syria, Mesopotamia and Arabia by the civilized nations."[2] Shortly thereafter, in January 1918, the President delivered his Fourteen Points, the twelfth of which called for "an absolutely unmolested opportunity of autonomous development" for the subject nationalities of the Ottoman Empire. He had intended to mention Armenia specifically in this declaration but was dissuaded from doing so by his trusted adviser, Colonel Edward M. House.[3] Still, in issuing an interpretive statement on the Fourteen Points, Walter Lippmann, Secretary of the Inquiry, and Frank Cobb, editor of the New York *World*, emphasized that Armenia should be assigned a "protecting power" and given a Mediterranean seaport. This implied that the strategic region of Cilicia should be included in the projected Armenian state, whether that was to be autonomous or independent.[4]

In September 1918, in the closing phase of the Great War, the Department of State under Robert Lansing issued preliminary guidelines regarding the future peace settlement. The Ottoman Empire, that is, the new Turkey, was to be reduced to Anatolia, historic Asia Minor, and possibly deprived of Constantinople/Istanbul and all other territory in Europe. The guidelines continued: "Armenia and Syria to be erected into protectorates of such Government or Governments as seems expedient from domestic as well as an international point of view; the guaranty being that both countries be given self-government as soon as possible and that an 'Open-Door' policy as to commerce and industrial development be rigidly observed."[5]

---

[1] On the organization and activities of the Inquiry, see United States, Department of State, *Papers Relating to the Foreign Relations of the United States, 1919: The Paris Peace Conference*, 13 vols. (Washington, D.C.: Government Printing Office, 1942–7) (cited hereafter as *Paris Peace Conference*), vol. I, pp. 9–200, Lawrence E. Gelfand, *The Inquiry: American Preparations for Peace, 1917–1919* (New Haven and London: Yale University Press, 1963).

[2] *Paris Peace Conference*, vol. I, p. 52.

[3] Laurence Evans, *United States Policy and the Partition of Turkey, 1914–1924* (Baltimore: Johns Hopkins University Press, 1965), p. 74.

[4] *The Intimate Papers of Colonel House*, arranged by Charles Seymour, vol. IV (Boston and New York: Houghton Mifflin, 1928), p. 129; David Hunter Miller, *My Diary at the Conference at Paris: With Documents*, 21 vols. (New York: Appeal Printing Co., 1924–6), vol. II, p. 79.

[5] Robert Lansing, *The Peace Negotiations: A Personal Narrative* (Boston and New York: Houghton Mifflin, 1921), pp. 195–6.

Professor William L. Westermann, the adviser on Western Asian affairs, elaborated on these points by urging that, in addition to the principle of self-determination, religious, economic, topographic, strategic, and linguistic factors should be considered in determining the future boundaries of Armenia. Because so many Armenians had perished in the deportations and massacres, the survivors would form barely 35 percent of the population in their new state, which would require strong external supervision.[6]

After the defeat of Germany, the Ottoman Empire, and their allies in the latter part of 1918, the United States Inquiry was reorganized as the Division of Territorial, Economic, and Political Intelligence of the American Commission to Negotiate Peace, that is, the US delegation to the Paris Peace Conference. Figuring among the intelligence division's first recommendations was the creation of a separate Armenian state combining the historic Armenian territories in the Russian Transcaucasus region and the Ottoman eastern provinces (Turkish Armenia) and Cilicia. The country should be placed under the protection of a mandatory power serving under the aegis of the soon-to-be-formed League of Nations. Again addressing the principle of self-determination, the intelligence division wrote:

The principle of majorities should not apply in this case, because of the conditions under which the Armenian people have lived in the past. They have suffered from every handicap of nature and man; they have been massacred and deported by hundreds of thousands; they have been subject of international political intrigue; and at this moment, helpless and weak as they are, they are being pressed for the unfavorable settlement of their affairs by big Powers seeking to define spheres of future political and commercial interests. It would be a departure from the principle of fair dealing if at this time their every claim were not heard with patience, and their new state established under conditions that would in some manner right historic wrongs.[7]

Despite these favorable recommendations, President Wilson was reluctant to commit the requisite US resources necessary to force the Turkish armies still in control of the territories of the proposed Armenian state to withdraw and to repatriate the Armenian refugees, or to press Congress to authorize him to assume a mandate for Armenia. Meanwhile, Armenophile organizations such as the American Committee for the Independence of Armenia (ACIA) dispatched hundreds of telegrams and letters calling for US support of Armenia.[8] As early as January 1919, 75

---

[6] Gelfand, *The Inquiry*, pp. 248–9.   [7] Miller, *Documents*, vol. IV, pp. 259–60.
[8] See *A Report of Activities: The American Committee for the Independence of Armenia, 1918–1922* (New York: ACIA, 1922) (cited hereafter as *ACIA Activities*); Gregory L. Aftandilian, *Armenia, Vision of a Republic: The Independence Lobby in America, 1918–1922* (Boston: Charles River Books, 1981).

Congregational ministers urged Wilson to champion Armenia's right to a free and independent national existence and to uphold his own stated principle that "the interest of the weakest is as sacred as the interest of the strongest."[9] On the initiative of the ACIA, 85 bishops, 20,000 clergymen, 40 state Governors, and 250 college and university Presidents petitioned President Wilson to assist in the formation of an independent Armenia extending from the Black Sea to the Mediterranean Sea.[10] This was followed on 22 June 1919 by the appeal of a group of prominent Americans – Charles Evans Hughes, James W. Gerard, Elihu Root, Henry Cabot Lodge, John Sharp Williams, Alfred E. Smith, Frederic Courtland Penfield, Charles W. Eliot, and Cleveland H. Dodge – to restore to Armenia its independence, unity, and integral lands and to give its people means for self-defense by helping to equip an army of 50,000 men.[11]

President Wilson, while participating in the Paris Peace Conference during the first half of 1919 until the imposition of the Treaty of Versailles on Germany, maintained that he could not bind the United States to accept the mandate for Armenia. He made no secret of the fact, however, that he personally favored assumption of the mandate. On a trip back to the United States in February, he told the Democratic National Committee:

I think there is a very promising beginning in regard to countries like Armenia. The whole heart of America has been engaged for Armenia. They know more about Armenia and its sufferings than they know about any other European area . . . That is a part of the world where already American influence extends, a saving influence and an educating and an uplifting influence . . . I am not without hope that the people of the United States would find it acceptable to go in and be the trustee of the interests of the Armenian people and see to it that the unspeakable Turk and the almost equally difficult Kurd had their necks sat on long enough to teach them manners and give the industrious and earliest people of Armenia time to develop a country which is naturally rich with possibilities.[12]

The King–Crane Commission

Notwithstanding his call to the National Committee to advocate an American mandate for Armenia, Woodrow Wilson returned to Paris in March

[9] *New York Times*, 27 January 1919, p. 8; James B. Gidney, *A Mandate for Armenia* (Kent, Ohio: Kent State University Press, 1967), p. 79.
[10] United States National Archives, Records of the Department of State, Record Group 59, 763.72119/4142, and Record Group 256, 867B.00/62; *ACIA Activities*, p. 24. See also *Congressional Record*, 66th Congress 1st Session, vol. LVIII, pt. 1 (23 May 1919), p. 156.
[11] US Archives, RG 59, 860J.01/12; *ACIA Activities*, p. 25; Gidney, *Mandate*, p. 169.
[12] Joseph P. Tumulty, *Woodrow Wilson as I Know Him* (Garden City, N.Y.: Doubleday, Page, 1921), pp. 376–7.

with the view that it would be "premature" and "unwise" to press for acceptance of the mandate prior to US entry into the League of Nations. It was planned that the Covenant of the League, which was to regulate the mandate system, should be incorporated into the forthcoming German peace treaty. Moreover, faced with the growing opposition of the Republican Senate majority led by Henry Cabot Lodge, Wilson now asserted that time was needed to prepare American public opinion.[13] The longer the Turkish settlement was put off, however, the graver became the competition and rivalry of the European Allies and the more precarious became the future of Armenia. Perhaps as a way of putting off a final decision on the hotly contested spoils in the Near East, the Allied heads of state in Paris agreed to send a mission of investigation to study the prevailing conditions and make recommendations about the future administration of the area.

It was on Wilson's initiative that the Supreme Council of the Paris Peace Conference reaffirmed on 20 March 1919 that

it is the purpose of the Conference to separate from the Turkish Empire certain areas comprising, for example, Palestine, Syria, the Arab countries to the east of Palestine and Syria, Mesopotamia, Armenia, Cilicia, and perhaps additional areas of Asia Minor, and to put the development of their people under the guidance of the Governments which are to act as Mandatories of the League of Nations.

Several peoples formerly subjected to Turkish rule could now be recognized as independent nations under the supervision of a mandatory power. An inter-Allied commission was to visit the regions in question to determine the sentiments of the inhabitants and to report on the social, racial, and economic conditions that would help in the division of territory and the assignment of mandates for the tranquility and development of these peoples and countries.[14] As it happened, however, the intensifying rivalry of Great Britain, France, and Italy, and their reluctance to allow the true desires of the affected peoples in the Near East to become known, prompted them to renege on their decision and turned what was to have been an inter-Allied commission into an American-only team.

The resultant US commission was led by Henry Churchill King, President of Oberlin College, and Charles R. Crane, an industrialist friend of President Wilson and a trustee of the American-sponsored Robert College in Constantinople. The small party included technical adviser Professor Albert Lybyer, Arab specialist Captain William Yale, and

---

[13] Seth B. Tillman, *Anglo-American Relations at the Peace Conference of 1919* (Princeton: Princeton University Press, 1961), p. 368.
[14] *Paris Peace Conference*, vol. XII, pp.745–7.

adviser on the non-Arab regions George R. Montgomery.[15] During June
and July of 1919, the King–Crane Commission conducted numerous interviews in Constantinople, Palestine, Syria, and Lebanon with American
diplomatic, missionary, and relief personnel and with spokesmen for the
various communities of the now-defeated Ottoman Empire.[16]

In Cilicia, American Relief Director William Nesbitt Chambers reported that 25,000 Armenian survivors had returned to the city of Adana
alone and that there now seemed to be a little hope for better times.[17]
To Turkish representatives who attempted to shift the blame for the
Armenian Genocide to the deposed Young Turk regime and to plead
for the territorial integrity of the empire, King's pat response was that
the peace conference had already decided to separate Armenia and other
territories from Turkey and that therefore the discussion should focus
on rectification of recent wrongs, emancipation of captive Armenian
women and children, and determination of suitable boundaries between
Turkey and Armenia.[18] American relief and missionary officials Dr. James
Barton and William Peet reported on their travels through the former
Armenian-inhabited provinces, where the horrible evidence of the scenes
of massacre and wanton destruction were visible everywhere. They insisted that to submit the Armenians to Turkish rule again would be an
unforgivable crime. No witness advocated Armenian independence more
fervently than Mary Louise Graffam, a long-time Oberlin missionary and
teacher at Sivas (Sepastia). As a witness to the genocidal atrocities, she
told the commission that to leave the Armenians with the Turks would
be "beyond human imagination."[19] Her testimony was echoed by Dr.
George White, President of Anatolia College at Marsovan, who stated
that unless the Armenians were liberated from Turkish domination, there
could be "no real security for the life of a man, the honor of a woman,
the welfare of a child, the prosperity of a citizen or the rights of a father."
Armenia should be made independent with American supervision. Like
other Americans he maintained that the liberation of Armenia required
external supervision also over Anatolia and the Constantinople-Straits
zone.[20]

[15] Ibid., pp. 747–8; Harry N. Howard, *The King–Crane Commission: An American Inquiry in the Middle East* (Beirut: Khayats, 1963), pp. 36–82.

[16] For the commission's interviews in Constantinople, see Walter George Smith, "Journal of a Journey to the Near East," ed. Thomas A. Bryson, *Armenian Review*, vol. XXIV, no. 3 (1971), pp. 72–5; Howard, *King–Crane*, pp. 87–8 (for its activities in the Arab provinces, pp. 88–154).

[17] Howard, *King–Crane*, pp. 140–1; *Hairenik* (Boston), 30 August 1919, p. 4.

[18] Howard, *King–Crane*, pp. 163–9.   [19] Ibid., pp. 183–4; Smith, "Journal," p. 76.

[20] Howard, *King–Crane*, pp. 187–8. See also George E. White, *Adventuring with Anatolia College* (Grinnell, Iowa: Herald-Register Publ. Co., 1940).

The findings of the King–Crane Commission supported the creation of a greater Syrian kingdom (inclusive of Lebanon and Palestine), were somewhat critical of the Zionist program in the Near East, and accepted a British mandate for Mesopotamia (Iraq).[21] The region of Cilicia, according to the recommendation of George Montgomery, was linked with the north rather than with Syria and was the most suitable outlet to the sea for Aintab, Marash, Kharput, and even Bitlis, "all Armenian towns." The commission pointed to the complexities of the Armenian settlement, as the boundaries had not been even approximately defined as yet and most of the native Armenians had been driven from their historic lands. To bring stability to the region, the European powers should be prevented from partitioning Anatolia, which should be kept as a Turkish homeland. Still, there had to be a "proper division" of the Ottoman Empire because of the "misgovernment and massacres of the Turkish rule." The Turks had many attractive personal qualities, but "the Government of the Turkish Empire has been for the most part a wretched failure . . . characterized by incessant corruption, plunder and bribery." Speaking of the treatment of the Armenians and the unrepentant attitude of the Turkish authorities, the commission emphasized that "these crimes black as anything in human history cannot be simply forgotten and left out of account in seeking a righteous solution of the Turkish problem." If the "rankest conceivable wrongs" were not to be passed over in silence, then any settlement "must contain that small measure of justice which it is now possible to render in this case."[22]

The report summarized the recommendation regarding the future of Armenia as follows:

The reasons for a separate Armenia, then, may be said to be: because of the demonstrated unfitness of the Turks to rule over others, or even over themselves; because of the adoption of repeated massacres as a deliberate policy of State; because of almost complete lack of penitence for the massacres, or repudiation of the crime – they rather seek to excuse them; because practically nothing has been done by the Turks in the way of repatriation of Armenians or of reparations to them – a condition not naturally suggesting a repetition of the experiment of Turkish rule . . .; the Armenians have surely earned the right, by their sufferings, their endurance, their loyalty to principles, their unbroken spirit and ambition, and their demonstrated industry, ability and self-reliance, to look forward to a national life of their own; because such a separate state would probably make more certain decent treatment of Armenians in other parts of Turkey; and because there is no adequate substitute for such a state. In the interests of the Armenians, of the Turks, and of the peace of the world alike, the formation of a separate Armenian State is to be urged.[23]

[21] *Paris Peace Conference*, vol. XII, pp. 751–802.
[22] Ibid., pp. 802–48.   [23] Ibid., p. 814.

Such a state, in order not to impose Armenian minority rule over a Muslim majority, should, however, be circumscribed and made up of the Russian Armenian provinces in the Caucasus and a large part of the Ottoman four eastern provinces of Trebizond, Erzerum, Bitlis, and Van. With the anticipated influx of Armenians from around the world and the probable emigration of many Muslims (who would opt to move into the new Turkish state or another Muslim country rather than to submit to Armenian rule), the Armenians could become a majority within five years. A state of even these modest proportions would be economically viable and have both geographic unity and defensible boundaries, thus decreasing the responsibilities of the mandatory power and hastening the time for full self-government. An important safeguard for the new Armenia would be the establishment of mandatory supervision also over both Anatolia and the Constantinople-Straits zone, preferably with the same mandatory power in order to facilitate exchange of populations, repatriation, and regional economic development. The United States, Henry King and Charles Crane concluded, was the only nation having both the moral fiber and the material resources to assume that obligation. It was better to spend millions to preserve the peace than billions to wage another war.[24]

The report of the King–Crane Commission was delivered to the White House in September, shortly after President Wilson had collapsed from nervous exhaustion in Colorado and then suffered a stroke. Although he had an outline of the commission's recommendations before beginning his ill-fated national political tour, during which he made reference to Armenia several times, he apparently never read the full report.[25] Even if he had not been incapacitated, however, it is unlikely that he would have submitted to Congress a program that required the acceptance of substantial military and financial responsibilities and that also included supervision over Turkish Anatolia. Moreover, the exclusion from Armenia of three of the six Turkish Armenian provinces, namely Sivas/Sepastia, Kharput/Kharpert, and Diarbekir/Dikranagerd, as well as the Mediterranean coastal region of Cilicia, would not sit well with the Armenians or their supporters. In any event, while the future direction of American foreign policy was being debated in the United States, another mission set out to study conditions in Armenia and the Near East.

---

[24] Ibid., pp. 819–28, 841–7.
[25] US Archives, RG 59, 763.72119/6457/7161/7162; Howard, *King–Crane*, pp. 218–19. The report of the mission was eventually published in *Editors and Publishers* 55:27 (1922).

The American Military Mission to Armenia

Reluctant to put the Armenian issue to Congress prior to US entry into the League of Nations, President Wilson consented to the dispatch of a second field mission to "report on the political, military, geographic, administrative, economic and such other considerations involved in possible American interests and responsibilities in that region."[26] Armenian spokesmen and Armenophile societies were distressed by this development, as it was clear that the United States already had amassed more than enough information on the subject and that the longer the peace treaty with Turkey was delayed the more precarious would become the future of the Armenian people. The political pragmatism of the moment was expressed by a member of the US delegation in Paris who rationalized that Americans "should know to the fullest the horror of the situation there and that pending action by Congress the President was doing all he could by sending someone for moral effect and to get information."[27]

The American Military Mission to Armenia, headed by Major General James G. Harbord, Chief of Staff of the American Expeditionary Forces in Europe, was formally appointed in August 1919 and included two Brigadier Generals and nearly sixty other officers, enlisted men, and specialists, who were carefully selected on the basis of training, experience, and expertise.[28] The mission was given broad publicity in the United States, where there was widespread speculation that the findings would determine the fate of Armenia and that General Harbord would probably be the Governor of that country if the United States did become the mandatory power. While still in Paris, members of the mission studied the extensive materials already at hand and conducted numerous interviews with persons knowledgeable about the state of affairs in the Near East. American relief officials who had recently returned from the region painted a grim picture of the wretchedness of the Armenian survivors and the renewed persecution of those who attempted to return to their native towns and villages.[29] On the other hand, repeated caveats were received from the United States High Commissioner in Constantinople, Acting Rear Admiral Mark L. Bristol, who discounted any threat posed by the emerging Turkish Nationalist movement headed by Mustafa Kemal (Ataturk) and complained that appointment of the Harbord mission was showing inordinate sympathy and concern for the Armenians

[26] US Archives, RG 256, 184.021/142.
[27] US Archives, RG 256, 184.021/106/122; 867B.00/209.
[28] Biographical sketches of the mission's officers and listings of all personnel are in US Archives, RG 256, 184.021/42/43/44/48/60/90/101.
[29] US Archives, RG 256, 184.021/106/113.

and would stir unrest among the Muslim population. Throughout the post-war years, Bristol would continue to press for the "big point of view" and resort to every means possible to dissuade Washington from allowing itself to be left holding the Armenian "lemon."[30]

The American Military Mission set sail from France during the last week of August for an investigation that would last two months and take it to Constantinople, Anatolia, Cilicia, the denuded Turkish Armenian provinces, and the small Armenian Republic that had been formed in the Transcaucasus during the final phase of the world war and that was now regarded as the nucleus of any future united Armenian state. Both before and during the journey, the mission gathered information that would be vital if the United States assumed a role in the region: climate, geography, and demography; ethnic and religious composition; flora and fauna; existing and potential facilities for communication and transportation; public and private finance and trade; health and sanitation; natural resources and production; and many other subjects that would be helpful to a mandatory power or to foreign investors.

In Constantinople for four days in early September, General Harbord exchanged many courtesy calls and gathered additional data before traveling with his mission by railway to Cilicia via Ismid, Afion-Karahisar, Akshehir, and other Anatolian towns. Along the way Armenian repatriates led by their priests welcomed the Americans with flowers and fruit and told of their tribulations and hopes. In Konia, American Relief Director Mary Cushman reported that half a million deportees had passed through the city in 1915 and that currently she had several hundred Armenian orphans under her care. Harbord later recalled that, after hearing so many graphic descriptions of the Armenian suffering, his mission "literally dreamed Armenia and Massacres."[31]

Passing through the Taurus tunnels near the historically strategic Cilician Gates, the mission descended to the rich alluvial plain around Adana, where American and Armenian relief agencies were trying to accommodate thousands of repatriates. General Harbord was struck by the large number of Armenian women and girls who tried to shield their faces to hide tattoos on their lips, cheeks, and foreheads – the glaring evidence of captivity among Muslim tribesmen. American Relief Director William Chambers recounted, as he had for the King–Crane Commission, the

[30] Library of Congress, Division of Manuscripts, The Papers of Mark L. Bristol, Box 65, Armenia file, Bristol to Ammission, 21 August 1919; Box 31, Bristol to Harbord, 20 August 1919.
[31] US Archives, RG 256, 184.021/141/142/147/250; James G. Harbord, "Investigating Turkey and Trans-Caucasia," *World's Work*, vol. XI (May 1920), pp. 36, 38–9.

horrors of the massacres, accused the Turkish population of complicity, and gave reasons for including Cilicia in the new Armenian state.[32]

Continuing on to Aleppo, which had been the principal dispersal point of the Armenian deportees during the war, the American Military Mission heard US Consul Jesse B. Jackson voice his outrage at the genocidal policies of the Turkish authorities. He estimated that of the million Armenians who had been deported to Syria, only about 100,000 survived and that countless other women and children were still held in captivity. He believed that only the "wise dictatorship" of a mandatory power could overcome the difficulties caused by the racial and religious heterogeneity in the region and by the fanaticism of the population.[33]

In mid-September the mission left the railway at its terminus near Mardin and traveled by automobile towards the Armenian Plateau, where Mustafa Kemal's Nationalist forces were in control. In remote towns and provincial capitals, a few American missionaries and relief workers were trying to recover Armenian women and children and feed the destitute. At Mardin, Agnes Fenerga reported that the massacres had been so thorough that not one Armenian was left, and Rachel B. North at Diarbekir explained that, of the 6,000 Armenians who had recently congregated in the city, few if any of them were the original native inhabitants. As the Armenians had been extirpated and the Turks had never been numerous in the province, Diarbekir had become overwhelmingly Kurdish.[34]

The largest American relief station on the Armenian Plateau was at Kharput (Kharpert), despite the ruin of its Armenian quarters. More than 3,000 orphans were housed in what was left of the American-sponsored Euphrates College and twenty other shelters. Dr. Henry H. Riggs of a prominent missionary family reported that about 25,000 of the province's 175,000 Armenians remained. Because of the lack of government support and a state of anarchy, most Armenian children still had not been freed from their abductors, and some 20,000 other forcibly converted Armenians were terrorized and prevented from reclaiming their Christian faith. Notorious cut-throats appeared on the streets of Mezre, the provincial capital, without fear of punishment for their part in the massacres, and Muslim squatters refused to relinquish goods and properties of returning Armenians. Riggs predicted that unless the United States

[32] US Archives, RG 256, 184.021/243/255/257/259/263; Harbord, "Investigating" (May 1920), pp. 40–1.

[33] For Jackson's reports relating to the Armenian deportations and massacres, see US Archives, RG 84, Foreign Service Posts of the Department of State: Aleppo; and RG 59, File 867B.48.

[34] US Archives, RG 256, 184.021/96; Harbord, "Investigating" (May 1920), pp. 46–8, and (June 1920), pp. 176–8.

took charge of both Anatolia and Armenia, the outlook for the Armenians would be bleak.[35] At Malatia, in a fertile plain south-west of Kharput, the American Military Mission to Armenia learned that, of the 12,000 original Armenian inhabitants, fewer than 1,000 remained. Two relief workers reported that prior to Harbord's arrival the authorities had been removing evidence of the massacres and had threatened reprisals against any Armenian who dared complain to the Americans.[36]

In Sivas, General Harbord met with Mustafa Kemal, who had just presided over the organizational meeting of the Association for the Defense of the Rights of Anatolia and Rumelia, among whose chief objectives was the prevention of an Armenian state on Ottoman territory and abolition of any and all special privileges for religious or ethnic minorities. In his discussion with Harbord, Kemal defined the Turkish Nationalist movement in Wilsonian terms. He denied rumors that the Nationalists were inspired by the Bolsheviks or Young Turks and expressed appreciation of the fact that the Americans recognized the goodness of the Turkish people and had stood up against the secret wartime agreements of the European powers on partition of the Ottoman Empire. When Harbord voiced concern for the surviving Armenians, Kemal disclaimed any malice towards them and condemned the wartime massacres, observing, however, that the outrages had been the work of "a small committee which had usurped the government." Greek outrages at Smyrna (Izmir), on the other hand, were now occurring under the cover of an Allied fleet, and the Armenian government of the "Erivan republic" was trying to exterminate the local Muslim population in a "wave of sanguinary savagery." Harbord left the interview impressed with Mustafa Kemal's authority, perception, and patriotism.[37]

Sivas had become a major American relief station, staffed by seventeen Americans and their assistants who operated shelters, workshops, and schools, and cared for 1,500 orphans. Harbord was told by Dr. Ernest Partridge and his sister-in-law Mary Louise Graffam that, of the nearly 200,000 Armenians of the province, only about 10,000 survived and these in a completely servile status. The General was particularly moved by

[35] US Archives, RG 256, 184.021/258. For accounts by Riggs and the former US Consul in Kharput, Leslie Davis, regarding the wartime Armenian decimation, see Henry H. Riggs, *Days of Tragedy in Armenia: Personal Experiences in Harpoot, 1915–1917* (Ann Arbor: Gomidas Institute, 1997); and Leslie A. Davis, *The Slaughterhouse Province: An American Diplomat's Report on the Armenian Genocide, 1915–1917*, ed. and intro. Susan Blair (New Rochelle, N.Y.: A. D. Caratzas, 1989).
[36] US Archives, RG 256, 184/021/329; Harbord, "Investigating" (June 1920), pp. 178–80.
[37] Harbord, "Investigating" (June 1920), pp. 185–8. See also Bristol Papers, Box 66, Caucasus file, Bristol to Ammission and to Secretary of State, 2 October 1919; US Archives, RG 256, 184.021/77/253/288/342.

seeing some 150 rescued "brides," Armenian girls who had been abducted and abused: "Many of these are still no more than children, and the stories of the treatment received by these little girls of tender years would be beyond belief in any other part of the world." Harbord had special commendation for Mary Graffam, whose harrowing experiences "have never been duplicated in the story of womankind."[38]

Everywhere that the mission traveled – Amasia, Marsovan, Samsun, Zara, Erzinjan – the story was the same. Few of the original population remained; those who survived were sequestered in Muslim households; exiled persons brave enough to return were unable to regain their homes and properties; fear and intimidation were ever present. Signs of the devastation and depopulation became all the more evident as the American Military Mission moved eastward on the Armenian Plateau towards Erzerum and the pre-war Russo-Turkish boundary. In Erzerum, General Kiazim Karabekir insisted that the Armenians had never formed a significant element in the region and complained that thousands of Muslims were being driven from their homes by the Armenian armed forces in districts on the Russian side of the 1914 pre-war boundary. He warned, however, that the Armenians would be taught an unforgettable lesson if, prodded on by the British, they dared to venture into the province of Erzurum or anywhere else on the Turkish side of the frontier.[39]

At the end of September, the Harbord mission passed beyond the last border post to Sarikamish on the territory of the Caucasian Armenian Republic and then proceeded to the fortress city of Kars and under the shadow of Mount Ararat to Echmiadzin, the Holy See of the Armenian Apostolic Church. There, Harbord met with His Holiness Gevorg V, "whose fine expressive face strengthened his words when he trusted himself to say something of the woes his people endured for so many generations."[40] When the motorcade arrived in the capital city, Erevan, on 29 September, it was greeted by rows of orphans and schoolchildren, backed by thousands of cheering townspeople, who looked upon the Americans as saviors. General Harbord conferred with Prime Minister Alexandre Khatisian and other ministers of state as his mission went about its business gathering information and data from various sources. Khatisian made the case for US military support pending a decision on the

---

[38] Harbord, "Investigating" (June 1920), pp. 189–90; US Archives, RG 256, 184.021/96. Mary Graffam died in Sivas in August 1921.

[39] Harbord, "Investigating" (June 1920), p. 192. General Karabekir included in his political–military memoirs a copy of the memorandum he submitted to Harbord. See his İstiklal Harbimiz (Our War of Independence) (Istanbul: Türkiye Yayinevi, 1960), pp. 305–18.

[40] Harbord, "Investigating" (July 1920), p. 271; US Archives, RG 256, 184.021/323.

mandate issue. He was surprised that Harbord dismissed any immediate threat from Turkey and that he seemed to take seriously Mustafa Kemal's assent to allow "non-offending" and "properly documented" Armenian refugees to return to their homes. Harbord later wrote: "To the mind of Dr. Khatissian, there is no promise, no guarantee, no bargain, that will ever justify the return of the Armenian refugees to their former homes in Turkey, except the complete separation from the Ottoman Empire of the territory containing those homes . . . To him it is unthinkable that his brethren shall ever again depend upon Turkish mercy or good faith."[41]

Sailing from the port of Batum to Constantinople in early October 1919, the American Military Mission to Armenia continued its labor without interruption. In the Ottoman capital, General Harbord listened to Admiral Bristol extol the Turkish Nationalists and denigrate "the constant cry from our relief people, missionaries and the Armenian propagandists in America that the Turks are massing on the Russo-Turkish boundary for an attack on the Armenians and a general massacre." He reiterated his arguments for a single mandate over the entire Turkish Empire and against the creation of a separate Armenian state.[42]

The Armenian Patriarch of Constantinople, Archbishop Zaven Der Yeghiayan, and the heads of the Armenian Catholic and Protestant communities, on the other hand, warned that the Nationalists had absorbed many of the followers and methods of the Young Turks – the Committee of Union and Progress – and were conspiring to keep the Christians in the status of chattels. American intercession was critical. Otherwise the children of the nation would continue to languish in exile, and the survivors would be in constant danger of new massacres. Unless the United States accepted the Armenian mandate soon, there would be no one left to save or protect.[43]

The report of the American Military Mission to Armenia

By the time the American Military Mission set sail for the return trip, General Harbord had concluded that, rather than making outright recommendations, he would list the main points both for and against accepting the Armenian mandate. Most members of his mission felt an overriding

---

[41] Harbord, "Investigating" (July 1920), pp. 139–40. See also *Haradj* (Erevan), 30 September 1919, pp. 1–2.

[42] Library of Congress, Bristol Papers, Box 65, Armenia file, Bristol to Polk, 1 October 1919, Bristol to Heck, 16 October 1919; Box 1, War Diary, 11–15 October 1919. See also Evans, *United States Policy*, pp. 185–9.

[43] US Archives, RG 256, 184.02102/5, exhibit B; *Erkir* (Constantinople), 15 October 1919, p. 2.

obligation to answer the humanitarian call, as expressed by Lieutenant Colonel Jasper Y. Brinton: "This is the hour of crisis for Armenia. If she is to exist as a nation, preserving her institutions and developing her national existence, rather than to continue as a refugee and persecuted people, she must have the immediate support of a great power." American relief efforts to save the starving Armenians would be like "pouring water into a sieve" unless the United States established control over the territory. Finance specialist William W. Cumberland added: "The Armenians are entitled to a better lot than has been theirs in the past. A sense of fair play demands that they be no longer subjected to promiscuous massacre, deportation, abduction and plunder." Other members stressed that world peace and America's unmatched qualifications to resolve the disastrous Eastern Question warranted circumvention of the Monroe Doctrine and a bold plunge into the trouble-ridden region. Arguments against the mandate, wrote John Price Jackson, represented the views of the "hard-hearted business man, who . . . reasons on the premises of dollars and cents," whereas those in favor based their case on "demands of the heart." The entire mission agreed, however, that for the best interest of the Armenians themselves, Turkish Anatolia and possibly the Transcaucasus region, too, should be placed under external supervision. Harbord himself believed that the drawing of the final boundaries of the Armenian state should be put off until there had been time for Armenian regeneration and the natural unraveling of the races through voluntary immigration and emigration.[44]

Major General Harbord submitted his report on 23 October 1919 to Undersecretary of State Frank L. Polk, who was then heading the American delegation in Paris. Polk cabled Secretary of State Lansing a summary of the findings, adding "General Harbord has presented a remarkable report on the Armenian situation."[45] Harbord arrived back in the United States on 11 November and the next day delivered copies of his report to the White House and War Department.

The documents submitted by the American Military Mission to Armenia consisted of the primary report and twelve appendices. The report, which was written by General Harbord, reviewed the history of Armenia and the record of broken promises and massacres since 1876, the current prevailing conditions in Anatolia and Armenia, and the feasibility of a mandate. His brief and forceful passage regarding the Armenian Genocide left no doubt about what had occurred and the judgment to be rendered: "Mutilation, violation, torture, and death have left their

[44] US Archives, RG 256, 184.021/329 enclosures.
[45] US Archives, RG 59, 860J.02/25; RG 256, 867B.00/296.

haunting memories in a hundred beautiful Armenian valleys, and the traveler in that region is seldom free from the evidence of this most colossal crime of all the ages." Women and children had been infected with venereal diseases; orphans and refugees were suffering all the woes "that flourish on the frontiers of starvation"; towns and villages were in ruins; brigandage was rampant. Conditions, he continued, "shriek of misery, ruin, starvation, and all the melancholy aftermath, not only of honorable warfare, but of beastial brutality unrestrained by God or man."[46]

Although the peace conference had decided to end Turkish sway over Armenia, Harbord continued, ethnographic and economic problems complicated the emancipatory process. To overcome the difficulties, it was recommended that the entire region from Constantinople to the Transcaucasus be placed under a single mandatory power. Only under a unitary or joint mandate could the ultimate boundaries of a self-contained Armenian state be decided. The Armenians needed a chance to prove their capacity for self-government, but they could not be allowed to rule a Muslim majority towards whom they held deep resentment for the terrible persecutions they had suffered. A federal-type mandate was the most feasible solution. Only a power with a strong sense of altruism and a willingness to make available its most gifted sons for at least one generation should assume the obligation: "No nation could afford to fail, or to withdraw when once committed to this most serious and difficult problem growing out of the Great War."

Finally, instead of making a clear-cut recommendation, General Harbord listed in parallel columns thirteen arguments for and against an American mandate for Armenia. Perhaps the fact that he then listed a fourteenth point in favor without a corresponding negative counterpoint bespoke the true sentiments of the American Military Mission to Armenia:

14. Here is a man's job that the world says can be better done by America than by any other. America can afford the money; she has the men; no duty to her own people would suffer; her traditional policy of isolation did not keep her from successful participation in the Great War. Shall it be said that our country lacks the courage to take up new and difficult duties?

In a concluding paragraph, General Harbord attested to the esteem, faith, and affection with which the United States was regarded by all

[46] US Archives, RG 256, 184.02105/5. The report, in a slightly different form and without the many photographs accompanying the original text, was published under the title, *Conditions in the Near East: Report of the American Military Mission to Armenia* (Washington, D.C.: Government Printing Office, 1920), Senate Document 266, 66th Congress, 2nd. Session.

peoples of the region, including "the wild, ragged Kurd, the plausible Georgian, the suspicious Azarbaijan, the able Armenian, and the grave Turk." Certainly the power-shouldering responsibility for the mandate would face extremely trying circumstances, but "if we refuse to assume it, for no matter what reasons satisfactory to ourselves, we shall be considered by many millions of people as having left unfinished the task for which we entered the war, and as having betrayed their hopes."[47]

The aftermath

Both the King–Crane and the Harbord missions, while listing practical reasons for avoiding American entanglement in the Near East, pleaded humanitarian arguments and implied that world peace was a powerful stimulus for active involvement. The recommendations did not satisfy Armenian aspirations for immediate unification and independence, but they did point the way to emancipation, repatriation, reconstruction, and eventual full sovereignty. Ironically, Woodrow Wilson did not use the reports to advance the Armenian cause, and the recommendations of the Harbord mission were actually turned against the mandate by its opponents. Because Wilson was ill, Harbord could not present the findings

---

[47] *Conditions in the Near East*, pp. 25–9. The twelve appendices to the main report demonstrate the breadth and the depth of the information gathered by the American Military Mission. They are preserved in the mission's papers in the National Archives, as follows:

184.021206/6	Political Factors and Problems	Captain Stanley K. Hornbeck
184.021206/7	Government	Lieutenant Colonel Jasper Y. Brinton
184.021206/8	Public and Private Finance	William W. Cumberland
184.021206/9	Commerce and Industry	Trade Commissioner Eliot G. Mears
184.021206/10	Public Health and Sanitation	Colonel Henry Beeuwkes
184.021206/11	Peoples	Lieutenant Colonel John P. Jackson
184.021206/12	Climate, Natural Resources, Animal Husbandry, and Agriculture	Lieutenant Colonel Edward Bowditch, Jr.
184.021206/13	Geography, Mining, and Boundaries	Major Lawrence Martin
184.021206/14	The Press	Major Harold W. Clark
184.021206/15	Military Factors and Problems	Brigadier General George Van Horn Mosely
184.021206/16	Transport and Communication	William B. Poland
184.021206/17	Bibliography	Major General James G. Harbord

directly to him and the report was filed away in the White House. Requests by Secretary of State Robert Lansing and members of Congress to have the document released were ignored for several months, thus increasing speculation that the mission's recommendation was against acceptance of the Armenian mandate. When at last the report was forwarded to the Senate in April 1920, the arguments in favor of the mandate were obscured by the skillful oratory and political manipulation of Wilson's opponents. By the time the President finally submitted a request to Congress in May 1920 for authorization to assume the Armenian mandate, it was already clear that this was a dead issue. The Senate quickly delivered the *coup de grâce* by "respectfully declining" the request.

By 1920 the United States Congress was recoiling from foreign obligations, except in territories where there were direct and immediate strategic or economic interests. The Senate refused to ratify the German peace treaty, which contained the Covenant of the League of Nations, and President Wilson was unable to form an effective coalition to battle the forces of isolation. In the Treaty of Sèvres with the Ottoman government in August 1920, the European Allies ultimately created on paper a united Armenia within the more moderate limits advocated by the King–Crane Commission and other experts, but they did nothing to enforce the provisions of the treaty. Indeed, as it happened, both the mandate for Armenia and the Armenians themselves were abandoned by Europe and the United States, as the Turkish Nationalist armies invaded and annexed half of the small Caucasian Armenian Republic at the end of 1920 and put an end to the prospect for a revived, united Armenian state. The "demands of the heart" fell far short of balancing the demands of pragmatic politics. This was demonstrated by the Allied Powers in their extensive concessions to Mustafa Kemal in the Treaty of Lausanne in 1923, which by and large acknowledged the current boundaries of the Republic of Turkey and effectively buried the Armenian Question by omitting any mention of Armenia and Armenians. It was as if they had never existed.[48]

This outcome notwithstanding, the post-war American field missions were important initiatives that still provide powerful historical testimony about the reality of the Armenian Genocide and its continuing consequences even after the defeat of the Ottoman Empire. The extensive records of the King–Crane Commission and especially of the American

---

[48] For details on the Senate debates about the Treaty of Versailles, the League of Nations, and the mandate for Armenia; on the drafting of the Treaty of Sèvres by the Allied Powers and the Turkish reactions; and on the Turkish invasion of the Armenian Republic and the failure of the Armenian people to attain an enduring independent state after the First World War – see Richard G. Hovannisian, *The Republic of Armenia*, 4 vols. (Berkeley, Los Angeles, London: University of California Press, 1971–96), especially vols. III and IV.

Military Mission to Armenia leave no doubt as to the scope and enormity of the crime and the fact that it was acknowledged by the entire American political and social spectrum. These materials, along with other extensive primary documentation preserved in the United States National Archives, can be used to give an effective response to those who would obscure or deny the truth of the Armenian Genocide or who would claim that the information is too ambiguous for the United States Congress and other bodies to reaffirm what was universally acknowledged during and after the First World War. Indeed, the United States response at the time was such as to be deserving of integration into the collective human narrative.

11   Congress confronts the Armenian Genocide

Donald A. Ritchie

The United States Congress's inability to come to terms with the Armenian Genocide underscored its limited role in American foreign policy. Under the constitutional system of division of powers, with its checks and balances, the executive branch has traditionally taken the lead in shaping foreign policy. Presidents have regularly made major policy decisions without prior consultation with Congress. The national legislature has exerted its influence chiefly through the power of the purse – by appropriating funds needed to carry out the policy – and through the Senate's confirmation of diplomatic appointments and its approval or rejection of treaties. Congress can legislate to mandate or restrict executive branch actions, especially if it can muster the two-thirds vote to override a presidential veto. Either jointly or separately, either house of Congress can also declare its positions on issues through formal resolutions, which Presidents may embrace or ignore. Being divided between two legislative bodies, and further between two political parties that lack the political discipline of a parliamentary system, Congress has needed to build consensus on each new complex and controversial issue. It proceeds by holding hearings and taking testimony, using the collected evidence to formulate bills and resolutions and then debating the proposals and amending them if necessary to gain majority support in both the Senate and House of Representatives. Congressional hearings, debates, and statements to the news media are further intended to educate and sway public opinion. As representatives of the people, answerable to public opinion whenever they stand for re-election, members of Congress must take prevailing sentiments into account. The inability to agree on an issue within Congress tends to reflect a lack of public consensus and support. Yet even debates that do not produce legislation can generate a copious record that can influence public opinion and form the foundation for future action, sometimes generations later.[1]

---

[1] As an authority on neither Armenian nor Turkish history, I approach this subject as a congressional historian, attempting to explain the ways in which the US Congress reacted

In the many hearings and debates that Congress held on the Armenian
Question between the 1890s and 1920s, the legislative branch amply
demonstrated its awareness of the Armenian Massacres, and yet other
than opening some avenues of immigration it did little to ameliorate the
Armenians' plight. When attitudes in Congress seemed predisposed towards intercession in the crisis, the executive branch resisted. By the time
a President finally proposed military intervention, shifts in political and
public sentiment had made Congress unreceptive. At the critical juncture in 1920, the American public's post-war weariness, and the titanic
clash between the President and the Senate over the Treaty of Versailles,
the League of Nations, and the role of the United States as a world
power, would overwhelm Congress's humanitarian impulses towards the
Armenians. Offered an opportunity to engage in an early form of "nation
building," the United States declined a mandate over Armenia, a decision
for which Congress bore the ultimate responsibility.

1894–1896: First reports

For most Americans at the end of the nineteenth century, the Ottoman
Empire appeared remote, exotic and dangerous. The little news that
appeared about the region in US newspapers concerned wars, massacres, and atrocities, and European protests against the mistreatment of
Christian minorities within the 500-year-old multi-ethnic, multi-religious
Ottoman Empire. A typical turn-of-the-century account by an American
visitor to Constantinople, the heart of the Empire, described the "core of
red violence that heart has always had!" Americans' most direct contact
came through the Protestant missionaries who had ventured into Asia
Minor. Otherwise, the United States maintained a scant diplomatic and
commercial presence in the region. This nation was not a party to the
1878 Congress of Berlin, where the Western powers had sought to bolster the "sick man of Europe" against Russian expansionism. There a
delegation of Armenians had petitioned the Congress in Berlin for protection for their people, and the Western nations had exacted a pledge
from the Sultan to protect his Empire's Christian minorities. Before long,
however, it became clear that the fearfully suspicious and despotic Sultan

---

to the plight of the Armenians. Reading through the transcripts of the many congressional
hearings and floor debates regarding the Armenians has been a sobering but enlightening
experience. The congressional hearings on the Armenian situation between 1894 and
1923 eerily foreshadow the "ethnic cleansing" that sent US peacekeeping forces to Bosnia
and Kosovo. The ample documentation that these past hearings provide would make
useful reading for today's lawmakers as they ponder future policy. Congressional records
also hold much potential for further historical scholarship.

Abdul-Hamid II had no intention of honoring that pledge, nor did the Western powers possess the resolve to enforce it.[2]

Reports reached the United States in 1894 that Turkish troops and Kurdish tribesmen had brutally massacred Armenians in Anatolia, and by 1896 Americans read about the violence that had spilled over into Constantinople, in full view of the foreign embassies. These reports undermined the Sultan's reassurances and sparked protest meetings first in London and Paris and later in New York and Chicago – although in the United States news of these atrocities competed with the more nearby atrocities in Cuba, which preoccupied the "yellow press." A hub of protest in the United States emerged in Massachusetts, which at that time was home to the largest concentration of Armenian-Americans. Congress received its first petitions about the Armenian Massacres from Massachusetts and members of the Massachusetts delegation responded to their constituents by introducing the first resolutions on the subject in the Senate and House. Congress also heard from the American Board of Commissioners for Foreign Missions and from American missionaries who had returned from the region, who lobbied either individually or through their denominations. These interest groups generated considerable sympathy within Congress towards the Armenians during the 1890s, but not enough to overcome America's traditional neutrality in European affairs and the lack of precedent for active intervention outside the Western hemisphere.

On the first day that the new session of Congress convened in December 1894, Senator George Frisbie Hoar, a Massachusetts Republican, introduced a resolution – which the Senate adopted by unanimous consent – requesting from President Grover Cleveland any information he might have received regarding "alleged cruelties committed upon Armenians in Turkey," and to inform the Senate whether he had protested to the government of Turkey or planned to "act in concert with other Christian powers regarding the same."[3] A week later, President Cleveland responded that essentially all he knew was what he read in the newspapers. He also provided two contradictory telegrams from the US minister at Constantinople. In the first telegram, dated 28 November 1894, the minister had insisted that:

Reports in American papers of Turkish atrocities at Sassoun are sensational and exaggerated. The killing was in a conflict between armed Armenians and Turkish soldiers. The grand vizier says it was necessary to suppress insurrection, and that

[2] Robert Hichens, "Skirting the Balkan Peninsula: From Triest to Constantinople," *Century Magazine* 86 (July 1913), pp. 377–9; Lord Kinross, *The Ottoman Centuries: The Rise and Fall of the Turkish Empire* (New York: Murrow Quill, 1977), pp. 528–34, 554–63.
[3] *Congressional Record*, 53rd. Congress, 3rd. Session, p. 12.

about fifty Turks were killed; between three and four hundred Armenian guns were picked up after the fight, and reports that about that number of Armenians were killed. I give credit to his statement.

This telegram relayed the Turkish government's official interpretation of the events; but a second telegraph from the same minister, dated on 2 December, reported: "Information from British ambassador indicates far more loss of lives in Armenia attended with atrocities than stated in my telegram of 28th." Despite this alarming message, President Cleveland explained to Congress that the United States had not participated in the Treaty of Berlin of 1878, by which Turkey had guaranteed protection to the Armenians, and for that reason he had declined to join in the international investigation of the alleged atrocities. Given, however, the conflicting evidence from his own minister, Cleveland had decided to send the US Consul to the scene of the alleged atrocities so that he might inform the US government of "the exact truth."[4]

At a time when some Americans were anxious to flex the nation's muscles internationally, President Cleveland remained a non-interventionist, bent on maintaining American neutrality outside the Western hemisphere. Cleveland's aloofness towards the Armenian situation caused the Massachusetts Republican Party and its delegation in Congress to protest against the administration's "immoral" lack of concern. One Massachusetts Congressman who expressed that view, and who would play a major role in the later congressional response to the Armenian Massacres, was Representative Henry Cabot Lodge. He had introduced the petitions from a mass meeting that had been held at Malden, Massachusetts, in December 1894. As much as Lodge was concerned about the Armenians, he was perhaps more concerned about establishing the United States' "place among nations." To achieve standing among the world's great powers, Lodge believed that the American people would have to shoulder the responsibilities that great power entailed. That meant willingness to use military force to achieve moral ends. Lodge publicly supported the humanitarians who rallied to the Armenian cause, but privately he considered it a waste of moral energy to protest against events in a place where the United States had little practical ability to shape the outcome.[5]

Congress's first encounter with the Armenian issue set a pattern that would repeat over the next century. Confronting the unwillingness of the

---

[4] Ibid., pp. 214–15.
[5] *Congressional Record*, 53rd. Congress, 3rd. Session, 232–3; *Congressional Record*, 54th. Congress, 1st. Session, 1972; William C. Widenor, *Henry Cabot Lodge and the Search for an American Foreign Policy* (Berkeley: University of California Press, 1980), pp. 74, 95, 155.

incumbent administration to intervene, those members of Congress who supported the Armenians could do little more than express their outrage. The longest debate on the first Armenian Massacre took place on 24 January 1896, over a resolution that Illinois Republican Senator Shelby Cullom had sponsored urging President Cleveland to take more "vigorous action" in protecting American citizens in Turkey. Senator Cullom was appalled over the newspaper reports of the "awful carnival of havoc, destruction, and blood" in Turkey. Other Senators had heard complaints from the "religious people" in their states that Congress was proceeding too slowly in response to the crisis. Republican Senator William P. Frye of Maine pointed out that Congress had passed the previous resolutions that the protestors had requested, but beyond that he did not know "how far the United States of America can interfere in Turkey." Senator Wilkinson Call, a Florida Democrat, dismissed the previous resolutions as meaningless declarations of sympathy that offered neither relief nor protection to the Armenians. Senator Call conceded that the United States was living up to the principles of the Monroe Doctrine by keeping out of European affairs, but he argued that Turkey had violated those principles with its "wholesale murder" of Armenians. There the argument stood. Nothing more was resolved because the national debate over foreign policy – whether or not the US should take a greater role in the world – shifted almost exclusively to Cuba. The events leading to the Spanish–American war overshadowed the plight of the Armenians.[6]

1914–1920: rejecting the mandate

The Armenian issue faded from congressional view until the First World War erupted in Europe. For three years the United States struggled to stay out of that fight, but US public opinion registered compassion for the many refugees whose lives had been disrupted and endangered by the war. In 1916, Henry Cabot Lodge, by then a Senator from Massachusetts, introduced a concurrent resolution relating to what he called "the evil plight" of the Armenians in Turkey. His resolution was designed to facilitate the raising of private funds in the USA for relief of Armenians in Turkey. Lodge described his resolution as identical to earlier resolutions on Poles and Jews, and insisted it should not "cause any debate whatever." Democratic Senator William Stone of Missouri endorsed Lodge's resolution, describing it as "a very proper appeal to the generosity, the sympathy, and the liberality of the American people in the hope of affording some measure of succor to a large number of men, women, and

[6] *Congressional Record*, 54th. Congress, 1st. Session, pp. 959–65.

children who are suffering from the sad effects of the war." Lodge's resolution, however, did differ from previous resolutions, all simple resolutions passed by the Senate and the House. His was a concurrent resolution, requiring identical language in the resolutions that both bodies passed, demonstrating a unified congressional response to a foreign policy.[7]

The Senate adopted Lodge's resolution without hearings or debate, but the House referred the resolution to its Foreign Affairs Committee, chaired by Representative Henry Flood, a Virginia Democrat. Here Congress began to do what it does best: collect testimony and create a record to build public support and a national consensus on an issue that might lead to legislation. The published transcripts of those hearings provide the testimony of the general counsel of the US Armenians, and the Prelate of the Armenian Church in America, who stressed the urgency for action due to the mass deportations of Armenians, which they estimated as involving between 750,000 and 800,000 people. Witnesses pointed to cooperation in the relief effort from the Rockefeller Foundation along with the Congregational, Baptist, and Roman Catholic churches in the USA. Their testimony educated the committee and strengthened its resolve in the floor debate that followed in the House. When some House members voiced concern that the resolution would stimulate a flood of similar resolutions to create what one midwestern isolationist called a "national tag day" for other beleaguered people, Chairman Flood replied that the world faced conditions that had never existed before. Wisconsin Republican William Stafford rebutted: "Oh, the gentleman knows that Armenia has been a sore spot for many years, by reason of massacres similar to those now being perpetrated." Flood responded that he was well aware of previous Armenian Massacres, "but there never has been a time before when seven or eight hundred thousand Armenians were driven out into the desert and were there starving, or living on grass and roots, as they are today." Ultimately, the Armenian resolution passed both houses and was signed by President Woodrow Wilson. Just as significantly, the hearings provided first-hand accounts of Armenian conditions in an official publication of the US government.[8]

Early in 1917, the United States abandoned its neutrality and declared war on Germany and Austria, although not against their essentially defeated ally Turkey. Reports filtering out of Turkey indicated that conditions for the Armenians were far worse than previously realized. Although no Armenian American served in Congress, some members had personal

[7] *Congressional Record*, 64th. Congress, 1st. Session, pp. 2335–6.
[8] House of Representatives, Committee on Foreign Affairs, *Hearings on Relief of Armenians*, 64th. Congress, 1st. Session (Washington, D.C.: US Government Printing Office, 1916), pp. 4–6; *Congressional Record*, 64th. Congress, 1st. Session, pp. 11235–6.

experiences in the region and felt a special bond with the Armenians. Representative Edward C. Little, a Kansas Republican, rose during a debate over appropriations for the Diplomatic and Consular Service, in 1918, to reminisce about how he had served as US Consul-General in Egypt during Benjamin Harrison's administration. He had traveled extensively throughout the Middle East and met the Ottoman Foreign Minister, an Armenian Christian through whom he "began to learn about the Armenian race." Painting a broad historical portrait, Representative Little exclaimed: "When our Aryan ancestors left the roof of the world and entered Europe north of the Caspian, our Armenian cousins, for such they were, marched to the south of that sea, and after a bit established themselves around Mount Ararat, where they have lived more than 3,000 years." The Turks coveted the land the Armenians occupied and were warring against them. If Turkey won that war, Little warned, it would annihilate the conquered and "the first Christian nation will disappear from off the earth." He then lectured to the House on events in Turkey since the beginning of the Great War. Of the 1.5 million Armenians he estimated had lived within the territory of Turkish Armenia, Little thought it "a fair statement to make that at least 500,000 Armenians have been killed." Americans were well aware of Germany's atrocities in Belgium, but Armenians had suffered "a thousand time as much as Belgium has endured." Little's impassioned oratory apparently made little impact on House members, because when three months later he raised the issue again he suggested that "a little aid financially from the allies would enable the Armenians and the Georgians to raise a couple of hundred thousand men and defeat the Turks on the Armenian front."[9]

In 1919, the Armenian cause gained another eloquent champion in Senator William H. King of Utah. King, a conservative Democrat whose name is more usually associated with opposition to his party's liberal economic programs, was also a Mormon who felt a deep empathy for persecuted religious minorities. He not only became an outspoken advocate of the Armenians in Turkey, but a generation later would speak with similar passion for the Jews in Nazi Germany. In an address to the Senate in August of 1919, Senator King described Armenian history as having been "written in blood" and "full of tragedy and sorrow." Senator King was the first member of Congress to assert "that the Turkish Government deliberately sought the extermination of the Armenian race." He attributed this policy to the war and Armenian support for the Allied cause, which he thought "doubtless increased the hatred of the Turks for the Armenians and intensified their purpose to destroy the

[9] *Congressional Record*, 65th. Congress, 3rd. Session, Appendix 175–82, pp. 5953–4.

entire race." King charged that Turkey had carried out a "predetermined policy to destroy the Armenian people," and had inflicted "the most savage cruelties" upon defenseless men, women, and children.[10]

To buttress his charges, Senator King cited Associated Press reports and articles from the *New York Times* indicating that a million Armenians had already perished. The situation called for immediate aid, he insisted: "This nation and the allied nations will be guilty of a great delinquency if they fail at this juncture to protect Armenia from the peril now impending and which threatens her destruction." King introduced a resolution calling on the Paris Peace Conference, which was then underway, to demand the eviction of Turkish forces from all Armenian villages.[11]

Reports from Americans returning home from the Middle East further fanned public opinion. In October 1919, Senator Frank Brandegee, a Connecticut Republican, commented on the many letters he was receiving, mostly from clergymen who demanded government intervention to prevent the extermination of all Armenians in Turkey. Newspapers indicated that Great Britain was withdrawing its forces from the Caucusus and wanted the United States to send troops to replace them. Then came word from Paris that the European allies had asked the United States to accept a mandate to protect Armenia. This proposal enraged isolationist Senators, who suspected a British maneuver to burden the USA with a thankless chore. Senator William Borah, the progressive Republican from Idaho, scoffed: "Are there not any undeveloped oil fields in Armenia or Turkey, then?" Borah cynically implied that if oil had been found in Armenia, British troops undoubtedly would have remained.[12]

The Senate Foreign Relations Committee established a special subcommittee to consider a joint resolution calling for an independent Armenian Republic and authorizing President Wilson to send US peacekeeping forces to Armenia. This resolution would also have suspended laws that prohibited Armenian Americans from raising and equipping their own armed forces "to go to the aid of their countrymen in Asia Minor." Chairing the special committee was an Ohio Republican whom political lightning was soon destined to hit. Warren G. Harding's subcommittee held four public hearings and heard many witnesses. Among them was Miran Sevasly, General Counsel of the US Armenians, who recounted the service that Armenians had rendered during the Great

---

[10] Laurence M. Hauptman, "Utah Anti-Imperialist: Senator William H. King and Haiti, 1921–1934," *Utah Historical Quarterly* 41 (Spring 1973), pp. 116–27; *Washington Post*, 28 November 1949.

[11] *Congressional Record*, 66th. Congress, 1st. Session, pp. 3483–4.

[12] Ibid., pp. 7051–4.

War. They had provided 100,000 soldiers to the Russian army, and after the Russian collapse had continued fighting the Turks in the Caucusus. The Armenians had thereby aided the British in their military campaigns against Turkey, enabling the Allies to conquer Syria and to take Jerusalem. Having rejected Turkish efforts to entice them over to their side, Armenians had suffered enormously. "I do not like to exaggerate numbers," Sevasly told the committee, "but I think about 750,000 Armenians have actually disappeared – have died from deportations or massacres."

A shocked Harding interrupted: "You say 750,000 Armenians have disappeared?"

"At least that many," Sevasly replied, explaining that he based those statistics on reports of travelers through the region and from US Ambassador to Turkey Henry Morgenthau.

The subcommittee's ranking Democrat, Mississippi Senator John Sharp Williams wanted to know what moral effect this resolution might have "upon Turkey and upon these people who are now trying to exterminate the Armenian race in order to put an end to the Armenian question?" Sevasly assured the Senators that the resolution would "act like magic" on the whole Middle East: "Once they know out there that the eagle is soaring around Ararat there will be no trouble whatever." He warned, however, that Armenians needed troops and relief as quickly as possible or else by the time the Great Powers got around to creating an Armenian Republic, there would be "no Armenians left to make it."[13]

Other Armenian-American witnesses combined appeals to American religious and patriotic sentiments. They called on the USA, as "a Christian nation," to send troops and battleships to help the Armenians who had "sacrificed much blood to defeat Germany and her associate, Turkey." Senator Harding asked if sending troops would not be "an act of war," but the witnesses insisted that the military were needed for relief and protection, not to wage war. A skeptical Harding reminded them that there existed "a tremendous clamor in this country" for withdrawing US troops sent to Russia after the Communist revolution, and that he could see little public sentiment for sending more troops abroad.[14]

The State Department provided the subcommittee with additional information. Assistant Secretary of State William Phillips reported on the famine in Armenia, which he blamed on Turkey's "deportations

[13] United States Senate, Subcommittee of the Committee on Foreign Relations, *Hearings on Maintenance of Peace in Armenia*, 66th. Congress, 1st. Session (Washington, D.C.: US Government Printing Office, 1919), pp. 4–6, 8–10.
[14] Subcommittee of the Committee on Foreign Relations, *Hearings on Maintenance of Peace in Armenia*, pp. 13–14, 26–8.

and massacres of the Armenians." So many Turkish Armenians had moved into the Transcaucasus, having left their worldly goods behind, that the densely crowded territory could not sustain the refugees and famine had set in. The State Department further reported collusion between the Turkish National Party, the Azerbaijan Tartar government, and certain Kurds, as part of a Pan-Islamic movement. Assistant Secretary Phillips explained that Turkish officers were organizing the Muslim forces, and that the Azerbaijan government was financing and backing the movement. "They want, if possible, to get rid of all these Christians," Phillips said, "and they may think that this is a good moment to do it." He called this "a political design seconded by a religious movement."

"Does the political program involve massacre?" Senator Harding asked.

"I am afraid so," Phillips responded, " – and history has shown it – because the Christian people are in their way, and that is the method they have of getting rid of anything that is in their way." At the birth of modern Turkish nationalism, the Armenians had the misfortune of being a non-Turkish, non-Muslim population "whose geographical position, besides their religion, race, and civilization," had gotten in the way of Turkish aspirations. American representatives "on the spot" had confirmed an Armenian situation that was "horrible beyond description." Captain George B. Hyde, an American doctor who served with the Red Cross, described the mass of women and children and paucity of men among the refugees, because so many of the Armenian men had been killed. Another Army Captain, Abraham Tulin, had visited Armenia as part of Herbert Hoover's relief efforts, and offered eyewitness testimony of the famine and of the massacres by Turks, Tartars, Kurds, and Georgians. Tulin assured the committee that Armenians in Turkey looked to the United States "as their great protector."[15]

Another relief commissioner labeled the massacres "deliberate and arranged for, through starvation," estimating that half of the victims had been killed outright, while the other half died of "exhaustion or starvation" via deportation. Similarly grim testimony came from the President of Grinnell College, J.H.T. Main, who had gone to the Caucusus as a Special Commissioner. He described encountering a half-million starving people and seeing refugee graveyards, where bodies had been thrown indiscriminately into pits. A shaken Senator Harding interjected: "Now, I want to tell you, I am a lot in sympathy with this whole situation." Harding, however, thought that leadership ought to come out of the Paris Peace Conference than from the US government. Dr. Main replied:

15 Ibid., pp. 34–7, 43, 53.

"I think it is up to us to do something to vindicate ourselves as the promoters of Christian civilization and good order in that part of the world, where the people are looking to us to do it."[16]

Despite this bulk of compelling testimony, the subcommittee reached an impasse because of what Senator Brandegee described as an inability to get information from the Wilson administration on "what sort of a situation the President had created in relation to Armenia and Constantinople." Without full information, subcommittee members felt they could not act on the resolution. By then, President Wilson had suffered a debilitating stroke, and in deference to his health the subcommittee did not press its demand, allowing the Armenian resolution to sit in abeyance. When citizens continued to agitate in favor of protecting the Armenians, Brandegee pointed out that the only apparent way to protect the Armenians was "to send an army over there to fight off the Turks," but he could detect no public sentiment for sending troops abroad so soon after the Great War.[17]

Congress clearly had to decide whether to put action behind its words. A seeming advantage to the supporters of Armenians was the heightened influence of their most consistent advocate, Senator Henry Cabot Lodge, who was now the Senate majority leader as well as the Chairman of the Foreign Relations Committee. In 1920 Lodge authored a resolution favoring recognition of Armenia as an independent state, and served on the executive committee of the American Committee for the Independence of Armenia, together with Senator John Sharp Williams and eminent leaders of both parties. Lodge had long believed in backing foreign policy with force. Yet, when the opportunity to act arose, Lodge failed to grasp it, allowing his contempt for President Wilson and the Treaty of Versailles to supersede his sympathies for the Armenians.

Utah's Senator William King continued to press the Armenian issue by introducing a telegram from the Secretary of the American Committee for the Independence of Armenia reporting on the deteriorating situation of Armenians. "It is a pitiful thing to see an entire people destroyed by a cruel and merciless foe," King told the Senate:

What are the allied nations doing to prevent this martyrdom? What are the Christian nations doing to preserve a heroic and suffering people from destruction? The blood of millions of Armenians cries aloud for vengeance; the starving, afflicted, and terrorized people who survive piteously cry out for protection. We are deaf. Europe is deaf. The tragedy continues, and with tearless eyes we behold its consummation.

[16] Ibid., pp. 67, 79–81, 98, 101, 108.
[17] *Congressional Record*, 66th. Congress, 1st. Session, p. 7052.

A month later, Senator King called for President Wilson to recognize Armenia and for Turkish Armenia to be united with Russian Armenia.[18]

Meanwhile, Senator Harding – on the verge of becoming the Republican presidential nominee – reported a resolution based on the evidence that his subcommittee had collected, which "clearly established the truth of the reported massacres and other atrocities from which the Armenian people have suffered." Harding's resolution sympathized with the Armenian people's nationalistic aspirations and encouraged the President to send an American warship and a force of marines to protect American lives and property in Armenia. After Harding described his resolution as "wholly advisory," the Senate adopted it by unanimous consent.[19]

President Wilson quickly seized on the Harding resolution, informing the Senate that he had read it with "great interest and genuine gratification" because it embodied his own feelings regarding the Armenians. He took this opportunity to request "urgently" that the Congress grant him power to accept a US mandate over Armenia. Wilson's maneuver towards a mandate triggered an intense reaction in the Senate. As Foreign Relations Committee Chairman, Senator Lodge responded with his own resolution, respectfully declining to grant the President power to accept a mandate over Armenia. The Republican majority rallied to Lodge's corner. The Democratic minority, led by Nebraska Senator Gilbert Hitchcock, realized that the mandate was a lost cause and introduced a variety of amendments designed to further Armenian independence, but none of these efforts mustered a majority. In defending his position, Lodge insisted that he had no desire "to turn a completely deaf ear to their cry for help, for they are a brave people who have struggled for centuries to preserve their religion and their liberty, and they, I think, must appeal to every American sympathy; but that is wholly different from taking the mandate and assuming the care of that country for we can not say how many years to come."[20]

Senator John Sharp Williams, a Democrat of Mississippi, rebutted:

In my private relations I have never, as far as I now remember, been confronted with a situation where I was willing to accept all the benefits and advantages while shirking all the burdens and responsibilities. I am not willing, as a Senator of the United States, to see these United States put themselves in that attitude before

---

[18] Lodge similarly authored a resolution endorsing a Jewish national home in Palestine; Herbert Parzen, "The Lodge–Fish Resolution," *American Jewish Historical Quarterly* 60 (September 1970), pp. 69–81; *Congressional Record*, 66th. Congress, 2nd. Session, pp. 3907, 6076.

[19] *Congressional Record*, 66th. Congress, 2nd. Session, pp. 6978–9.

[20] Ibid., pp. 7533–4, 7875–6; see also Rayford W. Logan, *The Senate and the Versailles Mandate System* ([1945] Westport, Conn.: Greenwood, 1975), pp. 97–102.

the world, and I think we would put ourselves in that attitude if we declined to do even this much – to accept the invitation of civilization to act as police regulators in Armenia until the Armenian people can stand upon their own feet.

Williams felt sure that if the United States accepted the mandate, "the mere presence of the American uniform in Armenia" would settle the issue "by preventing Kurdish and Turkish attacks and leaving the Armenians at peace to work out their destiny." Baring the intensity of his personal feeling, Senator Williams said that his heartstrings were "tied very closely to the history of this remarkable people." He placed into the record the report of the American Military Mission to Armenia, which traced the "organized official massacres" of the Armenians from 1895 through 1915, and asserted that massacres and deportations had been organized "under definite system, the soldiers going from town to town." Over 1 million had been deported, with the dead estimated at around 800,000.[21]

From the perspective of Capitol Hill, President Wilson seemed to be using the Armenian situation to win votes in the Senate for his League of Nations, since Senate defeat of the League would reduce the chances of America's accepting a mandate over Armenia. The isolationist bloc that opposed the League read the situation primarily in moral and economic terms. Rather than the USA coming to the rescue of a beleaguered people, Wisconsin's "Fighting Bob" La Follette equated the mandate with annexation and colonialism. Progressives like La Follette believed that Western powers would use the mandates as screens to gain concessions on natural resources in those regions. Nebraska's Senator George Norris expressed sympathy for the "suffering people" of Armenia but complained that the United States had drawn the barren lands of Armenia in contrast to the oil-rich Syria and Iraq, which went to the French and British. These "peace progressives" opposed any effort to inject the United States into what La Follette called "the turmoil of intrigue and imperialism which exists in the Near East and the Old World generally."[22]

During the Senate's lengthy floor debates, the depth of opposition to an American military presence in Asia Minor overwhelmed sentiments for protecting the Armenians. Senator Charles S. Thomas, a Democrat from Colorado, said that he had looked at an atlas and could not locate Armenia. "The political entity which we know as Armenia is indefinable," he asserted. Thomas believed that the pressures of Turkish nationalism on one side and Bolshevik expansionism on the other would make the

[21] *Congressional Record*, 66th. Congress, 2nd. Session, pp. 7877–83.
[22] Robert David Johnson, *The Peace Progressives and American Foreign Relations* (Cambridge, Mass.: Harvard University Press, 1995), pp. 101–2, 309.

mandate "predoomed and predestined to miserable failure," and that would "seriously jeopardize American prestige." Given the historical enmities of the region, Senator Thomas considered it "a little short of madness for the United States to enter upon this new and untried mission." Senator Joe Robinson of Arkansas, a rising leader in the Democratic Party, responded that rejection of the mandate would be "disastrous to the interests of a great, a brave, and a suffering people." Robinson endorsed an amendment by Senator King to authorize the President to cooperate with the League of Nations to protect Armenia. Robinson was furious at the suggestion by another Democrat, Senator James A. Reed of Missouri, that the massacres implied that the Armenians were cowardly and could not defend themselves. "Where else than in Armenia have cruelty and outrage been so persistent?" Robinson demanded: "In what other land has so much innocent blood been shed? What other people have sacrificed so much on the altars of Christian faith?"

The debate shifted back as Republican Senator Frank Brandegee brandished newspaper clippings reporting that Britain had grabbed the lion's share of the "Big Booty" in the Middle East, taking its oil riches while the United States received a "polite little invitation to finance and protect with armies the tiny Republic of Armenia." The *Congressional Record* noted that Brandegee's speech at this point was interrupted by "voices in the gallery pleading for the cause of Ireland," an incident that indicated the mixture and volatility of public opinion which Congress was then confronting. Anticipating that they would lose the vote, supporters of Armenia tried to recommit the motion for further study of the implications of a mandate, but Senator Lodge would have no delays. He insisted that the Foreign Relations' subcommittee had studied the matter so fully that there should not be the slightest doubt in any Senator's mind as to exactly what was meant by a mandate. The Senate supported Lodge and refused to recommit the resolution. The vote went largely along party lines, with most Democrats voting to recommit, and most Republicans voting "no." Senator Brandegee then offered an amendment to avoid the mandate issue and allow the President to enter into an agreement with other Allied nations or the League of Nations to offer protection and supplies to Armenians. This too was defeated by a vote of 62 to 12, the dissenters being mostly southern and western Democrats. The persistent Senator King then introduced an amendment simply to authorize supplies for Armenia, but this measure was similarly rejected, 46 to 28. Finally, the Senate voted 52 to 23 not to grant the President the power to accept a mandate for Armenia. This tally closely matched the voting that defeated the Treaty of Versailles. Of the 52 Senators who rejected the mandate, 39 (nearly all Republicans) voted against the Treaty of Versailles; and every one of the 23 who endorsed the mandate (all Democrats) voted for the treaty.[23]

1920–1923: the issue of immigration

With the mandate dead, Armenian supporters in Congress repackaged the issue as one of immigration. After the World War, Congress was bent on enacting legislation that established quotas to favor Northern Europeans over other peoples. However, Congress was willing to make an exception from these ethnic and geographic prejudices for the Armenians. Mississippi Senator John Sharp Williams defined the Armenians as "an old European race, placed by migration in Asia," adding that "in saying 'European' I am including the Americans, because we are all Europeans." The immigration loopholes can be dated back to 1910 when a California Representative, Everis Anson Hayes, of San Jose, took the lead in amending immigration and naturalization laws, to assist Armenians, Syrians, and Jews. Recognizing the intense public opposition on the West Coast to immigration from Asia, Hayes's bill sought to exempt these specific groups from restrictions on naturalization placed on "Mongolians and other Asiatics." Three years later, in 1913, Armenian immigration to the United States reached its pre-war peak at 9,353 new arrivals.[24]

Post-war immigration law permitted Armenians to come to the United States under three different quotas: the Armenian quota, the Turkish quota, and the Syrian quota – rewarding the Armenians at least one benefit from their diaspora. By 1920, estimates of Armenians in the USA ranged from 85,000 to 100,000. At a hearing of the House Committee on Foreign Affairs, the Revd. Mihran Kalaidjian, Secretary of the YMCA's Armenian Department, told Congress that he did not claim that the Armenians were "angels," but they were "substantially an honest people," and some of the most literate of all immigrants coming to America. Armenian Americans worked in the textile factories of New England, in the automobile and tire factories of the Midwest, and on the farms of California's San Joaquin Valley. Their numbers included university professors and medical doctors. Further attesting that they were upstanding citizens, supporters pointed out that only one Armenian immigrant was engaged in the brewing business – this being the start of Prohibition. Representative Merrill Moores confirmed that in his Indianapolis district nearly all of the Armenians were "in trade." Of the Armenians

---

[23] *Congressional Record*, 66th. Congress, 2nd. Session, pp. 8051–74.
[24] Subcommittee of the Committee on Foreign Relations, *Hearings on Maintenance of Peace in Armenia*, p. 113; House Report No. 1150, 61st. Congress, 2nd. Session, 1910.

who immigrated, 58 percent had been naturalized, a noticeably high rate compared to other immigrant groups.[25]

In response to complaints that federal authorities were turning back foreign nationals who exceeded their quotas, the House Committee on Immigration and Naturalization held hearings in 1922, and once again the Armenians were well represented among the witnesses. The committee heard from George R. Montgomery, Director of the Armenian American Society in New York, who described the large numbers of Armenian refugees who were literate, in good health, and could pay their passage to the USA, but were caught in a "very desperate" situation in Asia Minor. Some committee members worried that a million people in Asia Minor might be ready to move, but Montgomery reassured them that the potential immigrants numbered more in the tens of thousands. George Montgomery was an example of non-Armenian Americans who nevertheless felt a personal connection with Armenia. His parents were buried there. "They were missionaries, and their work has all been wiped out," he explained, "and I feel that I am doing a filial duty in trying to reestablish some of the work that they gave their lives to." The Revd. Miran Kalaidjian again testified. Through his work with the YMCA and as Pastor at Large for the Congregational Home Missionary Society, he specialized in helping Armenian immigrants "become assimilated and initiated into the mysteries of American citizenship." Kalaidjian assured the committee of the Armenians' loyalty to America. "The way I put it is this," he said: "A man does not have to hate his mother in order to love his wife, but the time will come when he has to follow the biblical injunction, forsaking mother and father to love his wife."[26]

By 1923, Representative Hays White, a Republican from Kansas, was promoting a bill to establish specific refugee status for immigration from Turkish territories. His measure gained support from Greek and Armenian Americans, from educators, philanthropists, ministers, missionaries, diplomats, and ex-servicemen. Some of the testimony before the House Immigration and Naturalization Committee was deeply emotional. Dikran Nazaretian, of Birmingham, Alabama, an Armenian who had served in the US army, begged Congress to let his mother immigrate, and pleaded that "The poor soldier needs Uncle Sam, too." The chief of Near Eastern Affairs at the Department of State, Allen

---

[25] House of Representatives, Committee on Foreign Affairs, *Hearings in Behalf of the Armenians*, 67th. Congress, 2nd. Session (Washington, D.C.: Government Printing Office, 1922), pp. 28–9.

[26] House of Representatives, Committee on Immigration and Naturalization, *Hearings on Immigration*, 67th. Congress, 2nd. Session (Washington, D.C.: Government Printing Office, 1922), pp. 301–3, 497–501.

Dulles – later Director of the CIA – testified of reports of great suffering among the refugees, who were in need of immediate relief. The committee also heard some odd testimony from Social Darwinists, who attempted to apply their theories to Armenian immigration. Lothrop Stoddard, of Massachusetts, author of a notoriously bigoted book, *The Rising Tide of Color Against White Supremacy*, argued that it would be "a great mistake" if large numbers of people from Asia Minor were admitted, and compared Armenians unfavorably to Western Christians. On the other side, Professor Ellsworth Huntington, a geographer at Yale University, insisted that centuries of massacres had made Armenians tougher and more able as a people. The Armenians were "stronger, mentally and physically" than the average person, and had "a character we can count on." The committee's Chairman, Albert Johnson, seemed less moved by these theories than by the wrenching eyewitness testimony the committee collected: "I may say that the committee admits the situation as it exists and has held hearings for two days, devoted principally to the massacres and the action of the Turkish Government in permitting those not massacred to move out."[27]

The Armenian American community then prevailed on Republican Representative John Jacob Rogers of Massachusetts to introduce a resolution calling on President Harding to express America's "moral protest" against Turkish persecution of "the Armenians and other Christian peoples," and calling for a conference of US and European powers to consider methods by which Armenians could become a nation. They modeled this call for an Armenian national homeland after Daniel Webster's resolution, back during the Monroe administration, in support of Greek independence. The House Foreign Affairs Committee heard another long line of witnesses testify on behalf of the Armenian cause, some of whom by now had become veterans at facing congressional committees. Walter George Smith, President of the Armenian-American Society, provided the historical background, explaining how Armenians were caught between Turkey and Russia during the World War. "That was the signal for what had already been determined upon," said Smith " – a deliberate attempt, by massacres, by starvation, by deportation, to obliterate the whole Armenian people." Other witnesses argued that Turkey took advantage of the World War to drive the Armenians from their mountain homes, because the war had cut off the chance of outside help. George Montgomery returned to testify again, explaining that the Armenian-American Society

---

[27] House of Representatives, Committee on Immigration and Naturalization, *Hearings on Admission of Near East Refugees*, on HR 13269, 67th. Congress, 4th. Session (Washington, D.C.: Government Printing Office, 1923), pp. 13, 79–80, 89, 99.

had kept the State Department fully informed about the resolution under consideration:

and I do not think that I am committing any breach of confidence in saying that there has been no objection on the part of the State Department, feeling that Congress does represent the public opinion; and it is not without precedent that the administration sometimes makes suggestions to the Congress with regard to certain actions where the initiative properly belongs with the administration.

Montgomery outlined how they had reduced the resolution down to the minimum. Resolutions had come in from all over the country "full of teeth," but supporters reasoned that Congress would be more likely to adopt a more moderate resolution. If the United States signed onto the plan, they hoped it would promote agreement among the European powers – Great Britain, France, and Italy – about a common policy on the Armenians. Nothing came of these efforts. Congress instead retreated into a decade of isolationism and allowed Armenian issues to fade from its agenda.[28]

---

[28] Committee on Foreign Affairs, *Hearings in Behalf of the Armenians*, pp. 1–2, 13, 16, 18–19.

12 When news is not enough: American media and Armenian deaths

Thomas C. Leonard

Americans entered the twentieth century with a vivid picture of Armenian victims in the Ottoman Empire. Headlines of "MASSACRE," "SLAUGHTER OF INNOCENTS," and "HOLOCAUST" ran in the *New York Times* in the 1890s. Outrages reported in the sober *Review of Reviews* and the *Independent* in New York became a book that was expected to reach beyond specialists: *Armenian Massacres or the Sword of Mohammed, Containing a Complete and Thrilling Account of the Terrible Atrocities and Wholesale Murders Committed in Armenia by Mohammedan Fanatics* (1896). Twenty stalwarts of benevolence in the Anglo-American world had their signatures reproduced in this volume, attesting to its truth. The cruel fate of Armenians caught the eye of many opinion leaders. Philanthropist Phoebe Apperson Hearst sent a check to the Armenian Agitation Association of America and her demagogic son, William Randolph Hearst, began his famous war cry over Cuba in the "yellow press" by invoking these martyrs of Anatolia. Among both elite and average readers of the news at the start of the twentieth century, it was common knowledge that the Ottoman Empire was a killing ground for Armenians.[1]

I wish to thank my research assistant Ferhat Birusk Tugan from the Graduate School of Journalism at the University of California, Berkeley. As a Kurd and a graduate of the University of Istanbul, he helped to enlarge my understanding of Turkish ethnic conflict and nationalism. Funds were provided by the Committee on Research at Berkeley for work in the Humanities.

[1] The early *Times* articles are conveniently available in *The Armenian Genocide and America's Outcry: A Compilation of US Documents, 1890–1923* (n.p.: Armenian Assembly of America, 1985). Frederick David Greene and Henry Davenport Northrop, *Armenian Massacres or the Sword of Mohammed, Containing a Complete and Thrilling Account of the Terrible Atrocities and Wholesale Murders Committed in Armenia by Mohammedan Fanatics* (Philadelphia and Chicago: International Publishing, 1896), pp. xi and 95 on sources. See also Edwin Munsell Bliss, *Turkey and the Armenian Atrocities: A Graphic and Thrilling History . . .* (Philadelphia: J. H. Moore, 1896), a book that begins with the suggestion by reformer Frances E. Willard that Armenians more closely resemble Christ physically than other races. Phoebe Apperson Hearst Papers, box 1 at the Bancroft Library, University of California, Berkeley: thank-you letter of 11 Jan. 1895. David Nasaw, *The Chief: The Life of William Randolph Hearst* (Boston: Houghton Mifflin, 2000), pp. 125–6.

The great European war of 1914 renewed ethnic bloodshed in Turkish lands and led the American press to pick up the thread of the earlier stories. Though overshadowed by the grand battles along European frontiers and sea-lanes, the assaults on Armenians were hard to miss in the news. Scanning the narrow columns, readers found arresting headlines:

BURN 1,000 ARMENIANS
SAW ARMENIANS GO STARVING TO EXILE . . . BABIES
THROWN INTO RIVERS
ARMENIANS KILLED WITH AXES BY TURKS

The *National Geographic* reported matter-of-factly in 1915 that, with Armenians in the hands of Turks, "the world has never seen a more furious effort to drive out a people, or more cruel methods in their execution."[2]

Body counts frequently drove coverage. Fragmentary reports in the spring of 1915 put deaths in the hundreds or a few thousands at particular places. By the beginning of August, readers of the *New York Times* were getting summary totals of 40,000 killed, up to the estimate, on 6 August 1915, that "tens and probably hundreds of thousands have been butchered." By September, the sketchy body count crept up on Lord James Bryce's authority that "perhaps half a million were slaughtered or deported." Three days later, on 24 September, Washington sources backed up the *Times* headline: "500,000 ARMENIANS SAID TO HAVE PERISHED." Lord Bryce's estimate jumped to 800,000 Armenians "slain in cold blood in Asia minor" since May. Armenian-American leaders made the total more than a million ten days later on 17 October 1915. Reckoning with a land where often "vultures were the only coroners," the total hovered in this range for a year in the *New York Times*. Looking at the Ottoman Empire in November 1916, the monthly magazine of this news organization compared the losses to the ranks of patriots who were filling American streets as the nation grew closer to war: "If the ghosts of the Christian civilians who have perished miserably in Turkey since the commencement of the great holocaust should march down Fifth Avenue twenty abreast . . . They would then take four days and eight hours to

[2] *New York Times*, 20 Aug. 1915, p. 7, and 6 Feb. 1916, II, p. 9. *Current History Magazine* 7 (Nov. 1917), pp. 339–40. A reproduction and index of coverage – Richard D. Kloian, *The Armenian Genocide: First 20th Century Holocaust* (Berkeley: n.p., 1980) – is immensely helpful and more complete than the third edition of 1988. Hester Donaldson Jenkins, "Armenia and the Armenians," *National Geographic Magazine* 28 (Oct. 1915), p. 349. The quote is from a caption, perhaps reflecting the editors' conclusions more than the author's observations. Jenkins wrote "there is little, if any, racial antagonism between Armenians and Turks. Had religion and politics never come to antagonize them, they could live together in essential harmony" (p. 348). *National Geographic* followed up with three articles on the plight of Armenians at the hands of Turks before 1920.

pass the great reviewing stand – in fact, longer, for most of them would be women and children."[3]

What we know today about the scale of deaths in the First World War may blind us to the meaning of these figures – and figures of speech. We are used to thinking of losses in great blocks of the hundreds of thousands. We would not think this way, however, if we were American readers in the years of the battles of the Somme, Verdun, and Gallipoli. Both the Allies and the Central Powers let their casualty figures dribble out over time, to mask their losses. "The whole history of war contains no more painful chapter of barbarity than this record of the slaughter of civilians," Joseph Pulitzer's paper thundered as it reported just over 4,000 non-combatants killed in the first year and a half of the Great War. The Armenian figures had shock value that the European catastrophe could not dim.[4]

Metaphors like "holocaust" could not register the mental image that was available decades later (when the term "genocide" was coined). Calling this the "Great War" did not produce a vision of mass killings stretching ahead in time. Indeed, in moments of marketing exuberance, the *New York Times* suggested that this might be the reader's last chance: "If this is, as many think, the last great war, the value of authentic photographs of it will increase every year. If carefully preserved, The New York Times War Pictorials will be extremely valuable." Readers were offered cloth bindings, or half-leather with gold trim to save their awful memento that "you will always enjoy referring to."[5]

---

[3] In the *New York Times*, see "Armenians Attack 2 Turkish Divisions," 17 May 1915, p. 3; "6,000 Armenians Killed," 18 May 1915, p. 3; "Russian Here for Cotton," 31 July 1915, p. 2; "Report Turks Shot Women and Children," 4 Aug. 1915, p. 1; "Armenian Horrors Grow," 6 Aug. 1915, p. 6; "Bryce Asks Us to Aid Armenia," 21 Sept. 1915, p. 3; "800,000 Armenians Counted Destroyed," 7 Oct. 1915, p. 3; and "Armenian Leaders Answer Djelal Bey," 17 Oct. 1915, II, p. 13. William W. Rockwell, "The Total of Armenian and Syrian Dead," *Current History* 5 (Nov. 1916), pp. 337–8. My conclusions square with those of Marjorie Housepian Dobkin, "What Genocide? What Holocaust? News from Turkey, 1915–1923: A Case Study," in *The Armenian Genocide in Perspective*, ed. Richard G. Hovannisian (New Brunswick: Transaction Books, 1986), pp. 97–109. Samantha Power, *"A Problem from Hell": America and the Age of Genocide* (New York: Basic Books, 2002), p. 9, counts 145 stories in the *New York Times* in 1915 and observes that "it helped that [Ambassador] Morgenthau and *Times* publisher Adolph Ochs were old friends." True, but the paper had warmed to this topic years before either man focused on the Near East.

[4] Walter Lippmann, *Public Opinion* (New York: Harcourt, Brace, 1922), p. 153, on the meager accounting. "Civilians Killed by the War," *New York World*, 11 March 1916, p. 10. Thomas C. Leonard, *Above the Battle: War-Making in America from Appomattox to Versailles* (New York: Oxford University Press, 1978), pp. 132–4, 164–7, on the overlooking of battlefield horror.

[5] *Mid-Week Pictorial* 1 (12 Nov. 1914), p. 23, and 2 (8 April 1915), p. 23. These were issued separately during the war and are not to be found in microfilm runs of the paper. A common title for the series was "The New York Times Pictorial War Extra."

The American press during the First World War provided substantial evidence documenting the Turkish ethnic killings and not just bulletins and cries of alarm. This was fortuitous, for American reporters were not in the field, filing reports. In the first year of the killings, just two regular US correspondents can be identified in Constantinople (Raymond Swing and George Schreiner). Only Schreiner of the Associated Press (AP) saw Armenian victims in the interior. In 1915, reporters schemed to get into one of the great theatres of the European war on the nearby Gallipoli Peninsula. Distant provinces were not a practical objective, no matter how disturbing the rumors of massacre. Schreiner found that a strict press censorship prevailed on the ethnic cleansing of Armenians. Nor were "stringers" (freelancers) of help. Signs of such a relationship – even the ability to speak several languages – were enough for an arrest around Zeitun where the AP made its lone attempt to reveal the war against civilians that the Turks wanted to hide.[6]

Yet relatively soon, the American press was stocked with detailed and compelling narratives of what had happened. Systematic accounts began with revelations from the Committee on Armenian Atrocities in September 1915. This New York committee got prominent and sympathetic coverage. Plain speaking set the tone: "The ostensible deportation of men, women, and children toward Mesopotamia is usually but a form of marching those starving, helpless, and frequently naked refugees out

---

[6] Raymond Swing, *"Good Evening!": A Professional Memoir* (New York: Harcourt, Brace, 1964), pp. 61–2. George A. Schreiner, *From Berlin to Bagdad: Behind the Scenes in the Near East* (New York: Harper & Brothers, 1918), pp. 183–4, 195–202. Eleanor Franklin Egan, "Behind the Smoke of Battle," *Saturday Evening Post* 188 (5 Feb. 1916), p. 12, underscored Turkish censorship. Schreiner filed no story about "Armenia's red caravan of sorrow" from Zeitun, having had earlier dispatches stopped by the censor. He sent a memo about the suffering to Ambassador Morgenthau. On the strength of Turkish authorities and a single Armenian woman who spoke broken English, Schreiner concluded that this civil population had been implicated in a revolt and that the aim was relocation not liquidation. In 1915 American readers learned, instead, that the Turkish attack was unprovoked: Dikran Andreasian, "A Red Cross Flag that Saved Four Thousand," *Outlook* 111 (1 Dec. 1915), p. 790. Schreiner's apologia for the Ottoman authorities in this region has not worn well. A genocide denier has conceded that Zeitun was one place where "the Turks did murder innocent civilians": Yitzchak Kerem, "The Armenian Catastrophe," *Jerusalem Post*, 22 Feb. 1995, p. 6. Hilmar Kaiser has concluded that the Zeitun expulsions were a historical first: "railway transport of civilian populations towards extermination." See Richard G. Hovannisian, *Remembrance and Denial: The Case of the Armenian Genocide* (Detroit: Wayne State University Press, 1998), pp. 72, 75. The *New York Times* mentioned Zeitun as a massacre site on 26 April 1915, p. 3, but had no specifics; this story did have a correspondent's inspection of Salmas and evidence of a massacre three weeks earlier. Later, the paper passed on a second-hand report that Armenians in Zeitun had revolted: "Armenians Attack 2 Turkish Divisions." Khoren K. Davidson, *Odyssey of an Armenian of Zeitoun* (New York: Vantage Press, 1985), recalls the armed clash as the actions of a small number of Armenian deserters who had come into the area (pp. 65, 200); on his seizure on suspicion of being a journalist, see pp. 68–9.

into the mountains to be outraged and butchered." A year later, Lord Bryce's reports were more vivid and comprehensive. Even today, it is a Bryce story that is likely to catch the breath of both author and reader in an Armenian-American family memoir. Highlights appeared in the *New York Times'* monthly magazine in November 1916, and the tales of grief stayed in the news.[7]

The output of publication centers such as New York was significant in a nation tied together by inexpensive subscriptions for readers and free exchanges among editors. The diffusion took some remarkable forms in the thousands of papers that served the countryside. Terse updates on the slaughter in the Ottoman Empire can be found in the files of hundreds of defunct, but once-proud, mastheads from small towns, across the continent.

As a sample, here are articles from Minnesota papers during the first year that news of the Armenian slaughter was being reported in New York and Washington, D.C. Each story is given in its entirety:[8]

At least the Armenian problem will be solved with the slaughter of the last of the Armenians.(*St. Paul Pioneer Press*, 8 Oct. 1915)

One of the most horrible things connected with the war, is the wholesale massacres of Armenian Christians by the Kurds and Turks. It is a war of extermination on their part.(*Montevideo Leader*, 8 Oct. 1915)

When the Armenians are all dead, the Turks will no doubt grant our request to stop killing them.(*Winona Independent*, 16 Oct. 1915)

The Turk must be given credit for one thing at least. He doesn't claim the Lord is an ally to his horrible atrocities.(*Owatonna Tribune*, 19 Nov. 1915)

Turkey has evidently decided that the present time of general slaughter is an auspicious one for her to end the Armenian problem by ending the Armenians.(*Red Wing Daily Republican*, 25 Oct. 1915)

"Squib" or "filler" does not do justice to this form of journalism, for it was an important bond between the public and the press. Compression was the watchword of editors who wanted to reach readers who were tired after a day at the farm or factory. This is a sensible communication

7 Andreasian, "A Red Cross Flag that Saved Four Thousand." Markarid Garodian, "Shadows of War," *Independent* 93 (5 Jan. 1918), p. 15. "German Missionary Aids," *New York Times*, 25 Sept. 1915, p. 3. "Tales of Armenian Horrors Confirmed," *New York Times*, 27 Sept. 1915, p. 5 (Quoted); "Tell of Horrors Done in Armenia," *New York Times*, 4 Oct. 1915, p. 1. "Woman Describes Armenian Killings," *New York Times*, 12 Dec. 1915, II, p. 6.
8 The Center for Holocaust and Genocide Studies, University of Minnesota maintains this archive that was assembled by Lou Ann Matossian at www.chgs.umn.edu under "Minnesota Newspapers Reportage About the Armenian Genocide, 1915–1922." There were meetings on the crisis in St. Paul and the Near East Relief was active in the state.

strategy when addressing people with little formal education or schooling
in the English language. In this era, E. W. Scripps built a chain of papers
across the United States that featured a sentence or two on remarkable
events of the day. A failure to elaborate was not a failure to care. Indeed,
terse statements of occurrences were at the historical root of American
journalism, featured in the Puritan sermons that were the printer's earliest
model of how to present news of importance. The one-line and two-line
items from the Near East that darted through the thousands of daily and
weekly papers is a hard flow of news to measure, but it seems to have had
the desired effect of starting conversations and even drawing people to
meetings on the Armenian Massacres.[9]

Nationally, the master contemporary narrative of the killings in
the Near East was by the former US Ambassador to Turkey, Henry
Morgenthau. His story broke in *World's Work* magazine in November
1918, and his book appeared before the year's end. American editors had
by then found other sources to confirm the scenes of horror: the memoirs
of victims, letters from Germans on the scene, and reports by eminent
Americans who were listening to missionaries in the region. "I am confident that the whole history of the human race contains no such horrible
episode as this," Ambassador Morgenthau concluded. Readers had no
reason to think of this as hyperbole in 1918.[10]

American media took the measure of the killings in the Ottoman
Empire much more quickly than the press was able to discern Hitler's policy for Jews a generation later. Compared to the performance of American
media on the politically directed famines in Stalin's Ukraine and Mao's
China, what Americans published on the Armenians seems remarkably
sound and timely. The press consensus that there was an extermination policy for Armenians in the Great War probably does American
journalists more professional credit than they can claim in coverage of
some mass killings closer to the US border. For example, the massacre at
El Mozote in El Salvador in 1981 took many years to register in the US
media. If we choose the 1994 genocide in Rwanda for comparison, then
journalists of 1915 appear to have been more skeptical that mass killings

[9] Gerald J. Baldasty, *E. W. Scripps and the Business of Newspapers* (Urbana, Ill.: University of
Illinois Press, 1999), pp. 122–4. David Paul Nord, "Teleology and News: The Religious
Roots of American Journalism, 1630–1730," *Journal of American History* 77 (1990),
pp. 9–38. On the diffusion of information in the marketplace, see Thomas C. Leonard,
News for All: America's Coming-of-Age with the Press (New York: Oxford University Press,
1995).

[10] "Ambassador Morgenthau's Story," *World's Work* 37 (Nov. 1918), pp. 92–116, quoted
p. 115. Print was the all-important medium at this time because news services and talk
shows were not part of early broadcasting and, in any case, the US government snuffed
out all civilian uses of radio after its declaration of war.

could be explained as age-old ethnic tensions. American media, with the aid of Ambassador Morgenthau, saw that a political elite in a faraway place were the master executioners. This insight was hard to find in the press as a half-million people were slaughtered in Rwanda.[11]

Compelling, documented records reached the reading public soon after the horrors of 1915 began. The political framing was sound, without ignoring cultural factors. Most journalists would say this is what a free press is for. The press of 1915 met the standard made famous in this era by Walter Lippmann: to act "like the beam of a searchlight that moves restlessly about, bringing one episode and then another out of darkness into vision." This is what newspapers and magazines did for Armenians in the play of their light across a vast theatre of death. (The *New York Times* ran a regular feature, "A Flashlight on Some Aspects of the War.") We might still ask, what good did it do?[12]

We live in a world of agile non-governmental organizations, celebrities eager to adopt causes, and governments with interventionist habits and principles. The language of human rights is accepted across a wide political spectrum and is commonplace in the press. Little of this world view was in place in 1915 and neither empathy nor action could be triggered the way they may be today. But American media coverage of the first years of deportation and killings of Armenians helped mobilize a large public. In New York, the Near East Relief deftly encouraged coverage and raised funds with no hint that it found what we now call "compassion fatigue." The American public listened through their press. Public opinion in war-torn Europe was, understandably, slower to grasp the crisis. Philip Knightley judged that atrocity reports were so discounted in Britain and

---

[11] On sluggish or worse coverage see Deborah E. Lipstadt, *Beyond Belief: The American Press and the Coming of the Holocaust, 1933–1945* (New York: Basic Books, 1985); David C. Engerman, "Modernization from the Other Shore: American Observers and the Costs of Soviet Development," *American Historical Review* 105 (April 2000), pp. 383–416; Mark Danner, *The Massacre at El Mozote: A Parable of the Cold War* (New York: Vintage Books, 1994); and on Rwanda, Robert I. Rotberg and Thomas G. Weiss, *From Massacres to Genocide: The Media, Public Policy, and Humanitarian Crises* (Washington, D.C.: Brookings Institution, 1996), pp. 120–3.

[12] Lippmann, *Public Opinion*, p. 229. "Flashlight" ran in the paper's *Mid-Week Pictorial*. One must not idealize the *New York Times* of this era. In a classic critique, Walter Lippmann and Charles Merz, "A Test of the News," *New Republic* 23 (4 August 1920 Supplement), pp. 1–42, read between 3,000 and 4,000 items on the Russian Revolution from March 1917 to March 1920 and found that, on basic questions of who was winning the struggle, the reporting was "nothing short of a disaster." This study puts the frequency of attention to Armenia in perspective. In her survey of the same paper in 1915, Dobkin, "What Genocide?" found about 10 items a month on the ethnic killings in the Ottoman Empire. Kloian, *The Armenian Genocide*, found about 4 items a month in his look at nearly six and a half years of *New York Times* coverage. The Lippmann–Merz survey works out to about 100 items a month on Russia's revolution in the *Times*.

France during the second year of the Great War that compelling reporting on Armenian deaths by Edmund Candler of The *Times* of London and Henri Barby of *Le Journal* in Paris left little impact.[13]

Did American readers hear from the Turkish side? In 1915, no less than today, that was a test of good journalism. Apologists for the Ottoman Empire should recognize that this state got its due from American journalists. On 8 April 1915, the Turkish War Minister commended the work of the AP in his country, "conditions having been described as they were." The attentive reader during the First World War could find what is now called "the revisionist position" on the genocide. In this analysis, Armenians took up arms to oppose lawful authorities and fought with the invading Russian armies. Lord Bryce's findings were "grossly exaggerated" and "severe measures" happened in all wars. Pictures of Armenians with guns aimed at Ottoman authorities documented the treason that no government could be expected to forgive. In October 1915, the *New York Times* reprinted a German newspaper's dismissal of the figure of 800,000 massacred. Readers were alerted here that pro-Armenian reports were skillful British propaganda. That is the way essayist H. L. Mencken saw it, dismissing the excitement as a sham. The *New York Times* requested and published a statement from the highest-ranking Turkish official in New York when the atrocity numbers spiked up in the fall of 1915 and a year later, the paper ran a defense of his government's policy by the Turkish Foreign Minister. Armenian subversion was his main theme. One Turkish letter-writer to the *New York Times* objected to the editing of what he saw put in print – the paper had cut him short at 26 column inches. The *Times* printed what it had deleted, allowing readers to consider if the expulsion of Armenians seemed any worse than driving Native Americans into reservations. Another Turkish view was noted in American dailies: American lynchings at home and atrocities abroad undermined outrage from the United States.[14]

---

[13] Philip Knightley, *The First Casualty* (New York: Harcourt, Brace, 1975), pp. 104–5. James L. Barton, *Story of Near East Relief (1915–1930) An Interpretation* (New York: Macmillan, 1930), especially ch. 26. On the limitations of modern journalism, see Susan D. Moeller, *Compassion Fatigue: How the Media Sell Disease, Famine, War and Death* (New York: Routledge, 1999).

[14] "Enver Says Turks had to Fight," *New York Times*, 20 April 1915, II, p. 2. A. S., "Guerrilla Warfare in Armenia" (letter), *New York Times*, 18 June 1915, p. 10. Zia Mufty-Zade Bey, "The Kind of Armenians a Turk Knows" (letter), *New York Times*, 18 Oct. 1915, p. 8 (quoted). "Armenian Protests Charged to Allies," *New York Times*, 13 Oct. 1915, p. 4. Mencken quoted in "Who Can Save Armenia?" *Literary Digest* 51 (30 Oct. 1915), p. 963. "Turkish Official Denies Atrocities," *New York Times*, 15 Oct. 1915, p. 4. "Turkish Foreign Minister's Defense of Armenian Massacres," *Current History* 5 (Dec. 1916), pp. 544–5. Zia Mufty-Zade Bey, "Undeleted" (letter), *New York Times*, 19 Oct. 1915, p. 10. "The Armenian Massacres," *Rochester (MN) Post & Record*, 13 Oct. 1915.

302 *Thomas C. Leonard*

At times, even the best news organizations contradicted themselves as they watched the Ottoman society turn on itself. This was inevitable in a war theatre where first-hand reporting by experienced journalists played almost no part in the story of these deaths. In 1916 the *New York Times* had a correspondent at a listening post on the eastern border (it is not clear whether he got close to bloodshed) who mused "it is a curious thing that here, as in Constantinople, the Armenians seem to allow themselves to be massacred, practically without striking a blow." Among other things, Charles Johnson was overlooking pictures and stories about armed resistance that had been appearing in the *Times* and other publications for more than six months.[15]

The list of flaws in coverage can easily be lengthened. Any historian will note that the press of 1915 proved to be a poor place to review the centuries of ethnic repression and expulsion that were the full context of the Armenians' plight. If, however, one came to journalism to learn what was going on in this distant place and what people on all sides of the dispute were saying about it, the American press met this responsibility.

Only one American journalist who worked to tell this story has been indicted as a fabulist: Burton Hendrick, a veteran muckraker who helped write Morgenthau's book on the Ottoman Empire and shepherd it into print as an editor of *World's Work*. In 1990 Heath Lowry concluded that this is a record of "crude half truths and outright falsehoods." A fairer judgment is that the Ambassador's memory differed from the written record he kept on the job and that Hendrick helped him to settle scores with other diplomats. This is not a rare thing in the memoirs of statesmen or a hanging offense for their collaborators in the press. If *Ambassador Morgenthau's Story* makes anything up about mass deaths, Lowry failed to find it. Indeed, that is not surprising. Hendrick's chief work, for a half-century, was the profiling of Americans in wartime, from the Civil War through the First World War. He was an old hand at reconstructing command decisions that took or saved lives. Hendrick won three Pulitzer Prizes, in both history and biography, in the decade following his collaboration with Morgenthau. Historian Joseph Frazier Wall, who worked on one of Hendrick's main subjects, views his entire career as marked with "accurate and detailed reporting" in "carefully researched" works.[16]

---

[15] Charles Johnson, "Something More About Erzerum and Trebizond," *Mid-Week Pictorial*, III (2 March 1916), p. 19; directly contradicting this is "With Armenians and Turks in Ancient Van," *Mid-Week Pictorial*, II (12 Aug. 1915), p. 9. Contrast the Johnson analysis with the refugee story from New York ten days later: "Beat Off 4,000 Turks," *New York Times*, 12 March 1916, III, p. 8.

[16] Heath W. Lowry, *The Story Behind Ambassador Morgenthau's Story* (Istanbul: Isis Press, 1990), quoted p. 60; other charges of fabrication, pp. 41, 44, 78–9. Lowry has raised legitimate questions about the gulf between Morgenthau's contemporary letters and

As a rule, scholars review press performance to explain professional malpractice. I have the unusual task of explaining competence and good judgment. I think this is just as much a puzzle as missing the story. In the early twentieth century, American journalists were certainly capable of monumental oversights. The *New York Times* botched coverage of the Russian Revolution in the very years that it got the Ottoman nightmare right. Many American newspapers were blind to some forms of domestic terror at the turn of the twentieth century. Lynchings of African-Americans approached the 3,000 figure, but editors North and South were tired of the race story and did little to keep this before the public. Running parallel to the Armenian tragedy in the Near East, King Leopold of Belgium created a personal colony in the watershed of the Congo River, with the loss of 10 million lives. This generated a photographic record as horrible as that which came out of the Ottoman Empire – a gallery of amputations suffered by the natives. Here was a story told in full force by lonely pamphleteers, not the mainstream press. In Africa, Lippmann's spotlight would not shine. Why were Armenian victims different? Why did the conventions of news-gathering work for them?[17]

Social-science literature has no template for addressing these questions and comparative historical treatments of slaughter from eras before the Holocaust are rare. As recent scholars of genocide have found, there is only a "sparse" literature on "the chemistry of the interactions between public exposure and international engagement."[18]

Press critics of a traditional bent look for economic motives to explain coverage. This is sensible, but a hypothesis that will not take us far. Attention to Armenian affairs was not driven by the demands of an ethnic readership or advertisers. There were only about 1,500 Armenian immigrants living in the USA before 1890. In the next quarter-century, the

diary and the 1918 narrative. He has not, however, properly weighed the importance of discrepancies or allowed for innocent explanations. His real discoveries in the archives do not challenge Morgenthau's testimony about planned massacres. For example, Lowry finds the journalist George Schreiner condemning *Ambassador Morgenthau's Story* in a letter of 1918. Schreiner did, but concedes in the same letter that with Armenians "the Turk went beyond all reasonable limits" (p. 62). Indeed, Schreiner could thunder like Morgenthau on Turkish guilt. In the field notes from 1915 he called the 1909 massacre at Adana the "most vicious crime of our age"; also in 1915 his own sources led him to note that "the Armenians are going through Hell again" in what he called a "shocking phase of barbarity": Schreiner, *From Berlin to Bagdad*, pp. 209, 332. Joseph Frazier Wall, "Burton Jesse Hendrick," *Dictionary of American Biography*, Supplement 4 (New York: Scribner's, 1974).

[17] Ida B. Wells-Barnett, *Crusade for Justice: The Autobiography of Ida B. Wells*, ed. Alfreda M. Duster (Chicago: University of Chicago Press, 1970). Adam Hochschild, *King Leopold's Ghost* (Boston: Houghton Mifflin, 1998).

[18] Rotberg and Weiss, *From Massacres to Genocide*, pp. 2, 10 n.4. See also Power, *"A Problem from Hell"*, pp. 514–16.

flight of Armenians to America was in an annual range of 2,500 to 3,500. Most of these newcomers, of course, were still learning English. In 1915, when wealthy donors formed a committee in New York to aid the victims of the Turks, no Armenian-American had the wherewithal to be listed. It is hard to believe that mainstream publishers or editors saw a business reason for coverage of this homeland.[19]

Of course these numbers also show that Armenians held little power in American elections. While domestic politics did not add to the news value of the killings, geopolitics certainly did. Turkey fought in the First World War with the Central Powers, often under the direction of Germans. American public opinion was never pro-Kaiser and after the spring of 1917, Germany was the declared enemy. Before Russia left the war in 1918 under the Bolsheviks, she was the US ally and the self-proclaimed savior of Christian Armenians. The equation of dead Armenians with a parade of Americans eager to fight was telling: foreign alliances brought a small minority in Asia Minor into the "we" of public discourse. Congolese natives, shot and clubbed to death in great numbers, never had this saving tie to American foreign policy.

Of course this was a time when a Black face was an enormous obstacle to the extension of empathy in the American press and it is important to note that Armenians were perceived as White victims. But news judgments about the Near East reflected far more than notions about race. Skin color – like foreign policy – simply made it easier to see a moral drama unfold.

The mental landscape of the Near East was crucial. Armenians died on "Bible Lands." Mount Ararat, Aleppo, Tarsus, and Constantinople were names that formed part of a common sacred tradition for American Catholics, Protestants, and Jews. As the journalist Thomas L. Friedman has argued, ethnic struggles in this region of the world form a sort of super-story because of these cultural associations. "CRUCIFIXION IS REVIVED" was the headline in the lead story of the *Los Angeles Times* in the Easter season of 1915. A dateline outside the Near East would have cast the story differently. A people slaughtered elsewhere – the Congo River basin of Africa or the Punjab region of the Indian subcontinent – cannot hope for the same solemn attention as victims on a Western heritage site.[20]

---

[19] Henry Morgenthau III, *Mostly Morgenthaus: A Family History* (New York: Ticknor and Fields, 1991), pp. 170–1.
[20] Thomas L. Friedman, *From Beirut to Jerusalem* (New York: Farrar, Straus, Giroux, 1989), pp. 427–31. *Los Angeles Times*, 29 April 1915. The crucifixion and Noah's ark show up in contemporary Chicago papers, see "Editorial Cartoons of the Armenian Genocide" maintained by The Center for Holocaust and Genocide Studies, University of Minnesota

There was another cultural inheritance that built news value: Americans understood that Turks did the killing. (Kurds were identified in many stories, but this proved a distinction without a difference, for press commentary held Turkish authority responsible.) As that book of 1896 about *Mohammedan Fanatics* reminds us, Islamic peoples of the Near East had assumed a role in the American imagination as the perpetuators of outrage. In an opinion piece featured in the *New York Times* before the first reports of killing in 1915, the Turk was summed up as "sensuous, lustful, indolent, deceitful, and incorrigible." Here Ottoman history was reduced to far-flung massacres. The "intolerable Turk" was the ethnic shorthand. "The Turk Reverts to the Ancestral Type" was the chapter title Ambassador Morgenthau used to tell the Armenian story. Mass deaths by themselves do not easily make news unless an aggressor has cultural resonance. In contrast, Belgians were not sinister people to Americans and this was an important reason why papers like the *New York Times* looked away from bloodshed in the Congo. In ancient Armenia, the press found an echo of the crusades and the *Mohammedan Fanatics* of Sunday school and schoolbook lore.[21]

What else can we learn about the American media over the nine decades that separate us from the Armenian slaughter? Reverence for the printed word and its preservation is one lesson. We are moving quickly into a digital record of current events where there need be no tangible artifact of what we know. To be preserved, data will simply migrate from one storage device to another as formats change. (Academics live with this limitation today with old drafts and notes on disks that cannot easily be read.) The generation of 1915 memorializes the stasis of print.

News of the uprooting and killing of Armenians in Turkish lands was not simply a story in print, it was a story that print made sacred. From

(www.chgs.umn.edu). Carried far enough, a biblical-centered view of events may reduce anything, even a holocaust, to a pale recapitulation of an ancient part of God's testing of his people. Thus, for all the religious emotion that charged the story of the Armenian Massacres, it is important to realize a secular mode of thinking at work. For recent writing on this distinction, see Gabrielle Spiegel, "Memory and History: Liturgical Time and Historical Time," Johns Hopkins University, Department of History Seminar Paper, 6 March 2000.

[21] "How Turkish Empire Should be Made Over After the War," *New York Times*, 24 Jan. 1915, VII, p. 1 (quoted). "The Greatest of Religious Massacres," *Independent* 84 (18 Oct. 1915), p. 83 (quoted). Henry Morgenthau, *Ambassador Morgenthau's Story* (Garden City, N.Y.: Doubleday & Company, 1918), ch. 22. Barton, *Story of Near East Relief*, p. 386, on the "Bible Lands" appeal to youth. *Minneapolis Tribune*, 8 Oct. 1915. Jared Diamond, *Guns, Germs, and Steel: The Fates of Human Societies* (New York: Norton, 1997), is a recent reminder of the unnoticed or unheralded elimination of populations into the nineteenth century. See, for example, pp. 53–4 on the genocidal Moriori–Maori encounter.

the first shock of discovery to the recovery of this story for a twenty-first-century public, print culture has played a sacramental role. "Bible Lands" was the cry of hundreds of activists who sought to awaken the American public, linking a *book* to a landscape of death. Lord Bryce and others tied the United States to Anatolia by a mystic bond of imprints – the vernacular Bibles that missionaries had spread through the region in the early nineteenth century. The printing press and periodical literature, he said, were American exports, introducing reading into this land. A striking feature of the genocide literature is its paths to treasures of print. Ambassador Morgenthau measured his grief, not against other deaths he knew about in a world at war, but instead against the tears he had shed as a child reading *Uncle Tom's Cabin* and *Evangeline*. Michael Arlen's *Passage to Ararat* (1975) begins with books he carried into the homeland and read there; he concludes with a long homage to the Bryce report. Peter Balakian fills more than twenty pages of the *Black Dog of Fate* (1998) with his conversion experience reading *Ambassador Morgenthau's Story*. He tells us where he sat and what he ate as he first devoured his parents' copy of the book. A rush of hymns, incense, and bells comes over this proudly secular English graduate student. The genocide is, at last, clear to him – something the actual survivors in his family had not been able to communicate.[22]

Ephemeral print – not just books – sanctified the massacres of the Ottoman Empire. The insistent pamphlets that burst on America in 1917 with titles such as *The Most Terrible Winter the World has ever Known* and *The Scourge of Summer (Follows "The Most Terrible Winter the World has ever Known")* were in part collections of cablegrams. They preserved the consular testimony that might have been lost or lay hidden in diplomatic files. Following up, activists filled the mails with replicas of these cablegrams so that Americans could hold and see the earliest words of despair from the Near East. *A New Harmony of the Gospels* was one of several pamphlets that set quotations from the cables in parallel columns with apt verse from the New Testament.[23]

---

[22] "The Turkish Atrocities in Armenia," *Outlook* 111 (29 Sept. 1915), pp. 262–6. "The Assassination of Armenia," *Missionary Review of the World* 38 (Nov. 1915), pp. 837–48. "Armenia's Need," *Literary Digest* 52 (17 June 1916), pp. 1782–3. Peter Balakian, *Black Dog of Fate: A Memoir* (New York: Basic Books, 1998), pp. 147–73. See also the Meline Toumani memoir at the Armenian General Benevolent Union web site (www.agbu.org/index.html).

[23] Edward L. Parsons Papers, container 25, folder 25 at the Bancroft Library, University of California, Berkeley, is a comprehensive collection of these materials, most sent to this clergyman in Berkeley from the American Committee for Armenian and Syrian Relief.

Journalism of the genocide easily assumed a central place in the rituals of remembrance. *Ambassador Morgenthau's Story* appeared first in a magazine and its crafted, narrative force comes from what the finest reporters had learned in an age of social activism. Rarely does journalism have this impact across generations. For the Armenian story, newsprint that was expected to have a brief life or to serve, at most, as a first draft of history, has become a tool of witness. For scholars today, Richard D. Kloian's anthologies of the breaking news of the Armenian genocide are in this tradition of recall by press replica. Kloian's preface invokes the "magic" of clippings. As the documentary *Back to Ararat* (1988) shows, Armenians have demonstrated for recognition of the genocide by standing in public with faded news stories from archives. Dozens of headlines from the Ottoman era anchor pamphlets issued by the Armenian Assembly of America. The reproduction of memory pieces of news is how the victims have been mourned for a century.

Emotionally it was easy to move from reverence for print to reverence for the physical house for words. Libraries were key venues for Americans who agitated for Armenian relief during the First World War. On California campuses in the 1970s, Armenian student organizations were launched with library displays of the printed records from 1915. I am unaware of any other protest movement by youth brought to life by a glass case with the assistance of librarians. At Berkeley, a global student movement had begun on Sproul Plaza. When the Chancellor told the Armenian students to display their documents in that bright sunny forum, however, these activists insisted that the genocide literature stay on display in the somber Doe Library. This drama on library stages has continued, most recently in the Capitol Hill première of the Atom Egoyan film *Ararat* (2002) at the Library of Congress. The largest community of Armenian origin outside Armenia – Glendale, California – has also relived the historical trauma through its library. The paper record of the Armenian Genocide, even the fragments of the truth written on deadline, has become a relic of a time that is nearly past for living memory.[24]

Sometimes the printed word is not enough – to rescue victims, to change policy, or even to silence deniers of terror. Some great calamities

[24] Kloian, *The Armenian Genocide*, preface. Pamphlet: *The Armenian Genocide – Facing Facts* (Washington, D.C.: Armenian Assembly of America, 1996). "Bowker to Decide Armenian Question," *Daily Cal*, 13 April 1978, p. 20. Hrag Vartanian memoir of the University of Toronto, Armenian General Benevolent Union web site (www.agbu.org/index.html). Carol Chambers, "Flap Leaves City Red, White and Bruised," *Los Angeles Times*, 30 Dec. 2001. Philip Kennicott, "Nearly Nine Decades After the Massacres, A Battle Still Rages To Define 'Genocide,'" *Washington Post*, 24 Nov. 2002.

of the past century remain unintelligible, perhaps untellable, with the passage of time. Thanks in part to journalism – and certainly thanks to the determination to preserve the printed word – the Armenian Genocide has not shared this fate. In this volume, Jay Winter draws our attention to the "mobilization of imagination" of the generation that endured the First World War. The Armenian story reminds us that libraries and archives are battle stations for our imaginations.

Index

Studies in the Social and Cultural History of Modern Warfare

Titles in the series: